The

BIG CHAIR

The
BIG CHAIR

THE SMOOTH HOPS AND BAD BOUNCES FROM THE INSIDE WORLD OF THE ACCLAIMED LOS ANGELES DODGERS GENERAL MANAGER

· ·

NED COLLETTI *with* JOSEPH A. REAVES

G. P. PUTNAM'S SONS

New York

PUTNAM

G. P. PUTNAM'S SONS
Publishers Since 1838
An imprint of Penguin Random House LLC
375 Hudson Street
New York, New York 10014

Library of Congress Cataloging-in-Publication Data

Names: Colletti, Ned, author. | Reaves, Joseph A., date.
Title: The Big Chair : the smooth hops and bad bounces from
the inside world
of the acclaimed Los Angeles Dodgers
general manager / Ned Colletti, with Joseph A. Reaves.
Description: New York : G. P. Putnam's Sons, 2017.
Identifiers: LCCN 2017021965 (print) | LCCN 2017031155 (ebook) |
ISBN 9780735215733 (epub) | ISBN 9780735215726 (hardcover)
Subjects: LCSH: Colletti, Ned. | Los Angeles Dodgers (Baseball team)—
Management—Biography. | Sports general managers—United States—
Biography. | Los Angeles Dodgers (Baseball team)—History—20th century.
| Los Angeles Dodgers (Baseball team)—Anecdotes.
Classification: LCC GV865.C6426 (ebook) |
LCC GV865.C6426 A3 2017 (print) |
DDC 796.357092 [B] —dc23
LC record available at https://lccn.loc.gov/2017021965
p.   cm.

Printed in the United States of America
1 3 5 7 9 10 8 6 4 2

BOOK DESIGN BY AMANDA DEWEY

Penguin is committed to publishing works of quality and integrity. In that spirit, we are proud to offer this book to our readers; however, the story, the experiences, and the words are the author's alone.

This book is dedicated to those who dream and wonder if life's dreams will ever blossom into realities. And to those who mentor, lead, and teach us dreamers—those who provide selfless opportunity and allow us to flourish and believe that all things are, indeed, possible.

CONTENTS

. . . .

TIMELINE

. . . .

November 16, 2005—Ned Colletti hired as the tenth general manager of the Los Angeles Dodgers.

December 8, 2005—Hires Grady Little to manage Dodgers.

December 13, 2005—Makes first trade, acquiring Andre Ethier from the Oakland A's for Milton Bradley and Antonio Perez.

December 14, 2005—Signs Bill Mueller to a two-year contract.

December 19, 2005—Signs infielder Nomar Garciaparra to a one-year contract.

December 20, 2005—Signs outfielder Kenny Lofton to a one-year contract.

February 7, 2006—Signs Japanese RHP Takashi Saito to a minor-league contract and invites him to Spring Training.

March 29, 2006—Signs second baseman Jeff Kent to a one-year contract extension with an option for 2008.

July 25, 2006—Trades Odalis Perez to Kansas City Royals.

July 31, 2006—Acquires Cy Young–winning pitcher Greg Maddux from the Cubs for infielder Cesar Izturis.

September 30, 2006—Greg Maddux outpitches Matt Cain to lead the Dodgers to a 4–2 win over the San Francisco Giants that puts Colletti's first team into the playoffs.

October 7, 2006—The New York Mets complete a three-game sweep to eliminate the Dodgers from the National League Division Series (NLDS).

November 22, 2006—Signs free agent outfielder Juan Pierre to a five-year contract.

December 8, 2006—Former Giants ace Jason Schmidt signs a three-year contract. Former Diamondbacks All-Star Luis Gonzalez signs a one-year deal.

August 24, 2007—Signs former New York Yankees and San Diego Padres star pitcher David Wells to a contract for the remainder of the season.

November 1, 2007—Announces hiring of Joe Torre as manager of the Dodgers.

November 8, 2007—Signs Korean star Chan Ho Park to a minor-league contract with an invitation to Spring Training.

December 12, 2007—Signs free agent Andruw Jones to a two-year contract.

December 16, 2007—Signs Japanese star Hiroki Kuroda to a three-year contract.

May 25, 2008—Future superstar Clayton Kershaw makes his major-league debut at age twenty against the St. Louis Cardinals in Dodger Stadium. Kershaw goes six innings, strikes out seven, walks one, and allows two earned runs. He gets a no-decision in a 4–3 L.A. win in ten innings.

July 28, 2008—The Dodgers acquire Casey Blake from Cleveland.

July 31, 2008—The Dodgers acquire Manny Ramirez at trade deadline.

August 19, 2008—The Dodgers acquire Greg Maddux from the San Diego Padres for a second time, the only two times in Maddux's career he was traded.

September 15, 2008—Brad Penny makes his final appearance for the Dodgers, giving up two runs on two hits in one inning of relief against the Pirates. Two days later, he is in the clubhouse showing a rookie pitcher how to shoot a hunting bow and arrow when Joe Torre is looking to put the rookie in the game. When the team comes off the road, Penny refuses to meet with team officials and is sent home. The media doesn't find out for nearly a month.

September 26, 2008—The Dodgers clinch NL West.

October 4, 2008—Hiroki Kuroda gets the win and Jonathan Broxton the save as the Dodgers complete a three-game sweep of the Chicago Cubs in the NLDS.

October 15, 2008—Chad Billingsley gets the loss as the Philadelphia Phillies eliminate the Dodgers four games to one in the National League Championship Series (NLCS). Greg Maddux pitches two innings in relief of Billingsley, striking out three, walking one, and allowing two unearned runs. It is the last appearance of his Hall of Fame career.

December 9, 2008—Re-signs shortstop Rafael Furcal to a three-year contract with a vesting option for 2012.

January 15, 2009—Releases Andruw Jones.

January 20, 2009—Signs closer Jonathan Broxton and catcher Russell Martin to one-year contracts, avoiding arbitration.

May 7, 2009—Manny Ramirez suspended fifty games for using a banned substance.

October 10, 2009—Andre Ethier homers for the second time in the series as he leads the Dodgers to a three-game sweep of the St. Louis Cardinals in the NLDS.

October 14, 2009—Frank and Jamie McCourt announce they are separating after nearly thirty years of marriage.

October 21, 2009—For the second year in a row, the Philadelphia Phillies eliminate the Dodgers from the NLCS in five games.

October 22, 2009—Frank McCourt fires his wife.

October 27, 2009—Jamie McCourt files for divorce.

September 17, 2010—Joe Torre announces he will step down as manager of the Dodgers and be replaced by Don Mattingly at the end of the season.

November 30, 2010—Signs free agent Juan Uribe to a three-year contract.

December 7, 2010—Divorce court judge invalidates a postnuptial agreement that Frank McCourt claimed made him sole owner of the Dodgers.

December 8, 2010—The Dodgers named Topps Organization of the Year.

April 20, 2011—Major League Baseball (MLB) takes control of the Dodgers. Tom Schieffer appointed monitor.

June 6, 2011—Infielder Dee Gordon makes his major-league debut as a pinch runner in a 3–1 loss to the Phillies in Philadelphia. Gordon scores the only run for the Dodgers.

June 20, 2011—MLB commissioner Bud Selig announces he has rejected a TV deal McCourt had negotiated with Fox.

June 27, 2011—Unable to meet looming end-of-month payroll, McCourt files for Chapter 11 bankruptcy.

July 31, 2011—Trades Rafael Furcal to St. Louis Cardinals.

October 17, 2011—Frank and Jamie McCourt reach a divorce settlement that calls for Jamie to receive $131 million.

November 1, 2011—Frank McCourt and Commissioner Selig make the surprise announcement that they have reached an agreement to auction the Dodgers.

November 14, 2011—First baseman James Loney sideswipes three cars in the evening rush hour. He tries to drive away, hitting another vehicle and breaking the axle on his Maserati. Loney is arrested on suspicion of driving under the influence. No charges were filed.

November 18, 2011—Matt Kemp finalizes an eight-year, $160 million contract.

February 1, 2012—Prosecutors say they won't file DUI charges against Loney for his November accident, citing insufficient evidence.

March 27, 2012—Guggenheim Baseball Management and Los Angeles Lakers legend Magic Johnson agree to pay McCourt $2.1 billion for the Dodgers.

May 1, 2012—New ownership takes over from Frank McCourt.

June 12, 2012—Outfielder Andre Ethier agrees to a five-year, $85 million contract extension.

June 28, 2012—The Dodgers sign Cuban defector Yasiel Puig to a seven-year, $42 million deal.

July 24, 2012—The Dodgers acquire three-time All-Star Hanley Ramirez and left-hander Randy Choate from the Miami Marlins in return for starter Nathan Eovaldi and minor-league pitcher Scott McGough.

July 30, 2012—Seattle trades former closer Brandon League to the Dodgers for minor-league prospects Leon Landry and Logan Bawcom.

July 31, 2012—Shane Victorino comes to the Dodgers in a trade with Philadelphia. Pitchers Ethan Martin and Josh Lindblom go to the Phillies.

August 25, 2012—Completes a nine-player deal with the Red Sox that the *Boston Globe*'s Dan Shaughnessy calls "the biggest Red Sox trade since Babe Ruth was dealt to the Yankees for cash in 1920." The Dodgers get four-time All-Star first baseman Adrian Gonzalez, four-time All-Star outfielder Carl Crawford, three-time All-Star pitcher Josh Beckett, and switch-hitting utility infielder Nick Punto.

October 30, 2012—Signs Brandon League to a three-year, $22.5 million contract extension.

December 9, 2012—Signs Korean All-Star pitcher Hyun-Jin Ryu to a six-year, $36 million deal.

December 10, 2012—Signs former Cy Young Award winner Zack Greinke to a six-year, $147 million contract.

June 3, 2013—Former Cuban star Yasiel Puig makes his major-league debut at Dodger Stadium at age twenty-two, going 2-for-4 and making a dazzling throw from right field to double up San Diego's Chris Denorfia at first base to end the game with a 2–1 win.

July 30, 2013—Signs former San Francisco Giants closer Brian Wilson.

September 19, 2013—The Dodgers become first team to clinch a playoff spot for the season with a 7–6 win over the Arizona Diamondbacks in Phoenix. About a dozen players, led by Matt Kemp, celebrate by diving into the outfield pool at Chase Field.

October 7, 2013—Juan Uribe hits a two-run homer in the bottom of the eighth inning to give the Dodgers a three-games-to-one win over the Atlanta Braves in the NLDS.

October 11, 2013—St. Louis right-hander Joe Kelly hits Hanley Ramirez with the ninth pitch of the NLCS, breaking a rib. Ramirez came into the game batting .500 with six extra-base hits, six RBI, and a stolen base during the four-game NLDS win over the Braves.

October 18, 2013—The Dodgers come within two games of reaching the World Series, losing to the St. Louis Cardinals in Game 6 of the NLCS.

October 21, 2013—Signs free agent Cuban infielder Alex Guerrero to a four-year, $28 million deal. Don Mattingly holds awkward news conference, saying he may not return as manager in 2014 unless he gets a long-term contract.

December 7, 2013—Signs Brian Wilson to a contract extension.

January 17, 2014—Ace Clayton Kershaw signs a Major League Baseball record seven-year, $215 million contract.

June 3, 2014—On the first anniversary of his Dodgers debut, Yasiel Puig shows up late for a night game and gets into a closed-door confrontation with manager Don Mattingly.

July 19, 2014—For the second time in forty-six days, Puig and Mattingly have a fierce closed-door confrontation during and after a loss in St. Louis.

September 24, 2014—The Dodgers clinch the NL West with a 9–1 win over the San Francisco Giants.

October 7, 2014—St. Louis first baseman Matt Adams hits a three-run homer off Clayton Kershaw in the bottom of the seventh to lead the St. Louis Cardinals to a come-from-behind 3–2 win and a three-game sweep of the Dodgers in the NLDS.

October 13, 2014—Colletti takes position as senior advisor to Dodgers president and CEO Stan Kasten.

October 14, 2014—Andrew Friedman, general manager of the Tampa Bay Rays, is hired as president of baseball operations with the Dodgers.

November 6, 2014—Friedman names Farhan Zaidi general manager of the Dodgers and former Arizona and San Diego GM Josh Byrnes senior vice president of baseball operations.

September 12, 2015—Corey Seager, the Dodgers' first-round pick in the 2012 draft, hits his first big-league home run off Arizona's Josh Collmenter in a game where he goes 4-for-5.

September 29, 2015—Clayton Kershaw throws a one-hitter as the Dodgers beat the Giants 8–0 to clinch the NL West for a third consecutive season, the first time in franchise history the team has won three straight titles.

October 15, 2015—Zack Greinke strikes out nine in six and two-thirds innings but loses 3–2 to the Mets in the deciding Game 5 of the NLDS at Dodger Stadium.

October 22, 2015—The Dodgers and manager Don Mattingly part ways after five winning seasons and an 8-11 record in the post-season.

October 29, 2015—Mattingly hired by Miami Marlins. A formal announcement is delayed until after the World Series, which the Kansas City Royals win on November 1.

December 4, 2015—After opting out of the three remaining contract years and $71 million of his Dodgers contract, Zack Greinke signs a six-year, $206.5 million deal with NL West rival Arizona Diamondbacks.

December 4, 2015—Dodger coaches Tim Wallach and Lorenzo Bundy follow Don Mattingly to Miami.

May 27, 2016—International free agent left-handed pitcher Julio Urias makes his major-league debut against the defending National League champion Mets in New York. At age nineteen, Urias is the youngest Dodger pitcher to make his big-league debut since Rex Barney in 1943.

July 11, 2016—Corey Seager hits fifteen home runs but is eliminated in the first round of the Home Run Derby at the All-Star Game week in San Diego.

August 2, 2016—The Dodgers leave on a road trip to Colorado without outfielder Yasiel Puig, who is batting just .260 and becoming a clubhouse distraction. Puig is told he either will be traded or demoted to the minors. Unable to work out a trade, the team sends Puig to Triple-A Oklahoma City.

September 2, 2016—Yasiel Puig is called back up to the big club after batting .358 with five home runs and fourteen RBI in twenty-four games at Triple-A.

September 25, 2016—In the final home game of broadcaster Vin Scully's sixty-seven-year Hall of Fame career, second baseman Charlie Culberson hits a walk-off tenth-inning home run against the Colorado Rockies. The win clinches a franchise record fourth consecutive NL West championship.

October 19, 2016—Julio Urias becomes the youngest pitcher to start a postseason game, giving up four runs on four hits in three and two-thirds innings of a 10–2 loss to the Cubs in Game 4 of the NLDS at Dodger Stadium.

October 22, 2016—It is Game 6 of the 2016 NLCS. Three generations of Collettis are sitting together at Wrigley Field, rooting for two different teams—Ned and his son, Lou, rooting for the Dodgers; Ned's uncle Frank and his son, Frank Jr., rooting for the Cubs. The Cubs shut out Clayton Kershaw and the Dodgers 5–0 to advance to the World Series for the first time since 1945. That was the year Ned's dad and Frank's other brothers told eleven-year-old Frank he was too young to go to the World Series and they promised to take him to the next one. His nephew would fulfill the promise.

AUTHOR'S NOTE

· · · · · · · · · · · · · ·

This book is a work of memoir; it is a true story based on my best recollections of various events in my life. I re-created dialogue to match my best recollection of those exchanges.

The

BIG CHAIR

One

THE EIGHT-OH-FIVE

· · · · · · · · · · · · ·

When you grow up in a blue-collar neighborhood where dads labor in factories and moms measure aspirations by packed lunchboxes, dreams for a better life don't have to travel very far. For me, the journey started on the 8:05 morning train from Mannheim station to Wrigley Field.

I took that train and then two buses at least a hundred times to sit in the bleachers and watch my beloved Chicago Cubs, never once appreciating that each trip was a divine wink at dreams and a life to come.

My mind drifts back often to my boyhood days in Franklin Park, Illinois. It was an honest place to grow up, a place where you knew the mailman and the mayor, the dogcatcher and the dentist. Parents worked, worried—then worked harder. Kids played baseball, went to school—then played more baseball. We played anywhere we could: in vacant lots without real bases, on the streets, and in organized leagues during the summer. We talked about the big leagues, memorized statistics of our favorite players, and dreamt of playing for the Cubs. A few even dreamt of playing for the White Sox.

I thought about those carefree times as I sat alone and stared at my cellphone. I was two thousand miles away, in Los Angeles, and the sun seemed to be shining brighter than it ever had. Back home, rain was falling. So were the leaves. Seasons were changing. Autumn was turning to winter.

My wife, Gayle, whom I had known for thirty-four years, since our days together at East Leyden High School, was wrapping up a shopping trip with her mother in the Chicago suburb of Elk Grove Village. Their dinner plans suddenly got canceled when I called.

In Oxford, Ohio, our daughter, Jenna, was having an early dinner with two college girlfriends in an apartment near the campus of Miami of Ohio. Her dinner was interrupted when Gayle called.

At the family home in Wood Dale, fifteen minutes west of Franklin Park, our son, Lou, answered the call from Gayle and got a lump in his throat.

My brother, Doug, had left Chicago at 6 a.m. for a daylong, in-and-out business trip to Houston. I reached him as he sat in a window seat on an American Airlines jet, engines turning, on the tarmac about to take off for the return trip to O'Hare International Airport.

Doug was off the phone in less than a minute and hustling to make two quick calls of his own before the plane took off. The first was to his wife, Val, asking her to meet him at the curb outside O'Hare with a fresh set of clothes when he landed around 8:30 p.m. The other call was to his travel agent, who booked him on a 10 p.m. flight to Los Angeles. By the time he landed in California, in the middle of the night after traveling more than 3,700 miles in one day, he had forty voicemails on his cellphone. Word was quickly spreading.

Two of the last calls I made that day were to my mom and to my uncle Frank.

My mom was in a retirement home in the Chicago suburb of Schaumburg struggling with the early stages of dementia. Mercifully, she was still sharp enough to savor the news. My voice cracked and I wept as we shared our feelings.

UNCLE FRANK, my late dad's lone surviving brother, couldn't have been prouder. He broke into tears of joy before I could. Then we both wept, knowing how wonderful it would have been if only Ned Louis Colletti Sr. could have been there to share the moment.

The day Frank McCourt made me the tenth general manager in the long, proud history of the Los Angeles Dodgers, November 15, 2005, was monumental for the Colletti family. I had just finished my twenty-fifth year in Major League Baseball, an accomplishment that was beyond my wildest dreams. And now, I would be taking over one of the most storied franchises in all of sports—albeit a franchise that was reeling after its second-worst season since World War II.

I was fifty-one, the age at which my dad died of lung cancer not far from where he made a home for his wife, Dolores, and sons, Doug and me, in Franklin Park. At the age when my dad was saying goodbye, I was saying hello to one of the most prestigious positions in professional sports.

Before it was over, I would get to know some of the best players and people in baseball's amazing history. I would become friends with men who I had idolized when they played.

We assembled teams that won with hustle and class. I added future Hall of Famers at trading deadlines and signed some of the best of all time. Over the course of my career, I had the chance to work for three of the most fabled franchises in the game—my hometown Cubs, the San Francisco Giants, and the Dodgers. I became one of the highest-ranking executives in baseball history to work for both the Giants and the Dodgers, two longtime rivals. And for one day, that magical day in November 2005, I actually worked for both of them—officially changing from one to the other at high noon.

I almost wish I'd had the chance somewhere along the way to work for the St. Louis Cardinals. Then I could say I worked both sides of the two greatest rivalries in the history of the National League—the Cubs and Cardinals in the Midwest and the New York/California Dodgers and Giants. Almost.

Then again, it would have been bittersweet to work for the Cardinals. They were the team I disliked most growing up. And the way my career unfolded, I disliked them even more as time moved on.

Over the years, I dined with Sinatra and Scully, and got to drink into the wee small hours of the morning with Santo, Caray, and Brickhouse—and a long parade of wordsmiths, some extremely talented and some not so much, who earned their livings the way I began my career, writing about sports.

I saw the World Series up close and personal and sat helplessly as the teams I helped put together stumbled in the postseason, the worst possible time. Former commissioner the late A. Bartlett Giamatti said it best: "[Baseball] breaks your heart. It is designed to break your heart."

While my career unfolded, I was blessed to raise a loving family and have two children who graduated from great universities with advanced degrees. I began my life living in a Chicago garage and ended up with a place beside the Pacific Ocean and another in the Arizona desert.

For more than three decades, I attended an average of 225 baseball games a year. I traveled throughout the United States, Canada, and Latin America watching men and boys play baseball. I saw the Great Wall of China and the breathtaking harbor of Sydney, Australia, thanks to baseball. I spent more than a calendar year of my life in New York City. The same for St. Louis, Montreal, Denver,

San Diego, and other National League outposts—all accumulated in three-to-four-day increments. And all the while, I called Chicago, San Francisco, and Los Angeles my home.

I stayed in some of the best hotels. I knew bellhops, shoeshine men, restaurant servers, and receptionists by name. I watched cities change in the shadow of new baseball stadiums. I saw buildings come out of the ground, highways laid down, and said hello and goodbye to more than a thousand players. I learned to tell time by hearing the *Montreal Gazette* hit the floor outside my hotel room at 3:30 a.m. or by the honking of horns on the street below the Grand Hyatt in Manhattan.

I watched baseball played by young people on high school and college fields, in minor-league parks with dim lighting and outfield walls cluttered with gaudy advertising. All of us, even though we were generations apart, sharing the same dreams that revolved around the big leagues. I traveled to Latin America in airplanes that were forty years old to see youngsters work out on dirt fields cut into jungles; where players used milk cartons for gloves and sticks for bats, and cattle, chickens, and dogs roamed the outfield.

I scouted players in politically precarious Puerto La Cruz, Venezuela, on a cricket pitch in Australia, and in a makeshift stadium in Beijing that was built and torn down with Potemkin-like chicanery by the Chinese government to placate Major League Baseball and the International Olympic Committee.

Along the way, I had the honor to watch the best of the best play in Wrigley Field, before and after lights. Wrigley Field is where my dad took me to my first baseball game in 1961, and where my favorite team played. Wrigley Field is where my baseball career began. From there I went on to see every major-league stadium any team has called home since 1982. I worked alongside nearly two dozen Hall of Famers and went to more than a hundred World Series games and twenty All-Star Games.

For me, the pinnacle—the reward for a quarter century of tireless work, time away from my family, and 4 a.m. landings—came that fall day.

During the next nine seasons, the Dodgers would go to the playoffs five times. In my eleven seasons as an executive in L.A., the team went to the postseason seven times. We'd come within two wins of the World Series twice and within three wins twice. Our five postseason appearances matched the best nine-year run in Dodgers history, as did the seven playoff appearances in eleven years. I inherited a team that was staggeringly bad and, with the baseball operations staff, turned it into a perennial winner that rekindled the Dodger brand and set attendance and revenue records.

It wasn't always easy. We also had some historically difficult times. On my watch, the franchise and its fans endured one of the most challenging ownership eras in American sports. We survived, though, and somehow even managed to thrive. From 2006 through 2014, no National League general manager won as many games nor maneuvered around more land mines—all under the white-hot spotlight of the second-largest market in Major League Baseball.

Through ownership turmoil and public relations firestorms, I had a chance to use what I learned on the gritty streets of Franklin Park, from the wise men and women who were fortunate enough to finish high school and earn an hourly wage. Franklin Park was settled in the 1890s. Decades later it became a hub for industry, thanks in large part to the trains that rattled our house. By 1942, Franklin Park was the fourth-largest industrial city in the state of Illinois. It was blue-collar. The people of Franklin Park were tough and strong. People of different cultures supported one another in a time when that wasn't always the case.

The lessons I learned from watching and listening on street corners and porches with the wiseguys and hustlers of Franklin Park were put to the test time and again during my days as general manager of the Dodgers. From time to time, multimillion-dollar negotiations pitted Harvard Law education against Franklin Park street smarts.

With a focused, passionate approach, anyone has a chance. My dream as a teenager was if I had children, they would go to college and I would pay a mortgage rather than rent. Those were very bold dreams for someone from Franklin Park. But I came to realize, long after I left, from being raised in a blue-collar railroad town, that many times we learn without even knowing we are learning. And while a traditional education certainly has its value, street smarts and grit offer something different. Most of all, I learned that all things are possible.

Long after I exceeded my wildest dreams and became a front office executive with the Cubs in the 1980s and early '90s, I dared to dream even bigger. All things are possible. I began to believe I could be a major-league general manager.

"So you want to sit in the Big Chair?" two of my mentors at the Cubs, Dallas Green and Jimmy Frey, would ask me now and then. "Do you really know what that entails and how your life will change?"

They warned me the changes would be drastic—mostly for the good—but also that baseball would consume my life more than anything or anyone I'd ever known.

"Be careful what you wish for," they'd chuckle, knowing better than most that becoming a general manager in the twenty-first century was incredibly different than during their time.

I GOT MY WISH and never regretted it. Dallas and Jimmy were right, of course. Life in the Big Chair has changed drastically through the years. While the foundation of the game remains the same, parts have changed throughout the years. The seasons were changing, too, in the fading fall of 2014, just as I was entering the fall of my professional baseball life.

For the second year in a row, I watched from the same seat in the same suite as the St. Louis Cardinals beat the best left-handed pitcher I had ever been associated with.

On October 18, 2013, Clayton Kershaw was battered in a 9–0 loss that earned the Cardinals the National League pennant.

Less than a year later, 354 days to be precise, Clayton took a 2–0 lead into the seventh inning of Game 4 of the Division Series, only to hang a breaking ball to Matt Adams with two runners on. Right fielder Matt Kemp went as far as the fence allowed and watched helplessly as the ball sailed over it, thus ending my run with the Dodgers.

Two years in a row, I left Busch Stadium with the glow of a glorious regular season snuffed out by a crushing, season-ending October defeat.

A year earlier, on my way out of the stadium, I had stopped to wish Cardinals manager Mike Matheny well in the World Series. Mike is a good man. We'd been together in San Francisco and remained friends despite being intense competitors. That was the norm. Most general managers have great respect for opposing managers. They wear different uniforms and do everything they possibly can to beat each other but they are professionals. Everyone has put in his time. Managers and general managers work endless hours to make their players the best they can be.

This time, though, after losing to Matheny and his Cardinals for a second consecutive year, I didn't stop to see him. I kept walking, past the home clubhouse to security, and onto the bus that would take me to an airplane that would bring me back to Los Angeles for the last time as general manager of the Dodgers. I didn't know for sure the ride was over, but I couldn't help but think it was.

Night had fallen. The wind was picking up. The streets outside Busch Stadium were crowded with red-clad revelers.

Fall was moving into the Midwest right on schedule. The Cardinals and St. Louis fans were looking forward to more baseball. No such luck in Los Angeles.

A remarkable journey, one born amid the vines of Wrigley Field, nourished by the bay in San Francisco, and crowned in the heady heights near Hollywood, was destined for a new track.

Two
TRADE OF A LIFETIME

· · · · · · · · · · · · ·

I made my first trade before I was ten years old: an empty Pepsi bottle for a pretzel.

That's how things worked during the 1960s at Al & Joe's Delicatessen, the corner grocery store in Franklin Park. A pretzel cost a penny—the same amount as the refund for an empty soda bottle. You could buy a pack of five baseball cards with a stick of gum included for a nickel. Once, I saw a kid buy an entire box of Topps baseball cards for a dollar. I thought he must not live around here, because no kid I ever knew had a whole dollar. Except for him, I never saw anyone buy more than two packs of Topps cards at a time.

Al & Joe's was where I first met Ron Santo. I was ten. Santo was twenty-four and about to hit .313 with 114 RBI and thirty home runs in his fourth season with the Cubs. He'd stop in at Al & Joe's to buy prosciutto and we'd talk baseball. I was blessed with Ronnie's friendship for forty-six years before he died in 2010.

Aldo Conforti, an elevator operator, and his lifelong buddy, Joseph Gapastione, a bricklayer, opened their store in 1960 and worked side by side for forty-seven years. Their place was the neighborhood hangout, Al & Joe were friends with everyone. They knew who had money and who didn't. We were one of the families that didn't. Beneath the cash register at Al & Joe's was a small box filled with index cards, one of which had "Colletti" scrawled on it. It was for money owed. Most Wednesdays, two days before payday, we were out of money. My father never had a credit card and never wanted one. He hated to be in debt. But we had to get by a couple of days a week, so we'd get what we needed and the cost would get scribbled on our index card. Every Friday, my dad would settle up. And more often than not, we'd be back to the index card a few days later.

I spent the first five years of my life in a garage on the corner of West School Street and North Natchez Street in Chicago. My dad, Ned Sr., converted the garage to their home shortly after he and my mother were married on February 3, 1951. Nine years later, we moved into a brick house at 3502 North George Street—on the northwest corner of George Street and Pacific Avenue in Franklin Park. The new house had four rooms, no garage, and was exactly 899 square feet, which wasn't a whole lot bigger than the office I would eventually work from overlooking the field at Dodger Stadium. My dad paid $8,500 for the house on George Street and I turned the front yard into a wonderland for Whiffle ball. The dimensions reminded me of Fenway Park, at least the Fenway Park I occasionally glimpsed on NBC's *Game of the Week*. Deep to center and right, but short, very short, down the left field line. My "Green Monster" was neither green nor any kind of monster. It was a four-foot-high picket fence just forty feet from home plate. Pitchers in my neighborhood learned to keep the ball away to the right-handed hitters.

The George Street house was no more than five hundred feet north of the Milwaukee Road railroad tracks and adjacent freight yard. The thunderous clang of giant steel trains never stopped. Six sets of tracks were used by trains hauling freight east to west and back again. Two other sets of tracks carried suburban commuters to and from Chicago, fourteen miles to the east. Not many commuter trains ran late in the evening, but the freight trains rumbled past endlessly. We never had air-conditioning, so we slept—or tried to sleep—with the windows open on hot, humid summer nights. A tight-knit wire screen kept the bugs out but was no match for the thuds of the freight trains as they stopped and started, backed up, then slogged forward again. And then there was the diesel from the engines. The smoke and smells that wafted through the screens sent me face-first into my pillow more times than I can remember. The smell was strong and acidic, but it was home. Shortly after we moved into the house on George Street, O'Hare became Chicago's dominant airport, eclipsing Midway, located in a neighborhood on Chicago's South Side. By 1965, when I was eleven, the number of passengers coming through O'Hare exceeded twenty million a year. And each plane carrying those twenty million passengers seemed to use our house as a homing beacon on its final approach. The house would shake with the deafening noise.

From 1964 to 2008, when the New York Mets played at Shea Stadium, the roar of jets from nearby LaGuardia Airport was somehow just part of the "ambience" of the game. I'd had that "ambience" all my life. My front yard was like Fenway in its dimensions and Shea in its decibels. Big-league atmosphere in little Franklin Park.

BASEBALL HAS ALWAYS BEEN AN important part of my life.

Each morning and afternoon, from the last day of one school year to the first day of the next, I'd walk two blocks from the little house on George Street to play baseball on the vacant lot next to Banti's Tap. Banti's was the neighborhood tavern. It catered to the railroad men who worked overnight, so it was always open—late or early. The busiest hours were four to seven—both four to sevens.

There among the railroad workers with the salty language and the thirst for morning beer, we boarded the bus outside Banti's front door for the long ride to one of the four grade schools I attended. When you literally grow up on the other side of the tracks, school boundaries were changed regularly.

None of us who played baseball beside Banti's had uniforms. Gloves and bats were shared. A baseball had to last for weeks. And center field was a problem—but one easily solved. An old abandoned garage sat where Joe DiMaggio would have played if Banti's were in the Bronx. So we made do. A ball that was hit off the roof was a home run. Anything off the walls was in play. Our fans loved it. And we really did have fans. Inevitably, two or three patrons from Banti's would amble out of the dark tavern and stretch out beside our field, deciding whether to linger there and sober up or grab a quick nap before going home. They were all working-class men who had spent the night unloading freight trains, coupling and uncoupling railcars, and turning switches to keep the trains on the correct track. And one of my most vivid memories is their vocabulary. How shall I describe it? It certainly wasn't anything I'd heard at home, but it was preparation for the language of baseball that awaited me.

If I walked out my front door and turned right, I'd hit Pacific Avenue, which led to Front Street and Banti's, facing the railroad tracks. But if I turned left and walked one block, I'd find Addison Street, the same Addison Street that was home to Wrigley Field. Sure, Wrigley Field was ninety-four blocks away—just shy of twelve miles—but it was cool knowing my then-beloved Cubs played down the street from where I played.

In the spring and summer, I would pull a chair next to our refrigerator and bring down the black transistor radio that was my lifeline to baseball. The radio had just one frequency, AM, and the round tuning wheel rarely moved off of WGN. WGN once was owned by the *Chicago Tribune* and took its broadcast initials from the self-proclaimed *World's Greatest Newspaper*. On winter mornings, when the snow blew, we would listen to Wally Phillips, a WGN staple, tell us which schools were closing for the day. That's all radio had to offer me until baseball season.

The only baseball news you could get during the winter was an occasional tidbit on the five-minute sports show that aired every weekday evening at 5:55 p.m. on WGN Television, which, in 1956 became the first independent television channel in Chicago. It would be another twenty-seven years before WGN became the superstation that broadcast the Cubs to the world, but at least from the late 1950s on, Chicago was lucky to have a channel of its own outside the big three networks. Still, even in the late 1970s and early '80s, if you missed that five-minute sports broadcast, you missed everything about baseball until the next day's newspaper—and that was only for families who could afford a dime for the daily paper and a quarter for the Sunday edition. The Collettis couldn't afford either on a regular basis.

I know it's impossible to stop progress and technology. But I can't help but chuckle at how much simpler my time as a general manager would have been if I'd had to deal with just one five-minute local sports show a week during the off-season instead of today's unending national news cycle on Twitter, talk radio, Facebook, Instagram, YouTube, and satellite TV.

During the spring and summer of my youth, WGN radio was a heaven-sent blessing—for me and for most everyone in and around Franklin Park. Neighbors would perch on porches with their transistor radio tuned to the Cubs or the hated White Sox. Tired men sat drinking Hamm's or Schlitz beers—or in my dad's case, a twelve-ounce bottle of Pepsi. The sweet soda was his reward for yet another eight- to ten-hour day at the Division Street factory named Pharmacy, which cranked out cardboard boxes.

My dad had the ability to fix just about anything. His job was to keep the machines running in the factory. Outside of work, his job was similar—be it at the garage-turned-home on School Street, the tiny brick house on George Street, or when a neighbor or relative came calling. If anything broke—the washer or dryer, the stove, television or radio, the car, a bicycle—my dad would fix it. Buying anything new was a painful last resort. The same went for clothes. When the soles of our shoes wore out, it wasn't unusual for me and my brother to use cardboard in the inside of the shoes to cover the hole that playing and walking had created.

In his lifetime, my dad owned four cars—a 1951 Chevy, a 1959 Chevy, a 1963 Oldsmobile, and, finally, a 1975 Pontiac Grand Prix, which his brother Joe left him when Joe died a premature death at age forty-seven. In thirty-five years of driving, my dad never owned a new car. He bought used or inherited all four cars and drove them until he could drive them no more. Every one of them had Bondo putty covering rusted gaps, like Clearasil trying to mask an acne-riddled face. Mufflers that rotted through were bandaged with duct tape and urged on for another ten thousand miles. Winter or summer—didn't matter—when the oil needed changing, my dad would drive his car up a curb to give himself enough room to crawl under and drain the crankcase. It could be below zero in January and if the car wasn't running smoothly, we would go out to change spark plugs. I'd keep the flashlight shining on the engine while Dad and I froze in the biting cold. On winter nights my dad would go to sleep by 9 p.m. and wake at 2:30 a.m. to go outside and start the car. He'd keep it running long enough to convince him the battery would survive one more night. When you are paid by the hour and every working minute counts, you don't look for excuses to not go to work. You get the job done as quickly and efficiently as possible. My dad and my mom, Dolores, lived by that credo. And they passed it on to my brother, Doug, and to me. How your life goes is your responsibility. You own it, no matter the obstacles or hardships. It's something I came to wish later in my career that more than a few of the players I dealt with had learned and practiced.

I remember, as clear as yesterday, one of the lessons I received on how my life was my responsibility. It came at the dinner table on February 10, 1970—two months before my sixteenth birthday. I was about to start driver's education and I excitedly told my dad I planned to start driving in April. He never owned a fancy car, but he did have one with the best sound system—something called a Vibrasonic. You could flip a switch and music would come out of the speakers with a terrific reverb effect. I was looking forward to driving that car.

"So whose car will you be driving?" my dad asked, not bothering to look up between bites. "You won't be driving mine because when you have an accident, I won't have a way to get to work and we'll be out on the street."

He said "when" I had an accident—not "if."

"And what are you going to do about car insurance?" he added.

Hmmm.

Okay. So much for my ambitious driving plan.

As soon as dinner was finished, I walked to the north base of the nearby Mannheim Bridge to the Holiday Inn and applied for a job as a busboy, cleaning and setting tables in the restaurant. I got the job and started that Saturday, Valentine's Day, working six-hour shifts on Saturday and Sunday nights. The job paid $1.25 an hour plus anywhere from $5 to $10 a shift in tips. Twelve hours a week at a buck and a quarter. Fifteen bucks a weekend plus tips and minus taxes. It took me two years, not two months, to get enough money for insurance. But I did it. My life. My responsibility. Lesson learned. I was proud of myself, but the job had a major drawback: It cut into my baseball—both playing and watching. That hurt.

WHEN I TURNED FOURTEEN at the start of the 1968 season, I was old enough to take a train and two buses each way to Wrigley Field— forty times a season through the end of the 1970 season. I would leave Franklin Park at 8 a.m., get to Wrigley Field by 10 a.m., and then sit against the outfield wall facing Waveland Avenue with two dozen or so other young fans waiting for the gates to open. To this day, when I think of those years, two distinct aromas are a part of my memories: the thick, rich, smell of suntan lotion and the occasional, unmistakable scent of marijuana. My soundtrack of those years is a loop of Tommy James and the Shondells whining "Crystal Blue Persuasion" . . . Chicago thumping out "25 or 6 to 4," the classic hit by keyboardist Robert Lamm about struggling to write a song in the middle of the night—around 3:35 or 3:34 a.m. . . . And, of course, John Lennon's "Give Peace a Chance"—an anthem of those tumultuous times.

Going to a Cubs game cost less than three bucks. And that was if I ate. If I had to, I could catch a game for a little more than a buck. A bleacher ticket cost seventy-five cents. A soft drink was a quarter. And a dog was thirty cents.

Most days I went alone, and I was always among the first to sprint under the big green center field scoreboard when the gates opened. I would race to the front row of the left field bleachers, as far toward center field as possible. From there I taught myself the intricacies of the game and set myself on a life-changing path. I'd trace the movement of pitches by Ferguson Jenkins, Bill Hands, and Ken Holtzman. I'd watch how players set up and I learned the art of infield and outfield play. It was all right in front of me to watch and study as much or as little as I wanted. And because I was alone, there never were any distractions. Wrigley Field is a cathedral for many. It was that for me, too, but it was a classroom as well—for my favorite subject, baseball.

My textbook for those years was the *Baseball Dope Book*, a publication put out yearly from 1948 through 1985 by *The Sporting News*. The black-and-white paperback contained a preview of every major-league team, standings and statistics from the year before, each team's forty-man roster, and a diagram of the home stadiums. From the time I was seven until I was about fourteen, there wasn't a book I read more. Night after night and game after game, I pored through it as I listened to the radio and wrote down the names of players my Cubs should acquire to make them better. It was a fun exercise and it set forth some good groundwork and a foundation for what would become my livelihood.

Like many Americans of my generation, I felt that 1968 was a defining year. That was the last season before division play and the Cubs were surprisingly good. They finished third in the ten-team National League—a distant thirteen games back of the archrival St. Louis Cardinals, but with a respectable 84-78 record. My dear friend and boyhood hero, Ron Santo, slipped to a .246 batting average but still hit 26 home runs and drove in 98. Fergie Jenkins won twenty games—the second time in a remarkable six-year run in which he won twenty or more games for the Cubs.

Outside the ballpark, the world was changing. Jet planes were being hijacked. Neil Armstrong became the first man to walk on the moon. Race riots were occurring regularly. The Vietnam War was dividing the country. Authority was being challenged in America like never before. Life would never be the same.

In April, Dr. Martin Luther King Jr. was assassinated in Memphis, Tennessee, and the west side of Chicago erupted in flames. Rioters and National Guard troops clashed for days. Weeks later, Robert F. Kennedy was shot to death in Los Angeles while running for the presidential office his brother lost to an assassin's bullets just four and a half years earlier.

The Democratic National Convention delegates gathered in chaotic Chicago. More than ten thousand protestors amassed in Grant Park beside Lake Michigan and were met by twenty-three thousand National Guard troops and Chicago policemen. Riots ensued. As demonstrators and authorities battled, the Collettis watched live along with the rest of the country on national television. I can still hear the protestors, shrouded in clouds of tear gas, chanting, "The whole world's watching! The whole world's watching!"

Through the turmoil, baseball remained my bedrock and my refuge from the real-world realities that were closing in all too quickly. More than ever, I made it a point to get to Wrigley Field as often as I could. There the angry rioters of Grant Park gave way to the riotously happy Left Field Bleacher Bums.

I was still too young, in that troubled summer of 1968, to be an official, full-fledged, beer-swilling Bleacher Bum. But I witnessed it all and was more than a passing part of the unending party. Most of the "Bums"—a group of about thirty-five—were between the ages of eighteen and thirty, with a few middle-aged outliers. They gave unflinching devotion to the Cubs and unmitigating misery to the opposition.

One of the ringleaders, who would become a lifelong friend, was Mike Murphy, a bugle-blowing free spirit born to lead. Inning after inning and game after game, Murph would take the point, blaring his bugle, as he led a troupe of Bums marching Mardi Gras–style atop the bleacher wall from left field to right field and back again. It was a free-for-all celebration that had never happened before and hasn't happened since.

It was the closing years of the 1960s. And the world was a

different place. Thankfully, there was baseball in my world. I loved it then. And I love it still—more than a half century later.

GROWING UP IN FRANKLIN PARK, our lives had a rhythm—an unalterable rhythm I never questioned—accompanied by long-lost simplicity.

My mom cooked on a four-burner stove three feet across and four feet deep.

Monday was always pork tenderloin.

Tuesday meant meatloaf.

Wednesday was spaghetti night.

Thursday, for some reason, brought the famous "Italian" delicacy—chop suey.

Friday, ah, Friday, was my favorite. Pizza from Sil's, the sweet-smelling joint next to Al & Joe's. For a while, my dad was a deliveryman for Sil's, making fifty cents a pizza plus tips. He would bring home ten bucks on a really good night.

Saturday was lunch meat and, once a month, a trip to the truck stop south over the Mannheim Bridge to get hamburgers. My dad would splurge and add a tamale to his order. Tamales and hamburger. How well would that go over in Sicily?

Sunday was special: a nice, fatty beef roast with potatoes.

When she wasn't cooking or cleaning, my mom spent time watching baseball. She was the only mom in the neighborhood who'd play catch in the front yard from time to time. During the World Series, when all the games were played during the day, my mom would write out the lineups for me. She'd keep score until I raced home from school and took over. As she handed me her neat scorecard and a pencil, she'd fill me in on the headlines: "Bob Gibson is striking out a lot of hitters today . . . Sandy Koufax is missing a game to honor the Jewish holiday . . . Why did the Cubs ever trade Lou Brock? He was never any good with us, but he's great for the Cardinals."

My mom died April 29, 2013, almost exactly thirty-one years to the day after my dad's passing, on April 27, 1982. They were the loves of each other's lives. When Mom died, my brother, Doug, and I became orphans. Even in our fifties, on the back nine of our lives, the loneliness was hard to take. But we were blessed to be with her in her final days. She thanked us for loving and caring for her after Dad's death. She especially thanked Doug, since he stayed in Chicago after I moved west. But she always understood why I had to leave Chicago. And I never missed the chance to be with her—always rearranging my travel schedule to spend at least a few hours in Chicago on my way to somewhere else. One of the last times I saw her, she held my hand and whispered to me: "Every day, be a blessing to someone."

Mom was a blessing to me every day of my life. And I try to honor her by being a blessing to someone, somewhere, every day.

My dad had a similar bit of character-building advice before he left this earth three decades earlier. The cancer that would kill him had spread from his lungs to his larynx and it was both painful and difficult for him to talk. But I remember him looking at me and saying in a whisper: "Son, always remember—you get far more out of life by giving than by receiving."

Give to others.

Be a blessing.

My parents lived by those beliefs. I have tried my best to do the same.

ON SUNDAY NIGHTS IN FRANKLIN PARK, while savoring the beef and potatoes from our special dinner, my job was to walk to Al & Joe's and buy the five thinnest slices of ham. A single-slice ham sandwich was all my dad afforded himself for lunch every week.

Al and Joe loved teasing me. One Thanksgiving, we were hosting a family dinner with three relatives joining Mom, Dad, Doug, and me. Al knew we were too poor to afford a turkey so he pulled me aside and jokingly asked if I wanted to place a special order for a Cornish hen.

Funny, Al. Funny.

He was a great guy, though. When he wasn't teasing me about the Colletti fortunes, he and Joe loved riding me about the Cubs and how badly they played.

I recall vividly one newspaper in particular—the *Chicago Sun-Times*, Sunday, March 13, 1966. I woke up early that morning and made a beeline three blocks to Al & Joe's. I couldn't get there fast enough. The night before, Bobby Hull, the Chicago Black Hawks' great left-winger, had scored his fifty-first goal of the season—setting what then was a single-season NHL record. There were no television highlights, no way to see history except to have been at Chicago Stadium the night before. But the moment is etched in my mind forever. The *Sun-Times* ran a back-page picture of Hull, just across the blue line, his stick in the follow-through position, the puck already in flight. Little black arrows mapped the path of the puck as it soared past Cesar Maniago, the New York Rangers' goaltender. I'm not sure why I remember all that detail. I guess it was just special and I was just a kid—a kid who loved hockey nearly as much as baseball and who was proud of Chicago. It wasn't until two years later that my dad and I had the chance to go to a Black Hawks game together.

I can watch Hull's goal anytime I want on YouTube, but the grainy black-and-white video will never replace that photo on the back page of the *Sun-Times*, just as the best television broadcast will never replace a radio play-by-play for me.

Baseball was made for radio. Thanks to legendary Cubs broadcasters Vince Lloyd and Lou Boudreau, I could see the incline of the outfield terrace in Cincinnati's old Crosley Field without ever being there. I could imagine the gigantic horseshoe shape of the Polo Grounds, which the expansion Mets called home on Manhattan's northern tip. Without ever setting foot in the Polo Grounds, I knew the upper deck hung ever so slightly over the playing field warning track, stealing fly balls from outfielders who were sure they were ready to make a catch. I knew, too, thanks to Vince and Lou, that the hallowed grounds they were describing was where, a little more than a decade earlier, Bobby Thomson hit the famous home run that helped *"The Giants win the pennant! The Giants win the pennant!"*

As I listened to Vince and Lou—and Jack Brickhouse on television—I could practically feel the cold winds of Candlestick, the soft summer breezes wafting across Chavez Ravine, and the boiling humidity rising from the carpet at Busch Stadium. Between pitches, I could hear the aggravating noise of the wondrous Astrodome, baseball's first indoor stadium, and the funny French accent from the public address announcer at Montreal's Parc Jarry, Major League Baseball's first international venue.

I saw every stadium, felt every stadium, smelled every stadium, through the words of Vince and Lou. I knew the light-tower power of McCovey and the majestic grace and greatness of Mays; the long stride that produced mid-90s fastballs and the soft, wicked twelve-to-six curveball of Koufax; the lightning-quick wrists of Banks, his fingers gripping the bat as if it were red-hot; and the ferocity of Gibson, who stared down the strongest and greatest hitters of his time from sixty feet, six inches.

Thanks to Vince and Lou, I saw it all on the radio. I fell in love with baseball because of the game, because of the strategy, and, equally, because of the storytelling that went hand in hand with the game—especially on the radio.

. . .

I DISLIKED BEING away from the radio because it meant I was away from my Cubs. Three times in the mid-1960s, my dad scraped up enough money to take us on vacation—all three to visit my mom's parents in Fort Lauderdale, Florida. Getting there meant a two- to three-day drive down two-lane highways that my dad would navigate by himself because he was the only driver in the family. All three times, he drove the '51 Chevy with a rusted-through hole in the backseat floor. We'd drive through the outskirts of Indianapolis, Louisville, Nashville, Chattanooga, Atlanta, Macon, and Orlando.

Once, a fierce thunderstorm forced us to the side of the road in Tennessee. We didn't have enough money for a hotel room, so the four of us slept in the car and waited for the worst to pass. We awoke to find we were no more than ten feet from the edge of Lookout Mountain outside Chattanooga, where I would visit regularly years later to watch the Dodgers' Double-A Lookouts. It was a time devoid of McDonald's, and Disney World in Orlando was still nothing more than Walt Disney's vision. If there were such a thing as Marriott points then, the Colletti family wasn't collecting them.

I said I hated being away from the radio because it meant being away from my Cubs. Well, that wasn't always the case. Sometimes I could be with the radio and still be without the Cubs. Such as on those vacation trips to Florida. The AM car radio would be playing Sinatra, Nat King Cole, Dean Martin, the Beatles, the Rolling Stones. Or at least it played most of the time. Now you would hear it—then static—and then you wouldn't.

Depending on where we were—how far we were from the nearest town—and what the weather was like, we'd get a whole song, part of one, or nothing but a steady symphony of static.

We couldn't hear the Cubs on the car radio, but, on our trips, I'd ask my dad to drive us by major-league stadiums every chance we had. Unfortunately, on the route from our house outside Chicago to my grandparents' in Florida, there were only two big-league parks. We had Comiskey Park on Chicago's South Side and then nothing until the then-new Atlanta–Fulton County Stadium, which sat astride Interstate 75/85.

I'd wake up the morning we were hitting Atlanta and be excited at the thought of driving past a major-league stadium. I'd look out the car window a good half hour in anticipation, then Fulton County would come into view and slip out of view—all in about ten seconds. We could never stop because we were always in a hurry to get to my grandparents'. And there was no way we could afford four tickets to a Braves game and stay overnight in a major city. The places we stayed at were roadside hotels—hours outside of town between one outpost and another—the kind that had a flashing vacancy sign out front and where you parked the car in front of the room you had rented.

At my grandparents' house, the newspaper would be delivered at 3 p.m. I would wait for the delivery boy, then open the Fort Lauderdale newspaper to the sports section immediately. I couldn't care less about the news. I'd go straight to the sports section to see how the Cubs had done—twenty-four hours earlier—and I'd check the standings. The Cubs were always near the bottom of the National League, usually a good twenty or so games out of first place. I would study the box scores and try and piece together what must have happened a day earlier. A week later we would be driving back north and I couldn't wait to get within range of WGN's signal so I could listen to the men on the radio talk about the Cubs. I couldn't wait to get home.

Those days and nights, listening to baseball and playing it, spawned my love and passion for the game—a love and passion that would grow beyond even my childhood dream.

I wasn't the only one in my family who loved and lived baseball.

Besides my score-keeping, let's-play-catch mom, my uncles on my dad's side were fanatics. Pasquale, whom everyone called Oscar, was the oldest brother of eight children born to Sicilian immigrants, Luigi and Louise Colletti. Luigi died in 1939, leaving seven children; an eighth had died in childbirth. Frank was the other baseball-crazy brother of that generation. His wife, Charmaine, knew her nephew was a baseball fan. She also had a meticulous home and once cleaned out a closet and gave me a baker's dozen of Cubs yearbooks from 1946 through 1958—a treasure that did nothing but fuel my passion for baseball and the Cubs.

The unquestioned ringleader of the Colletti Cubs Fan Club was Oscar. He would go to Wrigley Field many times a season. To make a living, Oscar sold scrap metal. He would pull furnaces out of basements in the morning so the furnace company could install a replacement in the afternoon. Then he'd head to the junkyard, which paid cash for the old furnaces.

An enterprising soul, Oscar would stop at home on the way to the junkyard and fill the furnace closest to the front of his old rickety truck with water so it would weigh more when he cashed in. Oscar had four kids and every penny helped.

Oscar went to Wrigley Field so often in the early 1940s that he befriended more than a few Cubs players. Once in a while, he'd get a player to give him a ride home. One of the players he befriended was an outfielder name Lou Stringer. He was an infielder for the Cubs in 1941, '42, and '46—becoming one of many major leaguers to have his career interrupted by World War II, which he spent as a physical training instructor before returning to play for the Boston Red Sox from 1948 to 1950. Lou eventually moved to Hollywood, became a bit actor and a car salesman, and loved to talk about the time he sold a Corvette to Elvis Presley.

In 2001, I was in Orange County, California, with a friend of mine whose parents were retired and living in Freedom Village in

Lake Forest. My friend introduced me to his dad and mentioned I was working for the Giants and had once worked for the Cubs. My buddy's dad perked up and said one of his retirement center friends once played for the Cubs. When I asked his name, he said, "Lou Stringer." A few minutes later I was talking to someone who had befriended my uncle Oscar forty years before. Lou's scouting report on my uncle was the same as mine: "He was a character." What are the chances that meeting would take place?

Oscar had a heart of gold. Somehow every holiday season he had an abundance of television sets and eight-track and cassette players that his nephews could sell around the neighborhood to give them cash to buy their parents and siblings gifts at Christmas. They said if Oscar was in a tavern after work in the winter and a stranger came in and asked for directions, Oscar would end up buying the guy dinner and a couple of beers before he was sent on his way.

In 1945, the last time in his lifetime the Cubs would ever be in the World Series—the last time in a lot of people's lives the Cubs would play in the World Series—Oscar conspired to take two of his brothers and a friend to Game 5. Tigers and Cubs. Hal Newhouser versus Hank Borowy.

The night before the game, Oscar, then twenty-eight, announced he would take his brother Joe, eighteen, who sold blocks of ice door-to-door for a quarter a day; my dad, who was just about to turn fifteen; and a buddy to the game. They would ride the streetcar—three cents for a child and nine cents for an adult—to the ballpark, where they "borrowed" some bedsheets from neighborhood clotheslines to stay warm against the Chicago October chill. Then they slept out on the sidewalks bordering Wrigley Field.

In that era, fans could buy bleacher tickets the morning of the game. The bleachers for the last World Series Wrigley Field would host for seventy-one years sold for $1.25. Left on the curb at the corner of Division Street and Oakley Boulevard was little Frankie, the youngest of that generation of Collettis. His brothers told him he was too young to go with them and he stood on the street corner crying, begging to see his beloved Cubs in the World Series. To calm the situation, the brothers—Oscar, Joe, and Ned—made a promise that cancer, the calendar, and the Cubs prevented them from keeping.

"We'll take you the next time the Cubs are in the World Series," they swore. "We promise."

Joe died in 1975. My dad died in 1982. And Oscar died in 1985.

Frankie Colletti, who was eleven years old when Game 5 of the 1945 World Series was played, is eighty-two years old as I type this. He and his brothers were the men who took me to my first games, put a glove on my hand, played catch with me, and taught me how to swing a bat. And because they struggled to make ends meet and fought, literally and figuratively, they taught me that family and friends needed to stay together no matter what. And they taught me how to compete. They taught me about teamwork and just plain old-fashioned hard work. They taught me baseball and, more important, they taught me life.

In 2016, seventy-one years after my dad and his brothers laid out the promise to Frank, the Cubs and I fulfilled it.

So that is how I began this journey. Simple and carefree. A little boy growing up in a garage and then in a little house with freight trains to the south, jets just above, and a yellow brick road named Addison Street twenty-five houses to the north.

I can't tell you I ever dreamt about working in Major League Baseball as an executive or being the general manager of the Cubs or the Dodgers or any other franchise. As grand and magnificent as any young person can dream, that fantasy was just too far away to even imagine. I can tell you I loved baseball and it was a part of every day for me.

Like so many young people I wanted to play major-league baseball and I wanted to play for the Cubs. I never had the extreme talent necessary, or the chance, but the chances I did get were absolutely precious. After fifty-plus years and after attending more than 7,500 professional games, baseball remains part of my soul. It always will be.

It was a helluva ride. More than I ever deserved.

Three

ANSWERED PRAYERS
AND SAD ENDINGS

. . . .

From January 3, 1982, to December 29, 1993, I worked for the Chicago Cubs, my hometown team. I started as the low man in a three-person public relations department and rose to a senior position in the front office, serving as a top aide to three general managers.

I worked with some accomplished baseball executives and players in that time: Dallas Green, Jim Finks, Jim Frey, Don Zimmer, Andre Dawson, Greg Maddux, Ryne Sandberg, Rick Sutcliffe, Mark Grace—just to name a few.

Working for the Cubs was a dream come true. I'd been a fan since I was a boy. My dad set the hook when he took me to my first game at Wrigley Field on April 15, 1961, the day before my seventh birthday. A Saturday afternoon game, Cubs against the Milwaukee Braves. Billy Williams, Ron Santo, Ernie Banks for the Cubs. Hank Aaron, Eddie Matthews, Joe Adcock for the Braves.

Dad bought box seats behind the Cubs' dugout. How he could afford them I never knew.

I remember it snowed a little that day—the wind was bitterly cold. The game ended on a walk-off grand slam by a Cubs out-fielder named Al Heist. I can still see it all: the grand slam, the snow, and my dad.

MY DAD'S LUNG CANCER LED me home. And, in a sense, launched my career in baseball.

His dying got me into baseball.

I was a twenty-six-year-old sports reporter covering the Big Ten for the Danville, Illinois, *Commercial-News* in August 1980. That month, the *Philadelphia Journal* hired me to be their hockey writer, covering the Flyers. It was a major career move and one that initiated a series of opportunities to come.

On our way to Philly, my wife, Gayle, and I decided to stop off in Franklin Park to spend a night with my parents. The house on George and Pacific was tiny. Not just the house, but everything in it, too.

Gayle still tells the story about the first time I took her home to meet my parents. She walked in and saw how small the stove was—maybe three feet wide by four feet high, with four small burners. My dad was five foot seven. I'm five eight. My brother, Doug, was twelve years old at the time, so he was maybe five five. My mom was five three.

We always had a cat, too. But when Gayle came for that first visit, the cat was a kitten.

"Everything in here is miniature," she said as soon as no one else could hear. "The people are miniature. The furniture is miniature. Even the cat is miniature."

By the time we came back in the summer of 1980 for the visit on our way to Philadelphia, Gayle was used to the miniature size of things in the Colletti household. And by then, at least the kitten had grown into a full-size cat.

We had a nice visit. My dad was proud my career was taking off. He had always been proud of his two sons, but he never was one to show his emotions. And he never was one to let us know he was satisfied. He always pushed Doug and me no matter how much we achieved.

Gayle and I were in our car, a classic old beat-up Chevy Chevette, just about to head to Philly when my dad came outside and leaned against the window frame on the driver's side. He never did anything like that. He put his hand on my arm, looked me in the eyes, and said in a heartfelt hush: "I'm so proud of what you've done."

I told him I loved him. I drew a deep, silent breath and drove away. As soon as I turned the corner onto Ernst Street, I looked over at Gayle.

"That was sort of out of character from my dad," I said. "I know he is proud of my brother and me, but it's the first time he ever said it. I think something's bothering him. The look in his eyes . . ."

"Why would you say that?" Gayle asked. "What he just said was so beautiful."

"That's just it," I said. "It's how and what he said. It's almost like he knows he has a problem that he doesn't want to talk about. I think something is wrong."

Unfortunately, I was right.

THE PHILADELPHIA FLYERS TRAINED in Portland, Maine, but I had to get settled in Philly before I headed off to camp. I rented a little place at 3819 Mary Street in Drexel Hill. It was early September 1980 and the weather in the Delaware Valley area was sweltering. Gayle had gone back to Danville to wrap up a few things before moving out. I was living alone in a one-bedroom apartment that was utterly depressing. I had only a few belongings—a sleeping bag, some pots and pans, a few knives and forks, an old hard-sided Samsonite suitcase, and a tiny black-and-white television with a built-in antenna. I would eat dinner off the suitcase, take the paper plates away, then turn the suitcase into a stand for the TV.

The place had a single window-unit air conditioner. I would sit with my back propped against the wall watching TV with the cold air blasting me. At night, I'd sleep right under the air conditioner and I'd wake up freezing. I would struggle to get up and shut it off, go back to sleep, and wake an hour later soaked in sweat. It's a wonder I didn't catch pneumonia or Legionnaires' or some other disease from sleeping on the rancid carpet in ever-changing temperatures. But that's what I did. I was making more money than I'd ever dreamt of—$18,000 a year—and I was writing about a sport I loved—hockey.

I was there about a week when my mom called and gave me the news.

"Your dad is sick," she said.

I never let on to her that I had had a premonition something was wrong, and I still felt as if I'd been punched in the gut. I asked her what was up.

"Your dad thought he had pneumonia, but he has a lung tumor," my mother said, her voice breaking. "In a few days, they're going to operate."

I was due in Portland for the start of Flyers training camp and didn't want to let anybody down. So I flew to Maine and was there a day or two when I realized things were bad enough that I had to get home to help my mother. Doug was in school at Northern Illinois University and couldn't afford to break away. I didn't want him to, anyway. He was more than halfway to a degree and it was very important to my parents that both their sons graduate from college.

So I told my boss at the newspaper I needed to get away for a couple of days. He was great. He said fine, even though I had been on the job less than a month.

The person who took me to the airport in Portland was the radio voice and public relations director of the Maine Mariners, the Flyers' American Hockey League affiliate. Today's hockey fans will recognize the name. Mike Emrick is the top hockey play-by-play announcer in North America and a member of the Hockey Hall of Fame and a nice, nice man.

A few days later, when I returned to Portland, the person who picked me up was Bernie Parent, the great goalie, who then was an executive with the organization.

The kindness of Emrick, Parent, and their longtime publicity man and traveling secretary, Joe Kadlec, was typical of everyone in the Flyers organization. Even though I was a writer who covered the team and often had to write critical stories, the Flyers always treated me with great class and dignity. They always watched out for me, and never more so than in those tough first few days.

While I was in Chicago, my dad had surgery to remove half his lung. Afterward, the doctors told us Dad had a 10 percent chance to live five years. Neither number was good. But the doctors were right. While I had been at funerals for my grandmother, an uncle, and two aunts, my dad's sickness and death took away the innocence I'd been able to cling to for my first twenty-eight years. Thirty-plus years later, I still miss him so much. Rarely has a day gone by that I haven't thought about him. He was a simple man who taught me so much by the way he lived.

WHILE MY DAD WAS FIGHTING for his life, and losing, Gayle settled in Philadelphia and we decided to start a family. We were blessed.

She became pregnant in February, and on October 29, 1981, our son, Lou—Ned Louis Colletti III—was born.

But, as with most young families, the blessing came at a tough financial cost.

A month before Lou was born, Gayle quit her job as a legal secretary. We had a combined income of about $30,000 before she quit and I wanted my son to grow up in a house, not an apartment. So we bought a duplex in Lansdowne, Pennsylvania, west of Philly, for $47,000. The interest rate at the time was 18 percent, which made our house note about $800 a month.

We were going to have to struggle to meet the mortgage as it was, but, then, on December 17, 1981, the *Philadelphia Journal* closed and I was out of a job. In a matter of two months, we went from having a combined income of about $30,000 to nothing. We went from a being a young professional couple to being a young couple scrambling to raise a newborn without a paycheck. We went from paying reasonable rent on a small apartment to facing a huge monthly mortgage. And, all the while, my father was dying in Chicago, about to leave behind a woman who depended on him so much that she never even learned how to drive and, true to the old traditions, had not worked outside the home since I was born.

Luckily, at what seemed like our darkest hour, we were blessed with another miracle.

Bob Ibach, who covered the Flyers before me at the *Journal*, had just moved to Chicago to become public relations director for the Cubs. Dallas Green, the former Phillies manager who had been hired as GM of the Cubs on October 15, 1981, knew Ibach in Philadelphia and brought him to Chicago.

Bob called me out of the blue. "I've got two job openings here for you to consider if you want to come back." "One is in media relations and the other is in publications. I know your dad is sick. I know you love the Cubs, love baseball. I know the paper's folding. If you want to come home, I've got a spot for you."

My first question was the obvious: "What does it pay?"

"Thirteen thousand," Bob said.

I was making $19,000 in Philly before the paper folded. "Let me think about it," I said. "I need to make some calls." I called home and I told my dad.

"You can't do it," he said, emphatically. "You're a new father. You're not just out of college. You're twenty-seven years old. You can't take a pay cut like that."

He was right.

Reluctantly, I turned down the opportunity.

While I continued to look for work, I was talking to my mom and dad every day. About a week after I turned down Ibach's offer, my dad had a change of heart. His health was declining rapidly.

"If you can still take that job, you should do it," he told me, clearly worried about my mother, knowing she would need a lot more physical and emotional support soon.

I called Bob and asked if either job was still open. He said yes.

"Is there any way you can increase the salary or help me pay for the move? Because I don't have any money—I'm in a bad spot."

He said he would talk to Dallas. I asked if I could speak with Dallas for a minute. He set up a call.

Dallas told me flat out there wasn't any more money and that there were many candidates for the positions if I didn't want to take one of them.

I asked him if he would give me sixty seconds. He said, "Go ahead."

"I'm hoping you can give me $15,000 a year and $1,000 to help me move back," I began.

"I told you there's not any more salary for these jobs," he interrupted.

I followed by saying, "You told me you'd give me sixty seconds. I've got thirty seconds left." I continued on. "If you can give me $2,000 more and help me a little with the move, I will do both jobs."

"Both jobs?" Dallas replied.

"Yes, I can do both and I need every dollar I can get. If you don't like the work by April, you can take one away and take the money back. But I know I can do them both."

"I'll have Bob call you back" was all Dallas would say.

When Bob called back, he was excited. Dallas had agreed to the proposal.

It was still going to be a financial struggle, but it would help. I took the job—actually, the jobs.

I wasn't able to distinguish myself from others academically, culturally, athletically, or intellectually, but I did get Dallas's and Bob's attention by my willingness to think differently and offer a productive compromise for the organization. A little more than one thousand days later, Dallas continued to increase my responsibilities by bringing me onto the baseball side. Perhaps my willingness to be different and take on as much as possible was still part of Dallas's scouting report on me. Whatever it was, dividends were being paid.

TO THIS DAY, I feel my prayers were answered on January 3, 1982. That was the day I started with the Cubs. Here it is, more than thirty-five years later, and I've had an incredible career. And, really, it was born out of the folding of a newspaper, me losing a job, and needing to get back to Chicago to be with my dad in his final days so I could help my mom and make it possible for my brother to finish college.

During my first year with the Cubs, my paychecks on the first and fifteenth of the month were for $501. I was clearing $1,002 and we still had an $800 mortgage back in Philly. Plus I had utilities and taxes on the house. So Gayle and I moved in with her parents in the Chicago suburb of Schiller Park. That was uncomfortable, but necessary. We lived in the basement, sleeping on a rollaway bed with Lou in a crib next to us and my mom and dad a mile away in the Little House of the Collettis.

I was scraping by financially. I was driving a 1972 black Ford LTD with a leaky radiator. I couldn't afford to have it fixed, and besides, the car was rusting out. Every morning, I would fill two plastic containers with water and drive the five miles to the end of the Addison Street bus line at Cumberland Avenue. I parked under a streetlight, not knowing how late or dark it would be when I returned via the bus. The car would be overheating as I locked it up—I still couldn't afford to have it stolen—before boarding the bus. At the end of the workday, I would ride the bus back to the end of the line—the same route I had taken as a teenager fifteen years earlier. By then the radiator was safe to open. I would fill it up with water from the plastic container and head back to Franklin Park or Schiller Park, arriving just as the hissing would begin. I did that every day for six weeks. It was cheaper than a new radiator, or a new car, which I couldn't afford.

Gayle's parents were nice people. But her dad wasn't fond of Italians and certainly wasn't happy that his only daughter was married to one. Eventually, it was time to move on. We moved out of his house and into an apartment nearby.

Meanwhile, to help make ends meet, I did something that turned out great for my career. I asked Dallas Green if I could travel with the team. I needed the expense money. We weren't receiving meal money back then, but if I was on the road I wouldn't have to buy groceries for myself. The bonus was that I became closer to the players, coaches, and managers—forging friendships and relationships that would help me for years to come. I was always respectful of the opportunities to sit with Dallas; our manager, Lee Elia; and members of the coaching staff. I sought wisdom. I craved the chance to sit and listen to those who came before me, who experienced what I had yet to experience. During my first two years, I rarely offered an opinion. I listened. As the thirtieth president of the United States, Calvin Coolidge, once said, "No man ever listened himself out of a job."

Another blessing was that we sold the Philadelphia house in April because, believe it or not, interest rates were going even higher. Everyone kept telling us how lucky we were to have an assumable 18 percent mortgage. But that kind of luck was about to drive me into another kind of house—the Poor House.

MY DAD DIED on April 27, 1982—three weeks after we sold the house. The season had just started. I wasn't even four months into my baseball career. I remember thinking how sad it was that my dad never was able to go to Wrigley Field with me while I was working for the Cubs. But as we were waiting to bury my dad, the Cubs gave us a small spiritual gift. The day of my dad's wake, Wednesday, April 28, 1982, as we were sitting around the living room of the four-room house in Franklin Park waiting to go to the funeral home, my uncle Frank and I turned on the Cubs. As usual, the hometown team, losers of twelve of their first eighteen games, was off to a miserable start.

It was a midweek afternoon game between two mediocre teams—the Cubs and the Reds—at a sorrowful time in my life. But it was baseball. And gradually, as the afternoon unfolded, a little magic happened. Dickie Noles, whom Dallas had just brought to the Cubs from Philadelphia, threw the first complete game of his then-young career—a one-hit shutout completed in just one hour and fifty-one minutes. The lone hit was a single by Reds right fielder Eddie Milner to lead off the fourth inning. I'll always be grateful for baseball, to Dickie Noles, for that game. He didn't know my dad had died, but he took our minds off the sorrow for a couple of hours.

THE NEXT TWELVE YEARS were more than a bit brighter. They were wonderful. I rose through the media relations department to succeed Bob Ibach as the Cubs' PR director. In 1990, I won Major League Baseball's Robert O. Fishel Award for Public Relations Excellence and, along with winners before and since, was honored in a special section of the National Baseball Hall of Fame in Cooperstown, New York. I helped lead the transition to the first night baseball game in Wrigley Field history, coordinated an All-Star Game, was part of the first two Cubs playoff series since World War II, and became friends with more than a dozen Hall of Famers and scores of great people. Dallas had helped turn the franchise and the culture around and I had the benefit of having a front-row seat for it all.

During the 1984–85 off-season, I made the rare migration from PR into the inner sanctum of the Cubs' baseball operations department, initially preparing the club's side of arbitration cases and eventually negotiating some of the biggest contracts in baseball. I was always good at public relations. The job was a perfect fit for my personality. In fact, years later, when I was general manager of the Dodgers, a columnist for the *Los Angeles Times* labeled me the "schmoozer." And I guess I was. I like people. And that ability to get along with people—to schmooze with the best of them—helped open the door to the front office for me. The baseball world is built on competition and confrontation. A good PR person has the ability to deal with both and remain friends with just about everybody. Granted, like everyone, I had my moments with people when personalities clashed. But they were few in number.

I was fortunate to be mentored by the late Jim Finks, probably the best "people person" I ever encountered in the executive ranks of sports. Few fans knew Jim Finks and probably fewer still remember him, but he single-handedly changed the losing cultures at the Chicago Bears and New Orleans Saints and helped Dallas change the culture with the Cubs. He was a gifted and insightful leader. More than thirty years later, I was having dinner with longtime NFL executive and Pro Football Hall of Fame inductee Bill Polian and we were talking about building culture and winning teams. I told him about my respect for Jim Finks and the impact he had on me. Polian looked at me and smiled. He told me Finks had done the same for him when he was just starting in the NFL.

Of course, there had been rough times during my twelve years. But never, even in the worst moments, did I think I would leave the Cubs. And I wouldn't have if it had been my choice. But it wasn't. Gayle and I came home from Gayle's birthday dinner on December 28, 1993, to find a message from my boss waiting on our answering machine.

Larry Himes had been general manager of the Cubs a little more than two years—since November 14, 1991—and in that relatively short time, we had worked closely on everything from negotiating what was then the biggest contract in MLB history, for Ryne Sandberg, to the sad, and unnecessary, losses of Greg Maddux and Andre Dawson, both of whom should have played out their career with the Cubs.

To say that Larry and I weren't particularly close on a personal level would be a laughable understatement. But we did make a solid professional team. He was a good judge of baseball talent but, in my opinion, didn't have the "people skills" that Jim Finks had in his pinky finger.

Larry's message on the answering machine that depressing December night was short and sweet. Give him a call. I felt my stomach knot as soon as I heard it. Larry never called me—especially in the dead of winter; especially between Christmas and New Year's. That wasn't the relationship we had. And that wasn't his style.

I looked at Gayle and said: "I'm getting fired tomorrow."

"Get outta here," she said.

"Why else would this man be calling me?" was all I said.

HIMES MADE AN ATTEMPT to sound upbeat when I reached him. "Hey, Ned, how are you doing?"

I said I was all right and asked what was going on.

"How about coming down to the office about ten o'clock tomorrow for a meeting?" he said.

"Really? You want to tell me what it's about?"

Himes hemmed and hawed for a second. "Just come by tomorrow. I'll talk to you when you get here."

As soon as I got off the phone, I called Mark McGuire (not to be confused with Mark McGwire, former player), whom I'd worked with for twelve years. Mark was executive vice president of business operations at the Cubs. "Mark, do you have any idea why I'm going to see Larry Himes tomorrow?"

There was silence on the other end of the phone.

"Um, well, there's been some talk . . ." And he couldn't finish. He didn't know what to say.

"About firing me?"

"Well, there's been some talk."

Needless to say, I couldn't sleep that night. I was so jittery, I left the house early. Instead of driving down Irving Park Road straight to Wrigley Field, as I usually did, I took the Eisenhower Expressway to Tribune Tower, about five miles from Himes's office.

The Tower stands at 435 North Michigan Avenue, but beneath Michigan Avenue at that point is a vast underground world. The famous Billy Goat Tavern is down there. So, too, are the VIP parking spots for Tribune Company officials. I knew where the Tribune Company's chief financial officer, Don Grenesko, parked. (Grenesko had held a senior leadership position with the Cubs until 1991, when he moved full-time to the Tribune Tower.) At about 8:30 a.m., an hour and a half before my meeting with Himes, I spotted Grenesko's car and decided I needed to talk to him.

When we were together, I asked Grenesko point-blank if he had heard anything about me getting fired.

"You're kidding me, right?" he said, seemingly genuinely surprised.

"I'm not," I said. "I think I'm going to get fired in about an hour."

He said, "I can't believe that."

"Well, call Mark McGuire. If anyone would know, he would."

Grenesko dialed McGuire. Obviously, I could hear only one side of the conversation, but when Don hung up he looked at me and said, "I think you're right. I can't believe it."

BEFORE JIM FREY replaced Dallas Green as general manager of the Cubs on November 11, 1987, I'd straddled two worlds: leading the PR department and doing special projects for the baseball front office. When Frey took over, he wanted me full-time in the baseball front office. Grenesko wanted me to make the move as well, and personally approached me about it.

"Don, I don't want to be one of those guys who get pushed out when Jimmy Frey leaves because I'm tied to Jimmy," I said. "As much as I love Jimmy, I work for the Cubs, not any one person."

"That will never happen," Grenesko assured me. "You're too good here. We think the world of you. The executives who run the company think the world of you. You'll be here for life if you want."

I made the transition and worked with Frey for the next few years. When he was fired and replaced by Larry Himes, I stayed on.

Himes made sweeping changes. He fired, or demoted, a number of good people, including farm director Billy Harford and scouting director Dick Balderson. But I survived—for another two years, anyway.

Then came the meeting two days before New Year's Eve in 1993.

HIMES, AS USUAL, hemmed and hawed and seemed nervous and uncomfortable.

"I'm going to have to make a move," he finally mustered.

My instincts and my calls to McGuire and Grenesko had prepared me and I was ready to make my case. "What have I done wrong?"

"You haven't done anything wrong," Himes said, averting eye contact. "I'm just not comfortable having you here."

I've been blessed to be a better negotiator than most because I can usually see beyond the emotion of the moment to the heart of the issue on the table. "Larry, after twelve years with the Cubs, that's kind of a weak answer, don't you think?"

All he could come up with was the same lame "because I said so" answer that underperforming parents fall back on when all else fails. "Well, I'm the boss and that's what I'm going to do."

"Larry, I haven't done anything wrong," I said. "I've been loyal to you. I've been loyal to the organization. I just don't understand it."

More awkward silence ensued.

"So you think you'll be going back to your hometown in Philly now?" he asked, hoping to wrap up the conversation with a personal touch.

I was stunned—more stunned than I had been an hour or so earlier when Grenesko confirmed my fears about being fired. "My hometown, Philly?" I said.

"Yeah. Aren't you from Philly?"

"I grew up in Chicago," I shot back, stifling the f-word. "I've been coming to this ballpark since I was six years old. I've been coming here for thirty-three years."

Himes got the deer-in-the-headlights look that fit his personality so perfectly. "I didn't know that," he mumbled.

"You didn't know that?" I squeaked. "I've worked for you the last two-plus years and you don't know where I'm from or anything about me, do ya?"

The rest of our meeting is best left unprinted.

I walked out and we didn't speak for nearly a decade.

TIM KURKJIAN, the talented baseball writer and broadcaster, wrote an article in *Sports Illustrated* in May 1994 calling Himes "one of the least-liked executives in baseball"—a label the Chicago media quickly embellished into "the most-hated man in baseball."

I'd be less than honest if I didn't admit it provided me with some measure of satisfaction. I try not to be a vindictive person. But I wasn't saddened when Larry was fired in October 1994, just ten months after he shattered my world.

Himes managed to stay on with the Cubs for years as an advisor. As I said, he is a solid judge of baseball talent.

I joined the San Francisco Giants in November 1994 and rose to be assistant general manager of a team that went to the World Series in 2002.

Years later, when I was named general manager of the Los Angeles Dodgers, one of the first messages I received was from Larry Himes.

"Very happy for you," it read. "Congratulations."

Four

THE BEST

• • • • • • • • • • • • •

Himes and Andre Dawson also didn't see eye to eye. Larry had made the tough decision to let Andre leave the Cubs as a free agent following the 1992 season. Dawson played longer in Montreal than Chicago and had his No. 10 retired by the Expos. Yet he was revered by the fans and his teammates in Chicago.

In my thirty-five-plus years in baseball, I have been in awe of just one player, and that was Dawson.

"The Hawk" was the best. I remember the day he walked into my world. It was early in Spring Training 1987 and I was standing in the parking lot of Fitch Park, then the Chicago Cubs' minor-league complex, just down the street from HoHoKam Park in Mesa, Arizona. I heard an unexpected buzz of excitement and looked up to see Andre and his agent, Dick Moss, walking purposefully down a sidewalk toward the cinder-block building where Dallas Green had his office. I was struck by how Dawson was dressed. He was wearing a suit that was all class and style in a setting where everyone around him was wearing shorts and T-shirts. The Hawk was the epitome of class—that day and every day.

This will be interesting, I thought.

Dawson was a free agent. He had broken off negotiations with the Montreal Expos on December 10, 1986, and Moss had said publicly and repeatedly for six weeks that Dawson wanted to go to the Cubs. As a visiting player he had a .346 lifetime batting average at Wrigley Field. He loved playing day games. And he desperately wanted to take his aching knees off the artificial turf at Montreal's Olympic Stadium, where he'd played for ten seasons.

At almost any other time in its history, the Cubs organization would have been falling all over itself to woo a player of Dawson's professional talent and personal class. But 1986 was smack in the middle of a three-year period when major-league owners conspired to hold down salaries of baseball's top free agents. Against federal law and specific provisions in the collective bargaining agreement (CBA) they had signed with the Major League Baseball Players Association, the owners colluded to cap salaries and limit the maximum length of contracts to three years for position players and two years for pitchers. Collusion was an enormous success for the owners—at least until the courts stepped in later to rectify the injustice.

During the 1985–86 off-season, none of baseball's thirty-three free agents signed with a new club. Twenty-nine of the thirty-three signed back with their existing clubs. Four others were unable to find a job. The only free agent that year who even drew an offer from another club was future Hall of Fame catcher Carlton Fisk. Yankees owner George Steinbrenner quickly withdrew his offer to Fisk when he was reminded he wasn't playing by the new rules.

During the 1986–87 off-season, Dawson was the most prominent free agent among a particularly strong class that included the Hawk's Montreal teammate Tim Raines, plus Ron Guidry, Jack Morris, Lance Parrish, Bob Boone, and Bob Horner. Even with strong career borderline Hall of Fame careers, three-fourths of the free agents on the market had to settle for one-year contracts and only four had signed with new organizations. For the first time since free agency began, salaries for players on the open market declined 16 percent.

Of course, by the time Andre and Dick walked into the Cubs' complex in February 1987, everyone who had even passing interest in the bargaining process knew the owners were colluding against the players. Nobody could prove it, but the Hawk was about to make it clear to all the world.

"DALLAS, YOU'RE GOING to have a visitor in a minute," I said, slipping into Green's office. "Andre Dawson and Dick Moss are headed this way. They're coming here to see you."

The eighth general manager of the Chicago Cubs looked exasperated. Moss had come to the Cubs' camp twice the week before. After his first visit, Moss told the media he believed Commissioner Peter Ueberroth and the Tribune Company had banned Green from negotiating with Dawson. When Moss returned to camp the next day, Green refused to meet him. Frustrated, Moss wrote Green a personal letter and had it hand-delivered by legendary scout Hughie Alexander, one of Green's closest advisors. Green responded by calling a press conference at which he demanded an apology from Moss and said Dawson should fire his agent.

"I have always had a good rapport with Dick, but the blatant innuendos and accusations he allegedly told the press is a perfect example of why so many people in baseball intensely dislike the man," Green said. "Peter Ueberroth and [Tribune Company executive VP] John Madigan deserve apologies. I am very upset at being characterized as being a puppet for baseball and Tribune Company, two groups accused by Dick Moss of doing something improper.

"If that's his approach to negotiations and trying to bring out all of this baloney and back me into a corner that he thinks is going to embarrass me or make me step forward, he'll find that Dallas Green has a little bit different approach. I don't like to get backed into a corner, and I don't like to be called names."

Just four days after that public rant, Moss and Dawson were in camp yet again—clearly determined to back Green into a corner. If Moss had come alone, Green would have again refused to see him. But Green couldn't be rude to Dawson, especially a Dawson who was dressed up for the big date.

The conversation between Moss and Green was strained. Dallas clearly didn't know what to make of it or how to handle it.

Finally, Moss came to the point. He asked Green, "Do you have a blank contract? You know, a boilerplate National League contract."

"I do," Green said, still unsure where Moss was headed.

"Can you get me one?" the agent asked.

Dallas had his longtime assistant, Arlene Gill, bring in a standard Major League Baseball player contract. Most of the contract is preprinted, covering everything from provisions on personal conduct to ownership of club clothing and uniforms. Section IV, which covers "Duration and Conditions of Employment," contains blank spaces for salary and length of the contract. The final page, under the heading "Execution of This Contract," contains blank lines for the signatures of the player, the general manager, and the commissioner.

Moss took the blank green contract, handed it to Dawson, and had the Hawk sign the back page.

"I want to be a Cub," Dawson said to Dallas. "You can fill in the rest."

In a two-page memo he handed out to the media, Moss said Dawson was willing to take a one-year contract on "whatever terms Mr. Madigan and Dallas Green think is appropriate."

"Dallas knows who Andre is, what other players are being paid and what kind of role Andre will have with the Cubs," the memo read. "We will give our opinion of what is fair, but it will only be for information and advice—the Cubs will decide. [Andre] is willing to report to camp within the next few days on the basis of such a contract, or if the club needs more time to consider our offer, he is willing to report without a contract, with no obligation on the part of the club to sign him at all. If the Cubs feel that they want to see how Andre looks before signing him, we are perfectly willing to accommodate their desires. We are making this offer as a sincere attempt to bring about a result we believe everyone involved wants— Andre, the Cubs, and their fans—Andre Dawson in a Cub uniform, helping the club achieve greater success. It is not a ploy or a public relations gimmick. We so strongly believe the goal is correct, that Andre is willing to, and has, put himself out on a limb."

Officially backed into a corner, Green responded with another angry outburst. "In my heart I don't feel that we need Andre Dawson. We need every one of those guys in that locker room. They are signed, they're Chicago Cubs. And some of them have not performed too well in the past. If they perform up to their past capabilities, and what we feel are their present capabilities, I'm not sure we need Andre Dawson."

How Dallas even managed to say those words with a straight face still baffles me. But he was mad as hell and he let everyone know it.

"It's a bunch of bull," he said of the blank contract ploy. "I find it rather strange that we come to Spring Training and the guy that is in charge of a particular free agent wants to put on a dog and pony show at my expense in my complex, using my press. . . . I'm not sure that's the correct way of putting a free agent in a Cubs uniform. I really resent the way we've gone about this thing. I mean, it's a circus. This is the way the man operates. I was hoping he wouldn't choose to do that. But he chose it. Let him lie in the bed. He's the one with the free agent."

Two days later, Green was the one with the free agent. On

March 5, 1987, he returned Dawson's signed contract with the blanks filled in and his own signature added to the back page. The contract was for one year at $500,000, less than half the $1,047,000 Dawson was paid by the Expos the year before.

Moss was disappointed at the salary but had represented Dawson with class.

"We had hoped that the club's definition of fairness would have been more realistic, but our offer was unconditional and we will, of course, honor our commitment," he said in a prepared statement. "Andre will be paid a salary, in my opinion, less than one-half of what he would be entitled to if he were properly slotted into baseball's salary structure. However, none of this detracts in any way from his enthusiasm of joining the Cubs or his eagerness to make a contribution to the team's competitiveness."

Dawson backed up those words. He played in 153 games, led the National League in home runs (49) and RBI (137), scored 90 runs, stole 11 bases, and won a Gold Glove. He became the first player in history to win the Most Valuable Player Award for a last-place team. Yeah, the team that didn't need Andre Dawson finished at the bottom of the National League East in 1987. Just think what the year would have been without the Hawk.

I HAD THE PRIVILEGE of knowing and working with Dawson for six seasons in Chicago. As I said earlier, he was the only player I ever truly was in awe of. That's not to diminish Greg Maddux, Ryne Sandberg, Barry Bonds, Manny Ramirez, Clayton Kershaw, or any of the other great players I know. In Manny's case, our time together in Los Angeles was brief and after his prime. In the case of Maddux and Sandberg, I got to know them when they were still young players and working to get established. I saw Maddux post records of 2-4 and 6-14 with a 5.59 ERA his first two seasons. I watched Ryno hit seven home runs his rookie season and eight the next, while batting just .266. And Barry's personality at the beginning of our relationship certainly didn't promote "awe."

The Hawk was in a class by himself. In 1983, four years before Dawson came to the Cubs, *The New York Times* conducted a poll of major-league players to see who they considered to be the best player in baseball. Dawson was the overwhelming favorite. Getting to know him—his class, his humility, his passion for playing—was phenomenal.

Anyone who watched the Hawk or played with or against him can reel off countless examples of his heart and hustle. One of my favorites came early in his first season in Chicago. The Cubs were playing the Houston Astros at Wrigley Field on June 2, 1987—a rainy Tuesday afternoon. Dawson hit a two-run homer onto Waveland Avenue in the third inning, just one batter before the umpires stopped the game because of rain and darkness. It rained so hard that water was pouring into the clubhouse. The delay was two hours and forty-six minutes.

Dawson suffered mightily with bad knees his entire career. He had twelve surgeries in twenty-one seasons. And he needed hours to get taped and stretched out for a game and nearly as long in a hot tub postgame. His home run had given the Cubs a fairly comfortable 4–1 lead and no one would have thought twice if the Hawk pulled himself out of the game after sitting nearly three hours in the damp clubhouse. But the thought never crossed Dawson's mind. He went out and played the rest of the game, hitting a triple and another home run—finishing the day 4-for-5 with seven RBI, a stolen base, and two runs scored in a 13–2 win over the Astros. Before his final at-bat, hitting coach Billy Williams let Dawson know he was just a double away from hitting for the cycle. Williams jokingly told Andre that if he hit a home run, he should touch first base, touch second, then miss third so he would be called out and credited with a double. Dawson did, in fact, hit a home run. But he ignored Billy's advice and circled the bases with his head down.

As impressive as Dawson's offensive display was, and as admirable his grit in coming back after the long rain delay, the moment I remember most about that afternoon was a foul ball by Glenn Davis in the top of the sixth inning. The Cubs had a 9–1 lead and the game was more than five hours old, counting the rain delay. The outfield, which hadn't been covered during the downpour, was dangerously wet. When Davis hit a looping fly ball toward the visitors' bullpen, Dawson sloshed full bore and made an amazing catch before crashing into the low brick retaining wall beyond the bullpen.

After the game, Fred Mitchell, the Cubs' beat writer for the *Chicago Tribune*, asked Dawson why he put himself, and his crippled knees, in such danger to go after a foul ball in a blowout game.

"I went after it the way I did because the ball was in play," said Dawson, clearly confused that anyone would think he should have done anything else.

And if all that weren't enough, an inning after crashing into a brick wall chasing a foul ball, Dawson dove headlong to make a dramatic catch of a sinking line drive by Houston rookie Chuck Johnson. The Cubs were leading 11–1 at the time. Most other players simply would have played the ball on one hop.

Not the Hawk.

The ball was in play.

THE FIRST WEEK of the 1992 season, Dawson's last with the Cubs, a reporter asked Shawon Dunston how many games he thought he would play that season. Dunston had back problems in 1991 and still was struggling a year later. In fact, he would wind up having surgery in May. But the first week of the season, he was trying to play through the injury.

Dunston's locker was next to the Hawk's. When the reporter asked Dunston how many games he expected to play that year, Dawson listened to the answer.

"I'm hoping maybe 120 games, 120 or 130."

Dawson exploded. "The season's just starting and you're writing off forty-two games? What's wrong with you, Shawon?" Hawk walked off, shaking his head in disgust, headed to the trainer's room to have his thirty-seven-year-old knees iced and taped.

EVEN ON THE RARE OCCASIONS when he dressed them down, Dawson's teammates loved him. So did everyone associated with the team. Traveling secretary Peter Durso thought the world of the Hawk. One of Durso's many roles was being in charge of the team bus, deciding when it left the hotel for the ballpark and when it pulled out for the return trip after the game. Traditionally, the bus would leave forty-five minutes after the last pitch. That was plenty of time for most players. But Dawson had to meet the press, ice his knees, get a shower, try to squeeze in a light workout, grab some dinner, and do any number of things to keep his painful body from shutting down. He was always the last player out of the clubhouse, no matter how much he rushed. But as long as Durso, who worked with Andre in Montreal as well, was in charge, the bus wasn't going anywhere until Dawson was ready.

"Is the Hawk on the bus?" Durso would ask every night as he climbed into the front right seat reserved for the traveling secretary. "We ain't leaving till the Hawk's on the bus."

More often than not, Dawson's soft, deep voice would come from the back.

"I'm on the bus, Peter."

"All right, we're out of here."

ONE OF THE TOUGHEST THINGS I have ever had to do in my professional career was be involved in an arbitration case against the Hawk after the 1987 season.

I was in a mixed role with the Cubs at the time. I was still overseeing media relations, but I was continually building my career on the baseball side, including preparing management's arguments in arbitration cases.

On Valentine's Day 1988, I spent three hours sitting across from Andre and Vanessa Dawson as arbitration judge Stephen Goldberg listened to the arguments I had helped put together. After winning the MVP Award on a cut-rate salary, Dawson was asking for $2 million in 1988. We offered $1.85 million.

Goldberg had to choose one or the other, no middle ground. He ruled against Dawson.

"I think Andre Dawson is a terrific athlete and he had a spectacular season," Goldberg said at the end of the hearing.

Yet when rendering a decision Goldberg said, "But weighing all the considerations, which I must under the guidelines, I just could not see my way clear to give him the amount demanded in the case."

As he was leaving the hearing, someone asked Dawson what he thought about the process.

"That's the damnedest three hours I've ever spent anywhere," he said.

I couldn't have agreed more.

In the end, though, it all worked out fine. We respected Dawson so much that six weeks later, just before Opening Day, we added two more years to his contract, offering additional incentive clauses on top of the $1.85 million he would be getting for 1988, and guaranteeing $2.1 million a year for 1989 and '90.

Even after that awkward arbitration hearing, Andre and I became close friends. He once gave me a collection of custom-made neckties, which I still have, honoring his kindness and our friendship. Even though many people have come into my life in the last thirty-plus years, I still consider him one of the top five people I've met in the game. When I do see him now, it's still special for me just to say hello. The man is class. I am, and always will be, proud to be his friend.

Five

MADDUX—
"NO ONE IS BIGGER"

· · · · · · · · · · · · · ·

Dawson and Greg Maddux are two Cubs who are honored in Cooperstown. Both were tremendous performers for the franchise and both were fan favorites.

Both left the Cubs within days of each other on Himes's watch and both signed elsewhere—Dawson with Boston and Maddux with Atlanta—on December 9, 1992. A difficult day at the corner of Clark and Addison streets on Chicago's North Side.

Dawson's moment in time was different than Maddux's. Andre was thirty-nine years old. Though he was still productive in his final Chicago season, age and knee surgeries were beginning to take a toll.

Maddux, however, was nearly twelve years younger and entering his prime. In the nearly thirty years before that wintry December day in 1992, Cubs fans had bemoaned Brock-for-Broglio as the franchise's low-water mark in the player marketplace. And that it had been—two key words: *had been*.

To briefly touch on the first misstep, on June 15, 1964, the most one-sided trade in Cubs history took place when the Cubs acquired right-handed starting pitcher Ernie Broglio from the Cardinals in a six-player deal that sent outfielder Lou Brock to St. Louis.

Broglio, who won eighteen games in 1963, had pitched poorly in 1964 and, in fact, hadn't been used regularly for three weeks prior to the deal. He pitched once between May 24 and June 12—a span of twenty days. Hampered by a sore elbow he brought with him from St. Louis, Broglio pitched fifty-nine games with the Cubs during the next two-plus seasons. His record was 7-19 with a 5.40 ERA.

Little more than two years after the trade, Broglio was out of baseball. Brock, one of the greatest leadoff hitters of all time, went on to produce a Hall of Fame career with more than 3,000 hits and a then–MLB career record of 938 stolen bases. From 1967 to 1971 alone, he stole more bases than the Cubs did as a team—and those Cubs teams were the best the franchise had in the second half of the twentieth century. They were led by four Hall of Famers—Ernie Banks, Billy Williams, Fergie Jenkins, and Ron Santo. Just think if they had a fifth Hall of Famer with them.

Ask Cubs fans today, and many would say the loss of Greg Maddux to the Atlanta Braves in 1992 was worse than Brock-for-Broglio.

I was deeply involved in the Maddux negotiations. His agent was Scott Boras, and Scott and I have been involved in many deals, including one with Barry Bonds and another with Manny Ramirez. But the Maddux negotiations may have been the most historic for many reasons, including how the outcome dramatically changed both franchises.

When Maddux signed as a free agent with the Braves after two years of talks with the Cubs, the Braves already had won two consecutive division championships, but would go on to run off another twelve and go to the World Series three times, winning once. The Cubs, meanwhile, would win one division title and have four ninety-loss seasons during those eleven years in which Greg pitched in Atlanta.

In the end, the final offers were a mere $100,000 a year apart for five years—a difference of less than 2 percent of the deal. With major incentive bonuses attached to the Cubs' offer, Greg might have earned more as a Cub than he did as a Brave.

Most negotiations have backstories and a clouded history—the more prominent the deal, the more twists and turns. This one is no different.

Greg's backstory began in the spring of 1990, when, at twenty-three, he signed a two-year deal for $275,000 and $437,500, covering the 1990 and 1991 seasons. The deal bought out Greg's first year of salary arbitration and was a good one for the Cubs. Boras didn't represent Maddux in those negotiations, but he probably used that deal as ammunition to convince Greg to let him represent him soon thereafter.

The first time Scott negotiated a contract for Maddux was before the 1992 season. Greg signed for $2.4 million as a second-time arbitration player.

In the fall of 1991, Greg had Boras as an agent and a career record of 75-64. He was coming off a very good 1991 season, in which he went 15-11 with a 3.35 ERA.

He had yet to win a Cy Young Award but, after a combined 8-18 record his first two major-league seasons, it was clear Greg was becoming one of the best in the game.

The question was whether he was going to exceed all expectations—which he did. But at the time, no one knew. And that made negotiations difficult (since Scott was about to accurately predict, by way of his salary demand, a future that far exceeded every other pitcher in the game at that point). Would Greg want a long-term deal that offered him security? Or would he opt to sign year by year at more money with the chance to cash in time and again?

On December 3, 1991, I flew to Phoenix, Arizona, with Dennis Homerin, the lead negotiator at the Tribune Company, which owned the Cubs, to meet with free agent pitcher Mike Morgan. Mike's agent was Joe Garagiola Jr., who later would help bring the Arizona Diamondbacks to life and be their general manager when they won the World Series in 2001. We met with Mike and Joe at a Doubletree hotel on Forty-Fourth Street near Sky Harbor International Airport and after four hours agreed to terms on a three-year, $12 million deal.

Homerin was tough, with book and street smarts, and gave me an education in negotiation techniques and styles. Legend had it that before he was forty he had suffered a serious heart attack while driving from one high-level meeting to another, and drove himself to the hospital.

I had the baseball expertise and he had the legal and negotiating background so we teamed up to do the contracts for the Cubs. We had arrived in Phoenix that Tuesday morning, negotiated a contract with Morgan, and then took a quick flight to Las Vegas to meet with Boras, arriving near dinnertime in Maddux's hometown.

We stayed at the newest Vegas hot spot—the Mirage hotel and casino, then just a little more than two years old.

On Wednesday morning, Dennis and I met with Scott at a coffee shop in the hotel. We laid out our plan and where we thought the deal should end up. We were prepared to make Greg the highest-paid pitcher in major-league history.

The highest-paid National League pitcher on that December morning was Dwight Gooden of the New York Mets, who earned $15.45 million over three years—a contract he agreed to in April of that year. The average annual value (AAV) was $5.15 million a year. When Dwight signed that contract he was twenty-six years old.

Here was his track record when he signed: In 1985, he finished twenty games over .500, with a 24-4 record and 1.53 ERA, and won the Cy Young Award, after finishing second for baseball's top pitching award during his Rookie of the Year season in 1984. He had three other top seven Cy Young finishes on his resume along with season won-loss records of 17-6, 15-7, 18-9, 9-4, and 19-7. He was the dominant pitcher in the National League and helped the Mets win the 1986 World Series.

Gooden's equal on the other side of that historic 1986 World Series was Boston Red Sox ace Roger Clemens—the highest-paid American League pitcher at that time. Clemens signed a four-year $21.521 million contract prior to the 1991 season. The average annual value of Roger's deal was $5,380,250.

Roger's career numbers were even more impressive: Clemens, twenty-eight, also had a season in which he was twenty games over .500. In 1986, he won his first Cy Young Award with a 24-4 record and also won the AL Most Valuable Player Award. He followed that up with a 20-9 season in 1987 and won a second Cy Young Award. After an 18-12 record in 1988 and 17-11 in 1989, he was 21-6 in 1990 and finished second in the Cy Young Award voting, which led to the four-year deal.

As we sat down with Scott that morning, Clemens, one year into his four-year deal, had also won his third Cy Young Award a couple of weeks earlier.

Greg was coming off a 15-11 record in 1991 and had been 15-15 in 1990, both years he had ERAs in the mid-3s. In 1988, Greg had an 18-8 record. In 1989, he was 19-12 and finished second in the Cy Young voting.

Unlike Gooden and Clemens, Greg, twenty-five, had yet to win a Cy Young Award, let alone two. He hadn't won twenty games in a season, much less win twenty more games than he lost in a single season, as Gooden and Clemens had done in their 24-4 years.

In spite of that, all of us recognized that Maddux was at or near the top of the pitchers in Major League Baseball. And the Cubs, being aggressive both in an offer and in its timing, since Greg still had a season to go before free agency, had Homerin and I offer $25 million over five years during breakfast with Scott.

The offer was a few dollars behind Gooden and Clemens in average annual value but included an extra year—always a value point to a pitcher who could be one pitch away from a career-altering injury. We were willing to go the extra year because of Greg's age and the smoothness of his delivery.

We had expected a positive response or, at the very least, some momentum toward a deal. We received just the opposite. We were told we weren't close to what it would take.

As we drove down Las Vegas Boulevard on the way to McCarran International Airport we passed the MGM Grand, where Greg's dad, David, dealt blackjack. I had played at David's table when I would go to Vegas every fall with Don Zimmer and Jimmy Frey. I looked across the car at Homerin and said, "I wonder if David Maddux will know what his son just turned down. Seems like a lot to be walking from at this stage of life."

Greg grew up in Las Vegas and appreciated the art of a gamble. He believed in himself and was willing to take a chance on what he could accomplish during the upcoming season, just ahead of free agency.

Greg and Scott were a perfect fit. Scott rarely negotiates a long-term deal before a player reaches free agency, unless it is a clear overpay. He believes in his clients and is confident the player will earn more than those who came before him, even if another player's career trajectory is relatively the same or even less. The agents also know when they represent top-end talent that clubs don't want to lose and hence can be persuaded to move higher and higher and higher even if there aren't players at that lofty salary—it's the price of doing business to secure those considered among the very best.

And Scott's clientele come at contract negotiations with the same approach. The players believe in his process. They have seen success and patiently wait for him to call with an offer that typically will exceed everyone's expectations—except maybe Scott's.

As we were trying to lock up Maddux, Scott probably knew Baltimore was going to extend Cal Ripken Jr. a deal that would continue to move the position-player market upward. Also looming out there was free-agent-to-be outfielder Barry Bonds; a potential new ownership group in San Francisco; and the possibility the Giants would make an historic, franchise-altering move that off-season by signing Bonds, which they did—at the Louisville Winter Meetings for a record $43.75 million, six-year contract.

The Winter Meetings are the exclamation point to the baseball calendar year. Held every December, the Winter Meetings are baseball's annual convention. They are hosted by the National Association, which is the umbrella organization for all minor-league teams. The Winter Meetings have changed a lot since my first meetings in 1982.

Back then, front-office staffs were smaller. Trade discussions took place in the hotel lobby and in hallways and back rooms. There was a lot of socializing and beverage consumption. The storytelling was robust.

Since the early 1980s, the influx of agents and the explosion of media have steadily moved baseball's decision makers out of the lobbies and into the privacy of suites. The social aspect of baseball's annual convention has been diluted.

Scouts still fill the lobbies, trading information with other scouts and helping set up clandestine meetings between GMs and each team's inner circle. But these days, it's possible to spend four days/ nights in a sprawling hotel and not see half the leaders from the other clubs. During my Dodger years, I typically would be in the lobby when I checked in and checked out—and maybe two or three other times for a few minutes. That was it.

Fading from the Winter Meetings are the sessions filled with long-winded war stories from seasons gone by. But it was where a young executive could learn the game and gain respect from those who had already walked the road during the previous decades and years. In the early years, I knew people who had known Babe Ruth, watched Ty Cobb, spoken with Joe DiMaggio. Now, modern technology is drowning voices with the barely audible click of texts and tweets. The Winter Meetings are becoming a mirror of the rest of society.

The Winter Meetings are also where agents, like Scott, can put the intense focus on their clients and the agents' ability to score big contracts.

THE LACK OF A LONG-TERM contract for Greg hung over the Cubs front office all of 1992. Other clubs began an earnest effort to scout this player who normally would never be available. Early in the 1992 season, the Yankees sent major-league scout and former pitcher Dick Tidrow (an associate of mine with the Giants years later) to see Maddux at Wrigley Field. Tidrow watched Maddux take batting practice before a game he was due to start. He saw Maddux leave the field and return to the clubhouse. Tidrow, who had pitched for the Cubs, knew the Cubs' clubhouse manager, Yosh Kawano.

Tidrow went down to the clubhouse and knocked on the door. Yosh answered. Tidrow asked him if he had any chewing tobacco. Yosh invited him in and they went to get the tobacco. They walked down the stairs and through the long clubhouse. Tidrow walked by a table where Maddux, the only player in the clubhouse, was playing cards by himself. Maddux looked up but didn't say a word and kept shuffling cards. Tidrow had wanted to see how Maddux prepared for a game. Tidrow sought every edge he could.

Months passed and the Cubs had played probably 120 games

since that day. Maddux had only a few starts remaining when Tidrow returned to Wrigley Field. The same routine followed: Maddux took batting practice, left for the clubhouse; Tidrow knocked on the door; Yosh answered; they both went downstairs and walked the length of the clubhouse; Maddux was sitting in the same place, shuffling cards at the long table; Tidrow walked by; Maddux looked up and this time said, "You again?"

Whether it was reading a hitter's swing, recalling previous idiosyncrasies of hitters and fielders, or reading body language or anxiety in a conversation, Greg missed very little.

While the Cubs front office watched the gathering storm clouds, being a free agent didn't seem to faze Greg in the slightest.

Homerin, GM Larry Himes, and I went to San Diego in July for the All-Star Game. Greg was on the NL roster. On the eve of the game, Himes said he wanted to go meet Scott by himself. Homerin and I sat together for a couple of hours in the Marriott by the marina, awaiting Larry's return.

Late that evening, Larry returned without any promising news. He had upped the offer to $27.5 million for five years, adding $500,000 per season and increasing the AAV to $5.5 million a year. That was higher than Clemens and Gooden and also a year and two years, respectively, longer than either. But with free agency just ten weeks away, the new offer didn't do anything for the Cubs. It just moved the floor of the deal up another level. Himes used the meeting to try to get close to closing a deal; Boras had used the meeting to get another $2.5 million as the end of the season was drawing near.

Maddux continued to improve his and Scott's position. By the end of that 1992 season, Maddux checked off two more major accomplishments. He won twenty games and a Cy Young Award, completing a five-year run in which he won more games than any other NL starter and threw more innings.

So if he was worth $27.5 million for five years without a

twenty-win season, without the Cy Young Award, without the value of free agency, what was he worth with that added trifecta?

Boras had played it perfectly, so long as Greg was fine with rolling the dice and prepared to play wherever Scott could get him the best deal.

On the morning of November 19, 1992, Homerin, Himes, and I flew out of Chicago's Midway Airport on the Tribune Company jet. We landed at John Wayne Airport in Southern California and went across the street to a hotel where we met Scott and his troupe of personnel. I can't recall how many people Scott had at this meeting, but it was more people than I had ever seen at a negotiation session that wasn't a salary arbitration hearing. Scott had some of his younger agents with him and an economist as well. It was heavy duty. Scott had driven fifteen minutes from his Newport Beach office, loaded with data and people. We flew two thousand miles west from Chicago and had nothing more to offer except some additional incentive bonuses. The bonuses were Cy Young Award–related and valued at $1.5 million. They were valuable, but really meant very little at this point since the bonuses were not guaranteed and wouldn't move the needle.

The one person we had asked to be present wasn't there—Greg Maddux. We wanted Greg to hear our pitch and to understand the value of our proposal relative to the other, comparable pitchers, namely Gooden and Clemens.

When we sat down at the meeting we learned that Greg wasn't going to be there and we also learned there wasn't any comparable pitcher in Scott's mind. Gooden and Clemens were tremendous, but they were older than Greg and their contracts had been signed before the previous season. Boras wanted us to know that Dwight and Roger were old news; Greg was the new frontier.

Boras told us it would take $32.5 million for five years—an AAV of $6.5 million—more than $12 million more than Clemens's guaranteed money. From the Tribune Company's point of view, it might as well have been $325 million. I knew immediately this negotiation was over. There was no way the Tribune brass was going to accept this demand. Maybe it was the money, maybe pride or gamesmanship. At the time, player salaries were on the rise, but at much slower levels than today.

Perhaps Stanton Cook, the Cubs' chairman and leader of the Tribune Company, had taken some heat earlier in the calendar year and didn't want it coming back to him just months later. The previous March 1, the Cubs had signed future Hall of Famer Ryne Sandberg to a major-league-record $28.4 million, four-year deal with an average annual value of $7.1 million. The Cubs had skipped right past the $6 million in AAV—Bobby Bonilla had signed three months earlier for a then-record $5.8 million AAV. To duplicate that with a Maddux signing beyond the $27.5 million threshold may have been more than Cook and the organization wanted to endure.

In those days, to raise an offer by a million dollars was a significant move. Today, on a contract for one of the best pitchers in baseball, a million-dollar increase—or even a five-million-dollar negotiation increase—wouldn't be a deal breaker; it would be more of a throw-in.

Scott was trying to raise the bar with another historically valued contract and he had the perfect pitcher to lead the cause. The highest-paid position player had just been established when Baltimore gave Ripken Jr. $30.5 million, surpassing Sandberg's $28.4 million.

As the dynamics and body language predicted, the meeting was one-sided.

Himes, Homerin, and I returned later that day to Chicago and spoke to Cook. He was miffed. He was pissed there wasn't a deal to be made. And his attitude wasn't going to change. He was dug in.

A couple of days later, we met as a staff at Wrigley Field and

Himes laid out the plan. We were not going to sign Maddux and we needed to sign a starting pitcher and upgrade the bullpen as soon as possible. Maddux was off the table. Himes had money to spend and a team to build, minus the staff ace. He decided to add quantity over quality.

Within ten days, Himes signed right-handed starter Jose Guzman for four years and $14.35 million.

Then we were off to the Winter Meetings in Louisville. Sunday night in Louisville, I received a call from Mike Morgan, who was six-plus years older than Greg, attended the same high school, and was friends with Greg. The call was telling.

Morgan wanted me to know that Greg had found out about the offer of $27.5 million and wanted us to put it back on the table so he could accept it. This was good news, except Larry had already signed Guzman and we were working on signing two relievers, Dan Plesac and Randy Myers. (Before the Louisville week was over, Himes signed the relievers on back-to-back days to multiyear contracts—Plesac for $3.2 million and Myers for $11 million.)

I found Himes and Cook in the team suite and told them of the Morgan phone call. We could get Maddux back in the fold, I told them. The conversation was dismissed in seconds. "We've moved on," I was told. "Tell them we have moved on."

"But there isn't anyone as good as Maddux that we are considering," I offered. "He's young, he's one of the best in the game, and he's our own—we drafted him."

"We've moved on," I was told in a harsher response.

I reconnected with Morgan and gave him the news. We were both disappointed. Mike took the news back to Greg.

Monday night Morgan called back. The message was that Greg would accept the deal and the Cubs could backload the payments—even defer money—so long as he could remain in Chicago and make $27.5 million for the next five years.

I went to the team suite to meet with Cook, the most powerful person in the Tribune Company media conglomerate, and Himes, my boss. I tried one last time and again the conversation went no-where. "I told you last night that we were done with this," Cook said. "I don't want you bringing this up to us again. Understand? It's over. Nobody is bigger than the Chicago Cubs and the Tribune Company. We've moved on. Now you need to move on. I'm done listening to this."

It was a monumental moment in Cubs history. Not a very good one, however.

I called Morgan back and gave him the message.

Former Cubs manager Gene Michael, then the GM of the Yan-kees, had flown to Las Vegas a week earlier, to play golf with Greg and try and sell him on New York. Greg then flew to New York during the Louisville meetings to meet with Gene again. He and his wife, Kathy, went to Broadway musicals and met Donald Trump, but New York wasn't a city he was interested in. Scott reportedly told the Yankees he expected a contract in the $32.5 million range, plus an additional million-a-year payout for the inconvenience of living in New York City. A contract with the Yankees would need to be in the $37.5 million range.

The Yankees reportedly offered a $9 million signing bonus and a deal worth $30 million. Also reportedly, that deal quickly ex-panded to $34 million.

And then something very smart and clandestine took place. The Atlanta Braves were waiting in the background. Most people in baseball felt the Braves needed to move payroll in order to do any-thing at the Louisville meetings. And that's exactly what happened.

General Manager John Schuerholz moved pitcher Charlie Lei-brandt and his $3.1 million contract to the Texas Rangers. That deal put them in a position to go after Maddux. Schuerholz and Stan Kasten, then president of the Braves, played it perfectly. They offered Greg $28 million over five years—a mere $500,000 more than the Cubs' offer, not including the incentives. As the meetings wound down in Louisville, Maddux signed with the Braves.

The next baseball season began on April 5, 1993, in Chicago when Greg, wearing his familiar No. 31, but in an unfamiliar Atlanta road jersey, pitched 8⅓ shutout innings. The Braves beat the Cubs 1–0 at Wrigley Field on Opening Day.

The next day, an hour or so before game time, there was a knock on my office door. The knock came from the right hand of Greg, in full uniform.

"Can we talk?" he asked.

"Sure."

"Can you tell me what happened?" he asked. "I can't believe I'm not here anymore."

We talked for several minutes. Greg intimated all he had heard until the eve of the Louisville meetings was that the crosstown White Sox had offered a four-year deal in the Clemens range. And then came the Yankees' offers.

(No one ever really knows the full, absolute truth about both sides in the negotiating process. Negotiations are always complicated and people many times use other people, conversations, and innuendo to get what they want. They use the press. They posture. They use time as an ally. I have used all those techniques.)

Did Greg always want to be a Cub?

It was reported that Greg had asked influential Cubs players to speak to management during the 1992 season, echoing his desires to stay in Chicago. The phone calls I received from Morgan in Louisville and my meeting with Greg the day after the 1993 opener would indicate he had wanted to stay in Chicago. Reports circulated that Scott had also reached out to Cook and Himes in the final hours trying to strike a deal.

Did Atlanta get Scott out of a box with an offer that was

$100,000 a year more than the Cubs' offer—giving Scott and Greg a deal with slightly higher value and also the opportunity to say Atlanta was always the place he wanted to be?

Perhaps at the outset of the negotiation, Scott wanted to use time to put pressure on Himes and push up the Cubs' offer with his sights set on a Winter Meetings signing—only to have the timing backfire because Himes took Scott's reputation and his word at $32.5 million and moved on quickly to spend the money on Guzman, Myers, Plesac, and outfielder Candy Maldonado, who signed two days after Maddux for $1.65 million.

Was the Braves' offer of $28 million so much better than the Cubs' offer of $27.5 million, with high-valued incentives, or better than the Yankees' offer of $34 million with a $9 million signing bonus included?

If so, that would mean Greg always wanted to be in Atlanta and used the Cubs and the Yankees to get there. Did that really happen? Or did timing and Scott's reputation for doing market-setting record deals, coupled with Himes's reluctance to wait it out, force the end result?

Most of what everyone was thinking, saying, doing, and posturing stays buried. We do know Maddux went on to win the next three Cy Young Awards, giving him four in succession. His record during his last season with the Cubs and his first three with Atlanta was 75-29, with an ERA of 1.98.

He became the only pitcher in history to win fifteen or more games seventeen consecutive seasons. He also won a record eighteen Gold Glove Awards. Greg is the only pitcher in history to win more than 300 games, strike out more than 3,000, and walk fewer than 1,000 hitters.

When the Dodgers and I acquired him from the San Diego Padres in August 2008, he was in the homestretch of a tremendous career.

A few days before the end of the season, after the Dodgers had clinched the 2008 NL West crown, Maddux stopped in to see Joe Torre and me in Joe's office. We had begun discussions on the postseason roster and were also formulating our pitching plans for the final days of the season—trying to provide enough light work to have a prepared pitching staff.

Joe asked Greg what his preference was in regard to pitching in the final days before we met the Cubs in the first round.

"I'd like to start, guys," Greg said. "And, Joe, if I have the lead after five innings feel free to take me out. But I want a chance to win the game."

I have known Greg since he was eighteen years old and I never viewed him as someone who had his eyes on personal accomplishments. After the meeting, I looked up Greg's career totals and there it was: He was tied with Clemens for eighth place all-time in victories. Clemens had been mentioned in the December 2007 Mitchell Report about suspected use of performance-enhancing drugs (PEDs). Greg, whose name was never remotely associated with PEDs, was competing once again with Clemens.

Greg got the start in San Francisco on September 27, 2008. It was the 161st game of the season. He went six innings, allowing two hits, and won the game 2–1.

Maddux finished his career with the Dodgers. He won 355 games, the eighth-highest total of all time.

His last major-league appearance came at Dodger Stadium. It was the fifth and final game of the NLCS against the Phillies. Greg came into the game in relief in the fourth inning and with the Dodgers trailing 3–0. He allowed a couple of unearned runs in two innings of work. In the last play of the fifth inning, Cole Hamels grounded out to first baseman James Loney. As the Dodgers returned to the dugout, Loney flipped Maddux the ball. Greg put the ball in his back pocket and walked off the field for the last time as an active player.

Guzman, the pitcher who was signed to take a rotation spot, pitched two of the four seasons of his contract. He was 12-10 in 1993 and 2-2 with a 9.15 ERA in 1994, before an arm injury ended his career.

Morgan, who was thrilled to pitch with his Las Vegas friend and be the No. 2 starter, became the ace. After posting a 16-8 record as Greg's wingman, he slipped to 10-15 the first season Greg was gone and then was 2-10 with a 6.69 ERA in the last year of his Cubs contract.

Ironically, Mike finished his career with the Diamondbacks, playing for his former agent Joe Garagiola Jr. and helping the team win the 2001 World Series.

Then came my firing by Himes, with Cook's blessing, on December 29, 1993.

Larry Himes was replaced as the Cubs' general manager ten months later, on October 4, 1994.

In 2004, Greg re-signed with the Cubs. He had been gone eleven seasons. In that time, he posted a 198-88 record and a 2.63 ERA, becoming one of the greatest pitchers in the history of the game.

Exactly fifty years and forty-three days after the Brock-for-Broglio trade, on Sunday, July 27, 2014, Greg Maddux was inducted into the National Baseball Hall of Fame, joining former Cub Lou Brock, inducted in 1985. Two historic mistakes that changed history.

Maybe Stanton Cook was right: Greg wasn't bigger than the Cubs or Tribune Company. Regardless, history tells us not signing Greg Maddux was the *biggest* mistake in Cubs history since at least 1964. Or perhaps of all time.

Six

CRYING IN BASEBALL

. . . .

Tom Hanks's character, manager Jimmy Dugan in the movie *A League of Their Own*, was wrong when he screamed, "There's no crying in baseball!"

There's plenty of crying in baseball.

I'm not ashamed to admit I've had real tears in my eyes three or four times. Thankfully, they were mostly tears of joy.

The first was in 2002, when Kenny Lofton singled off Steve Kline and drove in David Bell to give the San Francisco Giants the National League pennant. *The Giants win the pennant! The Giants win the pennant!*

I wept again in 2008 when the Dodgers beat the Cubs in the NL Division Series. We were massive underdogs and we swept the Cubbies. It was the first playoff series the Dodgers had won in twenty years and the first time as a general manager I put together a team that reached the League Championship Series. I was proud and overwhelmed.

Two other times, I wasn't really in the games, but I cried anyway. They came as my old team, the San Francisco Giants, surprised almost everyone in 2010 by beating the Philadelphia Phillies in the NLCS and the Texas Rangers in the World Series. About a month after the Series, John Shea of the *San Francisco Chronicle* asked me how I'd felt watching my former team win it all.

"I've got to admit I had tears in my eyes when they won," I told Shea. "I had tears in my eyes when they beat Philly because we [the Dodgers] had been there the last two years. I know how tough it was. I knew what they were up against. When they beat Texas, same thing. It was a very emotional time for me. But it happens to me every year because I know how hard it is to reach that level."

Steve Dilbeck of the *Los Angeles Times* saw Shea's story and used it to write a blog post under the headline "Say It Isn't So: Are Dodgers GM Ned Colletti's Giants Roots Still Running Strong?" Dilbeck pointed out that my son was a scout with the Giants, that I had brought several former Giants to the Dodgers, and that I was close friends with Brian Sabean, my former boss and the general manager. "Here is the fear," Dilbeck wrote. "The man whose job it is to make the Dodgers a winner, secretly loves the San Francisco Giants."

My answer to Dilbeck and everyone else who criticized me for not rooting against the Giants in 2010 and 2012 in the World Series was straightforward. It is the same answer I gave a woman and her son who came up to me at Scottsdale Stadium in Arizona just hours before the Giants won the 2010 pennant in Philadelphia. I was at the tiny, beautiful ballpark in Scottsdale with Vance Lovelace and Rick Ragazzo, whom I'd recruited from the Giants. We were scouting prospects at an Arizona Fall League game. I was headed to the restroom on the lower concourse when the woman approached. I'd met her son a few times and seen the two of them at Fall League games every now and then.

"I hope you're not rooting for those Giants tonight," the mom said.

"Well, you know what?" I said. "We're out of it. We're not playing. And I certainly can't root for Philadelphia after what they've put us through—beating us the last two years." I told the woman that my son, Lou, worked for the Giants, and pointed to her own son at her side. "Tell me, is there anything in the world that your son was trying to accomplish that you wouldn't root for him—no matter what—as long as it was good?"

The woman looked at me, glanced at her son, and looked back at me with a smile. "I'll root for the Giants, too."

Let's hope for Dilbeck's sake his son isn't on the baseball beat and up for a Pulitzer Prize while writing for a rival paper. He might end up pulling against his son.

THE DAY HIMES FIRED me was the worst of my baseball life. But I can think of few others that still make my stomach churn. They didn't bring me to tears. But sometimes my family wept.

One of the worst days I remember was Sunday, October 7, 1984—a dream day that ended in a baseball nightmare. The weather was typically picture-perfect in San Diego for Game 5 of the best-of-five National League playoffs between the Chicago Cubs and San Diego Padres. Leon "Bull" Durham hit a two-run homer in the first inning and Jody Davis added a solo shot in the second to give my beloved Cubbies an early 3–0 lead. I had only been working for them for thirty-three months, but it seemed my timing was perfect. Nineteen eighty-four was a magical season, and here we were in the deciding game of the National League Championship Series with soon-to-be-named Cy Young Award winner Rick Sutcliffe on the mound. In the top of the seventh, with one down, the Cubs were eight outs from going to the World Series for the first time since World War II when everything fell apart.

I could feel it coming. The flow of the game told me what was about to happen. Sutcliffe, who came to the Cubs in a June 13 trade that sent Joe Carter to the Cleveland Indians, had won twenty games that season, including a 16-1 record with the Cubs. He had beaten the Padres 13–0 in Game 1 of the NLCS just five days earlier and was cruising through five innings. In the sixth, though, he started to falter. He gave up a pair of sacrifice flies by Terry Kennedy and Graig Nettles. We still had a 3–2 lead going to the seventh, but the game was moving too fast. Our at-bats weren't lasting long enough. We weren't keeping the defense off the field. We weren't giving Sutcliffe enough time off the mound. I could feel it. And it finally caught up with us with one out in the seventh.

Carmelo Martinez, a former Cub, led off the inning with a walk and went to second on a sacrifice bunt by Garry Templeton. Then came the infamous "Gatorade Play"—a play that MLB TV proclaimed years later to be the second-biggest blunder in the history of baseball, behind Bill Buckner's gaffe in Game 6 of the 1986 World Series.

Durham, a hero for his first-inning home run, became a goat when he let a weak ground ball off the bat of Tim Flannery shoot between his legs into right field, scoring Martinez to tie the game. Durham later said he muffed the ball because his glove was "heavy and sticky." Teammate Ryne Sandberg, the NL MVP that year, accidentally spilled a cooler of Gatorade on Durham's favorite glove ten minutes before the fateful game. Durham asked coach Don Zimmer what he should do. Should he use the soaked glove or get his backup mitt? Zim told Bull to stay with the gamer. The Gatorade would be good luck, Zim said.

With the score tied at 3–3, Alan Wiggins hit a soft wedge shot that dropped for a single in front of Gary Matthews in left. That put runners on first and second. Tony Gwynn followed with a dagger to the heart. He hit a scorching one-hop line drive that exploded past Sandberg, who never had a chance. The ball flashed out of the shadows into a bright band of blinding sunlight stretching across the infield. It rolled to the right-center-field wall. Gwynn's laser shot scored two runs and you could feel the air go out of the Cubs' confidence. Steve Garvey added a run-scoring single to make it 6–3 and Padres manager Dick Williams turned the game over to his closer, Goose Gossage, a future Hall of Famer. Gossage skated out of trouble in the eighth inning, striking out Matthews to end the inning with runners on second and third. And he allowed a one-out single to Keith Moreland in the ninth, but got Ron Cey on a pop-up and Jody Davis on a ground-ball force to send the Cubs home and the Padres to the World Series against Detroit.

I was devastated. I was nauseated. I know a lot of other Cubs fans felt the same, but for me, being part of the team that I grew up loving, to be there and be working for them when they finally got to the World Series, that probably would have been the ultimate reward. The only thing better would be to be the general manager of a team that goes to the World Series.

EIGHT OUTS FROM GOING to the World Series. That's how close the Cubs were in 1984. And that's how close the San Francisco Giants were to winning the World Series eighteen years later.

I felt a lot better about the Giants' chances in Game 6 of the 2002 World Series. I really believed we were going to win. We had a 5–0 lead with one out in the seventh inning when manager Dusty Baker came out to get starter Russ Ortiz. Russ wasn't getting hit particularly hard and didn't look particularly tired to me. He had given up four hits and none of them were worrisome—dribblers up the middle, pop flies that dropped in. But Dusty wanted to go to his bullpen. Then he compounded a bad decision with what has become a famous faux-pas in baseball lore. Dusty stopped Russ and gave him the game ball to take with him to the dugout, instead of taking the ball from Ortiz and handing it to the incoming relief pitcher. Angels fans and players took Dusty's move to be a cocky gesture—a sign the Giants were sure the Series was wrapped up and were being disrespectful to the home team. While Felix Rodriguez was coming in from the bullpen and warming up, the video board started playing that damn Rally Monkey rally video and 45,000 Angels fans went nuts.

It's interesting how I can remember so many of the games I've seen so vividly. I remember pitches, situations, turning points. I remember Rodriguez, working in his sixth straight World Series game, throwing eight straight fastballs to left-handed hitting Scott Spiezio. He was between 94 and 96 mph and kept the ball away for the first seven pitches. After falling behind in the count early, 1-2, Spiezio saw five straight two-strike pitches. He took two for balls, fouled off two, and then hit the eighth, and final pitch, of the at-bat—a fastball down and in—into the first row of seats just to the foul pole side of the Anaheim bullpen. To me, it looked as if the whole play were in slow motion. I can still see Reggie Sanders going back to the wall and looking up.

We still had a two-run lead, 5–3, but suddenly it felt like we were losing. I had a sick feeling in the pit of my stomach—the same feeling I had in the final game of the 1984 NLCS when the Cubs blew that 3–0 lead to the Padres. If you watch enough baseball, you can viscerally feel the momentum of a game. We lost 6–5.

Game 6 in Anaheim was worse than Game 7. Once you blow a five-run lead like that on the road, when you've been that close to ending it, it's almost impossible to come back. And I knew it. I was sure we were dead. We got an early lead in Game 7 on a sacrifice fly by Sanders in the second inning, but it really was over pretty quickly. The Angels answered back with a run on a two-out walk by Spiezio and a double by Bengie Molina. A bases-loaded double by Garret Anderson in the third sealed the deal. We never really threatened again. That was the final score, 4–1.

That was the closest I've ever come to a World Series ring.

So many factors have to line up perfectly to win a World Series. The players, the talent, the lack of injuries to key players at key times, playing teams when they are cold and not hot, staying hot as long as possible and cold as little as possible. There is no fooling the game of baseball. The season is too long to be able to do that. If you are flawed in any way, eventually the long season will expose that flaw and you will be home on the couch watching the postseason. Being part of a team that makes it through all the trials and is one of only two teams still playing is a major accomplishment. So when you get there, you don't want anything to be amiss. It may never come your way again.

As miserable as Game 6 was, and as painful as it was to lose the Series, I do have a funny memory of that night—the night of Game 7. We were down by three in the ninth inning and I knew where it was going, how it would end.

Attendance that night in Anaheim was 44,598 and I'm guessing no more than three hundred or so were Giants fans, most of them sitting in the family section the Angels had reserved for us near the top of the lower deck between home and first base. I watched most of the game from a booth with Sabean and members of the baseball front office. But I decided in the top of the ninth inning to go check on my family, to make sure they were going to be okay in all the craziness. I got down there just in time to see Kenny Lofton fly out to right center for the last out of the Series.

Delirium breaks out. People all around us are going crazy. I'm just sitting there and my daughter, Jenna, eighteen years old at the time, is beside herself, crying.

I've seen Jenna cry only a few times in her life and, I guess fortunately, most all were baseball related. Once was when I got fired by the Cubs. Once was when I was with the Giants and we lost a one-game tiebreaker for a shot at the playoffs at the end of the 1998 season. In that one, we were sitting behind the visitors' dugout at

Wrigley Field when Joe Carter popped out to Mark Grace right in front of us to end the game. Everyone was yelling and screaming. I looked over and Jenna was just sobbing.

"You okay?" I asked her.

Jenna just looked at me and said, "I hate this place," and buried her head in her hands and wept.

She was weeping even harder after Game 7 of the 2002 World Series. The scene was a repeat of the pandemonium she'd suffered through at Wrigley Field just four years earlier. Only worse. The Rally Monkey is dancing across the scoreboard. Everybody is beating those obnoxious thundersticks. It's just a madhouse of jubilation and we are sitting together in a tiny huddle of Giants fans, hurting.

"Dad, can I say something?" Jenna asked between sobs. "You're not going to like it, but can I say something?"

"Jenna, whatever you want to do."

My daughter, my sweet, innocent daughter, turned and looked at the crowd around her, focusing on the most obnoxious ones who were watching her cry, and raised both middle fingers high in the air. "Fuck you people!" she screamed.

I laughed out loud. "Well done. Now, let's get out of here."

Seven

GETTING TO THE BIG CHAIR

· · · · · · · · · · · · ·

I was driving southbound through the Waldo Tunnel in Sausalito and the view was so spectacular I had to pull over. The Golden Gate Bridge was in front of me. To the far left, Alcatraz rose out of the dark waters of San Francisco Bay. The city was off to the near left and the ocean spilled out as far as I could see to the right. It was never more breathtaking than on this Saturday fall afternoon with my life at a crossroads.

I loved being in San Francisco. I loved how much the city had become part of my life. It suddenly hit me how humbled I was to even have had the opportunity to live in San Francisco, let alone spend eleven years trying to help bring winning baseball to the city. The time since Himes fired me had been a blur.

Tears welled in my eyes as I sat in my car at the Marin Headlands.

I had spent the day at V. Sattui Winery in Napa Valley, buying a case of wine for my boss and dear friend Brian Sabean, who was getting married in a week. I wondered why I hadn't gone to Napa and Sonoma more often. Now, though, I rued the missed opportunities.

My emotions were getting the better of me and I knew it.

Exactly two weeks earlier, on Saturday, October 29, 2005, I had been in Chicago with my family to celebrate my son's twenty-fourth birthday when I got a phone call from Jeff Kent, one of my favorite hard-nosed, old-school players. Gayle and I were driving to one of our favorite Italian restaurants, Piano Piano, in Park Ridge, to have dinner with longtime friends Mike Murphy, the left field bleacher bugler, and his wife, Dana, when Kent's number showed up on the caller ID of my cellphone. Earlier in the day, it was announced that Paul DePodesta was not coming back as the Dodgers' general manager.

Kent had spent five years with us in San Francisco and was a key reason the Giants emerged as one of the dominant teams in the National League. He was a gamer who should be in the Hall of Fame. Jeff made the great Barry Bonds even greater. In 2000, when Kent won the National League MVP, I told people it was the best thing that could have happened to the Giants because it would motivate Bonds. The next season, Barry hit 73 home runs and drove in 137 to win the fourth of his seven MVP Awards. Then, in June 2002, Kent and Bonds went after each other in the visitors' dugout in San Diego. The two former National League MVPs had to be separated by trainer Stan Conte and manager Dusty Baker, while television cameras caught the altercation. It was a case of iron sharpening iron and was a key moment that drove the team to the World Series.

In 2003, Kent went to the Houston Astros for two years before signing a two-year, $17 million deal with the Dodgers in December 2004. We hadn't spoken much the last three years, except for occasional pleasantries and on the night in 2003 when I presented him his 2002 National League Championship ring. To get a call from him on a Saturday night in the off-season was surprising.

Kent told me he had just finished a meeting with Frank Mc-Court, owner of the Los Angeles Dodgers. Jeff said he told Mc-

Court he didn't want to play for the Dodgers another season if an analytics-driven general manager was going to run the team.

McCourt stopped him right there and said he was open-minded on who succeeded Paul.

Kent told me he brought up my name to McCourt and said the Dodgers should hire me, or at least, interview me. Needless to say, that was flattering. I let him know that the terms of my contract allowed me to speak to another club after November 1 if the club asked and received permission from the Giants.

We had parked and Gayle had gone ahead into the restaurant by the time I finished the call. When I joined her, she wanted to know what Jeff wanted and I filled her in. We were both surprised by the nature of the call.

FIVE DAYS AFTER JEFF KENT'S CALL, just after 5 p.m. on Thursday, November 3, 2005, Peter Magowan, president and managing general partner of the Giants, called me into his corner office on the third floor of Pac Bell Park, now AT&T Park, overlooking the Willie Mays statue.

Peter sat behind his desk and began to speak with his head down. "Ned, I have some bad news."

My first thought was Barry Bonds. A little more than two weeks earlier, Victor Conte, founder of the Bay Area Laboratory Cooperative (BALCO), had been sentenced to four months in prison for his role in distributing performance-enhancing drugs. Steroids were all anyone was talking about at the time. And Barry's name was part of many of the conversations. Barry's personal trainer, Greg Anderson, had been indicted in the BALCO scandal and Barry had admitted using a clear substance and a cream that Anderson had provided him, though Barry insisted he had no idea he was actually using steroids.

Happily, Peter's "bad news" had nothing to do with Bonds.

"Frank McCourt from the Dodgers called and asked permission to speak to you about the GM position in Los Angeles," Magowan said, his voice low, thoughtful, and pensive. "I know I have to give you permission, but I can't tell you I'm happy about it. I would rather have it be any team but the Dodgers. Even the A's would be better. I know what I am required to do, but I really don't want you leaving to run our biggest rival. I can't see letting one of our best people leave—let alone for the Dodgers."

"Peter," I said, "I really appreciate that, but I would at least like to talk to Frank and get a feel for the situation."

The next morning, I called Frank McCourt and discussed the position. I told him I'd be willing to come down to L.A. for an interview. I called Peter and let him know what I'd told McCourt. I asked Peter to give the Dodgers the then-customary seventy-two-hour window to talk to me.

He reluctantly agreed, but said he wouldn't give permission until the following week. Peter had done nearly the same thing to me in 2001, when the Pittsburgh Pirates wanted to talk to me about their GM opening. Perhaps he hoped that in a week something would have changed and the problem he didn't want to deal with would resolve itself. That's what happened with Pittsburgh when it became clear Dave Littlefield had the inside track. I never had a chance.

But this was different.

Waiting a week created a timing issue. Sabean, Dick Tidrow, and I would be in Palm Springs, California, most of that time for the annual postseason General Managers' Meetings. We would be swamped. I'd have trouble finding time to prepare for my meeting with McCourt.

As soon as I got off the phone with Peter, I sought out Sabes. I consider Brian to be one of the smartest people I know and someone who became one of my best friends. Brian grew up in New Hampshire. He is well connected in the Boston area, where the McCourts had lived for generations before moving to L.A. He was the perfect person to help find out about the McCourt family and its business practices.

Sabean started making calls and it quickly became clear that I was going to have my hands full if the position were offered and I accepted. Many people warned that the McCourts were known for being very tough to work for. Whatever it took to get their way, they would do—not unlike many businesspeople. One thing seemed certain. Working for them would be a totally different dynamic from what I had experienced in my twelve years with the Cubs or my eleven years in San Francisco.

THE THREE DAYS SPENT in Palm Springs were a blur of emotions. I tried desperately to focus on the day-to-day business of the Giants, yet my mind always seemed to be scrambling to prepare for the all-important interview with the McCourts at the end of the week.

During the meetings, I approached Rich Levin. I'd known Rich for twenty years. He led Major League Baseball's public relations department and worked closely with Commissioner Bud Selig, who always addressed the general managers at their meetings. I asked Rich if he could ask Commissioner Selig to speak with me about the Dodgers. The request was extremely unusual, but I figured it was worth trying because the commissioner would know what was going on and he was someone I had somewhat of a relationship with for a number of years.

An hour before his address, Selig and I met on a veranda at the Hyatt Regency Indian Wells resort. I asked the commissioner to give me an overview of Frank and Jamie McCourt, but told him I didn't want him to reveal anything he was uncomfortable sharing. I was just seeking counsel since I'd heard things were sometimes tu-multuous in Los Angeles. While it was out of the ordinary to seek counsel from someone of his status, I also felt all information would be helpful and there wasn't any malice involved.

Selig said, yes, the situation in Los Angeles was challenging. But he also felt it was a great opportunity for me and thought I would have a chance to be successful. "Ned, you are smart and ex-perienced and, from what I can tell, you get along with many differ-ent types of personalities. I'm hoping you will have this opportunity and, perhaps, be able to calm and help steady things. I think you have to pursue this for many reasons."

I greatly appreciated Selig's time and willingness to share his thoughts. He didn't have to do that for me. And years later, when the McCourts and MLB went to war, I was especially glad I had approached the commissioner. No matter how difficult things be-came, I hoped Commissioner Selig was confident that I would do what was best for the Dodgers and baseball.

For the next three nights at the General Managers' Meetings, Sabean, Tidrow, and I ate at the same Italian place in nearby Palm Desert, Ristorante Mamma Gina. The dinners were great, the company terrific, and the conversations centered, as always, on how to improve our club—short and long term. But the closer the end of the week came, the harder I found it to concentrate. My immediate priorities were shifting to my meeting with Frank McCourt.

THE FIRST INTERVIEW began around 1:30 p.m. on Friday, November 11, in a suite at the historic Beverly Hills Hotel, the favorite haunt and setting for blockbuster negotiations among California's elite since 1912.

Charlie Chaplin, Gloria Swanson, and Rudolph Valentino

swanned through the hotel in the 1920s during the silent film era. In the 1940s, the hotel's El Jardin Restaurant was renamed the Polo Lounge in honor of a celebrity band of polo players that included Will Rogers, Spencer Tracy, and others who held their matches in a bean field near the hotel and celebrated their victories, and rare defeats, at the hotel. Howard Hughes, the reclusive billionaire, lived at the hotel on and off for three decades. Humphrey Bogart was a regular and Katharine Hepburn once dove into the hotel pool fully clothed after a tennis match. The Beatles were hotel guests, as was Elizabeth Taylor. The list of movie stars and moguls who played and parlayed at the Beverly Hills Hotel on Sunset Boulevard is simply staggering. And here I was cloistered in a three-room suite in secret negotiations, which, if all went well, could conclude with me being named general manager of the Los Angeles Dodgers, one of the most respected and prestigious organizations in all of sports.

Frank and I met through the afternoon and early evening, discussing a variety of topics and philosophies. There were no breaks. No lunch. No dinner. Just water and endless questions.

Periodically, Frank's wife, Jamie, would come in the suite and join her husband in peppering me with questions. The two of them were relentless. As the seven-hour grind began to wind down, I remember silently putting things in perspective for myself. I already had a great job. And while the opportunity to become general manager of the Dodgers was a tremendous honor, I didn't want to leave a good position with good people for a situation that wouldn't at least have the chance to equal that. But it was the Dodgers and it was the top position in the baseball operations department.

When the meeting finally ended, I drove to Los Angeles International Airport, returned a rental car, and grabbed the last flight of the night back to San Francisco. I thought I had a real chance for the job, but the ebb and flow of the interview had been typical. I saw my own pluses and minuses and was left in a mental no-man's-land. All I knew for sure was that, if nothing else, I was better for the grueling experience.

THE NEXT MORNING, I made my private, emotional pilgrimage to Napa to buy the case of wine for Brian and Amanda's upcoming wedding. As I sat parked in the Marin Headlands outside the Waldo Tunnel, reflecting on my eleven years in San Francisco and enjoying the beautiful view, I marveled at the bounty of blessings I had in my life, the experiences and opportunities and challenges and celebrations I had enjoyed, and the number of good people I had encountered along the ride.

As you can imagine, the rest of the weekend was filled with anxiety, waiting to hear something, anything. All I got was agonizing silence. Late Sunday, I called Magowan and asked if we could meet.

"Don't tell me you took the job" were his first words.

"No, no," I said. "I haven't heard anything. But I do want to talk to you. I want to sit down and just meet with you."

I'd been in San Francisco from the cold and lonely Candlestick Park days when few came to a frigid, windy ballpark, to the birth of privately funded, forever sold-out Pac Bell Park and its beauty by the bay. I'd been there with teams that were losing 90-plus games a year, to teams that were winning 90-plus and going to the World Series. Our group had been through the record-breaking and sobering days of Barry Bonds. We'd been to the playoffs in 1997, 2000, 2002, and 2003; were eliminated in 1998 in a one-game playoff; were eliminated on the last day in 2004; and were still in the hunt with three days left in the season in 2001. From 1997 to 2004, the

Giants had played just fifteen games in which they were mathematically eliminated from making the postseason.

It was a successful run and Peter had been the leader of it all. I wanted to sit down and thank him, regardless if I were leaving or staying. When you are on the ground floor of building something that is turning out special, you and those you have been closest with share a bond that is unique. You feel it. You know it.

"Okay, I'll meet you tomorrow morning," he said. "Come by about six o'clock."

The hour-long meeting was emotional. Our working relationship was a friendship founded on mutual respect and the pride we shared in our accomplishments.

Afterward, I also sat down with Larry Baer. Larry was Peter's right-hand person, who would replace Magowan as president of the organization in 2008. Our offices were all in a row, starting with Peter in the corner, then Larry's, mine, and Brian's. I'd spent a large chunk of my life with those men, trying to put together the puzzle of making a major-league franchise a vibrant success that was woven into the culture of a magnificent world-class city.

Each meeting was more emotional than the one before. Then, about 9 a.m., my phone rang. It was Frank McCourt.

"Are you still interested in the general manager job?"

"Yes," I said simply.

"Well, I am interested in continuing the discussion."

I explained to Frank that he would have to get an extension from the Giants if he wanted to talk to me past noon. The seventy-two-hour window he had requested, and been granted, was expiring.

About ten minutes later, Peter came into my office. He felt he had fulfilled his obligations in letting the Dodgers talk to me in the first place. He didn't want to grant an extension for the talks to go any further. "You know, ethically, morally, legally, I needed to give you permission to talk to them. I have fulfilled my end of the bargain," he said to me. "But I don't need to give you permission for an extra day."

"Peter, I've come this far," I said. "It's not as if I want out of San Francisco and not as if I have grown apart from the people here. But this is an opportunity I've worked twenty-five years for and I want to see it through."

Peter relented.

I LEFT THE OFFICE and drove south on 280 to 101 to my condo in San Mateo. I packed my only suit and a sport coat into a carry-on bag, put on my only other sport coat and a black sweater, and headed to the airport for a flight to Los Angeles that left around 11:30 a.m.

Frank had arranged for a car and driver to meet me when I landed and took me to Dodger Stadium. I'd been coming to Chavez Ravine for twenty-five years, but never in November, and never in a limo with a driver to shuttle me there. While I was familiar with many of the surroundings, the emotions were strange. A visiting ballpark in November has a vastly different feel than it does in season.

When I arrived at the stadium, Frank got into the car and we rode to the Beverly Hills Hotel. Again, no lunch. No dinner. No breaks. Just water and questions. And I was wearing a black sweater that was perfect for San Francisco, but a personal sauna under intense, deposition-like questioning in a hotel room in Los Angeles where the temperature felt like ninety degrees. I was sweating and gulping water nonstop, but I kept the sport coat and sweater on through it all. Hour after hour ticked by.

At around 9 p.m., we finally broke and headed down to the Polo

Lounge. I thought we might be winding down, but the questions kept coming as I tried to pick through a salad—my first meal in thirty-plus hours.

"How many people have you fired?"

"Tell me about the most difficult firing you ever had to do."

"How bad do you want this position?"

"Do you prefer college players or high school players when you draft?"

"How lengthy is your checklist when you are trying to sign a free agent? Or trade for a player?"

"Do you believe signing players from the international market is a necessity or a luxury?"

"What are the qualities of a good major-league manager?"

"Do you have candidates in mind and how long do you think it will take to have a manager in place?"

"What are the main attributes of successful coaches? Would you select the coaches, or would the manager, or would it be a combined effort?"

"If you had the choice between a very talented player who wasn't a great teammate or a tremendous teammate who was an average big-league player, who would you choose?"

"Are you willing to manage up, across, and down?"

"Are you comfortable dealing with the media, both national and local?"

"Tell me about your negotiation experience."

"What are the biggest deals you have negotiated?"

"You are a veteran baseball executive. Are you averse to using analytics?"

"How do you make your decisions? How much information to do you gather and what types of information do you obtain before you make a decision?"

Philosophies on player development, on scouting, on international scouting, player acquisitions, managers, and coaches: We discussed them ad nauseam.

SOMEWHERE IN THE MIDST OF an interview that had morphed into a cross-examination, Frank asked a poignant and insightful question I wasn't expecting:

"What will you do to keep the tradition this franchise has of being pioneers in the sport and in society?"

It was a great question—one I wish I had thought of in advance. But I hadn't and I didn't dare let more than three seconds pass without offering an answer. "Frank, we know the Dodgers have been first in many social advances—first to bring an African American player to the big leagues, first to have an academy in the Dominican Republic, first to have a prominent Japanese player, first to have the vision to move Major League Baseball west. I think the Dodgers should be one of the first two teams to play a game in China and develop that country both from talent and marketing standpoints."

McCourt looked at me. He didn't say a thing, but I felt I had struck a chord.

Twenty-eight months after I was hired, the Dodgers and San Diego Padres played the first major-league exhibition game in China, at Wukesong Olympic baseball stadium in Beijing, thanks in large part to Joseph A. Reaves, a former foreign correspondent for the *Chicago Tribune* who came home from overseas to cover the Cubs when I was there. (Reaves is the coauthor of this book.)

Joseph was the only person I knew who lived in China and worked in baseball, and I convinced Frank McCourt to hire him in September 2007 to help coordinate our historic trip to China. Reaves later was instrumental in helping the Dodgers host the

finals of the 2009 World Baseball Classic, play a two-city exhibition tour in Taiwan in 2010, establish Dodger-sponsored tournaments in Spain and Brazil, and bring in teams from Mexico, Italy,
and Korea to our Spring Training complex in Glendale, Arizona.

BY 10 P.M., we were back in suite 117, hammering away.

Frank's inquisition ended after midnight. I learned that day how
smart, intense, and relentless he was. I have worked for many smart
and savvy people. Frank stood out for how quick, thorough, and
organized his thought process was. He listened very intently, with a
perceptive eye for body language.

There are many people who take umbrage with Frank—some
have known him while others have forged their opinions through
hearsay. I viewed him as someone who, like any owner of a high-
profile business, could be a challenge to deal with from time to
time. But he was also going to provide me with an education. Remember, I came from a blue collar, street-corner background, so
education to me wasn't always from a book, and wasn't always going
to be easy. For me Frank was a healthy challenge.

"We have until noon tomorrow before the deadline expires?"
he asked.

"That's right, and I don't believe Peter will give us a minute past
noon," I countered.

"All right, I'll see you at six to continue this," he said.

Six, I thought. That's a nap away.

My mind was swimming. The process of interviewing with the
McCourts was invigorating, challenging, and draining. I felt like I
was in a heavyweight fight.

I assumed I would be sleeping in the suite since Frank had sum-
moned me on a moment's notice, whisked me directly from the airport, and spent the last eleven hours grilling me. It was customary

for an employer to provide lodging to a candidate if the interview process exceeded one day.

"It's okay for me to stay here tonight?" I asked.

Frank seemed to be caught off guard. "Stay where?" he asked.

"Stay here," I said.

"I hadn't planned on you staying here," he said.

"Well, I made an assumption that the Dodgers would secure me lodging for the night. That's customary," I said. "I didn't book a room and I don't have a rental car."

I guess he expected me to go out on Sunset Boulevard at one in the morning and hail a cab to take me to a hotel someplace without a reservation—and be back at the Beverly Hills Hotel in less than six hours.

Sunset Boulevard may sound like a busy thoroughfare. And it is. But not where the Beverly Hills Hotel is located. That part of Sunset runs through a posh residential neighborhood. It wasn't like I would be stepping onto Michigan Avenue in Chicago or Forty-Second Street in Manhattan. These were the days before Uber. I could go without seeing a taxi on that part of Sunset for at least fifteen or twenty minutes. And then when I did find a taxi, where was the driver going to take me? What was I supposed to do for the next three or four hours?

Frank relented. The room would be empty. So I stayed in a hotel suite that was beautiful—and, as I found out the next morning, very historic.

I took half an Ambien, knowing it would get me to sleep but not keep me asleep. In 240 minutes, I was awake—a big day ahead. Since the General Managers' Meetings nine days earlier, I had averaged about three hours of sleep a night. But this was the big day. Today was the ninth inning of Game 7, and I felt I was clinging to a one-run lead. I had to close it out.

JUST BEFORE 6 A.M. on Tuesday, November 15, 2005, Frank Mc-
Court knocked on the door of suite 117 with the second, and un-
doubtedly final, noon deadline just six hours away. He asked if I
wanted breakfast ordered in and I couldn't say yes quickly enough.
I was starving. I ordered a bagel and a cup of tea.

While breakfast was on its way up, Frank asked what I thought
of the day before.

"When I left, did you have any concerns about the conversations?" he asked. "Did you have anything that you wondered about?
Any aspect of our discussion that you were uncomfortable about?"

"No," I said.

"Are you sure?"

On second thought, I did have one concern. I told him I was hoping to get some sleep since I hadn't had much over the last few days.

"That's it?"

He looked surprised and I asked him why.

Frank's reply was interesting and offered an insight into how a
man like Frank McCourt could make someone like me keener and
sharper—and, even, tougher.

"Yesterday morning when I called you about coming back down,
I decided I was going to make the day as difficult for you as possible.
The heat was up in this room. You were in a jacket and a sweater
and I was in short sleeves. I figured you hadn't eaten much, if at
all, and I was going to keep this process at a high, productive level. I
didn't let us break for lunch or an early dinner. I kept pounding at
you because I wanted to know how much you wanted this position.
And then at the end of the night, I wanted to see how you would
react to me by not just simply allowing you to stay in this room
without a discussion. I made it as tough as I could."

"Well, how did it go?" I asked.

McCourt smiled and said: "It was a draw."

Frank's mind worked at a high level. He didn't become successful by chance. He was thorough, calculating, and visionary. And he was also very bold.

Many times in a negotiation I would watch him work the opposition to what would seem a logical finishing point. And then he would stop, recalculate and recalibrate, and move the target further in his favor. If he ever sensed weakness or desperation in the other party to a negotiation, he would attack it to the utmost, all the while with a stoic poker face. He rarely would expose his feelings and left the other side wondering. He was a magnificent listener—but a very challenging person to read.

I don't know many people who taught me more—and certainly about business dealings.

WITH THE NEW DAY just getting under way, I knew I had some momentum in my corner. But I knew, too, I still had a ways to go.

The room service server knocked on the door and came in with our breakfast. As he was laying out the dishes, he looked at me and asked: "Did you stay in this room last night?"

I thought, Oh no, is something missing? "Yes, I did."

"This is my favorite room in the hotel," the server said. "I've been working here for a while. Back in their heyday, the Rat Pack used to stay in this suite when they came to Beverly Hills. Frank Sinatra, Dean Martin, Sammy Davis Jr., and a lot of their friends. This was their place. And did they ever have fun here."

With a wide smile, I knew I not only had momentum, but I had a dash of kismet, as well. Martin and Sinatra were two of my all-time favorites, as well as my father's and uncles'. I figured it was a good sign.

After the server left, the questions started again. For more than three hours, the intensity built until finally, a little after 10:45 a.m., Frank offered me the position of General Manager of the Los Angeles Dodgers.

He offered me a three-year contract at not much more than I was making in San Francisco. I knew how much he had paid De-Podesta and how long a contract Paul had been given. My offer was not anywhere near Paul's in terms of dollars or length. And while money never has been the driving force for me, I couldn't—and didn't need to—sell myself short, especially for a job that was going to be as big and demanding as this.

Plus, it was early November, six weeks after a disastrous season for the Dodgers. Frank had no general manager, no field manager, and no coaching staff. Time was becoming an enemy for him and his baseball team.

Frank had spent a full twenty-four hours interviewing me over parts of three days. He wouldn't have done that if he didn't want me to be his general manager. I knew I had something valuable and that was leverage—an ounce of leverage I could use against someone I considered, and still consider, one of the best negotiators I have ever known. I also had a great job four hundred miles north that I wasn't desperate to leave. So I responded how only someone who lived in a garage as a kid, whose family ran short of money two days before every payday, and who had just been offered the opportunity to a lifetime, could.

I said no.

I had a briefcase with me. I closed it and thanked Frank for the offer. I told him that I was humbled that he had asked me to interview and offered me the position. But, also I told him, I had a great job and didn't need to leave it for the terms he was proposing.

Frank seemed surprised. "What do you need?" he asked.

"You are paying Paul for the next three years to not be the

general manager," I began. "And you want me to accept an offer for three years for far less money to be the general manager of a team that was seventy-one and ninety-one? I am basically being asked to clean up and to make less to do so in the same period of time that Paul will be getting paid to not clean it up. As much as I want to accept, it is too far short in term and money for me to feel comfortable doing it. I can't feel as if I am being taken advantage of. I won't do it."

I told him I needed an increased salary and at least a fourth year.

After more back-and-forth, and with the clock ticking toward the noon deadline, Frank relented and moved the deal higher. He increased the salary but also wanted to add a fifth-year club option.

I told him I needed to make it a mutual option on the fifth year, that I needed the same right at the end of four seasons.

He asked why would I need an option as well.

"I don't intend on failing or having you want me out of here. But, who knows? Maybe after four years I'll want to go. I plan on making this a success. We both need to be able to walk away."

We had a deal. That moment, Frank McCourt stepped up and gave me the chance of lifetime.

And we made it a success, going to the postseason three of those first four years, including two trips to the League Championship Series.

I ran the clock on the negotiations until less than ten minutes before Peter was going to close the door on Frank and the Dodgers—and me. In the end, we agreed on four years and a mutual option memorialized on a simple sheet of a yellow legal pad.

From my perspective, the length and depth of the three days of interviewing, along with the negotiation, were tense and grueling. Then again, Frank may have ultimately thought he had taken it easy on me.

Just before noon, I called Peter and Baer in San Francisco. While I was very excited, it was still not an easy call to make. But the deal was done. The next day, November 16, 2005, I was introduced as the tenth general manager in the proud history of the Los Angeles Dodgers.

Eight

BUILDING A TEAM

. . . .

I t's hard to believe that a suite at the tony Beverly Hills Hotel
could look like an East L.A. flophouse, but suite 117 looked just
like that the morning after I was hired.

It had been a short night. After Frank and I shook hands on a
deal, I called my family and a few friends. I invited Kim Ng to the
hotel to join me for dinner in the Polo Lounge. Kim had been an
assistant GM to my predecessor, Paul DePodesta, and his predecessor, Dan Evans. She would provide stability, but more important,
she had a great baseball mind and a pedigree with the Chicago
White Sox, New York Yankees, and Dodgers. I needed her, and was
looking forward to working with her.

The dinner ran late and I went upstairs to get a few hours of
sleep. Before I did, though, I stopped and left a spare key to my
room at the front desk. I told the night receptionist I was expecting
guests and to send them up. Before going to sleep, I turned on
ESPN and there on the scroll was a headline my family, parents,
uncles, and neighborhood buddies never could have imagined:
"Dodgers to Hire Ned Colletti as General Manager." I sat watching
a nondescript college basketball game playing out above the scroll,
which I kept reading over and over. This must be a dream. It was

not lost on me that I was inheriting the position once held by Branch Rickey, the man who brought Jack Roosevelt Robinson to the major leagues.

When I woke just before 6 a.m., my brother, wife, and son were sprawled across the room. They had flown from Chicago, arriving about four in the morning, and just flopped where they could without disturbing me. The only one missing was my daughter, Jenna, who couldn't miss her classes at Miami University in Ohio.

I laughed when I saw my family scattered around my room. I mean, the Beverly Hills Hotel is famous for its history of crazy celebrities partying nights away. And I'm sure there have been far wackier scenes in that very suite and others as the sun rose on a new day. But finding my family huddled under blankets on sofas and across the carpet struck me as a pretty funny way to start a new chapter of my life.

IF YOU WORKED for the McCourts, you were on call twenty-four hours a day, every day. They had purchased your time—not unlike any other general manager position.

Frank ran the two-day marathon sessions, while Jamie came in and out a few times. I could tell right away she was smart—very, very, smart—and had a lot of her own ideas. She and Frank would challenge each other from time to time in front of me, making some moments a bit uncomfortable. After all, this was an interview for the position of general manager.

Their marriage ended in divorce. As I watched them in those first days, I figured they had known each other for thirty-something years and had come to a level of acceptance.

Early on, I would talk to Frank a lot on the phone—an hour or two at a time. Then I'd hang up and Jamie would call and say, "What did you tell Frank?" and I'd have to go through the same thing. That was right out of the gate. It took a while for the dueling phone conversations to smooth out, where I didn't have to do everything twice—at least not at great length.

Clearly, Frank and Jamie both had a great passion for baseball. And both tried hard to figure out how to run a team. But unless you've owned another professional sports franchise, you can't possibly understand what you're getting into. Sports is not like real estate or construction or the newspaper or grocery business. Some fundamentals overlap, of course, but many don't. Probably the biggest difference between a professional sports franchise and most other businesses is that, in sports, the people who get paid the most have only limited accountability—and the best fail more than they succeed.

In many businesses, the people who draw the biggest salaries are the most reliable, the best leaders, and the most accountable employees or managers. In sports, athletes get the big bucks, while the people who run the franchise—those responsible for the decisions that make or break the business—get paid far less. Another major difference is that those decisions are dissected in the media every day for most of the year and all the while the public has a convenient barometer to measure success or failure—with just a glance at the standings.

If a businessperson is successful 33 percent of the time, they will be out of business. If a hitter is successful 33 percent of the time, there will be a statue of him outside the stadium after he's done playing.

All that takes some getting used to, but we're all expected to understand it upon walking in the door the first day. Most, if not all, new owners are forced to learn by trial and error. That certainly was the case with the McCourts.

My advice to an owner who has never run a professional sports team before would be to observe for six months to a year. Ask many questions, but don't make many decisions. Keep the existing staff in place. Watch them work. Listen, and learn. Then, after the first anniversary, start tinkering, start doing things your way. But not until then. That will never happen, of course, but it should, because it's tough to run a professional sports franchise on the fly. The Mc-Courts were an example. They were good businesspeople but still it took time and trial and error when running a Major League Baseball team for the first time.

I WAS IN SAN FRANCISCO when the McCourts took control of the Dodgers so I didn't know a lot about them before the interview process. But I could see from four hundred miles north that the *Los Angeles Times* in particular gave them a rough ride from the outset. Many fans and most of the media questioned their financial firepower and willingness to spend what they might or might not have. They had been successful at running their real estate business in New England, but they had nowhere near the number of staff, nor the spotlight, of the Los Angeles Dodgers. They went from Boston to Los Angeles, from a successful family construction and real estate business to one of the most hallowed franchises in all of professional sports.

The McCourts also had the disadvantage of taking over a franchise that only a few years earlier had been owned by one of the most revered families in American sports history. Many times, it seemed as though the McCourts were sailing into a headwind.

Walter and Peter O'Malley had owned the team for decades and had brought them west from Brooklyn. Their employees rarely left and were rewarded with trips to Italy and Hawaii.

In the years between the O'Malleys and McCourts, the Dodgers were owned by News Corporation, the parent company of the Fox network and movie studios. In just seven years, the franchise went from being owned by a beloved family that had been part of the community for five decades to an impersonal corporate giant. The Dodgers—the ultimate exemplar of the National League for decades—were then sold to a family few fans knew much about—only that they were suspected of not having the financial muscle to do business in a major market with a brand like the Dodgers. There's always suspicion whenever a major civic entity changes hands, but the whipsaw-turnaround the people of Los Angeles went through with the Dodgers meant Frank and Jamie were in a tough spot from day one. And they didn't always make crowd-pleasing decisions when it came to their employees, again not unusual in business.

The McCourts had their offices in a locked area of the front office behind another locked section of the stadium—a few hundred feet and a hallway apart from the bulk of the staff. Rarely did the two worlds meet. From time to time, Frank made the effort to mingle with the everyday staff. But Jamie seemed to have a tough time with it.

"What do you think we need to do to build the front office?" Jamie asked me on more than one occasion.

I always responded with the same sentiment: "If you spent a half hour—fifteen minutes twice a week—walking through the other side of the building, and sit down at a cubicle or two and build on that, it would do wonders."

I tried to bridge that gap because some of the people at Dodger Stadium felt isolated and often without value. I felt it was important to strengthen the bonds of the workforce to help further the franchise.

Early in my career, in 1983 and '84, I was low man on the totem pole with the Cubs. As I mentioned earlier, Jim Finks, the team president, was a legend in Chicago. He was a starting quarterback for the Pittsburgh Steelers in the 1950s. He was general manager of the Minnesota Vikings and the Chicago Bears for twenty years. He would later become general manager of the New Orleans Saints and be inducted into the National Football Hall of Fame.

During his fourteen months with the Cubs, Jim Finks didn't need to give me the time of day. But he went out of his way to give me—and everyone else in the organization—a lot more. He taught me a lifelong lesson and instilled a world of confidence by treating me as if I had more value to the club than I probably did at the time. No one was number 95 in the lineup when Finks was around. Everyone was somebody. He made his employees feel excited to be part of the team. He was going to help each person grow. He taught me how to do the same.

Finks encouraged me to be someone who could bridge the natural gaps between the talent side and business sides of professional sports. Nearly four decades later, I still remember how Jim Finks made me feel, what he did for me, and how much I appreciated it.

The personal touch counts. It always counts. But many felt the personal touch was lacking during those years.

MY FIRST FEW DAYS, and weeks, in L.A., were a blur. We had the news conference at Dodger Stadium announcing my hiring on Wednesday, November 16, 2005. Just before it started, I made four phone calls: to Vin Scully, Sandy Koufax, Tommy Lasorda, and longtime Dodger employee and friend Bill DeLury. I started right at the top.

I sensed Tommy had begun to be marginalized by a couple of the previous baseball regimes, and I didn't need to be on the wrong side of him. Admittedly, reaching out to him was a very calculated move, but it was genuine, as well. I have always respected those who came before me with rich histories and experiences. Experience is gained over time and trial, error and life lessons. Tommy added tremendous depth to our conversations both personally and with the baseball operations staff. I knew what he meant to the Dodgers and the fans of the franchise; I also respected what the Dodgers and their fans meant to him. It wasn't my business to ever disrupt those ties.

Lasorda never recorded a big-league hit or won a game in the majors. But he is still one of the most iconic figures in baseball. I was lucky enough in my career to see Tommy in a wide range of roles, from ebullient manager of the Dodgers to a top-level executive whose office was no farther from mine than home plate is from first base. Tommy was sometimes a caricature, and always a character. But, man, did Tommy love the Dodgers. He talked about "bleeding Dodger Blue," and he probably did.

Before I came to the Dodgers, I often wondered how much of his banter was bullshit and how much was real. I came to the conclusion it didn't matter. The players he managed heard the same stories over and over—the same motivational rants time and again. And all they did was go out and play hard for him and win.

One of my favorite stories about Tommy and his motivational speeches involved a visit he made to our Double-A club, the Chattanooga Lookouts. Tommy walked into the clubhouse an hour before game time and launched into a loud rant, calling out players and trying to inspire through sheer volume, historical anecdotes, and more than a touch of vulgarity. About three minutes in, a coach put his hand on Tommy's shoulder and broke some unexpected and unwelcome news: "Tommy, you're in the wrong clubhouse. Your team is across the field."

Long after he was through managing in the majors, he agreed to manage Team USA at the 2000 Sydney Olympics. Tommy donned an Uncle Sam top hat, launched into one rah-rah rant after another, and turned a group of ragtag minor leaguers and major-league cast-offs into a surprising gold-medal-winning team.

Tommy and I never had anything but a great relationship, although we did have one disagreement over a piece of jewelry in my early days as GM of the Dodgers.

"How long you going to wear that fucking San Francisco Giants championship ring?" he asked me a few times.

I was proud of that ring—and I still am. My thinking in those early days was that wearing a championship ring from the San Francisco Giants would help fuel the rivalry and instill a more competitive spirit in a Dodgers organization that was coming off a 71-91 record.

When I ran into Tommy again a couple of weeks into the job, he looked at my hand and was nearly apoplectic.

"Ned, while you are a fellow Italian, and make no mistake, I want you to do great here," he began, "I'm telling you right now, if I see that ring one more time I will cut that ring off your fuckin' hand."

I took the ring off.

THE DAY AFTER I was formally announced as GM of the Dodgers, I flew to Tampa, Florida, for Brian Sabean's wedding. I wasn't going to miss that, but I also needed to get to work. I had my three newly inherited top lieutenants—Kim Ng, Logan White, and Roy Smith—meet me in Florida. We were already a month and a half into the off-season and Thanksgiving was a week away. I had no manager, no coaches, and a staff I needed to get to know.

In Florida, I made time to sit down with Kim, Logan, and Roy. We also interviewed Jim Fregosi about the manager's job. I'd known Jimmy for a long time and had worked with him in San Francisco. He had managed fifteen years in the majors, taking the Phillies to the National League pennant in 1993 and winning 1,028 games with the Angels, White Sox, and Blue Jays. I thought he might be a good fit for our young club, or at least someone to start the hiring process and to be a gauge for the remainder of our candidates.

I also broke away and drove to Clearwater, Florida, to meet with Terry Collins, who was running player development for the Dodgers. Terry was on the verge of being hired to manage the team when DePodesta was let go. With Paul gone Terry's dream of managing the Dodgers was gone too. I felt I needed to make amends with him even though I had nothing to do with the sudden turn of events—other than being asked to take over.

I met with Terry twice, once in a restaurant and the next day at his house. Terry wasn't in a very good mood. Our conversation was like trying to put out a raging fire I didn't start. I think I finally convinced him I wasn't the person he should be irritated with. But it wasn't a warm and fuzzy parting. It has been good to see Terry have success managing the New York Mets and our conversations these days are far easier—even jovial.

At Sabes's wedding, the San Francisco folks were great. They were genuinely excited for me. So, too, was my old friend Don Zimmer, who had managed the Cubs when I was there. We had dinner with Zim and his wife, Soot, and then went to their house where I saw, for the first time, Zimmer's huge collection of Dodgers memorabilia. He came up with Brooklyn in 1954 and moved to L.A. with the Dodgers in 1958. Seeing all the old Dodgers jerseys, programs, pennants, and souvenirs in Zimmer's house was pretty cool, but it only reinforced how much work I had to do. I had a team to build. I had the *Dodgers* to build.

IN MY FIRST TWENTY-ONE DAYS as general manager, I was on eighteen flights. Every minute of every hour was filled trying to get my arms around a new organization—trying to figure out what I had and what I needed.

The first roster move I made came less than forty-eight hours after I got the job. We released third baseman Norihiro Nakamura, an all-star in Japan who had walked away from a guaranteed two-year, $10 million contract with the Kintetsu Buffaloes the year before to sign for $500,000 with the Dodgers. Nakamura had been an abysmal flop, hitting .128 in seventeen games, so the decision to release him didn't take up a lot of our time.

We took a short break for Thanksgiving. The day before, I flew to San Francisco for a going-away lunch with my former coworkers at the Giants. I was touched that so many people showed up on the eve of a holiday. It was wonderful. As soon as I walked in the room, they blared a tape of Russ Hodges's famous radio call of Bobby Thomson's home run to beat the Dodgers 5–4 on October 3, 1951:

"The Giants win the pennant! The Giants win the pennant! The Giants win the pennant! The Giants win the pennant!"

Yeah, yeah, I said, laughing. That was a long time ago. Let's see what happens next year.

The next day, Thanksgiving, I spent cleaning out my office at Pac Bell Park. It was a humbling, tough day, but I didn't have a lot of time to dwell on emotions. I was happy for the holiday and to be able to pack my things without a lot of people around.

The next morning, my new team and I really got down to work on building the Dodgers. We didn't have many tradable players, so we needed to make the club better through the free-agent market. The Dodgers had been 71-91—the second-worst record by a Dodger team since World War II—and we really needed to shore it up quickly.

Free agent negotiations are always complicated. All deals require thorough research and preparation, but with free-agent deals even more so. Before I would make a phone call to an agent, I had a step-by-step process I worked through. Information is king and I needed as much as possible from people I could trust.

Typically, I would begin with my inner circle of Kim Ng, Vance Lovelace, and Rick Ragazzo. We would navigate through a preliminary list of potential free agents and decide who we thought would be a likely target for our club—based on talent, age, injury history, personality, work ethic, and probable cost and length of contract.

Then I'd meet with the manager. I would never put a player in the room that the manager didn't want. That could only end badly. There are enough battles every day without creating new ones. If the baseball front office leader was high on a player the manager didn't want, we'd ask for specific instances to make sure he wasn't reacting to hearsay.

Next, I would get the medical staff involved. Stan Conte, our vice president of medical services who joined the Dodgers from the Giants before my second season, was kept in the loop. Obviously, it is imperative to have a working knowledge of a player's medical history. Anyone can look on the Internet and see how often a player has been on the disabled list and for what injuries. But sometimes a player will have an injury and never spend time on the DL. Perhaps he has a nagging injury that prevents him from running hard or stealing bases, but he plays through it. Perhaps a pitcher has abandoned a breaking ball because his elbow is barking. The best medical people know a lot more about a player than someone who simply checks a list. Every free agent acquisition is predicated on the player passing a physical examination. But research done ahead of time can help direct the medical staff and physicians who are doing the physical. They will know to check for problems beyond the obvious. In addition, the medical staff can usually provide keen insight into a player's personality—just as clubhouse workers and traveling secretaries can.

I sought as much information as I could get.

Was the player a good teammate? Did he get along with the players who were not only talented but respected the game and played hard? Did he look after the rookies and the twenty-fifth man? Did the manager and coaches consider him an asset to the team? Did he report to the clubhouse early? Did he leave a lot of tickets on his pass list for people other than family? How did he act and react when the team was going well? When the team was slumping? How did he treat the clubhouse kids who work for minimum wage and tips?

I would bring in the analytical department to provide insight into the player's performance numbers and prevailing trends in the game.

From there, I would simultaneously begin canvassing the scouts and reviewing their reports. While I read their reports, I also wanted to talk to the scouts themselves—to hear the inflection in their voices. Some scouts invariably said yes to anyone I asked them about and others were predictable naysayers. Some were better at scouting pitchers; others had a knack for knowing good hitters. Long before I sought their opinions, I had scouted the scouts. In order to properly evaluate, a leader needs to know how the evaluators evaluate—otherwise, opinion has no value.

Next we would study the market to determine how many teams might be interested in this player—based either on their needs or wants. We had to know the likely competition. That meant knowing what organizations had the payroll flexibility and the inclination to add a player of that particular talent and that likely cost. We knew the styles and gamesmanship of the other general managers—how they typically worked; if they had the money and the courage to invest at a financial level; if they would have a seemingly legitimate interest or just feint to raise the asking price for everyone else. It's not uncommon for some general managers and assistants to use the media to raise expectations and spur fan interest in players they have neither the interest in nor the dollars to sign.

Agents do the same. Many will tell you they have talked to a certain club about a particular player. Maybe they talked, but what did they talk about? Was the conversation to gauge interest, decline interest, make an offer, or end a conversation? Does it mean a team is interested? Not necessarily.

BESIDES ANALYZING OPPOSING GMS and their front offices, we also studied their ownership. Did the club need a boost on the field to help the turnstile numbers? Was the club on the verge of obtaining a new local television contract? Was the club saddled with a below-market revenue stream and for how long? Some owners get deeply involved in player negotiations, which is akin to sending a hungry man to the grocery store—beneficial to the player and the agent most times, but not so much for the payroll; and maybe not for the team.

Once I had all the background, I would find a quiet place to pull it all together. I would come up with my breaking point. If it was three years and ten million a year, I would set that as the goal—knowing I might have to go to three years at eleven million per year, or maybe even a tad more. But I knew my limit. I knew where I wouldn't go no matter what. Of course, my thinking could change if, say, one of our players went down and we needed a replacement. But other than that, I set my limits. And I did it in a quiet, private place so the agent, the player, the media, the fan base, even the owner—none of them—could emotionally sway me to a place I wasn't really comfortable with and didn't want to go.

If, after all our research, I decided to move forward on a potential free agent, I would take it to ownership or the president of the club. I didn't want to be in those high-level discussions with a player and his agent without a clear understanding and unanimous perspective about a player among the inner circle, manager, and owner/president of the club. I didn't want to waste a player's time and I wanted to be prepared for as many questions as possible. Agents know preparation and they know if the club negotiator is prepared.

And let's face it, you only want to have a discussion with ownership when you can answer all the questions. General managers don't sit in that position for long if the owner has more questions than they have answers, especially when financial commitments are at stake.

Only then, after those many steps, conversations, and internal debate, would I pick up a phone and dial the agent.

While I believe research and preparation are paramount in dealing with free agents, I believe listening and being willing to say no—not yes—are equally important and valuable once the negotiation starts.

In a two-hour conversation, I might spend 90 percent of the time listening. And in all that listening, there might be sixty invaluable seconds. In that minute, I may learn the most important element of this negotiation—or the most important element to the player, to the player's family, to the agent, to the union. Negotiators need to be able to listen intently and then be able to decipher the richest sentence or two in a marathon conversation.

Careful listening can keep negotiators from making a big mistake. Take this conversation from an agent:

"I think this player is going to get four and sixty," an agent may say.

What does that mean?

Does it mean the player is going to get a four-year contract at fifteen million per year for a total of sixty million?

If you're not listening closely you might take it as gospel.

But believing, thinking, feeling, and hearing isn't the same as being offered a contract.

And "four and sixty." What does that really mean?

The "four" and "sixty" aren't necessarily related; both could be separate. The agent might have an offer of four years at, say, ten million a year for a total of forty million, and a separate proposal worth sixty million, but spread over six years. So he's got "four" and "sixty," but not in the same package he believes, thinks, feels, or has heard the player is going to get.

Unless you get the agent to specifically lay out terms, and tell you whether those terms are in a real proposal, you might be getting nothing but speculation. And it may be just the agent's own speculation.

The key to good negotiating is to listen—and ask for clarity.

I scouted agents, just as I did players, scouts, executives, owners, and the media. I learned their styles, their favorite buzzwords, who relied on deception, how they liked to use the clock, whether they ran up to deadlines, what types of players they chose to represent, how they went about their profession. Preparation and research are invaluable tools.

So, too, is the Power of No. And no one used the Power of No more magnificently than Frank McCourt.

Until a GM tells an agent no and is willing to walk away, the value of a deal is going to continue to climb. The process only winds down when the GM says, "That's it. I'm done. This negotiation is over; it is now either a yes or a no from your side."

In my opinion, there is no clearer real-world example for this than buying a car from a dealer.

First rule: Make sure in the course of a conversation the salesperson gets your contact information.

The best opening: "There's one thing I know for sure right now and one I don't know for sure . . . I'm know I'm buying a car today. I just don't know from what dealer or salesperson."

If you've done the necessary preparation and research, and you are willing to say no and leave the showroom, chances are you'll get the deal at what you know is a fair price.

Whether we know it or not, we all negotiate daily—really from the moment we are born. The more we understand about the personality and position of the other side, the better prepared we are, and the better chance we will have at negotiating a successful outcome.

Major League Baseball's free agent market is a last resort—and nearly always the most precarious method to add a player. I would go to the free agent market when I didn't have a player who was already part of the organization who I felt could contribute at the level of the free agent. Sometimes, I used a free agent signing to produce competition or to give a young player additional time to mature and become a bona fide major-league player.

The problem with free agent signings is that they rarely return one hundred cents on the dollar. Unless the deal is very short—a year or two—chances are it will be an overpay. And then there is the issue of adding a new personality to the clubhouse. If a team is mostly composed of players who first signed professional contracts with the organization, they have been brought up in a specific culture. When you add from the outside, a player's priorities may be different. It may take time for the cultures to mesh, or they may never mesh.

Free agents are a gamble, but when I took over the Dodgers, they were a gamble we had to take.

THE MORNING AFTER THANKSGIVING 2005, I flew to Los Angeles from San Francisco and began the real work of building my first Dodgers team. I met Roy Smith, the vice president of scouting and player development, and the two of us drove down to San Diego. We wanted to meet with Brian Giles, one of three free agents on the market I thought would give us a chance to get better. Besides Giles, the other two free agents I targeted were Rafael Furcal and Paul Konerko. With up-and-coming first baseman James Loney in the system, Konerko was less of a priority and we didn't think he was going to leave the White Sox anyway. So I focused on Giles and Furcal.

Giles had been a productive outfielder with San Diego. He played with passion and was a solid run producer. Furcal, a shortstop, was entering free agency at a very young age, twenty-eight. He was a switch hitter who led off—adding even more value. In addition, he had signed originally with Atlanta, an organization known for its winning culture. He and Giles would be big upgrades for a team that finished twenty games under .500 and needed an infusion of talent, passion, and culture.

We met Brian in San Diego, then stopped on the way back to L.A. to talk with Alan Trammell, the six-time All-Star shortstop and former manager of the Detroit Tigers. Trammell was looking for a coaching position, if not the manager's job. And, of course, he wasn't alone. The entire next week we were interviewing a long line of possible candidates, including Grady Little, Manny Acta, and John McLaren, all three of whom would be managing in the big leagues by 2007 and gone from those jobs by 2013.

As the days sped by, Furcal quickly became my number one target. Rumors were strong he was going to go to the Cubs and Giles was going back to San Diego. But I wasn't ready to give up. Logan White, who oversaw amateur scouting, and I set up a dinner with agent Adam Katz at Il Fornaio restaurant in Pasadena. Adam was part of the group that represented Furcal but he wasn't Raffy's main agent. Paul Kinzer was. But I'd known Adam a long time and he had a direct line to Furcal and Kinzer. I asked him where things stood with Chicago.

Adam felt a $55 million, five-year offer was in reach.

I asked him: "What if we go shorter and more money?"

Adam looked at me quizzically.

"What if it was like thirty-nine for three?" I asked.

"Really?" Katz said. "I think that may be of interest."

I went into the Furcal conversation knowing that the allure of being a free agent again at thirty-one years of age may have had some value. There was also speculation that the Cubs were trying to add a clause to the contract because Furcal had had a DUI in Atlanta. That would be a change from the standard language, and players, agents, and the union typically balk at unconventional language.

A deal for $13 million a year was enticing, even if the term was two years shorter. I was gambling that Furcal and his agents would be enticed knowing his next contract would be building off a $13 million a year base—not $11 million a year—and he would be a free agent at thirty-one, not thirty-three. All points in their favor. Having Furcal and having him for three years, not five, was in our favor.

Shortly after I dropped the $39 million for three years offer on Katz, I excused myself and left Logan to carry on the conversation. I went to a pay phone—perhaps one of the last in the world at that time—in the back of the restaurant and called Joe Bick, who represented Giles. I could have used my cellphone, but I wanted privacy and the pay phone in the back of the restaurant was tucked into a tight space that was nice and secluded, plus I could guarantee the reception quality. Bick told me he was pretty sure Giles was headed back to San Diego. That left my three-man wish list down to just Furcal. And I really needed him. Our shortstop, Cesare Izturis, was out. He had Tommy John surgery and wasn't coming back until July. And we didn't have a shortstop or a decent leadoff man in the system.

Katz didn't know how desperate I was for Furcal. But I kept hammering away. We flew Raffy out to Los Angeles for a grand tour, counting on the legendary Manny Mota to help woo him.

Manny has been with the Dodgers either as a player or coach since 1969, eight years before Furcal was born, and is revered among players from the Dominican Republic. He's a great ambassador for the Dodgers and for baseball. Manny and Logan took Furcal to dinner on Friday night with the McCourts.

I skipped the dinner. I was on my way to my first Winter Meetings in Dallas as a general manager. But I had a few stops to make. First was Chicago. My home was still there. My family was still there. All the time I worked for the Giants, I lived in a small condominium in San Mateo. I planned to fly to Chicago and grab a few suits, a bigger piece of luggage, and a couple hours of sleep. Then I was flying to Columbus, Ohio, to interview Joel Skinner, a Southern California native and son of former Pittsburgh Pirates All-Star Bob Skinner. Joel had an impressive minor-league managing career and had managed the Cleveland Indians to a third-place finish in 2002. He was still a coach with the Indians but had an interest in managing the Dodgers and I was willing to hear him out.

My flight to Chicago was delayed, delayed, and then delayed again. I was supposed to land about midnight. Instead, a little after 4 a.m., I was standing at an empty luggage carousel with no bags that belonged to Ned Colletti on it. When the search was over, the news was bad.

"Sorry, Mr. Colletti. We saw that your flight to Columbus leaves at six a.m., so we just went ahead and put the luggage you checked in L.A. on the connecting flight to Columbus."

Great. So now I don't have time to go home. All I can do is crash at O'Hare and wait for my six o'clock fight.

I landed in Columbus and changed clothes in the airport restroom. I met Joel Skinner right there in the terminal. We had a nice conversation and as soon as it was over, I picked up a rental car and drove 120 miles to Oxford, Ohio, to see Jenna, my daughter. On the drive, I got a call from Kirk Gibson, hero of the last

Dodgers' World Series championship team in 1988. He wanted to manage the club. At the time, he had been a coach with the Detroit Tigers, but had never managed anywhere.

I was polite, but told Gibson we were pretty far down the path with someone who had been successful in a major market. I didn't tell Kirk, but we were strong on Grady Little.

Kirk was one of the game's greatest competitors and he let me know he didn't appreciate not having an opportunity to even interview. I was respectful and polite, but Gibby kept coming after me like I had just thrown a 98-mph fastball up and in on him. Eventually, the call ended civilly. But it took a while.

LATE THE NEXT DAY, Saturday, December 3, 2005, just as Jenna and I were about to reach sold-out Goggin Ice Center to see a big hockey showdown between No. 8 Miami of Ohio and No. 3 Michigan, I got a phone call from Kim. She told me one of our scouts, Vance Lovelace, was about to take a job with Tampa.

"How good is Vance Lovelace?" I asked, relying on Kim's experience to fill a void until I could get up to speed.

"He's pretty good," she said. "And he has potential to be a lot better."

The winter weather was moving in. I stopped under a tree with no leaves in the midst of a sleet storm to call Lovelace at his home in Florida. Baseball is a big business. Thousands of people work for nearly three hundred organizations, including minor-league baseball. But, it's still a small world.

In the winter of 1983, I had been in Dallas Green's office with the Cubs the night he acquired Ron Cey from the Dodgers. One of the two players he sent to L.A. was Vance Lovelace. Twenty-two years later, I was on the phone with Vance.

"You don't know me and I don't know you," I said without

any small talk. "Tell me why you want to leave. What do you want to do?"

"Well, I work hard and I don't think anybody appreciates what I do," Lovelace said. "They really don't care about my reports. I've got no say in the organization or what we do. And now I've got a chance to go and work for my hometown team."

The last thing I could afford my first few weeks on the job was to start losing good people. I asked Lovelace what he was making.

"Fifty thousand," he said.

"All right," I said. "And your goal is to really have a say in the organization and to have a presence in the baseball-making decisions, right?"

"Yeah."

"All right. Do you have any needs for any up-front money?"

"Yeah," Lovelace said with a chuckle. "What do you think? I have two kids in college."

I offered Vance twice his salary with some up-front signing bonus money. And just as important to him, I told him he was going to be my right-hand player personnel person.

"I'm going to give you the chance to work twenty-eight days a month and to have a say in everything we do," I said. "I'm going to trust that you are who you say you are, and this is who you are. And I'm going to start there."

"Really?" Lovelace said, seemingly taken aback. "Well, let me think about it for a couple days."

I told him no. "You can't think about it for a couple of days. You know what you want. You know what you need financially. You're going to have to trust me like I'm going to have to trust you. You've had plenty of time to think about it. Your words to me were well rehearsed. You weren't like you didn't know what you wanted to do or what you wanted it to look like or what you wanted to be paid. So that's what I have for you."

Lovelace hesitated a second. "So I don't have any time to think about this or call Tampa back?"

"No," I said. "When we hang this phone up, we're both going to know what team you will be working for."

Lovelace gave a booming, high-pitched laugh that I would come to know well and love.

"All right, I guess I'm coming back."

"Well, you made a good decision."

He *had* made a good decision. And so had I. Lace proved to be one of the best scouts in baseball and a tremendously loyal person, somebody who is probably on the road twenty-seven or twenty-eight days a month and never complains—except when the team didn't play up to its capabilities.

THE MIAMI REDHAWKS played well that night—incredibly well—upsetting No. 3 Michigan on a late unassisted goal by senior captain Andy Greene. But I missed most of it juggling work. And I nearly missed it all. My lovely daughter forgot to get tickets to the sold-out game. We had to talk our way in and finally got a couple of seats in the press box when Athletic Director Brad Bates learned the new general manager of the Los Angeles Dodgers was in the house.

Midway through the second period, I went out into the lobby to call Adam Katz about Furcal—from another pay phone, no less, since my battery was low and cell service unpredictable. I asked how Friday night's dinner with the McCourts had gone. Katz said it was great.

"So where are we?" I asked.

"Well, I think we can do this," Adam said. "Can you give me forty-two?"

"No," I said. "We can give you thirty-nine. That's all we're going to do. But we should do this."

"Well, let me think about it," Katz said.

"Fine, but you've got till tomorrow morning because I don't have time to waste on this," I said. "I can't afford to have you shop it. You know what you have out there. If he wants to be a Dodger, this is your last chance."

"Okay, let me call you back."

A few minutes later, Katz called back and said we had a deal. So, in less time than it took for the Redhawks to whip the Wolverines, I signed my right-hand man and a starting shortstop.

There are many factors to consider when signing a free agent. Most of the time, it is about adding a player who possesses a talent at a position of need that you don't currently have. Furcal's age, coupled with his ability to switch-hit and play in the middle of the field, made his signing imperative to me. It also provided our sales force with a key player to add to their marketing and sales pitches, though I wouldn't add a player solely for that reason. Winning is the best marketing tool available.

THE NEXT EVENING, after a wonderful weekend with Jenna, I was off to Dallas for the Winter Meetings. Before I left, I called Grady Little in North Carolina.

"Are you still interested in managing the Dodgers?" I asked.

"Absolutely" came his quick response.

"Okay, here's what I want you to do. I'd like you to fly out to Dallas tomorrow and stay at the Hyatt at DFW Airport. We'll get you set up with a room, but nobody can know you are there. I'll come by tomorrow. We'll have another set of interviews and see how it goes."

Logan, Roy, and Kim had sat in on the interviews the week before. But I really wanted to dig deep in a one-on-one setting since Grady was the leading candidate. Many of the conversations during a season between the manager and general manager are one-on-one sessions. I felt it imperative to begin that form of interaction as soon as possible and I wanted Grady to know this interview was different than the first one.

The session the next day went well. Frank flew in and spent another hour with Grady. He gave the thumbs-up and I asked Grady to come back with me to the Loews Anatole—now the Hilton Anatole—the main hotel off Stemmons Freeway in Dallas, where the Winter Meetings were getting under way. As fate would have it, as soon as Grady and I returned to the hotel, something awkward happened. We were stepping off an elevator together when, who did we run into? Jim Fregosi.

Fregosi had been on hold for the possible manager's job for a couple of weeks. I couldn't tell him I was going in another direction, because if things hadn't gone well with Grady, Jimmy would have been back in the picture. But they had gone well, and Grady was going to be my choice. Fregosi knew it the moment he bumped into the two of us coming off the elevator and gave me a disappointing glance. I felt bad about having Jimmy see Grady and me together—and in a crowded lobby where people could put two and two together. We were already well behind schedule in hiring a manager and a staff. We needed as much time as possible to bring Grady up to speed on the club with the scouts and player personnel staff present in Dallas and also to prepare for a press conference to be held the next day. Had I procured a signed agreement with Grady, I would have alerted the other candidates immediately. But that was still a little bit of a process and I figured the information exchanged with Grady wasn't going to be earth-shattering, plus the chance to interact would move the signing process with Grady to completion—which it did.

Meanwhile, Furcal had flown to Los Angeles for a physical. He passed and we asked him to get on a plane for Dallas. I told Grady he'd have to hang around for yet another night, and on Wednesday we made our two big announcements—Grady and Furcal—at a news conference. I was feeling pretty good. We were off and running.

ONE OF THE FIRST ASSIGNMENTS Frank gave me was to trade Milton Bradley. Frank told me that Milton had had trouble with Kent, among others, during the previous season and he thought it was best that we trade Milton as soon as possible.

Every owner handles the day-to-day decisions by the general manager in different ways. They all want to know when big deals are coming and the thought process that goes into making them. And that is their right. Most people I dealt with at the ownership level needed the same basic questions answered.

But Frank was a little different. He not only wanted the basics, he wanted more. A conversation about a deal that I thought would last fifteen minutes often continued for two to three hours.

I would try not to sit down in Frank's office, to keep the conversation short and concise.

As it turned out, I always ended up sitting down.

Frank constantly challenged my thought process. As he had done in my first interview, he always wanted to learn what I knew, what I had done to prepare, how many other options I'd considered, and why I had selected the option I had chosen. No other owner I worked for grilled me as relentlessly or made me justify my thinking as thoroughly as Frank did. It was one of his great strengths. I was a better thinker because of how he tested me.

I talked to Milton's agent, Sam Levinson, in the hotel lobby in Dallas and he agreed that it was probably better for everyone if Bradley went somewhere else. So not only did I inherit a team that finished with the third-worst record in the National League, but I also had a pretty good player that I now had to move.

I had known Billy Beane of the Oakland A's for a long time, having watched him closely from across the bay. Paul DePodesta had worked for Billy, so there was a strong possibility that Billy knew a lot about Milton's relationship with the Dodgers and vice versa. He approached me about Bradley during the Winter Meetings, but the players he originally talked about didn't appeal to us— pitchers who probably would be the eleventh and twelfth arms on our roster. I still had a couple of weeks before I would be forced to tender Bradley—that is, offer him a contract, or lose him. I wanted to see if I could do better than what Beane was offering.

Toronto had shown only a little bit of interest in Bradley. The Blue Jays' GM was J. P. Ricciardi. J.P. had also worked for Billy. If I were Billy, I would have wanted to get as much inside information as possible from two of my former lieutenants who were in a prime position to explain a few different views. It was looking more and more as if Oakland was our only real shot. I was sitting in a suite in the Anatole and we were tossing around names when somebody brought up an outfielder the A's had at Double-A.

One of our top scouts, Al LaMacchia, was in the room watching television and half-listening to the names.

Al pitched sixteen years in the minors and sixteen games in the majors before becoming one of the most respected scouts in baseball. Among the legion of players he signed were Dale Murphy, Cito Gaston, George Bell, Lloyd Moseby, Dave Stieb, and David Wells. He also signed Mike Coolbaugh, the onetime Brewer and Cardinal third baseman, who was killed by a line drive while coaching first base for the Tulsa Drillers in 2007.

LaMacchia, who died at his home in San Antonio, Texas, at age eighty-nine in 2010, was one of the best talent evaluators I ever knew. More important, he was a wonderful man.

As soon as the name Andre Ethier was mentioned, Al wheeled around and said, "Let me tell you about Ethier. If you've got a chance to get this kid, you should do it in a heartbeat," he said, and launched into a long description of how good Ethier was going to be and how good a hitter he already was.

As it turned out, Logan White had seen a lot of Ethier the month before I was hired because Andre was playing on the same team in the Arizona Fall League as a group of Dodger prospects. He liked what he saw and seconded LaMacchia's opinion.

When we got back to Los Angeles, I called Beane about Ethier. He originally said no. A few calls later, he said he might be willing to part with Ethier for Bradley if we threw in another player, third baseman Antonio Perez.

Perez was a utility infielder, primarily a third baseman, who had hit .297 in ninety-eight games for the Dodgers in 2005. That was solid, but Perez wasn't a full-time player. And he never would be. In fact, he played just fifty-seven games with the A's after we traded him, hitting just .102, and would be out of Major League Baseball after the 2006 season.

I was willing to give up Perez because, at the time, I was deep in negotiations that would bring Billy Mueller and Nomar Garciaparra to the Dodgers within a week and I really wanted Ethier after the rave reviews from Logan and LaMacchia. I didn't think Ethier could make our club out of Spring Training, but I liked the idea of adding a solid hitter to the group of promising prospects we had coming through the system. Ethier would be at just about the same developmental stage as catcher Russell Martin, infielders James Loney and Andy LaRoche, and pitchers Jonathan Broxton and Chad Billingsley. Just a touch behind them at that point was center fielder Matt Kemp. Adding Ethier to the mix sounded pretty attractive and getting veterans like Mueller and Garciaparra to bridge the gap until the young players were ready seemed like a solid plan. We traded Bradley and Perez to Oakland for Ethier on Tuesday, December 13, 2005. Two days later, we signed Mueller. Four days after that, we added Garciaparra. One day after that, we signed Kenny Lofton.

We needed to add quality, successful players. Mueller, whom I knew from my days in San Francisco, was one of my favorites. He played every game like it was his last and he poured all he had into baseball. He won a batting championship in the American League and was the starting third baseman for the 2004 World Series champion Boston Red Sox. When knee injuries ended his career, he sat in the clubhouse and wept.

Nomar was from Los Angeles and had been a two-time batting champion with Boston. Just a couple of years earlier, he was one of the best shortstops in the game. He had a great baseball mind, was intelligent and ultracompetitive, and I thought he would be a great addition—especially on a short, one-year deal.

Lofton was also a winning player. He came from Gary, Indiana, a place I knew well. Just thirty-two miles from Chicago, Gary had one of the highest rates of violent crime in the nation. Lofton competed in life and he competed on the baseball field. He could lead off and, while his ability to play center field had diminished a little with age, he was still a big upgrade for us. I had helped acquire him in 2002 from the White Sox during the Giants' run to the World Series. I knew he played with passion and without fear. We also signed him for one year.

In a span of thirteen days, we hired a manager, traded for a prospect who eventually would become an All-Star, signed All-Stars to play short and center field, and brought on a two-time American League batting champion to play first base and a former AL batting champ to be our starting third baseman. But we still weren't close to finished. We still needed a coaching staff.

We wanted to promote some coaches from within the organization, and we did. We brought Rick Honeycutt from a minor-league roving position to become the pitching coach for the big-league club. We gave longtime Dodger legend Mariano Duncan a well-deserved promotion from the minors to become first-base coach.

We went outside the organization to hire Danny Warthen from the Mets as our bullpen coach, Hall of Famer Eddie Murray came over from the Indians to become hitting coach, and Dave Jauss, who had worked with Grady in Boston, became his bench coach.

Those moves took another three weeks or so, which brought us to mid-January and the eve of Spring Training. In just two months, we'd built a team and assembled a coaching staff that would take the Dodgers from being a team twenty games under .500 in 2005 to the National League playoffs in 2006.

MY FIRST OPENING DAY as a general manager was a milestone, but one filled with its own challenges. I slept little the night before. After building teams with baseball cards as a ten-year-old on the kitchen table in Franklin Park, I was now going to get a look at a major-league team I'd put together for real. I was driving the bus. I knew there would be days the bus would run just fine and days it wouldn't. This was one of the days the bus started to break down before the trip even began.

I got to the ballpark and learned that the starting first baseman, Nomar, and center fielder, Lofton, were out. In the time between a Sunday Freeway Series exhibition against the Los Angeles Angels in Anaheim and a Monday afternoon regular season opener against the Braves, both Garciaparra and Lofton went on the disabled list.

We knew all along, of course, that Nomar was a bit of a health risk. He'd played just sixty-two games the year before with the Cubs and eighty-one games in 2004, split between Boston and Chicago. But we thought he was worth the gamble. Just a few years earlier, he was one of the game's premier hitters. He'd come to us privately, looking for a one-year deal and a chance to prove himself.

We had Furcal to play short and Mueller to play third, so Nomar, a natural shortstop, was going to have to play first. He was good with that. Our guys were convinced he could still hit if he could stay on the field. And they were right. Even though he started the season on the DL, Nomar played in 122 games, hit 20 home runs, batted .303, and made the National League All-Star team.

Along with Nomar, the team had a good year despite a slow start. We lost the opener to the Braves 11–10 and were 47-55 in late July after losing thirteen games in a fourteen-game stretch. I could feel the rumblings. Fans were wondering who I was, who Grady was, and what we were doing to their team. Then we hit our stride.

From July 28 to August 15, we won seventeen of eighteen to go from last place to first—up by three and a half games. But the defining moment for that team came a little more than a month later, on September 18, 2006, when, trailing the Padres by four in the bottom of the ninth, we did something only one other team in history had done: We hit four consecutive home runs to tie the game. Jeff Kent hit the first off Jon Adkins. Then J. D. Drew took Adkins deep. San Diego manager Bud Black called for his Hall of Fame closer, Trevor Hoffman, but he couldn't stop the onslaught. Russell Martin homered on the first pitch Hoffman threw and Marlon Anderson hit Hoffman's second pitch into the left field pavilion, sending what was left of the announced crowd of 55,831 into a frenzy.

Aaron Sele, who later would become one of my special assistants in the front office, gave up a run in the top of the tenth inning but became the winning pitcher when Nomar crushed a two-run shot off Rudy Seanez with nobody out in the bottom half.

The miracle win stopped the Padres from taking over first place and kept us atop the division with twelve to play. We held on to finish in a tie with San Diego and qualify for the playoffs as the NL wild card team.

After that four–home run comeback, I was almost at peace with the season. I think I would have been okay even if we hadn't made the playoffs because we never gave up. We had been in one of those situations where we could have faded and never gotten back in the race. But at least we'd made a statement that we were going to continue to play hard and continue to do everything we could to win.

We clinched a playoff spot on Saturday, September 30, 2006, in, of all places, San Francisco. Greg Maddux beat Matt Cain 4–2.

But I remember pulling out of the parking lot in the team bus headed for the Oakland airport after the final game of the season the next afternoon and driving past the plaza at Third and King. The place was a sea of blue. Dodger fans were everywhere—most of them right beneath Peter Magowan's office.

I remembered our conversation from a year earlier when he really didn't want to give me permission to speak to the Dodgers, because he didn't want to lose me.

If Peter's up there looking out the window right now, I thought, he's probably not having a lot of great feelings about me.

Nine

McVILLAIN? McBANKRUPT?
McBRILLIANT

• • • • • • • • • • • • •

arvard Business School should teach a course on the business acumen of Frank H. McCourt Jr.

It seemed that not many Dodgers fans liked the man. The commissioner of baseball seemed like he despised him. But there is no denying Frank's staggering business skills.

Frank came from a very successful family. His great-grandfather, an Irish immigrant, founded the John McCourt Company, which quickly became one of Boston's most respected road-building companies. His grandfather once owned a piece of the Boston Braves while expanding the family business into one of the top highway construction companies in New England, at a time when Americans were becoming increasingly dependent on the automobile.

Frank's father served with the Fourteenth Armored Division in Europe during World War II and returned to shepherd the McCourt Company's transition from road builders to general contractors, overseeing more sophisticated infrastructure projects, including the expansion of Boston's Logan International Airport.

After graduating from Georgetown University, Frank McCourt

Jr. established his own company and quickly made his mark, acquiring twenty-four acres of waterfront property in South Boston from the bankrupt Penn Central Railroad in the early 1980s and turning the land into lucrative parking lots while he waited for even more lucrative development opportunities.

In 2001, at age forty-seven, McCourt made a bid to buy the Boston Red Sox, offering ten acres of his waterfront property for use in building a new ballpark to replace historic Fenway Park, which, at the time, was deteriorating badly.

"Clearly the land is much more valuable for full-time commercial and residential development," McCourt told *The Boston Globe* in August 2001. "So the only rationale that would motivate us to take on a less-valuable ballpark project would be if it was fused with a controlling interest in the team."

That proposal quickly fell flat, but two years later, Frank made another bid to buy the Los Angeles Angels of Anaheim, losing out to Arte Moreno, who became the first Mexican American to be the primary owner of a Major League Baseball team.

On January 21, 2003, News Corporation put the Dodgers up for sale. Allen & Company, a New York–based company that specializes as an investment banking and advisory firm, helped broker the sale.

For six months, News Corporation courted Malcolm Glazer, the billionaire owner of the National Football League's Tampa Bay Buccaneers and the Premier League's Manchester United, who died in 2014. Both sides tried hard to reach a deal, but the NFL's cross-ownership rules made it impossible. (The NFL allows its owners to purchase sports franchises outside the United States, but banned cross-ownership of teams within the country.)

The prolonged negotiations only made News Corporation all the more impatient to sell the Dodgers and played right into Frank McCourt's hands. On October 10, 2003, Rupert Murdoch's Fox media conglomerate agreed in principle to sell the Los Angeles Dodgers to McCourt for approximately $431 million. The deal, which was approved by Major League Baseball on January 29, 2004, was highly leveraged—so leveraged that longtime local radio talk show host Joe McDonnell of KSPN stopped using McCourt's name and started calling him "McBankrupt." That was just days after the sale and a full seven and a half years before Frank actually filed for bankruptcy. It was a sign that from the very beginning the media were bent on giving the McCourts a tough ride.

There was a curiosity about how leveraged the deal was and few really knew until Frank and Jamie's divorce trial, when Frank's attorney, Steve Susman, acknowledged publicly that "not a penny" of the McCourts' own money went into the deal.

Not a penny of his own money?

And eight years later, he sold the team for $2.15 billion. *Billion!* That's a pretty good return on investment. I'd call it McBrilliant. Worthy of a course at Harvard Business School.

Frank and Jamie took over the club in February 2004. Within two months, they bought a home in the Holmby Hills portion of Brentwood, near the University of California, Los Angeles campus in Westwood, and a few hundred yards from the main gate to Hugh Hefner's Playboy Mansion. They paid $21.25 million for the five-bedroom, six-bathroom, 11,637-square-foot mansion, then spent another $14 million on renovations that included an Olympic-sized indoor swimming pool—Jamie was an avid swimmer—and transporting the entire kitchen from their Massachusetts home. For good measure, a few months later the McCourts bought a neighboring house for $6.5 million with the intent of using it as a guesthouse. Media, citing divorce documents, reported the McCourts spent an additional $4.8 million in basic improvements and architectural fees to that property.

The first year they owned the Dodgers, the team made the

postseason for the first time since 1996. Then things went south. After losing three of four to the St. Louis Cardinals in the 2004 National League Division Series, the 2005 team started 12-2, only to stumble to a 71-91 record—the second-worst record by any Dodger team since World War II. General Manager DePodesta and Manager Jim Tracy weren't seeing eye to eye. Outfielder Milton Bradley had a series of high-profile run-ins with his teammates and fans. The franchise was in dire straits.

As the 2005 season was winding down—unbeknownst to either one of us, it would be Paul's last with the Dodgers and my last with San Francisco—the Giants were playing the Dodgers in Los Angeles the first few days of September 2005. My son, Lou, and I decided to drive over from Phoenix, where the Giants had just finished a series against the Diamondbacks and Lou had wrapped up a season coaching at the rookie level. On our way to Dodger Stadium, Lou and I stopped for lunch. We sat down and heard a commotion coming from a raised row of tables nearly adjacent to us in the restaurant. It didn't take long for me to recognize the voices. DePodesta and Tracy were having a respectful yet emotional exchange that would have best been kept private, not carried out in a popular Pasadena restaurant.

LITTLE MORE THAN A MONTH LATER, Tracy and the Dodgers parted ways and Paul was let go with three years remaining on his contract. I had replaced Jim with Grady Little. We turned the 71-91 debacle into a team that won 88 games and went to the postseason. Frank and Jamie were ecstatic. Two of their first three teams had made the playoffs. Attendance was healthy. So were sponsorships. Healthy enough for the McCourts to go shopping again.

In 2007, the McCourts added a $27.3 million beachfront home previously owned by Courteney Cox and David Arquette at Carbon

Beach in Malibu. The home had eighty feet of private beach. Frank and Jamie bought the neighboring house in 2008 for $19 million.

According to media reports from divorce documents, the L.A. homes were added to a portfolio of properties in Vail, Colorado ($6 million), Cabo San Lucas, Mexico ($4.6 million), the Yellowstone Club in Montana ($7.7 million), and a one-hundred-acre Cape Cod estate that at one point was on the market for $50 million.

Life was good for Frank and Jamie, as the public divorce reports displayed. Late evening dinners in Brentwood, Bel-Air, and Beverly Hills. Personal drivers, private jets, expensive daily hairstylists, florists, a "healer" in Massachusetts, and a staff of assistants at their home and at Dodger Stadium.

In 2008, the Dodgers advanced to the National League Championship Series, against the Philadelphia Phillies. We lost in five games but the following year played the Phillies again in the NLCS. In the moments immediately before the opening of the 2008 NLCS, I ran into my first baseball boss—Dallas Green, at that point a special assistant in the Phillies front office.

We saw each other in a hallway. He came toward me with outstretched arms and we hugged.

"I am so very proud of you, Colletti," Dallas said. "You've done very well here."

I thanked him. His words meant a lot to me since he provided me with my first baseball opportunity.

"But make no mistake, we are here to kick the Dodgers' ass."

Ah, yes. The same man I knew twenty-six years earlier.

Then, on the eve of the 2009 NLCS, the marital cracks began to reach the public. Media speculation had been rampant that the McCourts were having issues. They were seldom seen together. I had been trying to block it all out, but the night before Clayton Kershaw would match up against Cole Hamels in Game 1 at Dodger Stadium, I was with a friend, Bill Connor, who had worked for decades on *The Tonight Show* with Johnny Carson and Jay Leno. We were dining at Morton's near the NBC lot in Burbank and I'd just sat down when Frank called.

He told me they were separating and he wanted me to know ahead of the news reports.

I thanked Frank for the heads-up and within days the firestorms erupted. The fire would burn for nearly three years.

On October 16, the day after we lost the series opener 8–6, Frank and Jamie each publicly declared ownership of the team— Frank claimed 100 percent ownership. Jamie said she was entitled to 50 percent under California community property law.

Six days later, the day after the Phillies eliminated us and moved on to the World Series, Frank fired Jamie as CEO of the Dodgers, telling her to clean out her office and report to Human Resources. I don't remember ever hearing of a husband firing his wife. Publicly, no less.

On October 27, Jamie formally filed for divorce and demanded her job back as Dodgers CEO.

All those chaotic and headline-grabbing events were playing out as I was coming up to the fifth-year option I had negotiated when I originally signed. The deadline was October 31. We'd been negotiating a possible extension during the NLCS and amid all the ugly legal maneuvering. Without the fifth-year mutual option, the Dodgers would have had all the leverage. Frank could have taken the club option for the fifth year and left me in a weak negotiating position. But since I had an option, too, and other clubs were beginning to send out feelers, I had a touch of leverage. The Dodgers had gone to the postseason three of my first four years and were coming off back-to-back NLCS appearances for the first time since 1977– 78. People had taken notice.

A position with another team was there for the taking if I wanted to leave, but there was something about the challenges of leadership and the competition in L.A. that fueled me. Although a different organization might have had less drama, and perhaps even as good a chance to be successful—if not better—I decided that if Frank would negotiate with me fairly, I would stay. Like a free agent deal for a player, I had done my research and felt I was prepared. I knew where my break point would be in deciding to stay or leave. The next move would be up to Frank and I was at peace with whatever his decision would be. He was still the best negotiator I had ever been up against, but I felt confident that between the respect we shared and the research I had done and explained to him, he would be fair and realistic. If not, there were options.

It was also important to me to be able to keep the staff together. They had earned the opportunity to stay and prosper. If I left, they would fall into the purgatory that comes with a new leader in the GM chair. I felt I owed them stability as well.

Besides taking the 71-91 team from 2005 and turning it into three postseason clubs, the organization had been very successful at the gate and we were making deadline deals without paying the salaries of players we were acquiring.

In the end, we settled on a three-year extension with a pair of one-year options—both club options. We signed the deal in the lobby of the Philadelphia Ritz-Carlton, which is a block from City Hall and about a mile or so west of where the Declaration of Independence was signed.

The day of the signing was an off day between Games 4 and 5 of the NLCS. I went to the meeting alone. Frank was there with Dennis Mannion, the club president; Sam Fernandez, the Dodgers' legal counsel; Peter Wilhelm, CFO; and Jeff Ingram, a longtime aide to Frank in real estate and Dodgers ventures. The dynamics of that day are still very interesting to me. I was running a team trying to get to the World Series and managing 180 or so people in the front office while dealing with all the outside noise and uncertainty of the McCourts' marriage and my own future. We were sitting at a table in the lobby with five men on one side of the table and me on the other side. Then, one night later, the Phillies beat us. The 2009 season was over and Frank's fight to keep the team took center stage, and I had the additional task of walking a fine line of support to the people who hired me and maintaining credibility in the public eye.

A prominent sports columnist once told me point-blank that as long as I continued to support McCourt, he would do everything he could to make me look bad and damage my credibility and career. And he did at least try.

All you can do in a situation like that is live with it. In a job like the one I had, you live with a lot of things. You try to take the high road and be as classy as possible. Don Mattingly and I talked about that all the time after he became manager of the Dodgers. Focus on what you can control in a positive way.

Former Navy SEAL Mark Owen laid it out clearly when he said that the best focus on what they can control and stay within their three-foot world.

You keep those things riveted in your sight line—on your goal path. If we had gotten distracted by everything we dealt with during the McCourt era, we wouldn't have had time to do anything but feel sorry for ourselves and bitch and moan.

Frank had his faults. We all do. But I truly relished my time with him, particularly our conversations. Frank is a sharp man—very, very intelligent. He would challenge my thought process constantly and relentlessly. In the beginning, he was more than a little intimidating. But I came to realize he was doing it for the good of the organization, and for my own personal growth. I would have an idea and tell his assistant, Hannah Shearer, I needed fifteen minutes. By the time Frank stopped grilling me, we'd be in there for an hour and a half or two hours. In the end, he nearly always agreed with me, and I remember asking him once, "What did I say to give you the confidence to agree with me?"

"I agreed with you before you walked in the door," he said. "I just wanted to make sure you had thought it through and let you see how you had done it."

That was an amazing ability. I miss those sessions.

IN MY OPINION, the next two and a half years were the most tumultuous the Dodgers or, for that matter, any American major market sports franchise ever endured. Frank and Jamie's divorce trial led to a seemingly endless marathon of demoralizing news reports about their lifestyle, which the media used to question whether the team had the best chance to succeed. But those reports were only part of the landscape. Commissioner Selig went to war against Frank— MLB claimed publicly that $189 million had been "looted" from the franchise. It got mean and personal. MLB tried to take over the team and vetoed a television deal with Fox that Frank hoped would put the team on very solid financial footing.

As with any business leader, Frank wanted to make money, but he also wanted to be seen and respected as a "success." He had a genuine passion for baseball and understood how privileged he was to own the Dodgers. Frank wanted to be seen as a good steward of the franchise. But each passing news report undermined any hope the fans and media would see him that way. All along the way, Frank fought every assertion.

On June 26, 2011, McCourt struck back. He had threatened to drag the commissioner and Major League Baseball into court, but held off. Then, over dinner with a trusted associate, he struck business genius. He decided to file for bankruptcy, a strategy that changed the course of events dramatically. The decision did not come easily. But it was his only choice.

"He fought the idea," a longtime business associate offered. "It wasn't something he had ever wanted to consider, but after having that dinner, there were a couple of discussions and then it was full on. In less than two weeks he had filed. It easily turned out to be the best choice."

Frank hired the international law firm Dewey & LeBoeuf to lead the charge—an ironic move considering Dewey & LeBoeuf filed for bankruptcy itself and went out of business just two years after McCourt sold the team.

The bankruptcy move, which took less than a week to put into action once it began, gave Frank leverage and took potential control of the franchise out of the hands of Major League Baseball. No one I knew used leverage better than Frank McCourt. The United States Bankruptcy Court was now in control of the Dodgers, and, as is the case with most bankruptcies, the court has two primary goals: try to get creditors as close to one hundred cents on the dollar owed, and settle the case. Frank could argue strongly that the scuttled Fox deal offered creditors the best possible remedy.

THE DODGERS MISSED the playoffs in 2010 and 2011, which is hardly surprising considering what we were dealing with off the field and how we were hampered financially. Our payroll dropped. We had signed players to deals based on one payroll, only to see it slashed by $20–30 million. Now we were forced to fill out the rest of the club with low-salaried players. That helped balance the budget sheet while leaving an unbalanced roster—in the second-largest market in the country, no less.

The members of the organization kept the ship afloat and moving forward while a hurricane of distractions swirled around us. We were 162-161 those two seasons—not what we wanted. We had a better record combined in those two seasons than any team in our division except the San Francisco Giants—and a record better than nine of the sixteen teams in the National League at the time. And no other organization was going through what we were going through with ownership.

Cost-efficient, homegrown talent dwindled at a time when the franchise lacked the financial resources to fill holes from the outside. We had basically abandoned international scouting and signing players in Latin America for financial reasons and it was taking its toll.

With ownership set to change on May 1, 2012, the team began that season with a payroll of approximately $90 million. By comparison, between 2013 and 2017, the Dodgers total payroll exceeded more than $1.3 billion during those five seasons. The organization also paid more than $113 million in CBA-required competitive-balance tax, in addition to the payroll costs. (Clubs that exceed a predetermined payroll threshold are subject to a Competitive Balance Tax, which is commonly referred to as a "luxury tax." Those who carry payrolls above that threshold are taxed on each dollar above the threshold, with the tax rate increasing based on the number of consecutive years a club has exceeded the threshold.)

Each day brought more bad news, courtesy of the press, which had a field day with all low-hanging fruit. We just needed to hang on and do whatever we could to have a positive effect on the few things we could control. That was the greatest lesson learned in those days—spend your energy on what you could affect in a positive manner; tune out the noise, and ignore what you had no chance to change.

As emotionally draining as those two and a half years were for all of us, no one survived them better than Frank. Sure, he was a villain to the fans and Selig. But in the end, he came out the financial winner. He paid Jamie off with a $131 million tax-free divorce settlement plus property. Then he won an important, unprecedented, and staggering concession from the commissioner. For whatever powerful reasons, Selig agreed to let Frank hold an auction among MLB-approved bidders and sell the team to the group of his choosing. He broke the oligarchy that is Major League Baseball.

The group Frank eventually chose was headed by Mark Walter, with Los Angeles basketball legend Earvin "Magic" Johnson and four others—investors Todd Boehly and Bobby Patton, Hollywood executive Peter Guber, and longtime sports executive Stan Kasten. Doing business as Guggenheim Baseball Management, the new owners paid $2.15 billion for the franchise, parking, and real estate around Dodger Stadium. The sale price was a record for a U.S. sports franchise, far surpassing the previous high of $1.1 billion, which New York real estate mogul Stephen Ross had paid for the Miami Dolphins in 2009.

Pundits had predicted that the most Frank could get for the franchise was $1.5 billion. And few thought he would come close to that. Not only did Frank blow the doors off those numbers, but, according to media reports, he also got Guggenheim to agree to let him keep 130 acres around Dodger Stadium *and* to invest $400 million with McCourt Partners—a joint-venture real estate development corporation he formed with his sons and Guggenheim. For good measure, Guggenheim paid him $5.5 million the first year to manage the joint venture.

Think about that. And then remember, his attorney said the team was purchased with "not a penny" of the McCourts' own money. Love him or leave him, the bottom-line results were staggeringly impressive.

McVillain? McBankrupt? McBrilliant.

Ten

TIME TO MOVE ON

· · · · · · · · · · · · ·

Behind the scenes, there are many subplots and story lines that aren't limited to the ownership level. Let's face it, not everyone gets along, and when staff, players, and management spend months side by side, there is bound to be some friction and some personalities that simply don't mesh.

Through decades of management, I worked with a few players who didn't fit for me—nor me for them.

Both Odalis Perez and Brad Penny had talent, and both had reached a place in the baseball timeline where a free agent contract came their way.

I couldn't always tell if the riches had overtaken the drive, passion, desire, and work ethic that brought a player to his highest financial earning years—only to have the checks seemingly become the dominant motivator.

Players' rights are protected by contracts and also by the collective bargaining agreement. A team has almost no recourse if a player decides to forgo his conditioning or decides to alter his competitiveness or his willingness to fully participate. While I'm fairly certain most GMs have wrestled with those issues, incidents such as these are difficult to prove. After signing long-term contracts, some players lower the bar on performance in comparison to salary. In turn, the system escalates the salary structure. When signed players under-perform, it raises the market value of the players who do perform. The salary scale keeps moving upward because the ceiling on salary becomes the salary floor when performance dips. So trust in the player is paramount—which is sometimes easier said than done.

If Odalis cared about his team, he had a bizarre way of showing it. In my opinion, his conditioning suffered and so did his perfor-mance during his free agent contract. I had a very difficult time watching and accepting it and was saddled with an $8.75 million contract that I had inherited.

That type of behavior has become more prevalent since I started three decades ago. Major League Baseball is a tough game. With-out a doubt, it's hard to play every day at the highest level, and some players lose their concentration and drive for a game, some for a week. Sometimes, a player will lose it for a season. In my opinion, Odalis lost it to the point that his career never rebounded. It was difficult to find him working out and preparing for his next start. Instead, Odalis seemed to care about the next party and the checks that rolled in on the first and fifteenth of the month.

During my first year with the Dodgers, we went to Arizona to play a two-game series against the Diamondbacks the first week of May. We had just come from San Diego, where we had a chance to sweep the Padres in a weekend series and move over .500 for the first time in the young season. Derek Lowe started the Sunday game and had an early 5–0 lead, but left after just six innings. The bullpen, which had worked nine innings in three previous days, im-ploded. San Diego scored five runs in the bottom of the ninth and one in the tenth to beat us 6–5.

The next day, Frank decided he would fly to Arizona for the

D-backs series. He wanted to talk about Sunday's collapse and how the team would respond. We sat in the small private booth on the press level and watched the Dodgers lose again, 3–2, to fall into fourth place, two games under .500.

An hour after the game, Frank went back to the team hotel on his own. As he walked into the lobby of the Westin Kierland in North Scottsdale, he saw Odalis sprawled out on a couch, drinking with his buddies. As someone later described the scene, Frank "walked by Odalis and saw him sprawled out on a couch, a drink in his hand, and a bunch of hangers-on surrounding him."

"Hey, Frank, hey, how ya doing?" Odalis said when he saw the owner.

McCourt asked Perez what he was doing.

"Hey, I'm just relaxing."

"You know you're pitching tomorrow night, right?" Frank asked.

"Yeah, yeah. Don't worry about it. I'll be there. Everything will be okay."

Frank didn't say another word. He walked up to his suite, called me, and said, "Your starting pitcher is on a couch in the lobby of the hotel and looks to be having a pretty good time."

I told Frank I'd take care of it and went back to the hotel, got things squared away with Odalis and sent him upstairs. One of my beliefs always has been I can only control myself. I can't control what others do with their opportunities or challenges. And I surely couldn't control Odalis Perez and his priorities, as skewed as they seemed to me and others.

The next night, Frank and one of his top associates, Howard Sunkin, caught the first inning of the game from box seats beside the visitors' dugout. The Dodgers jumped to a 2–0 lead in the first inning off Orlando Hernandez and Perez retired the side in the bottom of the first. From my booth up on the press level, I saw

Frank and Howard leave their seats to do a lap around the ballpark, something they liked to do to see how other teams ran their operations.

While they were walking the concourse, the Dodgers resumed their pounding of Hernandez. With one out, Oscar Robles tripled. Dioner Navarro singled home Robles, and Odalis came to the plate. He swung at the first pitch and got the only base hit he would get all year for the Dodgers: a single to center that he probably wished he'd never gotten because it meant he was on first base when Kenny Lofton tripled to the deepest part of center field. Odalis chugged around the bases and probably cursed when he saw third-base coach Rich Donnelly waving him home.

Odalis was in just ahead of the relay throw. He laid in the dirt next to the plate for several seconds, his chest heaving.

Just about the time Odalis was walking very slowly back to the dugout, Frank and Howard came into my booth. "What happened?" Frank asked.

"Odalis just scored from first on a triple, and it wasn't pretty."

Odalis went back to the mound in the bottom of the second with a 5–0 lead. He gave up a harmless single in the second, walked one in the third, and stranded a leadoff double in the fourth. But by the fifth inning, with the Dodgers now leading 6–0, he was cooked.

Shawn Green led off the bottom of the fifth with a home run. Andy Green followed with a bunt single. Chris Snyder walked. After a sacrifice bunt, Craig Counsell singled home the second run. Eric Byrnes singled to load the bases and Chad Tracy launched a grand slam. With the score now tied at six, Grady Little left Odalis in for one more batter. He walked Luis Gonzalez, and, in the booth with me, Frank was incensed.

I was incensed, too. But I knew I couldn't show it because you never know who is watching or when the cameras are on you. Frank was sitting beside me. He was screaming and yelling—not at me, but to me. He was gesturing like a conductor for the Boston Pops until I finally grabbed his arm.

"Frank, nobody's more pissed off than I am, but right now you're on television," I said.

Sure enough, everybody saw it.

We lost the game 10–8 and that night Frank told me to trade Odalis. "I don't care if you've got to eat the entire contract. Get him out of here."

Six weeks later, we traded Odalis to the Kansas City Royals for Elmer Dessens, and what did Odalis do?

He came into my office and cried.

Unloading Odalis wasn't easy. He had a 4-4 record with a whopping 6.83 ERA and had allowed 105 base runners in 59⅓ innings. Kansas City was the only team that would consider a deal and Royals GM Dayton Moore refused a straight-up trade. We had to throw in two minor-league pitchers—Blake Johnson, a second-round pick in the 2004 draft, and Julio Pimentel, a Dominican free agent— plus cash. But we still got the better of the deal. The personal elements aside, Perez was just as bad on the mound in Kansas City as he had been for us—going 2-4 with a 5.64 ERA. Ninety-nine of the 298 batters he faced for the Royals reached base.

In the newspapers, the day after we finally managed the trade, Odalis was politically correct in his comments to the newspapers. "This year has been tough. But at the same time, I really appreciate what the people in the front office and the fans have done for me since I've been here. I had a great time here. I didn't want to leave, but it's a business. It's time to move on. It's time to go to a different franchise and show I still have the skill to pitch and the stuff to do it."

But when he spoke in his native Spanish to ESPNdeportes.com, his tone was decidedly different. "They treated me like garbage with the things they did to me," he said, without mentioning me or

Grady by name, but telling reporter Enrique Rojas that his standing in the Dodgers changed when our predecessors, Tracy and DePodesta, had left. "I don't know if the new guys in the organization just don't like me or what, but I can say that I really have no respect for them because they didn't have the guts to tell me how things really were. I was always lied to."

If there had been any lying, it wasn't from management's side: Odalis said he was a professional.

BRAD PENNY WAS ANOTHER PLAYER with whom I didn't see eye to eye after originally getting along with him pretty well. He came to the Dodgers at the trade deadline in 2004 and was mediocre his first year and a half in Los Angeles, going 8-10 with a 3.85 ERA. In my first two years with the Dodgers, he was terrific. He was one of the league's best pitchers, going 16-9 in 2006 and 16-4 in 2007, finishing third in the Cy Young Award voting.

Going into the 2008 season, Penny had one year left on his contract and the club held an option for the following year. With one and perhaps two years remaining on his contract, he started pushing me about a long-term extension. I wasn't eager to make an early move, but I agreed to set up a meeting during Spring Training with Penny, his agent, Greg Genske, Frank, and myself. Penny and Genske were looking for up to five years and big money, so I wanted Frank in the talks because he was the one who would have to sign off on that kind of commitment, although I didn't have any interest in pursuing it myself. It was a method to cut to the chase: Frank would veto it.

Penny and Genske said all the right things in the meeting—how Brad was a team player who only wanted to win, how he wanted to stay with the Dodgers for the rest of his career, how he would do whatever it took to bring a championship to Los Angeles. It was just a preliminary meeting and nothing serious was happening as we moved into the season. But Penny was constantly pushing the issue. His attempts to convince me he was committed seemed staged. Brad was talented, but he wasn't a hard worker and never convinced me that he was dependable.

In May, we were wrapping up a weekend series with the Houston Astros at Dodger Stadium before heading to Milwaukee to play the Brewers. Penny, who is from Blackwell, Oklahoma, wanted to go home on the Monday off day and asked Joe Torre if it would be all right. Joe wasn't thrilled about the idea, but Penny was a veteran and Joe respected that. He told Brad he could leave after the Sunday game as long as he was in Milwaukee by Monday night, because he was pitching Tuesday.

Penny left and didn't show up until Tuesday, just hours before his start. He then went out and got rocked. He gave up five runs on nine hits and lasted just six innings in a 5–4 loss to the Brewers. Torre was livid. I was so disappointed. I had listened to all the talk about what a great teammate Penny was—how much he wanted to contribute to a winning team and all this other bullshit. This was his behavior and he was trying to get an extension? It didn't bode well if we were going to commit to him for even more money and more years. What then? He'd be a complete no-show?

I waited a day to let my anger subside.

We had a day game the next afternoon and I deliberately went to the press box area at Miller Park to call Genske because I knew with all the writers around, I'd have to keep my voice down and my temper under control. I was pacing back and forth as I told Genske he could take all those things he'd told me and Frank about dedication and team first and what a great teammate Penny was and put them where the sun doesn't shine.

That was May 14. By July, Penny still didn't have a long-term deal and now he was getting upset. He asked me one day why he should pitch if he wasn't getting an extension.

I reminded him that he was under contract to pitch and was being compensated per the contract.

He countered, asking why he should pitch if he didn't have a long-term contract and what would happen if he was injured without more long-term security? Maybe his arm was tender; perhaps he was afraid of getting hurt.

This was going on with the Dodgers in the midst of the pennant race. We were headed to the National League Championship Series for the first time since 1988. But Penny kept saying he was hurt and went on the disabled list August 14 for the second time that season. He was clearly in no hurry to come back, but when he did return, in September, he didn't want to pitch out of the bullpen. That was where the team needed him and because he had missed so much time, the bullpen would have been a better and a quicker option. But there wasn't much we could do. While major-league contracts don't specify a player's role, his position, or when he takes the field, executives have to trust that a player will fulfill his end of the contract and do what he is asked to do on behalf of the team.

The team was in Pittsburgh with a dozen games left in the season and I was back in Los Angeles when I get a call from Torre about Penny. "We need to move Brad."

I asked him what was wrong now.

We had just brought in several young pitchers for the September call-ups and Torre wanted to get one up in the bullpen, but the rookie was nowhere to be found. Turns out he was in the clubhouse with Penny and the two of them were practicing with a hunting bow and arrow. Penny owned a 2,200-acre ranch in Oklahoma and loved to hunt turkey and deer with a bow and arrow. He clearly was focused on the off-season, not the pennant drive.

When the team came back off the road, I went down to the

clubhouse looking for Penny. I couldn't find him, so I told Mitch Poole, our clubhouse manager, that I needed to see Brad as soon as batting practice was over. I didn't hear anything from Mitch, so I went downstairs to the clubhouse and Penny was nowhere to be found.

"Where is he?" I asked Mitch.

"He left."

The man was on the active roster. He was on the lineup card. And he decided to go home.

I told Mitch, "When he gets here tomorrow, tell him I want to see him." That night, I left a message on Penny's voicemail. "Brad, I need to talk to you. I'll see you at the park tomorrow."

The next day, Penny came in and went on the field during batting practice, but when I got down to the clubhouse, he wasn't there.

"He left again," Mitch said.

I went upstairs to my office on the fifth level of Dodger Stadium and called Penny's agent. "I need you to tell Brad that I don't want him here anymore," I said. "If he doesn't pick up his stuff by noon tomorrow, we'll pack it up and ship it to him. But he needs to be here before noon and out by one o'clock because I don't want him here anymore."

Genske was genuinely stunned. "What happened?"

I told him and he said, "You're kidding me. He would never do that."

"Greg, that's what he's done and he's gone."

That was it for Brad Penny and the Dodgers. Brad was the only player I've ever told to pack and not return. Sent him to the house, as they say.

Brad's banishment never made the papers. But a month after we sent him packing, Al Balderas of the *Orange County Register* did a story headlined "Dodgers' Penny Absent from Sight in Playoffs." The story ran on October 15, the day the Phillies eliminated us from the National League Championship Series, and quoted Torre on the missing pitcher's status.

"He was frustrated being here and not being able to do something," Joe said. "We talked about it and thought it might be better that since (he's) not going to be a part of this thing . . . not being able to contribute and not feeling all that good about how things went this year, I just did what I felt was best for both."

We bought out Penny's option for $2 million and he was granted free agency on November 5, 2008.

The Red Sox signed him a month later and gave him his outright release in August, before he even finished one season. The Giants picked him up for the final month of the 2009 season, then didn't bring him back.

Penny made nine starts for the St. Louis Cardinals in 2010 and was gone again. And in 2011, the Detroit Tigers were the next team to give him a shot. San Francisco brought him back for twenty-eight innings in 2012. He also pitched in Asia in 2013 and appeared in eight games for the Marlins in 2014.

Every year, a different team took a chance and every year they cut the cord.

In the six seasons after we sent him home during a pennant race, he made 74 major-league starts and changed teams every year. He compiled a 27-26 record with a 5.02 ERA. In 464 innings he allowed 552 hits and walked 144 hitters, striking out 241. His WHIP was a lofty 1.49 (WHIP is an acronym for walks and hits allowed per innings pitched). Had the Dodgers signed him to the extension he wanted, it would have been one of the worst deals we made—especially considering his approach, which we had witnessed when he had incentive and was trying to convince us to extend him.

With the Tigers, he got into a shouting match with his own

catcher in a game in Detroit and had a rocky relationship at best with Jim Leyland, one of the great managers of the game.

Penny was just one of many players I came across who proved a guaranteed contract never guarantees performance, continued effort, or focus.

Sabean may have put it best when he told me the vast majority of a general manager's time is spent on crisis management. Many days there seems to be some issue that centers on someone's behavior and unfounded expectations.

When I worked for the Dodgers, I was paid for twenty-one hours a day to deal with everything and everybody. The other three hours I worked for free: when I watched our games.

For many people, a great day is when something magnificent occurs, something that is rare and beautiful and memorable. For me, a great day in baseball was when nothing happened.

No arguments, disagreements, fights.

It's hard for fans to understand everything that goes into building, and holding together, a team. Few could even imagine a professional player who behaved the way Brad Penny did in those final months of his Dodgers career.

Eleven

A WEIGHTY CONVERSATION
THAT ENDED WELL

• • • • • • • • • • • • •

In baseball, like in every business, holding together a group takes managing the personalities and the idiosyncrasies—especially when big money is involved. Days were always interesting, with random conversations that have stood the test of time with all levels of talent, including some of the best players in the game.

I had many conversations with players and managers and staff members through the three-plus decades I called the clubhouse a workplace. I always felt it important to establish a relationship and a communications path with the players, even if someone was going to be part of the club for a short period of time. The clubhouse belonged to the players and the manager, in my opinion. The players didn't see me there every day, but they knew I was around enough to be available. It helped me keep a finger on the pulse of the club's dynamics. Along the way, there were some conversations that, even years later, I shake my head and smile. One of the more interesting exchanges happened during the last few weeks of the 2007 season with David Wells.

The Dodgers had improved from a record of 71-91 in 2005 to

tying for the NL West title a year later. But now we were trying to keep the air in a leaky balloon and I thought Wells could help. Our rotation was stumbling to the finish line and we had a chance to at least get to the wild card slot.

Without Wells, the long shot became longer—much longer.

Boomer was a gamer and a winner, and while not always a favorite of every manager he played for, he still won 239 games in his career, including a perfect game in Yankee Stadium. He also earned a pair of World Series rings with the Blue Jays and Yankees. But by August 2007, the sun was setting on his near Hall of Fame career. He had just been released by the San Diego Padres. His career seemed over. But I had seen enough to know that David knew how to pitch. He could figure out how to win a game. I thought he'd win enough games to keep us in the race in the National League West. At the very least, he would get us through the rest of the season. So I called his agent, Gregg Clifton, to talk about David finishing the year with the Dodgers.

When a player is released by another team, the team that signs him is only responsible for paying a prorated share of the major-league minimum salary. In 2007, that was $380,000 for the year. And with only about six weeks left in the season, we could get Wells for about $80,000. The Padres would be on the hook for something like $600,000, which was what Wells had left on his $3 million contract that year—minus the money we were picking up.

Early in the talks, Clifton made it clear Wells didn't want to pitch if there wasn't any additional money in it for him. He could go home and collect what the Padres owed him and never have to break a sweat again. Wells would only pitch for us if we guaranteed bonus money based on the number of starts he made down the stretch.

I didn't have a problem with that. At least, I didn't think so. But it didn't take me long to realize I should have.

I'd been dealing with contracts, arbitration, free agency, waivers, disabled lists, and all the staggering fine print and legalese of base-ball for nearly thirty years. I thought I knew all the rules and nu-ances. But every general manager has a backstop to protect him. Mine was Kim Ng, a very smart, conscientious, and experienced executive. Kim handled all the contracts for me and she went to work on Boomer's. We finally came up with a deal that would pay Wells somewhere between $700,000 and $800,000 if he ran the table on starts the rest of the season. Boomer signed and happily came up the I-5 freeway to pitch for us.

What neither I nor Kim realized immediately when we signed Wells was that if a team signs a released player to additional bo-nuses beyond the preexisting contract, that team is responsible for paying the bonuses, and the money comes off the amount the orig-inal team owes the player. In other words, we'd be paying the bo-nuses, which of course makes perfect sense and which we were committed to doing. But the amount we paid in those bonuses would be deducted from the money San Diego owed Wells. Wells wouldn't be making anything extra until the entire owed contract value had been paid back—in other words, it wasn't going to earn him another dollar.

David would end up getting exactly the same as if he stayed home. We'd be giving money to the Padres, our division rivals, and doing nothing for Wells, who'd essentially be working for free.

I can say that was the only mistake I ever knew Kim to make in the five and a half years we worked together. And it was as much my mistake as it was hers. David had made three starts for us, going 2-0 with a 3.71 ERA, when suddenly we were made aware of our screwup. Someone in the San Diego front office gave Kim a heads-up.

As soon as I realized what was happening, I called Clifton. He also represented Mark Mulder, who was making a rehab start with the Cardinals at the time, which meant Gregg was flying all over the place to see Mulder pitch. I guess that explains why he apparently didn't know what was happening with Wells. Every time I called, I got Gregg's voicemail. I kept leaving messages but I didn't hear back from Greg.

Meanwhile, San Diego—the team that released Wells—was charging to the playoffs and they were coming in to play us. Wells was scheduled to pitch the final game of the series on Thursday night, September 13. The day before, Wells said he got a call from Kevin Towers, then general manager of the Padres. Towers is a good guy, a talented executive, and probably as good a friend as I had in the game that I didn't work alongside. Like us all, he is ultracompetitive and wasn't too keen on watching the pitcher he had recently released and owed nearly $800,000 pitching against him with a chance to win a division. Friendships often finish a distant second to competitiveness in this business.

Towers is also a good friend of Wells. Releasing David was tough on him. But he called Wells and, according to Wells, told David he was not getting any additional money for all the starts he was making. The bonus provision was going against what the Padres owed him.

So, now it was about six o'clock on Wednesday, September 12, 2007, an hour or so before the second game of our series with the Padres, and I came up from the field to do a few things in my office. As I walked past Kim's office, which was next to mine, she waved frantically and called me in. She had a look on her face that I'd never seen before, one that wasn't exactly calming.

"What's up?"

"David Wells just called," she said. "He was told he's not getting paid bonuses and he is livid."

At this point, we'd been trying to reach Clifton for several days to explain the problem and assure him we were working to make everything good so he could give Wells a heads-up. But as soon as

Kim learned that Wells had gotten the news from someone else, she tried to call the MLB offices to make sure the powers that be were in the loop. Unfortunately for us, Rosh Hashanah, the high holy day marking the Jewish new year, had begun at sundown that day and would run through nightfall on Friday, September 14. The MLB offices were closed.

"All right," I said, "I'll go down to the clubhouse and deal with David."

The game was about to start. I walked down and saw our clubhouse manager, Mitch Poole, who had a look on his face that was not much different from the one I had just seen on Kim's face.

Before I could ask what was wrong, he said, "David Wells just packed up all his stuff."

"Okay, I'm going into Grady's office," I said. "Send him in there."

I was sitting on the couch in Grady Little's office and here comes David Wells, who is a big man—six foot four and about 260 pounds. And he looks a lot bigger when he's mad and in his underwear.

"David, I need to talk to you," I said as he came through the door.

"No shit," he said. "What the fuck is going on? I thought that I had this deal."

"David—"

And before I got another word out, he said, "You guys are ripping me off."

I said, "David, we're not ripping you off."

"I'm fuckin' leaving," he continued, not really hearing a whole lot of the conversation. "I'm getting fucked over and I'm done."

Hoping he needed a breath, I quickly wedged in a few words. "We didn't do anything devious. Why would I want to pay San Diego to have you start for me? Think about the dynamics of this. I want San Diego to pay everything.

"Helping San Diego is the last thing I'd do."

I could have said anything short of "here's a million dollars" and he wasn't hearing it. Wells was ranting and raving and walking all over Grady's closet of an office, just fuming. And every time I tried to explain it to him, he cut me off. He wouldn't listen to anything. He was beside himself. Finally, I said something that I find hilarious today. Looking back, though, I took a pretty big risk, personally, maybe physically and professionally, in saying all I could think to say.

"Hey, fat fuck!" I offered in my best oratory style. "Sit the fuck down so I can tell you what's really going on. I'm not screwing you."

And he looked at me with eyes as round and wide as a pair of slow-pitch softballs. "Fat fuck!?"

"Yeah, I say it lovingly," I said, forcing a weak chuckle.

"Fat fuck!?"

"Well, David—"

"You called me a fat fuck?" And he said again, with his voice cracking, "Fat fuck!?"

"Just sit down," I said, and, to my great relief, he did. "Let me explain.

"Where did you hear this?" I asked him.

Wells said Towers had called him earlier in the day.

"Oh, did he?" I said, my own voice going up an octave or two. "Well, he's got no business calling you because you don't play for him anymore." I explained to Wells that I had been trying to reach his agent for a few days to let him know we'd realized our mistake and were trying to find a way to fix it.

"Well, I tell you this," he said, his voice finally calm, but resolute. "I'm not pitching tomorrow if I'm not making more money to pitch."

"Fair enough," I said, and meant it. "But I don't want you leaving Los Angeles until you give me time to figure this out."

Wells had a home in San Diego but was staying at a downtown Los Angeles hotel.

"Okay, I'll stay overnight, but I'm out of here at three o'clock if I don't hear from you."

By now, the game was going on. I called Howard Sunkin, one of Frank's top aides, and asked him to see if he could bring Frank down to Grady's office. After I filled them in, Frank said, "You're kidding me. Kevin Towers called our pitcher?"

"That's what David told me," I said.

McCourt wanted to know what we were going to do.

"The guy's not going to pitch tomorrow and we don't have anybody else to pitch," I said.

"Well, what are we going to do?" McCourt asked again.

What I did was go straight to Mitch Poole. "Put some clothes in David Wells's locker," I told him. "Put some stuff in there so nobody knows he's not here and let's see what we can do."

I went upstairs to my office and called Bob DuPuy, who at the time was Bud Selig's right-hand man, and filled DuPuy in on everything, including the call from Towers to Wells that David said took place.

"That's not right," DuPuy said. He told us he was going to work on this and that we should tell David he was going to be compensated for the bonuses he would earn starting games for us.

I never knew what happened between the commissioner's office and San Diego. I do know I called Wells and told him he was getting paid and that he should come pitch. And he did.

We paid Wells the bonuses we agreed to in the contract, and we paid San Diego the offset portion of the contract. Wells pitched the game he nearly walked away from and beat Greg Maddux 6–3. He went six innings, struck out three, and walked one. In the end, Boomer started the final seven games of an excellent career for the Dodgers, going 4-1—and earning a few extra dollars, thanks to the commissioner's office.

. . .

TWO YEARS AFTER WELLS THREW his last pitch in the major leagues, we ran into each other in Philadelphia, where he was a broadcaster for TBS and the Dodgers were in the NLCS for a second consecutive year.

"How ya doing?" Wells said, giving me a big hug. "You remember—"

Before he could say another word, I cut him off, just as he had cut me off in Grady Little's office in tougher times. "We don't have to talk about that right now," I said. "Or ever again for that matter."

We both laughed.

I told that story to Jason Scheff, the former bassist and vocalist for the band Chicago, who is from San Diego and is a good friend of Wells. I've been a big fan of Chicago for years and have been lucky enough to become friends with all the guys in the group. On my way to one of their concerts a while after I told Jason the story, I got a phone call from Lee Loughnane, one of the founding band members.

"We just wanted you to know," Lee said, "that David Wells is going to be backstage tonight."

I told Lee it would be all right. And it was—so long as we talked music and baseball and left physical conditioning on the back burner.

Twelve

FISHING FOR WHALES

· · · · · · · · · · · · · ·

Joe Torre was a whale.

And a whale was exactly what the Dodgers needed.

The 2007 season had just finished unraveling in an ugly mess of clubhouse bickering, name-calling, finger-pointing, and near fistfights in the clubhouse. The promising playoff team from my first season as general manager in 2006 had morphed into a cast of aging veterans and entitled young players who were on totally different pages.

As late as July 21, the Dodgers had the best record in the National League. With just fourteen games left in the season, the Dodgers were only a game and a half out of the wild card. Then the bottom fell out. We lost eleven of fourteen games, including all seven against the Rockies, the eventual wild card winners, who went on to the World Series. Los Angeles finished fourth in the five-team National League West at 82-80—eight games behind the division champion Arizona Diamondbacks.

Grady, who managed twenty-two professional seasons and had a lifetime winning record at all six levels from rookie ball through A, High-A, Double-A, Triple-A to the majors, blamed himself for the shipwreck of 2007.

"It's my fault, Ned," Little muttered in his native Texas twang as tears snaked down his cheeks behind his closed office door minutes after the last out of the season. "You gave me a good team and I screwed it up. I'm sorry. I screwed it all up."

Grady, indeed, had "lost" the clubhouse the final month of the season—lost the confidence of his team, but Connie Mack, John McGraw, and the Holy Ghost combined couldn't have held that Humpty Dumpty together. An unholy mix of cocky, young, up-and-coming players and disgruntled veterans had split into rival gangs and gone to war wearing the same colors. The older players felt the younger players didn't play the game right; they didn't give the veterans the respect they were due. They were talented, but hadn't paid their dues yet. The younger players thought they were the stars, the future. The veterans may have put in their time, but their talents were fading.

"Bad chemistry" is a simplification, of course, but that's pretty much what happened in that clubhouse and nothing Grady could have done would have stopped it.

The Dodgers started the 2007 season with seven players who had two years of big-league experience or less. By the time rosters expanded in September, we had seventeen, including five starters. At the other end of the spectrum—the other side of a virtual boxing ring—were veterans Luis Gonzalez, Nomar Garciaparra, Jeff Kent, and Derek Lowe, who combined had fifty-seven years in the majors at that time.

Gonzo had been an icon with the Diamondbacks and probably didn't feel good at being cast aside by Arizona after the 2006 season. It must have been tough on him to accept that he was inching toward being just another outfielder in Los Angeles and that his skills were diminishing at age forty. It happens all the time; it is part of any athlete's life.

Lowe allegedly had other issues. He turned thirty-four that

June and was struggling through his second losing season in three years with the Dodgers after a 52-27 record his final three years in Boston. He had a sterling 21-7 record for the Red Sox in 2002 and, two years later, was the toast of Beantown when he became the first pitcher in history to win the final game of three consecutive post-season series as Boston captured its first World Series champion-ship in eighty-six years.

In spite of that impressive run, the Red Sox refused to re-sign Lowe and he came to the Dodgers.

Lowe's first wife, Trinka, alleged in a sworn deposition during their 2006 divorce proceedings that Derek's agent, Scott Boras, once suggested an "intervention" to help the pitcher cope with a drinking problem. Trinka also claimed in the deposition that Boston's bullpen catcher called her at home in Florida late in the 2004 season to tell her Derek was "falling apart" and that Boras later told her the reason the Red Sox failed to re-sign her husband was that club officials thought he had off-the-field issues. Lowe acknowledged that the Red Sox thought he had a drinking issue but he disagreed.

Late in the year, in the visiting clubhouse in New York before a game, Lowe started loudly voicing his opinion about some of the younger players when one of them jumped up and called out Lowe, challenging him to a fight. The hard feelings had been boiling for a while, including over an incident that had occurred at the end of the season between the two players.

"Shut up or I'll come over there and rip your head off," the younger player said.

It was not good.

GONZO AND LOWE, for all their grumbling, were mere foot soldiers in the fight against the Young Turks. The commanding general was

Kent, who—as far as I know—never backed down from a confrontation in his life. Witness the dugout battle with Barry Bonds in 2002.

Kent left the Giants after the 2002 World Series season and spent two years with the Houston Astros before coming to Los Angeles. He was already with the Dodgers when I joined the team and, as I mentioned earlier, was instrumental in me getting the interview with owner Frank McCourt that led to my getting hired.

During the final two weeks of the 2007 season, as the Dodgers were spiraling to fourth place, Kent erupted again—this time verbally. After a 9–4 loss to the Rockies at Coors Field on September 20, Kent vented to reporters, "directing vitriol," as one wrote, "at all things Dodgers this year." He hinted that he was upset about Grady's lineup choices and ranted that the younger players didn't understand how to be professional, didn't concern themselves with moving runners up, and didn't respect the veterans.

"I'm angry and disappointed, and perplexed," he said. "Bitter. I don't know what it is, especially when you have a lot [of young players]. It's hard to influence a big group. We have some good young players on the team, don't get me wrong. Please don't misinterpret my impressions. [But] it's hard to translate experience. I don't know why they don't get it."

Asked what the younger players failed to get, Kent said: "A lot of things. Professionalism. How to manufacture a run. How to keep your emotions in it. There's just a lot of things that go on with playing 162 games."

The tirade, of course, was national news and amounted to a public pronouncement that the season was over. We still had nine games to play, but Grady knew the team was lost, and I knew I had to find someone to fix things—someone with great stature and experience.

· · ·

THE FINAL WEEKEND of the season, we were officially eliminated from wild card contention and playing the Giants. That's when Grady broke down in his office. He said he knew he had to quit. I asked him if he was driving back to his home in North Carolina. He said yes.

"Well, take some time and think about it on the drive," I told him. "Don't make any decisions right now. We'll talk in a few days."

I wanted to keep all my options open. Grady was a good manager and a good man. More than a decade later, we both are happy to see each other or exchange messages. He received a bum rap in Boston in 2003 when he was fired despite leading the Red Sox to their second consecutive 93+ win season. The fans called for his dismissal after he left Pedro Martinez in to pitch the eighth inning of Game 7 of the American League Championship Series against the Yankees, who rallied to tie and win the game. Pedro tried to defend his manager, repeatedly telling reporters it was his choice to stay in the game and praising Little's leadership. But nothing could stop the public perception that Grady Little single-handedly kept the Red Sox out of the World Series. Jeff Merron, a writer for *ESPN Page 2*, declared Little's decision to leave Pedro in the game "the worst sports move of 2003." Almost everyone in New England agreed and Grady was gone in days.

Now, four years later—still without a losing season in the major leagues and a career .539 winning percentage in twenty-two seasons managing professional baseball—Grady was being skewered again. This time he was blaming himself. I didn't know if he had it in him to come back—or, if he did, whether he could bring the clubhouse together again. I needed to go fishing.

TWO DAYS AFTER I WATCHED Andy LaRoche fly out to left field off Brian Wilson of the Giants in Dodger Stadium for the final out of the 2007 season, I was sitting in Joe Girardi's living room in Florida. I'd known Girardi since our days with the Cubs in the late 1980s and early '90s. An engineering graduate from Northwestern University and a catcher by trade, Girardi was one of the smartest ballplayers I ever came across. We got along very well during the years our careers merged with the Cubs. It was unusual in those days for players and executives to spend any time together, but the Collettis and the Girardis did. Fifteen years later, Joe was my first choice to replace Grady Little as manager of the Dodgers.

Girardi had just one year of major-league managing experience—in 2006 with the Florida Marlins. He had been eager to get his first job, of course, but wasn't told during the hiring process that Marlins owner Jeffrey Loria planned to gut the payroll in yet another of his now-notorious "fire sales." Loria slashed the team payroll to a mere $14.98 million—less than the $15.5 million thirty-three-year-old Chan Ho Park was making pitching for the San Diego Padres that year. In all, a dozen players in the major leagues were earning more in 2006 than Loria was paying his entire twenty-five-man Opening Day roster.

In spite of the financial handcuffs, Girardi kept his team in contention until late September, when the reality of playing twenty-two rookies finally took its toll. The Marlins finished 78-84, fourth in the tough National League East behind the Mets, Phillies, and Braves.

Two days after that remarkable season, Girardi was fired. Hardly anyone was surprised. Girardi and Loria had been feuding, practically in plain sight, for months. The ugliest moment came during a game on August 6 when Loria, sitting next to the Marlins dugout, relentlessly berated home plate umpire Larry Vanover about his calls. Girardi listened, embarrassed, biting his own lip as long as he could, then walked over to Loria and told the owner in no uncertain terms to zip it. All Loria was doing was hurting his own team by alienating the umpires and undermining Girardi's authority in public.

Loria threatened to fire Girardi after the game, but held off until the season ended. A month later, an unemployed Girardi was named National League Manager of the Year—the first in history to win the award leading a team with a losing record. Girardi beat Willie Randolph, who had taken the Mets to a division title.

Girardi had opportunities to manage in 2007 but turned them down and went instead to the broadcast booth with the Yankees. He denied repeatedly that he was positioning himself to replace his old boss Joe Torre, who was in the final year of his contract. Girardi, at age forty, had been Torre's bench coach before taking the Florida job and never made any attempt to hide his ambition to either succeed Torre in New York or return to his native Illinois and manage the team that drafted him out of college, the Chicago Cubs.

In turning down offers from the Washington Nationals and Baltimore Orioles, Girardi politely said he was doing so for his family—that the fit just wasn't right for them. People believed he was waiting for the bigger opportunity.

I thought I could convince him the bigger opportunity he wanted was waiting in Los Angeles. At his home that day in Florida, we spent six hours talking about the possibilities and then met twice again the following week in Los Angeles. Girardi was on the West Coast to do studio work for Fox during the American League playoffs. One of the L.A. meetings was at the airport Marriott, where I brought along two of my most trusted assistants, Lovelace and former Detroit Tigers general manager Bill Lajoie, to get their impressions of Girardi. The other meeting was in Frank and Jamie McCourt's home in Holmby Hills.

Both sessions went so well that we made Girardi an offer to manage the Dodgers.

Then things got really wild.

. . .

THE JOE TORRE ERA with the Yankees ended on October 18, 2007, at Legends Field in Tampa, Florida, when the future Hall of Fame manager refused to accept a pay cut to return for his thirteenth season in New York. Torre had earned $7.5 million in 2006. The Yankees wanted to cut his base pay to $5 million and offer $3 million in incentives—$1 million if the team made it to the American League Division Series, $1 million if the Yankees played in the League Championship Series, and $1 million for advancing to the World Series.

Torre, who led the Yankees to the playoffs each of the twelve seasons he managed, including nine consecutive American League East titles, six AL pennants, and four World Series championships, felt slighted by the offer. Sure, $5 million was a lot of money. And, unless something dramatic happened, Torre was almost certain to make the playoffs with a strong chance to go to the World Series and cash in $8 million. However, the notion that his bosses thought he needed incentive clauses was insulting to him. Even more important than the money, though, was a measure of trust and security. The 2007 season had been a personal nightmare, with constant questions from the media about his future, endless leaks, and false reports that he was about to be fired. He couldn't come back and be a lame duck all over again. Torre wanted two years and was willing to write in a buyout for the second year if the Yankees wanted. They didn't. Their only offer was one year with a 33 percent cut in base pay and incentive clauses that implied Torre had lost his edge and needed to be financially motivated to win. Torre couldn't do it. The meeting reportedly lasted ten minutes, and less than two hours after he landed in Tampa on a private jet, Torre was sitting in the same plane headed back to New York without a job.

. . .

AS SOON AS I HEARD the Yankees had let Torre walk, I knew I needed to get an answer from Girardi.

"Look, Joe," I said to Girardi. "Your name is coming up as going to the Yankees—that you are one of their candidates. If you get the opportunity to have either position, either job—the Yankees or the Dodgers—where is your heart going to take you?"

Joe was straight with me and said in a strong voice: "I'd probably have to go with the Yankees."

"Fair enough," I said.

Girardi paused a second or two, then asked if I understood and if I would be upset with him.

"Yeah," I said. "It's okay. I understand, Joe. I needed you to be honest and, besides, there's another guy out there now that I'm interested in talking to."

I DIDN'T WANT TO APPROACH Torre directly. I didn't know if he wanted to manage again and I certainly didn't want to put him in the awkward position of having to say no to a direct offer. Plus, Grady was still technically our manager. Weeks had gone by without Grady calling and it was clear he couldn't continue. Instead of contacting Torre directly, I made a phone call to Robert Bartholomy, a longtime friend of Torre.

"Black Bart," as Bartholomy was known, was a former Northwest Airlines pilot who seemed to know everybody, including a lot of Major League Baseball players. He was single, was fun to be around, and knew the places in town to have a good time. When players visit a city, they are drawn to the people who know the places to frequent. As a pilot, Bart was constantly meeting the leaders of business, sports, and entertainment who flew on his flights. I thought he was the perfect person to get a read on Torre's state of mind. He and Joe talked often, and since they were such good friends, Torre wouldn't think it strange for Bart to ask him if he had an interest in managing again.

"Just ask him," I told Bartholomy. "Take your time. Do it when you feel comfortable, but get back to me and let me know."

Three days went by and I hadn't heard anything so I called Bartholomy again. "You think Joe still wants to manage?" I asked.

"Yeah, I think he does," Bartholomy said.

"Are you sure?"

"Well, not really, but I think so."

I asked Black Bart when he was going to talk with Torre again.

"We talk all the time," he said.

"Why don't you call him soon and see if he has an interest in doing it again for sure?"

A half hour later, Bartholomy called and said: "Yeah, he'd love to manage again."

"Okay," I said. "Call him one more time and see if the Dodgers would interest him."

I could hear the excitement in Bartholomy's voice. "Really?"

"Yeah, really," I said. "But listen, now, you can't take this anywhere, Bart. You're in the middle of it, but you can't take it anywhere except back to Joe. And if Joe has an interest, have him give me a shout."

Thirty minutes later, my cellphone rang. It was Torre. The conversation was short and sweet.

He was definitely interested.

I told Torre we should meet somewhere other than New York or L.A., maybe somewhere halfway for both of us. He suggested Las Vegas, which was an easy flight for me since I was in Scottsdale,

Arizona. He said he was going to be there with his wife, Ali, the next weekend for a lavish $75,000-a-couple, three-day charity gala hosted by Michael Milken.

"I'm staying at the Wynn," he said. "There's a bank of elevators in the back. I'll meet you there and we can go up to my room and talk."

On Saturday morning, October 27, 2007, I took a Southwest flight from Phoenix to Vegas and was walking past the blackjack tables at the Wynn shortly after 9:30 a.m. I phoned Torre when I landed and he was waiting by the elevators. We went up to his suite and spent the next six hours talking.

Part of the conversation centered on how long Joe wanted to manage. He said three years.

I asked how he felt about having his successor on his coaching staff to help with continuity when he was done managing. He had no problem with that.

When it came to the coaching staff, he asked for two men— Larry Bowa and Don Mattingly. I had known Bowa since 1982, and had heard many good things about Don from coaches who knew him, particularly Billy Connors and Dave Righetti.

"As you consider having the next manager on my staff," he said, "I'd like you to get to know and take a good look at Donnie. I think the more you get to know him, the more you will see him as a candidate."

I told him I would give Don consideration when the time came.

During the winter of 2009–10, both Cleveland and Washington came calling on Don—the time to either sign him as a future manager or start over as Joe was heading into his third and final contracted season.

I decided to give Don a contract that would make him the Dodgers manager whenever Joe left. I believed in Don. I'd watched

him for two years. Some people with his impressive playing resume might have felt entitled, but not Donnie. He was one of the
hardest-working coaches I had been around. I also believed he
would be pliable and would adapt to what we needed him to do. I
felt because of the career he had, and how he treated people, he
would be respected by the players. Coupling all those factors with
the cost of hiring him, it made sense. Don wanted the opportunity,
so I knew we could get the salary back in the "Grady Little range"—
less than $1 million a year—near the bottom of all major-league
managers.

ONLY NINE DAYS after the Yankees and Torre parted ways following
their take-it-or-leave-it offer, Joe was telling me that he'd think seriously about managing the Dodgers. I was excited about the possibility of pulling off what I considered a major "get," but I still had
one serious obstacle to overcome: Frank McCourt. I knew he would
be elated at the prospect of being associated with one of the biggest
names in all of sports—of standing in front of the television cameras and reveling in what he clearly would see as a big-time power
play, but would he be willing to pay for that power play?

Frank was a businessman first and foremost. He knew he was
owner of one of the most iconic franchises in sports and used that as
leverage to hire employees willing to work for less. Jobs in professional sports are scarce, and the number of people who want them
are plentiful. A determined owner can easily skew the salary scale,
but not when it comes to hiring quality people like Joe Torre. I
needed to know if Frank was committed before I brought Torre to
L.A. for serious negotiations.

From the gate at McCarran International Airport, I called
Frank and discussed the meeting and the next steps. Frank and

Jamie seemed to be excited about the chance to hire Torre. But the backstage pass they were about to buy was going to cost a lot of money—$13 million for three years, as it turned out. I didn't want things to go any further if the McCourts weren't willing to make that type of financial commitment.

"Frank," I said, using a quote Sabean often invoked in big-time negotiations, "you've got to be all in on this. We can't go fishing for a whale in a rowboat with a Kmart fishing pole."

Frank got it. He told me to get Torre to Los Angeles the next day and he would handle the rest. He knew it would be costly, but he also knew we needed Joe—and in some ways, Joe needed Frank and the Dodgers.

We met the next day at the McCourts' Holmby Hills house and within days we had a new manager.

JOE BROUGHT CREDIBILITY IMMEDIATELY. He was someone players didn't want to disappoint. His relationships were similar to the solid, productive bonds between parents and children. I would rather have had my mom or dad mad at me than ever disappointed in me. I believe players felt that way about Joe.

He had accomplished so much and had so many life experiences.

There wasn't anything a player was going to do that Joe hadn't seen himself ten times over.

Joe is shrewd and wise. When players were true to the cause, Joe was their best advocate. When players got off course, Joe would patiently, softly guide them back on course.

If they were careless and disrespectful repeatedly, he was done with them.

He looked out for many people—in and out of the game. The guys in uniforms wanted to be on that side of the relationship.

Joe had been around. Brooklyn-born, street raised, he was an excellent player before becoming a manager and a broadcaster. Torre became one of the prominent faces of baseball during his twelve years managing the Yankees.

Torre exuded class and experience. He hosted dozens of post-game dinners during a season for the coaching staff and front office personnel. Loyalty and team-building were important to Torre, as they are to me. Joe knew what he was doing, which certainly helped him rise to the heights he did in a sometimes cutthroat business, and in a city like New York, where you better understand how people and things work.

We had work to do after two mediocre seasons, but nothing was more pressing than getting our young players to meet expectations. Clayton Kershaw would make his major-league debut in 2008. James Loney, Andre Ethier, Matt Kemp, Russell Martin, Chad Billingsley, and Jonathon Broxton would be entering their third years. They were the core of our team and we needed them to perform up to their potential.

Our biggest off-season signing was Japanese starting pitcher Hiroki Kuroda. He would be a solid addition to a rotation led by Lowe, Billingsley, and Kershaw, when we called him up in May. We also added second baseman Orlando Hudson.

Unfortunately, that off-season I signed the biggest flop of my career with the Dodgers—former Gold Glove centerfielder Andruw Jones. Andruw had hit only .226 the year before, but had twenty-six home runs and ninety-four RBI. In his only season in L.A., he hit .158 with three homers and fourteen RBI. He was so bad we released him at the end of the season with a year and $18 million remaining on his contract. The combination of his play and the salary put a lot of strain on the club. The signing was my fault; the lack of preparation and passion and the dwindling production was on Jones.

The 2008 Dodgers needed to rally to finish 84-78, but still won the division and advanced to the NLCS—the franchise's first visit to that round since 1998.

The acquisitions of Manny Ramirez, Casey Blake, and Greg Maddux helped bring stability and talent, but it still wasn't enough to beat the Phillies, who were a far tougher team. If the series was a street fight, we would have had our collective ass kicked.

Instead we just lost a baseball series four games to one.

The next season, despite losing Ramirez for fifty games due to a PED-positive test, Joe led the team to 95-67 record.

On the Thursday night of May 7, when we learned Manny had tested positive—five weeks into a two-year, $45 million contract—the Dodgers were the best team in baseball. The team had jumped out to a 21-8 record and was 13-0 at home—a modern-day record for a home winning streak to start a season. And Manny had played a big role in that start, batting .348 with six home runs and twenty RBI in twenty-seven games. We led the NL West by five and a half games.

The first day of the fifty-game suspension, Washington rallied from a six-run deficit to beat the Dodgers 11–9, stopping our home winning streak.

Even with the stunning and disappointing loss of Ramirez, the team played on. This group was outstanding and geared up to go to the Fall Classic. Kemp and Ethier each drove in more than 100 runs, while Loney drove in 90 to make up for Manny's absence in the middle of the lineup. Ethier had the best year of his career, playing 160 games and hitting 31 home runs with 42 doubles. The young hitters were surrounded by a strong veteran presence with Brad Ausmus, Mark Loretta, Juan Castro, and Juan Pierre, who stepped into Manny's left field spot and became a fan favorite for his strong play and hustle.

On August 31, we traded pitching prospect Luis Garcia to the Washington Nationals for Ronnie Belliard, who hit .351 with five home runs the final month of the season. That team was as good as any Los Angeles had seen since the 1980s.

Yet again, in the playoffs, we stumbled in the make-or-break moments, while the Phillies stepped up. We lost the 2009 NLCS to Philadelphia in five games.

Prior to the 2010 season, I offered Joe a one-year extension. He said he wanted to think about it. Then, two weeks before the end of that 80-82 season—the only year in my nine years as the GM that we didn't finish over .500—Joe called me into the visiting manager's office in San Francisco.

"Boss," he began, "I think I've had enough. I can't give you what you need from me to do this job the right way. It's been a great run and you've done many good things for me, my family, and this team. It's time for me to go."

In more than thirty-five years in professional sports, that was one of the most genuine, selfless acts I witnessed. Joe could have negotiated another $4–5 million deal for another season and then, if it didn't go well, been paid anyway. But he wasn't that kind of guy. He was an honorable man—a true professional.

I will always respect Joe for that. And I will also always respect him for how he treated me. Never once did he play the "I'm Joe Torre" card: twelve straight postseasons, six World Series appearances, four World Series championships with the Yankees, a batting title, and an MVP Award as a player.

In an industry filled with big fish, Joe Torre was a whale and we were better for having him.

Thirteen

PLAYING WITH
HOUSE MONEY

· · · · · · · · · · · · ·

Joe Torre wasn't the only whale we landed during my days with the Dodgers. But many times, I was trying to land them with a rowboat and a cane pole. And more than once, the whale got away because the big-wallet financial backing that everyone thought should be there simply wasn't.

We were typically hampered in the free agent market. Many of the long-term contracts we had were backloaded and some contained buyouts on option years to increase the value and also lengthen the time it would take for the player to be paid. Backloading contracts was heralded as a creative move and made sense for us, especially considering we were hoping for the possibility of a financial windfall from a new cable television deal; plus the dollars we were committing now would be worth less five years from now when the money was paid.

The different method of doing business extended into our deadline dealings. For a few seasons, we were getting teams to pay for the players we were acquiring. The second time we acquired Greg Maddux, I remember Kevin Towers, then the Padres' GM, saying to me on the phone: "So, you are telling me the big, mighty Dodgers are going to require the little San Diego Padres to pay more than two million dollars for the right to trade Maddux to you? You've got to be kidding me."

The most memorable whale that got away was CC Sabathia.

It was the fourth of July weekend in 2008, and we were in San Francisco playing the Giants and chasing the Arizona Diamondbacks for first place in the National League West. We were a half game back, and with the trade deadline a little more than three weeks away, it was time to go fishing again. We'd finished eight games behind the Diamondbacks the year before and I wasn't going to let that happen again.

The day before we got to San Francisco, shortstop Rafael Furcal, who had been out since May 6, underwent back surgery. He would miss all but four games, only playing the final week of the regular season. Our infield was a mess. We were rotating Luis Maza, Angel Berroa, and an aging Nomar Garciaparra at short, and juggling youngsters Blake DeWitt, Andy LaRoche, and even All-Star catcher Russell Martin at third base. I was looking for infield help when I called Chris Antonetti, then the top assistant to Cleveland Indians general manager Mark Shapiro. Antonetti had two players that I thought would fill some big holes in our club. Casey Blake could play third and would provide the veteran leadership lacking that year. And Jamey Carroll was an all-out hustler who could play anywhere in the infield except first.

But the talks quickly became more interesting when I asked Antonetti about Sabathia, his ace starter. The Indians were looking to move salary. They loved CC, of course. Who wouldn't? But they knew they couldn't afford to keep him and I knew they wanted to start stockpiling younger, more easily affordable prospects. I had a nice supply of those.

Mark and Chris were close to a deal with Milwaukee, but we

felt we had made an offer that had gotten their attention. The Indians would get four prospects, all of whom eventually played in the major leagues—LaRoche, catcher Carlos Santana, shortstop Chin Lung-Hu or Ivan DeJesus Jr., and our minor-league pitcher of the year, James McDonald. We'd get Blake, Carroll, and Sabathia and be taking a lot of contract cash back.

I was excited when I went down to the visiting manager's office at the then newly renamed AT&T Park to let Torre in on the news. Joe was even more excited at the mere thought we might be able to pull off something like that. And I was glad to see his reaction because I needed his help. Frank and Jamie were coming in for the game that night, Saturday, July 5, and I intended to get Frank together with Joe and me to approve the trade. If Joe was enthusiastic and could help convince Frank what a potential season-changing deal it was, I'd have a better chance of getting McCourt to sign off. He was going to have to pick up more than $4 million in extra salary in addition to giving up some young talent—although I doubted whether the prospects, with the exception of Santana's bat, would be successful in a market that carried the expectations and distractions.

For Joe and me, the trade-off was well worth it, with us plugging the holes in our infield and adding a Cy Young–caliber starter to a team that was only a half game out of first place. Not only would we be adding talent, but the psychological boost it would give our players would be immense.

Torre was everything I hoped he would be—telling Frank what an amazing deal this was, how it could put the club over the top, how it filled all the needs, how impressive it would be if we could pull it off. But, surprisingly, Frank wasn't buying in and Torre was quick to pick up on it.

Within a few minutes, he excused himself. "Sorry, guys, I need to get out of here," he said. "I've got a game to manage."

With more than ninety minutes until the first pitch, Joe left the room. That left Frank and me alone in the visiting manager's office.

"We really ought to do this, Frank," I said.

He shook his head. "I'm not going to give up all those prospects and I'm not going to take on the extra money."

Knowing Frank and how much he wanted to win, I was surprised by his response. It was as if taking on the additional salary was going to cause outside issues.

He couldn't approve it, he said. He just couldn't. He suggested an alternative.

"You know, you should trade Derek Lowe," he said. "Trade Derek Lowe to Cleveland."

I said: "Frank, Cleveland's not in that position. They're trying to shed payroll—shed players for prospects. Derek Lowe is not going to get it done."

Frank said again he wasn't going to approve the Sabathia deal, and the meeting was over.

I went upstairs, watched the game, and sat there trying to figure out what I could do.

In about the third or fourth inning, I left the visiting general manager's booth and went to a little corner of the concourse up on the loge level of that beautiful ballpark I'd known since it was on the drawing boards.

Finally, I called Antonetti. "Chris, do you have any interest in Derek Lowe?" I asked, knowing the answer.

"Ned, that's not what we're trying to do," Antonetti said. "What are we going to do with Derek Lowe?"

"Well, you could probably move Derek Lowe."

"We're not going to take on the added responsibility of moving another player," Chris said.

I understood but was sick to my stomach. "All right. I think I'm out."

The conversation ended at around 10:30, Cleveland time, Saturday night—7:30 in San Francisco. By the next afternoon several media outlets were reporting that the Milwaukee Brewers had scheduled a Monday news conference to announce they'd acquired Sabathia from the Indians for pitchers Rob Bryson and Zach Jackson, first baseman Matt LaPorta, and outfielder Michael Brantley. LaPorta and Brantley became starters for the Indians, but Bryson failed to make the majors and Jackson was out of baseball within two years. We had a shot at doing a trade that would have changed the fortunes of the franchise that year and maybe for years to come. We couldn't make it happen and it was frustrating—especially considering what came next.

TEN DAYS AFTER THE SABATHIA deal fell through, I did manage to get Blake, one of the three players I'd hoped to land in the original blockbuster package. Part of the deal was we needed Cleveland to pay all of Blake's remaining salary.

Reporters and a group of disgruntled fans complained we included our top catching prospect, Carlos Santana, in the trade because we couldn't afford to take on the extra $2.2 million salary that Blake was going to cost us. To Cleveland's credit, once they knew we were even willing to discuss Santana, they dug in and weren't going to do any deal without him. The trade always was going to be Santana for Blake. We knew we would have to give up a key prospect to get a veteran player of Casey's caliber. And we felt pretty secure at catcher at the time with then-All-Star Russell Martin. Of course, that was before Martin's hitting started to wane, and before a serious leg injury, which he later recovered from. Still, as we worked on the trade, I sent one of my top talent evaluators, Assistant GM for Scouting Logan White, to San Bernardino, California, then home of our High-A minor-league partners, to watch Santana.

Logan told me he didn't doubt that Santana would be a good major-league hitter. But he questioned his defense behind the plate. Logan turned out to be correct on all accounts.

The Dodgers already had Martin, a young, All-Star catcher, and I had a proven, trusted scout telling me Santana probably wouldn't catch much in the majors. So I made the deal.

The Indians had been willing all along to send back some money to cover Blake's salary—most of it, in fact: $1.7 million. But Frank made it clear I needed to get all $2.2 million back before he'd approve a deal. So to get the extra $500,000, I added pitcher Jon Meloan, a fifth-round draft pick out of the University of Arizona. Meloan never panned out. He had appeared in five games for us in 2007 and would make it to the majors with Cleveland for two games. Then he finished his thirteen-game big-league career with six appearances for Oakland in 2009. Although a bit unconventional, our business model worked well most of the time. If a prospect had an exaggerated value and we knew who they were and it made sense to parlay it with both a major leaguer and the finances to cover his major league salary, we felt we were in a good position.

There is always going to be a balance in trades. The more accomplished the big-league player a team is acquiring and the more money he is making will determine the value of the prospect being dealt. If the acquiring team is also receiving money back along with the big-league player, the prospect's value will rise as well. The value points: big-league player talent, big-league player contract, who is paying what percentages versus prospect values, and relative salary plus controllable years.

The Santana-for-Blake trade proved key to our run to the National League Championship Series in 2008. Blake hit ten home runs the final two months of the season and was everything I hoped he would be in the clubhouse, where his calm confidence was just what our young players needed. We went to the National

League Championship Series that season and also in 2009 with Casey as our third baseman. He was a big part of that success. Besides being a productive player, he helped tremendously in changing the clubhouse culture. The Dodgers would not have reached the NLCS either year without Casey Blake.

And, yes, there is no denying Santana, more of an American League player, developed into a really good hitter in Cleveland. He was the best prospect I traded during my nine years as the GM. Of the fifty-seven trades we made, we accumulated players who had a WAR of 17.3 the season they were acquired and added a WAR value of 16.5 if we re-signed them. Of the nearly fifty prospects we dealt, only a few ever reached a WAR higher than 5.0. (WAR is an acronym for Wins Above Replacement—it is an approximation that quantifies the difference between a major-league player's value compared to that of a minor-league player, if, for example, the major-league player was injured and replaced by the minor leaguer.)

I always believe you don't back off on a player like Blake to hold on to a player who at that point is still a few years away and who you know would have a tough time defensively in the National League. You only have a few chances to go to the postseason, let alone to the NLCS. And in a city like Los Angeles, you never pass on a chance today when the future is never promised.

I CAN'T BEGIN TO COUNT the number of times I was asked if ownership handcuffed me and the Dodgers with spending constraints and a somewhat limited budget. I was always a loyal soldier, answering with carefully chosen, politically correct answers.

The questions became commonplace about the financial viability of the ownership. It put me in a tough spot many times, saying I wasn't interested in certain players even if we were from a pure baseball standpoint. The media would ask me, "So you really don't think so-and-so can help this team?" They weren't buying it.

I knew going in that I'd be facing big-market expectations without big-market financial flexibility, but the never-ending chess game became frustrating. I had to act as if we were a big-market team, but I couldn't follow through on it the way the GM of most big-market teams would.

The writers would ask me about this player or that player. I'd say: "No, we don't have interest in him." Until Frank finally announced he was selling the club in 2011, I never could say, "Hey, we don't have the money for it."

But the truth was, we had a budget and it was the owner's prerogative to set it. We heard a lot about debt service and being heavily leveraged until a cable television deal that was looming could be negotiated and be the life preserver for the franchise. In the meantime, we had to win and do it within a budget.

That reality led to constant, troubling discussions and evaluations. We had all sorts of scenarios where we could have become so much better with just a little more flexibility—like the vetoed Sabathia deal, for example, or the way we eventually landed Manny Ramirez. We didn't have to spend like the Yankees or Red Sox. We just needed to spend a little more in line with the revenue the club was generating.

Like every leader, I picked my battles. When I lost, I told myself, You know what? As long as you know the rules of the game, you can decide whether you're going to play.

Frank made the rules as clear as clear as could be and I chose to play. I told myself, Okay, I don't agree, but I get it and I'm not going to complain about it, or sing the blues about it. I'll make the best of what we have.

I have done that my whole life. I pride myself on being loyal. I pride myself on competing as hard as anyone, but always within the rules. I knew Frank's rules and I played within them.

Yes, the McCourts lived in a different world with different rules. Their ever-expanding empire of homes and high-profile outings at expensive restaurants were evidence enough. But nothing underscored the different world—especially Jamie McCourt's role in it—more than a report in the *Los Angeles Times* that revealed the existence of a seven-page action plan dubbed "Project Jamie." The goal of the plan, drawn up in March 2008, was to have Jamie McCourt, who had never held elective office, "be elected President of the United States."

I didn't know about "Project Jamie" at the time. I had bigger concerns. Baseball's 2008 Winter Meetings were upcoming and I had many challenges more pressing than the quest for some unfathomable presidential primary.

The Dodgers had just been to the National League Championship Series, coming within three wins of going to the World Series for the first time in two decades. One of the four losses to the Phillies was by one run, another by two. We'd come so close and I was fighting to get enough money to take us to the next level, or at least keep us close to the current one. But I was getting nowhere. No matter what I said, no matter how much I argued and pleaded, I kept hearing the same thing: The money's not there. It's just not there.

I readily admit I don't know all the principles of accounting, especially in an organization as complicated as the Dodgers. But the fact that we couldn't add *anything* to the payroll simply didn't make sense to me. Worse, we actually were going to have to lower payroll. For clarity, I finally turned to the organization's financial experts.

In frustration, I went to see Pete Wilhelm, who had earned an undergraduate degree in economics from Cornell and an MBA in finance and operations from the Graduate School of Business at Columbia University. He had been with Frank McCourt for a long time. Peter was very smart and was juggling a lot.

"Peter," I said, "let me ask you something. Do the Giants have more debt service than we do?"

"Yes," Peter replied.

"And we're drawing about five hundred thousand more fans than they do."

"Yeah, that's about right," Peter said.

"And our revenue is higher than theirs?"

"Yes."

"Why, then, is our payroll barely higher than theirs? It just doesn't add up. It doesn't make sense to me."

Coming just four months after the Sabathia setback, and as a lower budget was being set in place, I remember thinking after the meeting that I'd just had my most frustrating conversations as general manager of the Dodgers. But within a year came a day that topped it.

On October 28, 2009, I picked up the *Los Angeles Times* and read a story by Bill Shaikin headlined "Dodgers' Ownership at Stake in McCourt fight." The story was published one week to the day after we'd lost to the Phillies in the NLCS for a second consecutive year—falling short, as I had feared, in part because we weren't allowed to make even incremental additions to the team and payroll. Shaikin's article detailed Jamie McCourt's just-filed divorce petition, in which her attorneys spelled out the lavish lifestyle she enjoyed and felt entitled to continue. The context of the article was hardly surprising since Jamie was an estranged wife and trying to receive as much spousal support as possible.

The testimony and documents detailed the amount of property owned and the day-to-day lifestyle. Jamie told the court in her divorce plea that she and Frank had $400 dinners at world-class restaurants four to five nights a week, routinely stayed in $5,000-a-night hotel rooms, and flew everywhere on private jets.

In petitioning the court to award her enough money to maintain a lifestyle few could even imagine, Jamie made a candid revelation that enraged Dodgers fans:

"Many of our travel costs are paid by the Dodger entities," her attorneys wrote.

And documents revealed it wasn't only travel costs. As the divorce played out, and as more and more court documents were filed and released, the press reported that "the Dodger entities"—spinoff companies created specifically to keep the McCourts' financial house of cards from collapsing on itself—were basically being used as ATMs. In all, court documents cited in *The New York Times*, *Los Angeles Times*, *Vanity Fair* magazine, and numerous other media outlets showed Frank and Jamie spent more than $108 million from the Dodgers.

The article Shaikin wrote made many people think differently about the McCourts. Many who warned of the lack of financial firepower at the outset of their ownership now felt they had proof they were right. We had been told the Dodgers didn't have the financial wherewithal in some instances and we had to cut programs and not pursue upper-echelon players. The Dodgers, once the pioneers in Latin American scouting and player development, had slipped mainly due to financial decisions. Latin American players had buoyed many big-league organizations, while the Dodgers were beginning to see the negative effects of curtailing spending in Latin America. Also, the economic model of supply and demand was evident in our staff hirings. I could hire brilliant statistical and technical savvy graduates from prominent universities, but I couldn't pay them more than $35,000 a year. And when they'd worked their tails off for a year, the biggest raise I could give them was $500. Still, the line of people interested in working in Major League Baseball wound around the block.

From one perspective, you could ask whose business it is how someone else spends the money they earned. It's probably a safe guess that other leaders of profitable megacompanies also have lifestyles and holdings that are expensive and vast. Is it anyone else's business what they spend and how they invest? In the case of the Dodgers, though, it seemed to become almost everyone's business, thanks to the public records filed in an ugly divorce.

From another perspective, the Dodgers are viewed as a civic jewel—part of the community, shared by everyone in it. People care about how the team is run. Many fans feel the franchise should be run almost as a not-for-profit. Those viewpoints spurred enormous emotional conflict.

From my perspective, it wasn't my business how the McCourts spent the money they had earned from their investments; I just didn't like it being portrayed as if they were struggling to make ends meet. By my support of not pursuing big-name players, I became a focal point to the press and the public. Which I guess is better than knowing what was going on and having to craft statements that I didn't personally support. Nevertheless, it was a process that many people, especially the press, took exception to. I was forced to believe the financial restraints were real and carry that theme in a convincing way to staff, to Joe, to the media, to the fan base, to myself. And now the truth was revealed through divorce filings.

It wasn't right. I was doing all that, running a team with my hands tied, while the McCourts were using a complex and confounding checkerboard of legal shadow companies.

I felt conflicted and somewhat misled, although the situation was extremely complicated. I knew Frank well enough to believe he was being as straightforward as possible. Still, I felt I was in an awkward position.

So did many fans. They expressed their feelings the only way they could—by staying away from Dodger Stadium. The fans' reaction was a boycott.

We were in trouble. The franchise was in the eye of the storm.

Fourteen
MANNYWOOD

• • • • • • • • • • • • •

T he first time I had discussions about Manny Ramirez coming to the Dodgers was at the 2006 Winter Meetings in Orlando. Grady Little and I were just back from a visit to Campo Las Palmas, the Dodgers' training academy in the Dominican Republic, and were walking through Orlando International Airport when he told me that Boston might make Manny available. This caught me off guard but if Grady was bringing it up, I figured there must be something to it. (Grady, of course, had managed Manny in Boston in 2002 and 2003. And he still had strong baseball contacts within the organization and media.)

Sure enough, a few hours later, Theo Epstein called. Then GM of the Red Sox before moving to the Cubs in 2011, Epstein wanted to know if I had any interest in Manny.

"Yeah, I'd have interest," I said. "But are you really going to move Manny Ramirez?"

"We may have to," Theo said.

We agreed to meet one-on-one, no assistants, no managers, nobody. The only person I told was Grady. Theo and I met several times that week in Orlando, always one-on-one. If there was anything to this, neither of us wanted word leaking out while the baseball world was gathered in one place.

To this day, I don't know if that was just a fishing expedition on Theo's part to see what he could get. A lot of times, a GM will go fishing to see what the value is on the outside for one of his players, and at the same time have you rank your own players—make you say, well, I'll give up this player, but won't give up that player.

Theo kept asking me about Matt Kemp and I told him, I won't talk about Kemp. So I felt I knew where he ranked the Dodgers players starting with Kemp. And he knew I wouldn't move Kemp.

The talks never became serious and the whole episode had a shelf life of about four or five days. But now it's a year and a half later, July 2008, with hours to go before the trade deadline. Manny's having all kinds of trouble in Boston. People are saying he's burning down the clubhouse. They want him out. And I get a call from Theo. He asks about Andy LaRoche, a 39th-round pick who had come into his own in 2006, hitting .315 combined at Double-A and Triple-A, and followed that up with a .309 season and eighteen home runs in seventy-three games at Triple-A Las Vegas in 2007.

Epstein offered right-handed reliever Craig Hansen, a former first-round draft pick out of St. John's University who'd saved three games for Boston that season, but was 2-7 with a 6.22 ERA in 48 games. Hansen had walked 43 in 46⅓ innings.

I wasn't interested and Theo understood.

With about thirty-six hours to go to the trade deadline, the only deal I had working was to try to get Greg Maddux back to Los Angeles for a second time. We'd gotten him for shortstop Cesare Izturis at the trade deadline in my first season, 2006, but he'd left to go to the San Diego Padres in 2007 and 2008.

Maddux still had a lot of money left on his contract. He was making $10 million and, as usual, I wasn't in a position to pick any of it up. The more cash I asked then–Padres GM Kevin Towers to pick up, the better prospects he demanded. So as I was leaving the ballpark the night of July 30, I stopped in to Torre's office to fill him in.

"I don't know," I told Joe. "We really don't have much going on right now. I'm going to try to keep the Maddux thing alive and see what happens.

"At the end of the day, we may be able to wait on Maddux. He's got a no-trade clause and his contract is so big that he could clear waivers. I'm hoping we can get into the middle of August, he'll still be there, and will have cleared waivers. Maybe he'll want out of San Diego a little more than he does now and we'll be able to do something. But that's really all I got."

EARLIER THAT AFTERNOON, I'm watching ESPN before our game against the Giants, and I see a scroll that has Florida, Pittsburgh, and Boston working on a three-way deal to send Manny to the Marlins.

I don't really think too much about it until I get a call from Theo a few hours later. "Hey, I know I asked you about LaRoche the other day . . . You're sure you're not interested in moving him?"

"I'm really not," I said. "Besides, you've got [Kevin] Youkilis and Mike Lowell. What are you going to do with LaRoche?"

Epstein was honest. "I may have another deal," he admitted.

I was just as honest back. "I've got to get a pretty good deal to move LaRoche."

Theo said, "All right."

"By the way," I said. "I just saw on the scroll on ESPN that you've got a deal going with Florida and Pittsburgh for Manny. Good luck with that. I hope it works out for you."

I got the impression Theo wasn't real confident a deal would happen.

After the game—we beat the Giants 4–0 that night on a five-hitter by Chad Billingsley—I went down to the clubhouse to keep Torre up to speed. I mentioned the Maddux scenario, then said, "But you know what? There's something interesting with Manny Ramirez. He was supposed to be traded to Florida, but it hasn't happened so who knows."

"Really?" Joe said.

"Think about it overnight. You've managed him in All-Star Games. You've managed against him. Think about it. Think if we had a chance to get this guy, what your thoughts would be."

"Wow, that would be huge," he said. "On this club? With our young hitters? That would be huge. Can we do it?"

I told him I didn't have any idea. I just had a gut feeling that if Boston couldn't move Manny to Florida and Theo had to move him, I'd be getting a call. "All I know is this trade was supposed to go down. It's midnight and it hasn't gone down. And when I talked to Theo, he didn't seem real confident and he asked me, again, about LaRoche. I know, too, that Pittsburgh's had an interest in LaRoche all year. They've called a couple times asking about him. So let's just see."

I arrived home close to 1 a.m., just twelve hours before the 1 p.m. trade deadline, Los Angeles time. So I was up at 5 a.m. And back at the stadium an hour later. About 9:30 a.m., Theo's cell number lit up my phone. "Hey, would you have any interest in Manny?"

"Theo," I said, "we already did this. Remember the Winter Meetings? I had the feeling you were on a fishing expedition."

"This is no fishing expedition. I've got to move him. He'll agree to go to you and I need to do something."

"Well, I'm not picking up any money," I said, sensing leverage and being perfectly honest at the same time.

"Manny's got like $7.5 million left," Epstein said. "You've got to pick up something."

"I don't have anything to pick up," I said. "I don't have it. But do I have interest? Yeah, I think I've got interest. Who are you going to need back?"

"I need LaRoche back," he said, then started asking about some more pitching.

Did I want Manny? Absolutely. But I didn't think Theo would pick up all the salary and I didn't want to waste more time with him trying to get me to rank my pitchers. So we left it at that.

Minutes started ticking.

I called Frank. "I got an interesting call on Manny this morning. When do you think you'll be here?"

Frank said between ten and ten thirty.

"When you get here, why don't we call the Red Sox?"

Shortly after Frank got in, with about three hours to go to the deadline, he and I called Theo and Red Sox president Larry Lucchino. Frank reiterated what I had said. The Dodgers weren't going to pick up any money.

With the ground rules firmly established, the talks suddenly started to gain traction. But the complications were crazy. Theo, as smart a baseball executive as I have ever known, was juggling Pittsburgh and us at the same time, though even then, I wasn't sure whether he was working the Pirates, the Marlins, or some other team.

By twelve thirty, a half hour before the deadline, seemingly a million things needed to be done. The commissioner had to approve the $7 million or so that would be coming to us. Manny had signed off on his no-trade clause, but any players and agents involved had to be notified. And Theo was calling again to say he needed one more player.

"Look, Theo, tell me where you're going with this so I can help you," I said.

"Well, it's Pittsburgh," he said.

"All right," I said. "I know they want LaRoche."

So we got Pittsburgh on the line. They wanted one of two pitchers, either Bryan Morris, a first-round draft pick, or James McDonald, who was on his way to becoming our minor-league pitcher of the year in 2008.

It is now fewer than ten minutes to 1 p.m.—the deadline.

I moved quickly across the hall to the office of Kim Ng. With her, waiting on red alert for just something like this, were my most trusted advisors: Lovelace, Ragazzo, De Jon Watson, Logan, and Mueller.

"I need to know right now," I said. "We've got a chance to get Manny Ramirez. Who are we going to trade? Bryan Morris or James McDonald?"

They were all shocked. Nobody said anything for several excruciating seconds.

"I've got to know," I said. "I've got to know your opinions."

Getting a consensus was tough. But finally, we reached an adrenaline-fueled decision and I sprinted to Frank's office, where my always-efficient director of baseball administration, Ellen Harrigan, had the commissioner, the Pirates, and the Red Sox waiting on a conference call.

With Ramirez's contract being paid by the Red Sox, the commissioner needed to approve the transaction that was complicated and needed to be completed by 1 p.m. Pacific.

"We are trading Bryan Morris and Andy LaRoche to Pittsburgh. We are acquiring Manny Ramirez and cash from Boston—the amount he is owed for the remainder of the season," I said.

For a moment, there was nothing but nerve-shattering silence. Then a pair of voices, one after the other—Theo and Pirates GM Neal Huntington—both explaining their give-and-take on the deal and in agreement to the principles of the trade.

"We are good on this end," I said, completing the three-way deal.

That was the only time in my career that representatives from the commissioner's office and three teams' leadership groups were on a call to consummate a deal.

I WALKED OUT of the room and into my office, where I smiled when I heard the baseball experts on ESPN saying: "Well, it looks like the Red Sox are stuck with Manny. The Red Sox weren't able to trade him before the deadline."

But the Red Sox were able to trade him. The only reason the world didn't know yet was that a lot of loops had to be closed before the trade could be announced. Manny had to be notified. So did everyone else involved. Besides our two players—LaRoche and Morris, who were going to the Pirates—Pittsburgh needed to reach out to Jason Bay, who was going to Boston, and the Red Sox had to notify Hansen and outfielder Brandon Moss they were going to the Pirates.

Obviously, the paperwork and the notifications took a while. But the next day, August 1, 2008, I was sitting in the general manager's booth at Dodger Stadium with Lovelace watching Manny jog out to left field for a game against the Arizona Diamondbacks.

"Can you believe that's Manny Ramirez down there?" Vance said with a wonderful "ain't the world a great place" grin on his face.

The moment was shocking—completely shocking—because forty-eight hours earlier, Manny coming to Los Angeles wasn't even a whisper. It didn't have a breath of life to it. And suddenly it was done.

For the first time since I'd come to Los Angeles, the ballpark was electric.

Years later, fans still commented to me how different the park felt that night.

THE NIGHT OF THE TRADE, the night before he took the field as a
Dodger, Manny kept calling me. He was trying to figure out what
number he could wear. He wanted 24, the number he had worn for
fifteen and a half seasons with Cleveland and Boston before coming
to Los Angeles.

"Walter Alston wore twenty-four," I said.

Manny didn't know who Walter Alston was. Ole Smokey only
managed the Dodgers for twenty-three seasons, winning seven National League pennants and four World Series. Of course, Manny
was four years old the year Alston stepped aside and turned the
Dodgers over to Tommy Lasorda.

"Twenty-four's retired," I said.

Manny understood, so he said, "Okay, I'll take eleven."

Nope, I told Manny. Eleven belonged to Manny Mota, who'd
been a Dodger as either player or coach for thirty-nine years in 2008
and would be around for years to come. The number was untouchable.

Manny's next choice was a nonstarter, as well. "What about
thirty-four?"

"That's Fernando," I said. (The Dodgers haven't retired Fernando Valenzuela's number, but no one has worn it since Fernan-
domania reigned in Southern California.)

I could hear the frustration in Manny's voice. "Are there any
numbers I can have?"

"How about ninety-nine?" I said.

"Ninety-nine!"

"Yeah, I know nobody's got that one and it's not retired."

Manny said he'd think about it, but a second later announced: "I
think I might do ninety-nine."

That was it. With one phone call, 99 went from being an un-
heard-of number with the Dodgers to a place in team history.

THE NEXT AFTERNOON, Friday, August 1, Manny and his agent, Scott Boras, arrived at Dodger Stadium around one o'clock for a 7:10 p.m. game. I had gone up to the players' parking lot on the eighth level to meet them and take Manny down to Torre's office. We had a nice conversation for several minutes, then Joe looked at Manny's hair.

"Manny, we do have rules here about length of hair," Torre said, sounding for all the world like Marlon Brando in *The Godfather*. "So you're going to have to cut your hair."

Manny didn't hesitate. "Hey, whatever you want me to do, Joe. I'm not here to cause trouble. Whatever you want me to do, I'll do."

About ten days went by. There's no haircut and the media were starting to write about how Manny has his own rules.

So I went into Torre's office. "What are we going to do about the hair?"

"I've told him like three times," Torre said, rolling his eyes.

Around that time, stories were popping up that Manny was planning to cut his hair for charity, but Manny never said anything about it to any of us. Then one afternoon, after the team had returned from a six-game road swing to St. Louis and San Francisco, I was walking through the clubhouse. The team was on the field taking batting practice when all of a sudden I heard Manny.

"Hey, Papi, Papi," he said from the back of the clubhouse.

"What's up, Manny?" I asked.

"I need to talk to you."

So I said, "Let's go," and the two of us ducked into Torre's office.

"Papi, what about my hair?" Manny said. "What about my hair?"

"You told Joe and I you were going to get it cut," I said. "We told the world you were going to get it cut."

"But, man, I have been growing it a long time. Why would I have to . . ."

"Manny, you told us you were going to get it cut. We have a rule here and you said you'd get it cut."

"Aw, but . . ."

Well, now, Manny's played ten games for the Dodgers. He's batting .467 (21-for-45) with ten runs scored, sixteen RBI, and five home runs. He's on fire and the last thing I want to do is upset the applecart. But we also have a rule and Joe is telling him to get his hair cut.

"How 'bout we do this?" I told him. "How 'bout you cut it this much?"—holding my thumb and forefinger a few inches apart. "Like two or three inches. You got about a foot or so. Why don't you cut two or three inches?"

"If I cut it two or three inches that'll be good enough?"

"Well, then you will have gotten your hair cut, right?"

Manny flashed his smile of pure joy, jumped out of his chair, and gave me one of his famous bear hugs. "Papi, I like it here," he said. "I'll get it cut tomorrow, three or four inches."

And he did.

MANNY'S PERFORMANCE THAT AUGUST, September, and October was historic. He carried us and he loved every minute of it. He had the most dynamic impact on a club I'd ever seen in the middle of a season since my first boss, Dallas Green, acquired Cy Young Award winner Rick Sutcliffe, who went 16-1 after coming to Chicago from Cleveland in 1984.

Manny taught the young Dodgers how to win and he taught them how to relax. Within the first couple days of being there, he went from group to group, clique to clique, every three or four lockers. He'd pull a chair up and talk to people. He brought the clubhouse, which had been fractured and divided twelve months earlier, closer and closer.

The final days of August, we were in a stretch where we'd lost eight in a row and ten of eleven—including a three-game sweep at the hands of the last-place Washington Nationals—to go from four games over .500 to five under. We were tied for first place when the slump started. After Arizona's No. 4 starter, Doug Davis, beat us 9–3 in the first game of a crucial weekend series at Chase Field on Friday night, August 29, we were four and a half games behind the first-place D-backs. The season was rapidly winding down and we were in a tailspin with nothing but more bad news facing us. Arizona's starters for the next two games were their two studs, Dan Haren and Brandon Webb. Haren was 14-6 at the time. Webb was 19-5. They would finish the season with a combined 38-15 record.

A crowd of 49,045 had Chase Field rocking in the third inning of a scoreless game. Manny was due up third in the inning and was swinging his bat in the dugout while Haren warmed up on the mound.

"If this guy throws me a breaking ball off the plate, he's going to need a new ball," Manny said, loud enough for all his teammates to hear. Everyone howled in laughter.

Sure enough, after Russell Martin and Andre Ethier made quick outs, Manny crushed the first pitch he saw deep into the seats. As he jogged back into the dugout to fist bumps and high-fives, Manny turned and yelled out to the field: "Get a new ball! Get a new ball!"

That one at-bat, that unbridled confidence, turned everything around for us. We beat Haren that night and Webb the next afternoon. We won eight in a row, including five straight against the Diamondbacks in a nine-day stretch. We caught Arizona and moved into first place on Saturday, September 6, when Manny hit a three-run homer off Webb and drove in five in a 7–2 win at Dodger Stadium.

Then, six weeks later, in Game 2 of the division playoffs, Manny did it all over again. Cubs starter Carlos Zambrano struck Manny out his first two at-bats, once on a ball down in the dirt and the other on a low called third strike. After the second strikeout, Manny came back to the dugout and said simply: "It won't happen again."

Sure enough. In Manny's next at-bat, leading off the fifth inning, Zambrano threw an ankle-high fastball that Manny reached down and launched into the batter's eye in deepest center field.

He was a tremendous addition to the Dodgers. No denying it. He hit .396 with seventeen home runs and fifty-three RBI in fifty-three games.

But, as we learned later, what seemed too good to be true was mostly just that.

After an off-season of negotiations with Scott Boras, Manny signed during the first week of March. Spring Training had been under way for three weeks. Then, on May 6, 2009, Frank received a phone call from Rob Manfred in the commissioner's office. Manny had tested positive in Spring Training for a female fertility drug that is used by steroid users to restore testosterone production to normal levels. He was suspended for fifty games and in my opinion never returned to the caliber of player he was in 2008 and before.

At the time of his suspension, he was batting .346 with six home runs and twenty RBI.

We called up Xavier Paul to replace Manny Ramirez.

Life in the Big Chair: It doesn't always sit right.

One day the team is doing great, 21-8 with a 6.5-game lead after opening the season with a record thirteen straight wins at home, and then a phone call later, the team dynamics change instantly. It is like a kaleidoscope—the slightest move and the picture changes dramatically.

Manny's time in L.A. finished much the same as it did with Boston, with the exception being the production had dissipated greatly. His needs became more important than the needs of the club and he pushed his way out. Fortunately, the White Sox claimed him on waivers. After spending two days trying to get a prospect from Chicago for Manny, we more or less relented after a day of contentious conversations in Colorado first between Manny and Joe and then between Manny and myself. By sundown that day, August 29, 2010, Manny was moving on to the White Sox. No prospect necessary. Taking Manny and the $3.8 million left on his contract was enough of a return.

Fifteen
ARE YOU OKAY?

• • • • • • • • • • • •

O n a seemingly quiet April morning in 2011, the Los Angeles Dodgers persona changed drastically and dramatically as the leaders of Major League Baseball had seen enough and seized control of the franchise.

There had been rumors but only a few people knew what was being staged in the MLB offices atop Manhattan's Park Avenue.

It was chaotic. The flow of information was slow, and a franchise hallowed for its on-field successes and off-the-field social conscience was being placed squarely in high-stakes limbo.

It happened so fast that no one in Los Angeles could brace for the announcement or decipher what exactly would come next. Information, true and false, was coming from all corners. It was going to take a few days to sort it all out.

A former sportswriter, whom I hadn't spoken to in thirty years, informed me by email that MLB had taken control.

Did I find out from ownership?

No.

Did I find out from someone in Major League Baseball?

No.

Mike Sistak and I had been colleagues at the defunct *Philadel-*

phia Journal but had lost contact after the paper folded in 1981. He had emailed me just once since—out of the blue in 2010—when I was the talk of the sports world for a few days because I publicly called out Matt Kemp during a radio interview.

Almost a year to the day, Sistak emailed me again. "Heard on the Red Sox broadcast that the Dodgers are now under control of Major League Baseball. Are you okay?"

I thought I was . . . that is, at least until I got his email.

The news that Commissioner Bud Selig was sending his hand-picked deputies to monitor the shaky finances of the Dodgers wasn't exactly a surprise. That possibility had seemed increasingly real for a year and a half as more and more disturbing details emerged from court documents and testimony in the acrimonious and highly public divorce of Frank and Jamie McCourt. The story line was that the couple had put the financial stability of one of sports' most storied franchises in jeopardy by allegedly siphoning more than $100 million from the Dodgers to finance their lifestyle. The public learned through the media Frank was drawing a $5 million a year salary from the Dodgers and various related businesses. Jamie was bringing home $2 million a year until their divorce, when she was awarded $131 million in the tax-free divorce settlement.

While not exactly a surprise, the news that MLB had taken over the team was, to say the least, disconcerting. Adding to the moment was the fact that I had to learn about it from someone I hadn't had a verbal conversation with in thirty years.

RICK RAGAZZO, one of the Dodgers' special assistants, and I spent the morning of Wednesday, April 20, 2011, in El Segundo, California, at the practice facility of the Los Angeles Kings near LAX airport. The Kings were hosting the San Jose Sharks in Game 4 of the NHL quarterfinals at Staples Center that night. I had known

Dean Lombardi, general manager of the Kings, for more than a decade—back to the days when he was GM of the Sharks and Rags and I worked for the San Francisco Giants.

Lombardi reminds me a lot of Brian Sabean in his demeanor and decision making. Dean graduated with honors from law school at Tulane University with a specialty in labor issues and worked with famed agent Art Kaminsky before moving into the hockey front office with the Minnesota North Stars in 1988. Getting together with Lombardi was always enlightening, entertaining, and helpful—professionally and personally.

There is a kinship among GMs from other sports. While the playing surfaces may be different, as well as the cost of players, the character traits of accountability and the methods of motivation and team building cross over easily.

After spending time in Dean's office, Rags and I went downstairs to the rink to meet up with our friends from the Sharks, who were working out in the same arena. Sometimes, having good friends associated with both teams put me in a somewhat comical situation.

"So where do your loyalties lie?" someone would inevitably ask.

I always had the same response. "I root for a good game," I'd say, then added with careful timing, "And for the team that left me the tickets."

That afternoon, Rags and I spent time with Todd McLellan, then head coach of the Sharks, and the three of us found ourselves commiserating about the challenges we faced in our positions. Little did I know the challenges at the Dodgers were about to grow exponentially.

RAGS AND I LEFT the rink headed east on Interstate 105 and were approaching the 405 interchange when my BlackBerry started buzzing. The first message was Sistak's. Within minutes, I was deluged.

The Red Sox were playing the Oakland A's that day in an unusual 3:35 p.m. start at Fenway Park. That meant the game was on at lunchtime in L.A. The world of sports is a small one and word like that travels very quickly.

This was an historic move. That I would hear about it from a distant acquaintance and that he would get it from a Red Sox broadcast was, and still is, puzzling. It begged the question: Did MLB move quickly because it knew something was about to break that would affect the franchise or the league? Had the announcement been planned for weeks and merely unfolded as MLB had it scripted? If that were the case, wouldn't it have made more sense to have Commissioner Selig's monitor, former Texas Rangers president Tom Schieffer, on the ground in L.A. to take over immediately instead of withholding his name, not naming him that day and not sending him out to California for eight days? Considering how valuable and high-profile the Dodgers are, wouldn't MLB have wanted the transition to be as seamless as possible? Why have a leadership void for more than a week?

"Can you believe this?" I asked Rags, looking over to the passenger seat without really expecting an answer. "We need to get to the stadium."

IT WAS RARE for me to hold a team meeting. I planned one meeting a year—the morning the full squad reported to camp in the spring. But, obviously, there were times when I needed to speak impromptu—maybe a half-dozen times: when we were eliminated by the Phillies in the National League Championship Series in 2008 and 2009, when Manny Ramirez was suspended for fifty games in 2009, when Joe Torre decided he was stepping down as manager, when Don Mattingly was being appointed, and now, when Major League Baseball was taking over the Dodgers.

The time Manny was suspended was pretty typical of my rare group sessions. The day before we found out, Manny left a 10–3 win over the Washington Nationals a few minutes early and ducked out of the clubhouse before the team came off the field. I didn't find out what was happening until Frank called a little before 1 a.m. on Thursday, May 7, 2009. He told me Manny had tested positive and was going to miss fifty games. We got Joe Torre on a conference call and filled him in.

By the time I addressed the club that afternoon, the news was out. I kept my remarks short. I reminded the players how good they had become, that I thought they were a special group. I told them they needed to continue to get better without Manny the next couple of months. I wanted the players to use his absence as an opportunity to make a stronger positive impact themselves. Keep playing hard. Don't let this be a distraction.

Short and sweet. I used the same format this time with the MLB takeover: brief and to the point.

"Guys, as you may have heard, Major League Baseball is going to monitor the Dodgers," I said. "I don't have all the information, but from what I can surmise, they are doing this to make us better, to give us a better chance. I don't see them coming in to be a detriment or a hindrance. It is in everyone's best interest to have this franchise be a cornerstone and to be successful. So, as I said in Spring Training, your focus is on playing and winning. Leave the rest to myself and others."

I finished with a warning and a reminder: "The press is going to be all over you these next few days, but, again, your thoughts should be on what you do—you prepare, you play, and do the best at what you have control of."

The reaction was muted. No one had any questions. No one had anything to add. Everyone looked focused.

We beat the Braves 6–1 that night and beat them again the next day 5–3, then headed to Chicago for a weekend series against the Cubs. We got to our hotel on Michigan Avenue after midnight, grabbed a few hours' sleep, and had to be at Wrigley Field by midmorning for a 1:20 p.m. game.

Fans rarely appreciate the grind of travel during a major-league season. Yes, big-league players travel on chartered planes and almost never have to endure the long lines and aggravations of tedious security checks in most airports. They don't have to drive themselves to or from airports or most ballparks, don't have to carry their own luggage, and stay in nothing but the finest first-class hotels. But the constant flying, often through two or three time zones at all hours of the night immediately after and before games that are physically challenging and emotionally draining, is an ordeal few can relate to.

This trip was tougher than usual. Whether we wanted to admit it or not, we were reeling from the commissioner's announcement just seventy-two hours earlier. We were exhausted after the red-eye flight with little more than a nap to tide us over. Then we got to Wrigley Field and the weather was miserable. First pitch was delayed seventy-four minutes by rain. When we finally did start, the temperature was forty-one degrees and dropping, with a biting seventeen-mile-an-hour wind blowing in from right field. A quick game was exactly what everyone wanted and needed, but it wasn't to be. The two teams combined for twenty-two hits, thirteen walks, and fourteen runs over three hours and fifteen minutes. It was nearly 6 p.m. by the time the game finally ended, but we'd won again. Dodgers 12, Cubs 2. The joke going around the club was that we were 3-0 under Commissioner Selig.

Three weeks into the season we had been blindsided by MLB's intervention and been hit with injuries to shortstop Rafael Furcal, third baseman Casey Blake, and pitchers Jon Garland, Vicente Padilla, and Hong-Chi Kuo. Our planned infield of Blake, Furcal, Juan Uribe, and James Loney played exactly two games together through the first month of the season. And the schedule had been brutal. Our first twelve games were against division rivals and the next eight had been against the Cardinals and Braves—two of the toughest teams in the National League. Still, as April turned to May, we were a .500 club. It was not where we wanted to be, and not where we would finish, but—at the time—it wasn't bad considering everything we had been through.

A FULL WEEK AFTER MLB'S surprise announcement, Frank called me. Understandably, he had his hands full, but it was good to hear from him at last. He had just finished meeting in New York with baseball's top executives—minus Commissioner Selig—and wanted to explain his case to me. The Dodgers, unlike the financially troubled New York Mets, had never asked MLB for a loan, had met every financial obligation, and, despite published reports, had never been the subject of any investigation by the Internal Revenue Service.

Frank told me what he would later tell reporters: that he was convinced Selig had set in motion a predetermined chain of events designed to take the Dodgers from him. I listened and barely had a chance to say anything. His description was chilling, desperate, and sad.

We spoke for about thirty minutes. He was upset that Selig hadn't sat in on the meeting to personally hear his appeal and told me he'd asked then–MLB vice president Rob Manfred, Selig's eventual successor, to call the commissioner after the session. Frank was convinced he could bail himself and the Dodgers out of financial trouble by selling the team's long-term broadcasting rights for a windfall. Manfred agreed to make the call and Frank had waited to hear what the commissioner had to say. He needn't have bothered. He said Manfred came back looking somewhat ashen after a ninety-minute absence and said Selig wasn't going to approve any plan to bail out the Dodgers.

The next day, April 28, Selig's monitor, Tom Schieffer, sat down at the round conference table in my office overlooking left field at Dodger Stadium. He carefully explained what he was doing and how it related to me. He wasn't here to interfere with baseball operations. He wasn't here to second-guess. He came with the power to approve or disapprove any moves baseball operations might want to make that exceeded the existing budget.

Schieffer encouraged me to call Doug Melvin and Tom Grieve, two general managers who had worked for him while he was president of the Rangers.

"I don't need to do that," I said. "I believe in being a team player and if Major League Baseball and Commissioner Selig made this decision, and you are their choice to do the job, I will follow that direction."

Schieffer said he appreciated that, but I should call anyway.

When I talked with Melvin later, he confirmed everything I'd read or heard about Schieffer and had experienced in our brief meetings. He is an intelligent, highly principled, strong-willed man who loves baseball. A former U.S. ambassador to China and Australia, he also is discreet and extremely loyal. Tony Jackson, a columnist for ESPN.com, had a lunch interview with Schieffer and described him as "cryptic and transparent at the same time."

"The one thing Schieffer hasn't done, and wouldn't do over lunch, is pile on McCourt," Jackson wrote. "Schieffer gave McCourt credit for being cooperative, especially after everyone got over that initial awkwardness that Schieffer knew he would encounter when he arrived."

But the awkwardness would return soon enough. On June 27, 2011, McCourt, unable to meet a looming end-of-the-month payroll, had his attorneys file for Chapter 11 bankruptcy protection in a Delaware court—part of the reason was to try to buy time and also have a fair fight. As they filed, they notified Schieffer and his assistant, John Allen, that the bankruptcy filing meant neither MLB appointee had authority any longer to monitor the team's finances. Selig's watchdogs were rendered useless, forced to work out of the offices of MLB's attorneys in Los Angeles, without access to the Dodgers' books.

Frank called to tell me about the bankruptcy filing at 6 a.m., just as I was preparing to board a flight to Minnesota for an interleague series against the Twins. I took off with a mind-numbing sense of confusion and isolation.

I was a long way from Franklin Park.

I was a long way from Wrigley Field and my days with the Cubs.

San Francisco seemed a foggy memory.

I felt anything but okay.

Sixteen

NAVIGATING THE EYE
OF THE STORM

· · · · · · · · · · · · · ·

A mysterious off-season rush-hour traffic accident almost brought Prince Fielder to the Dodgers.

A torn ACL in Orlando, a day of high-stakes financial meetings in New York, and a determined eighty-two-year-old pizza salesman in Detroit combined to make sure it never happened.

Fielder and Albert Pujols were the two most coveted free agents on the market during the 2011–12 off-season.

Under an agreement between Major League Baseball and the MLB Players Association, teams could begin signing free agents at 12:01 a.m. Eastern Daylight Time on November 3, 2011—five days after the World Series.

Two days before the signing period began, on Tuesday, November 1, Frank McCourt suddenly, and surprisingly, announced he was selling the Dodgers. In a joint statement, McCourt and his bitter rival, Commissioner Selig, agreed they would seek approval from a federal judge in Delaware to auction the team.

Finally.

After two trying years, I could see a light at the end of our long, dark tunnel—hope on the horizon.

That off-season and the next few months were unpredictable. Few had a road map or guide to building a major-league team with a franchise in bankruptcy and up for sale. Obviously, Frank had less interest in making any major financial commitments. Our payroll was shrinking: We were in the second-largest market in the country, but we'd have to work with the payroll of a midmarket team.

At the same time, the baseball staff would be under the microscope of a new owner—whoever that would ultimately be. We were auditioning with one hand tied behind our back financially and without knowing who was doing the screening.

I could see panic in the eyes of the staff. Our baseball operations department was spread across the globe. We were all together once a year, if that. Cellphones and emails kept us connected and both were ideal conduits for the rumor mill.

I contacted all the baseball department leaders and instructed them to encourage their staffs to spend their time doing what they could—be professional, keep working hard, block out the noise, and, by all means, avoid spreading gossip.

Frank called me just before news of his agreement with Selig went public. I was in Scottsdale, at a drinking establishment named Eli's, which Sabean and I frequented for years during our relatively tranquil time with the Giants. I stepped outside into the perfect night air and sat on a bench while Frank filled me in on the next steps. McCourt typically held his feelings in check, but this time he was emotional. He explained the whole deal and said he had negotiated a process that basically would let him pick the new owners from a list of MLB-approved finalists. This was a change in MLB protocol, from the way Major League Baseball normally did business. The way things had played out certainly wasn't what he had in mind when he came out to L.A. from Boston. It was a very difficult decision for Frank to make, but he knew selling the team at that point was the best for everyone.

I felt it was also the appropriate decision and was relieved. Everyone in the organization desperately needed this transition. It was difficult to continue in the direction we were heading. Organizationally and personally, you need full-time leadership, you need a full-time commitment from everybody, including the people at the top. But with so many things going on, the court fights, a bankruptcy hearing, the negotiations with MLB, it was difficult for McCourt to provide that leadership. I was proud we had kept the organization afloat amid all the chaos. And Frank had also been able to pay one hundred cents on the dollar—somewhat unusual in bankruptcy situations. Now we were moving forward even though no one knew for sure what the future would look like.

There were so many variables that had to play out. When would the auction take place? Who would the bidders be? When would the new owners take over?

And for the Dodgers' staff and players, it became obvious that their futures with the club would be decided by people they didn't know and who didn't know them.

Selig said he hoped new ownership would be in place by Opening Day 2012 but that there were no guarantees.

Meanwhile, we had another team to build.

After coming within three wins of going to the World Series in 2008 and 2009, we had fought hard with a diminished payroll and the firestorm around us to finish a combined one game over .500 (162-161) in 2010 and 2011. For anyone who wasn't there on a daily basis during this period, it is hard to completely fathom what an historically unsettling time it was in Dodgers history. The more time passes, the more the events are muted. Suffice it to say that few, if any, people in American sports history went through what that staff went through.

In every big city or small town the scouts and player development people traveled to, someone from another club would ask: "Will you be working next year?" "What's going to happen to this guy or that guy?" "I hear they are going to clean house." "I hear that so-and-so is going to get the team and they have their own people in mind."

Professional baseball is a very public business populated by people who worry—with good reason. Job security is fleeting. The vast majority of scouts make between $35,000 and $70,000 and are on one-year contracts that typically expire on October 31. A few veteran scouts earn more, but not that many. A scout can work twenty years, be fifty years old, still be paying off college debt for his children, and then, one day, he is on the street. He can be loyal to a fault—spending twenty-eight days a month on the road, driving and flying, sometimes daily. And then suddenly it is over.

Outside of coaching or another scouting position, what comes next?

Like many middle-age people of the workforce, the tightrope walk of employment is tenuous. Unlike many industries, the world of baseball scouting is very small.

The same goes for the player development staff. Every September and October, you see the look of uncertainty in their eyes. And that's in a normal season. This year would be anything but normal in Dodger Land.

Uncertainty went on and on. The truth was that no one knew anything.

The experience was uneasy, but also educational. It taught us, among other things, what was and wasn't worth our time and effort. None of us could do anything about the McCourts' divorce, about the bankruptcy, about the decline. We had to concentrate on those small areas where we could make a difference and, hopefully, impact directions and outcomes. The rest of the conflict we had to let go. It was a true life lesson.

Frank still owned the team and made it clear payroll was going down in 2012. The 2011 payroll had topped at $114 million, but that included $22.2 million in "dead money," owed to seven former players, led by Manny Ramirez and Andruw Jones. The active payroll was just under $92 million.

Fans had protested McCourt's ownership by staying away from Dodger Stadium. Attendance fell under three million in 2011 for the first time in a decade. Because of the loss of attendance revenue, the bean counters had told McCourt he would lose money if he spent more than $80 million on player salaries in 2012. To Frank's credit, he recognized how unrealistic that would be. We would be in a financial no-man's-land. With all the prior commitments that came with a payroll of $114 million, cutting back that far would not make the team better. It made more sense to trade off the assets—Kemp, Kershaw, Ethier—and do something never done with the Dodgers before—rebuild.

He pushed the payroll upward to $90 million when he really didn't have to, with a pending sale.

We set out trying to fill in gaps—not trying to move big mountains. We wanted to plug holes with professionals who knew how to win with players like Jerry Hairston Jr., Tony Gwynn Jr., Juan Rivera, Mark Ellis, Adam Kennedy, and Chris Capuano.

I wanted to bring Hiroki Kuroda back. Kuroda won forty-three games for the Dodgers from 2008 to 2011, including the clinching game against the Cubs in the 2008 NLDS and our only victory in the 2008 League Championship Series against the Philadelphia Phillies.

When I met Kuroda's agent, after signing Rivera for $4 million,

I had about $12 million left in my budget. I was willing to spend it all on the gutsy pitcher and maybe even bust the budget by another half million, if necessary. But negotiations began, and essentially ended, when his agent kicked things off with one of the strangest lines I ever heard.

"He'll sign for fifteen million or more for one year."

Or more? Aren't agents always looking for more?

I laughed and told him, "We're looking for twelve and a half million. *Or* less."

There wasn't much left to talk about.

Agents use a wide range of tactics to push salary demands higher, but now, with a sale on the horizon and the uncertainty that went with it, they had fewer cards to play until the dynamics of ownership changed.

JAMES LONEY PLAYED all but eleven games at first base for the Dodgers from 2008 through 2011. Never a power hitter at a power-hitting position, he was nonetheless a solid defensive player who, for much of his career, had a penchant for driving in clutch runs. He had 90 RBI in 2008, 90 in 2009, and 88 in 2010. But in 2011, Loney drove in just 65 runs and had only 43 extra-base hits in 158 games. His slugging percentage was .416, third lowest among major-league first basemen with at least five hundred plate appearances. We needed a power upgrade but were planning to stick with Loney one more year, given the ownership uncertainty and payroll restrictions.

Then came the accident. On Monday, November 14, 2011, at 6:12 p.m., during rush hour traffic, Loney was driving a silver Maserati that sideswiped three cars on the 101 Freeway in Sherman Oaks, California.

A woman in one of the cars told KTLA TV that she rushed to

Loney and found him sitting with earbuds in his ears. She pulled the earbuds out and could hear music blasting, but Loney didn't move. "He was nonresponsive to everything I tried," said Judy Eckerling, who immediately dialed 911. Eckerling still had her head inside the window of Loney's car when he jolted to consciousness, looked around, saw the accident scene, started his car, and tried to cross four lanes of westbound traffic. He struck a fourth car before hitting a sound wall and coming to a stop a second time with a broken axle.

A police report said Loney was "restless, unsteady, aggressive, and irritable." He was handcuffed and taken to Sherman Oaks Hospital, where police said he remained "uncooperative" and bit off the mouthpiece of a Breathalyzer machine and spit it at an officer. Police then placed Loney in arm and leg restraints and medical personnel gave him an injection to calm him down.

Amazingly, no one at the Dodgers—or in the media—knew anything about what happened for weeks. In fact, the day after Loney's bizarre accident, I was being completely candid when I told Dylan Hernandez of the *Los Angeles Times*, in response to a question about the Dodgers possibly going after Pujols or Fielder: "As of today, it looks less realistic."

I was convinced the payroll restrictions and ownership uncertainty meant we were going with Loney at first base for 2012.

We learned about Loney's bizarre accident when one of the women whose car had been sideswiped got through to Ellen Harrigan, our director of baseball administration, and asked what the Dodgers intended to do about Loney. If you are a well-known professional athlete, it would seem to be difficult to hide in a city like Los Angeles. But how the accident stayed under the radar that long was both remarkable and troubling.

Ellen was dumbstruck. So was I.

I was on the phone with Loney's agent, Joe Urbon, but wasn't getting very far when James called me on the other line and downplayed the incident. He did little to clear things up and I was left wondering how a player is involved in a multicar accident during rush hour and does not say anything for two weeks. Doesn't come forward and say, "Hey, here's what happened." Especially if it was all innocent. The agent contended over and over again that had he believed the incident was important, he would have alerted me.

From the outside, it often looks as if the GM of a professional sports team simply puts together players to form a team and has fun doing it. Although it is a tremendous way to make a living, the job is far more than that.

The Loney car accident caper is a perfect example. Nearly every day, there is something that a GM needs to handle that goes beyond merely trading and signing players. The GM position is so deep and complex—far more than it was thirty years ago. The gap is even wider when you think of the combustible nature of young millionaires—some with college education, some without, with fame, athleticism, and time on their hands. A player goes to the ballpark most days around 3 p.m. and leaves around 11 p.m. postgame. Believe me, a lot goes on between 11 p.m. and 6:30 a.m. that has nothing to do with baseball. There are seven, sometimes eight, minor-league teams in each organization with perhaps thirty players per team—that's a lot of people to keep track of, and a lot of potential for trouble.

At the end of November, with the Winter Meetings just days away and Loney facing possible charges of driving under the influence and trying to leave the scene of an accident, I was in a difficult spot. His behavior raised a lot of questions and neither Loney nor his agent was offering many answers. Eventually, prosecutors refused to bring criminal charges against Loney, saying in early February 2012 that there was "insufficient evidence" because tests came back negative.

. . .

WHEN WE WENT to the Winter Meetings in Dallas, we knew we were going to have an ownership change. We knew that a new, potentially lucrative television deal was coming. And we knew we had a first baseman whose recent power numbers and personal behavior were questionable.

I figured I would float the idea of signing Prince Fielder and see where it went.

Fielder was represented by Scott Boras. And chances of a quick negotiation with Scott were slim. I figured we would have time to learn more about our financial situation. There really was no harm in getting in the game.

Dating back to Greg Maddux's early arbitration years, Scott and I knew each other well. That's a long time in the baseball business. I'd also spent three Christmas Eves on the phone with him during the negotiations for Bonds, Ramirez, and Fielder. Christmas Eve is not a good time to be missing the family after putting them on hold most of the other 364 days of the year.

I've had some passionate exchanges and more than a few good conversations with Scott through the years. He is smart and always prepared. He sees the long-term picture better than most and hones it to the specific needs and desires of his clients. He is different than most agents. From a club standpoint, sometimes that is good. Sometimes not. He has helped many players become wealthier than they ever imagined. A onetime minor-league infielder, Scott most likely surpassed whatever personal dream he may have had in his playing days.

The relationship between an agent and GM is typically of the love-hate variety. I considered a few agents good friends and have known some for thirty years. Most executives don't like the relationship between the two sides, and I can't say I did, either. But I knew I had to do business with agents so I put away "like or dislike" and just tried to make sound business decisions.

A GM needs the agent in order to make a deal for a player, but the GM also knows the agent isn't a middleman—he is squarely on the player's side.

Agents have changed the face of professional sports. They are the protector, guiding light, negotiator, and sounding board for the players. Before the advent of agents, club owners ran the sport. Now agents and the union have a lot of say on how the game is run and how the money is spent.

Before 1975, players had fewer rights than nearly anyone in the American workforce. While most workers could leave one job for another, a baseball player was bound to his team for the length of his career.

Marvin Miller changed all that. As executive director of the Major League Baseball Players Association from 1966 to 1982, Miller transformed the players' union into one of the strongest labor organizations in the United States. The great broadcaster Red Barber once told a writer from *The Village Voice*, "Marvin Miller, along with Babe Ruth and Jackie Robinson, is one of the two or three most important men in baseball history."

Scott also deserves to be listed among the most important men in baseball history. One of his strengths is his ability to get in front of ownership, and bypass the general manager. He has used that tactic many times to secure some of the richest contracts in sports. In my opinion, Scott's greatest strength is his talent for forecasting the long-range plans of teams and matching them to his potential free agents. Say a team has a third baseman who is two years from free agency and Scott has a client who is a better third baseman, who will also be a free agent that off-season. He will do what he can to drop a hint two years ahead of time. Boras knows teams' strengths and weaknesses and he knows what his personal free agent class will look like compared to the other options for a team.

I remember having lunch with Scott in Newport Beach in 2006. He was laying out how I would need a center fielder in two years and he had the perfect match for me. I remember thinking to myself, I'm trying to figure out how we are going to win a game today and he is moving players around like chess pieces two years down the road.

A classic example of this was the free agent class of the 2004 off-season, when Boras represented Atlanta outfielder J. D. Drew and Los Angeles third baseman Adrian Beltre.

Supposedly, Scott was struggling to find a multiyear deal for Drew but had action on Beltre. The Dodgers wanted to re-sign Beltre. Scott waited until many of the big bats were off the market and took Beltre to Seattle for five years and $64 million. With Beltre gone, the Dodgers needed a middle-of-the-order bat. Drew signed with them for five years and $55 million. Boras also negotiated an "opt-out" clause in Drew's contract so he could go back on the free agent market in two years, which he took in 2006, leaving Los Angeles for Boston on a five-year, $70 million deal. An ingenious move in a business that doesn't move quickly.

DURING THE 2011 WINTER MEETINGS in Dallas, I spoke with my inner circle of advisors about Prince Fielder. Then, on Monday of the following week, I sent a text message to Boras: "Hey, I've got an idea I want to run by you."

When we started talking, I laid out an initial offer for Prince. Did I think at the time the offer was going to get a contract done? No, but I wanted Scott to know we were serious and had a solid concept of how we might get it done. I offered $75 million for three years with two club options that would guarantee $80 million for three years or $125 million for five years if the options were executed.

Boras played the initial offer with a poker face. Usually, you don't know right away if you've caught an agent's attention. And I wasn't sure with Scott for about a week. But by the middle of December, it was clear Boras was interested in continuing the talks. If nothing else, he knew it couldn't hurt to have a big-market team involved when he was trying to drive up that player's value.

I told Scott right away I didn't want the conversation to go public. If it did, I told him, we wouldn't go any further. Boras assured me nothing would get out and he was true to his word. We talked once or twice a week. Most of the conversations were amicable, though we did have a few "passionate" exchanges. But overall, we had what I thought was a fairly tame negotiation by our standards. We wouldn't move a lot because I didn't know what we were chasing—what other offers might be out there—and of course I still didn't have a clue about our new ownership situation or what the new television package would bring.

I went up to five years and $125 million, taking out the option years, and stayed there for a long time waiting to feel out the landscape. Boras had visions of an Alex Rodriguez–type contract, the ten-year deal he renegotiated with the Yankees in 2008 that carried an average annual value of $27.5 million.

We were never going to go that deep, but we kept at it into January, when Boras nudged things forward by telling me, "If you want to meet with the player, I can arrange it."

Time is a valuable commodity in any negotiation. You have to use it to your advantage when you can. And we did in this case. We took several days, then agreed to meet Fielder in Dallas on Saturday, January 14. He was meeting with the Texas Rangers on Friday and would stay an extra night to sit down with us.

I asked two of my top assistants, Toney Howell and Vance Love-lace, to go to Dallas with me. Toney knew Fielder. He was a scout for the Brewers when Prince was making his way through the minor-league system. And Lace was a very good evaluator who could read people well.

We were determined to keep our pursuit of Fielder secret and I didn't have a confidant in Dallas I could trust to line up a meeting place. So I asked our traveling secretary, Scott Akasaki, to book me a suite at a hotel near DFW airport, the same hotel where I met Grady to hire him for the manager's job in December 2005. Akasaki is very good at his job. He never asked what or why. If I gave him half an idea of what I needed done, he somehow made everything happen. And that's what he did this time. When I got to the hotel, someone met me in the lobby and handed me a key. The room was in Akasaki's name so the media wouldn't know we were there, in case any enterprising reporters were trying to keep tabs on us.

Later, Akasaki told me he wondered why I needed a hotel room in Dallas, but when he saw on the news that Fielder was meeting the Rangers, he put two and two together. Fortunately, no one else did, or really could.

Toney, Lace, and I flew in separately and met at the hotel. We had dinner, then went up to the suite and designed a plan and discussion points for our morning session with Prince and Scott. The next morning, all of the parties gathered and chatted for nearly three hours with Prince, Scott, and Scott's associate Mike Fiore. It was a great conversation, all of us just being candid and relaxed. We didn't talk money. We talked about the Dodgers, Los Angeles, and the future. Prince was very open. He was eager to dispel any concerns about his conditioning. Officially listed at five foot eleven and 275 pounds, Fielder was all of that and probably more. But he wanted us to know how much he trained and how much it meant for him to be a solid player for a long time. He said he never wanted to be embarrassed, never wanted to let his conditioning slip to the point that he couldn't be as productive as he thought he should be.

When we broke up and headed in different directions, I felt good. The negotiations, the talks, and the meeting had all been among the best I'd ever been involved in. Despite all the chaos of the bankruptcy proceedings, the McCourt divorce, the pending sale of the team, we still had a shot at landing one of the premier free agents on the market that winter. Sometimes, money talks louder than circumstance.

The next week, we upped our offer from five years and $125 million to seven years and $168 million. We also offered Prince an opt-out after three or four years in the event he wanted another shot at free agency—an opt-out being one of Boras's trademark contractual points. But that still wasn't going to get a deal done. Fielder had averaged 40 home runs and 113 RBI for five seasons coming into the negotiations and was just twenty-seven years old. He was coming into the prime of his career and was someone I was convinced could make a drastic difference for our club. I was willing to go higher if I could get Frank to sign off on the offer.

On Friday, January 20, 2012, Boras called and said, "I've had an owner offer me nine years. They may end up going to ten years at a very high number. I just wanted to let you know that you're going to have to go to a strong eight, at least, in order to get it done."

I didn't know it at the time, but the owner who'd come forward was Mike Ilitch, founder of the Little Caesars Pizza empire. Ilitch had also owned the Detroit Red Wings of the National Hockey League and had enjoyed great success, winning four Stanley Cups. He wanted the Tigers to become champions, too. And he wanted it to happen now. Ilitch was eighty-two years old at the time and at least one Detroit writer speculated in print that Ilitch's age played a role in his willingness to do whatever it took to sign Fielder.

Adding to the urgency was news that one of the Tigers' top players, Victor Martinez, had just been injured in a freak accident. Martinez, who hit .330 and drove in 103 runs in 2011, tore the anterior cruciate ligament in his left knee while working out in Orlando just about the time we were meeting Boras and Fielder in Dallas. Two days after that meeting, doctors told Ilitch and the Tigers that Martinez would be lost for the 2012 season.

When Scott called that Friday and said we'd need to go "a strong eight, at least" to stay in the running, I gathered my inner circle. We decided, given that Prince was just entering his prime, we would consider eight years at $200 million if we could get Frank's blessing. We'd structure the deal in a way that the first three or four years would be $26 million each, with the salary tapering a bit toward the end. We'd include an opt-out clause after three years, so Fielder could explore free agency if he wanted and we would be off the hook for the other five years.

Throughout the negotiations, Matt Kemp and Tony Gwynn Jr. had been incredibly helpful, trying to convince Fielder how great it would be to have him with the Dodgers. Kemp made many phone calls. Gwynn and his family went on vacation with Fielder and his family. Tony was great pitching how good a place Los Angeles could be and what a change Prince could make for our club. And Tony's wife, Alyse, lobbied Prince's wife, Chanel, about the great California lifestyle. But, in the end, I never got that chance to put the $200 million offer on the table. The Tigers signed Fielder to a nine-year, $214 million deal on Tuesday, January 24, exactly one week after learning Martinez was lost for the season.

Just before the deal was announced, I tried to get Frank and his chief financial officer, Peter Wilhelm, to give me their thoughts on the concept of the eight years at $200 million with an out clause. Maybe all the efforts Gwynn and Kemp had put into wooing Fielder would have convinced Prince to give up the extra year and $14 million. We'll never know because we couldn't get Frank or Peter to the phone. They were locked in meetings about the sale of the team.

In the end, it worked out for the best. Seven months later, in an historic deal, we acquired power-hitting first baseman Adrian Gonzalez. And two years after that, Fielder was traded from Detroit to Texas, where he played just forty-two games in 2014 before undergoing career-ending surgery for a herniated disc in his neck.

Still, at the time, it would have been nice to give it one last shot.

Seventeen

A DAY IN THE LIFE

• • • • • • • • • • • • •

Some days are spent chasing big-time free agents and dealing in the $100 million to $200 million dollar stratosphere. Some days are spent maneuvering through the day-to-day that finds the GM juggling and looking through many different windows simply trying to figure out people.

In the sports world, there are young people who dream about being a professional athlete. At some point, those dreams dissolve into the reality that being paid to play sports isn't going to happen except for a very tiny percentage of people.

That is not the case with the Big Chair. There is no age limit, no physical appearance or conditioning that will stop people from aspiring to or playing general manager.

Fantasy sports leagues have exploded across the United States for decades since Dan Okrent, then a publishing consultant for *Texas Monthly* magazine and later public editor of *The New York Times*, invented Rotisserie League Baseball with friends at La Rôtisserie Française restaurant in New York City in 1979. Among one of the many reasons fantasy games are so popular is because they give fans the illusion they are running their own team. Anyone and everyone can be a general manager. Just pull the right players off the basement card table or on the Draft Day computer and build a championship team.

But, in twenty-first-century professional sports, evaluating talent and assembling a team are just a tiny fraction of a real-life general manager's job. Besides balancing budgets, placating owners, dealing with the media, reaching out to the community, negotiating with agents, and constant travel, a general manager has to be part-time psychologist, big brother, confidant, disciplinarian, punching bag, and voodoo doll.

There is no such thing as an off day or a typical day. Every day is frenetic and every day is different. But a look at just part of my day—thirteen and a half hours of it—on Friday, June 3, 2011, offers a glimpse at some of the craziness beyond merely assembling a team that real-life general managers have to juggle.

The Dodgers were in Cincinnati for a weekend series with the Reds. We were 26-31 and six and a half games behind the Giants.

I flew to Phoenix to see our extended spring staff and to meet with two of our top relief pitchers, who were going through difficult adjustments.

Hong-Chi Kuo, a gifted left-hander from Taiwan, had had two Tommy John surgeries and two other elbow surgeries. He'd come back so often that our trainer Stan Conte affectionately called Kuo the "cockroach," because "you can't kill him."

Besides the physical injuries, Kuo had battled anxiety issues for several years. He twice fell victim to the so-called Steve Blass disease, named after the Pirates pitcher of the 1970s who suddenly and inexplicably lost the ability to control his pitches. The same psychological problem derailed the careers of Mark Wohlers, Rick Ankiel, and Dontrelle Willis.

In 2009, one year after he went 5-3 with a 2.14 earned run average, struck out ninety-six batters in eighty innings, and won Game 2 of the National League Championship Series for us, Kuo suddenly developed Steve Blass disease. He was warming up in Dodger Stadium and threw a series of balls over the bullpen fence onto the field. When he went back to our training facility in Arizona to work on his control and consult with two sports psychologists, he was throwing off a mound one day and hit a trainer—who was walking on *another* field.

Another time, in San Francisco, Torre pinch-hit for our starter in the fifth inning, but he didn't have anyone warming up in the bullpen. I couldn't imagine Joe was making a mistake like that, but then I saw him go out to home plate and call over Giants manager Bruce Bochy. Torre let Bochy know that Kuo was coming in the game. He had been warming up under the stands because he couldn't keep from throwing his pitches onto the field from the visitors' bullpen, which is located down the first base foul line. I've never seen anything like that.

Kuo worked extremely hard with the two sports psychologists and made a phenomenal comeback. In 2010, he became the first Taiwanese player to make the All-Star team. He went 3-2 with twelve saves and a 1.20 ERA—the lowest ERA in the major leagues that season and the lowest ever by a Dodger pitcher with at least fifty innings of work. Kuo allowed just twenty-nine hits and eight runs in sixty innings. Opponents batted just .139 against him. The word *dominant* was an understatement.

His fabulous performance in 2010 earned him a huge pay raise, from $950,000 to $2.75 million, and he was, of course, a major part of our plans for the 2011 season. But in his first five appearances, covering just three innings, he walked five and gave up five runs. After allowing another two earned runs in his next two innings of work, Kuo came to manager Don Mattingly on May 10 and said he was letting the team down and wanted to quit.

I thought, Letting the team down? To me, walking away would be letting the team down.

Taking $2.75 million with him was letting the team down. Having a few bad outings in April and early May—was that letting the team down? No. It just seemed to me that this guy who had been a warrior for so long was suddenly overwhelmed by his challenges.

We put Kuo on the disabled list on May 11 and he went to Arizona with the young players who were either hurt or couldn't make a minor-league club out of Spring Training. I met with him at about 11 a.m. in an office at Camelback Ranch, our Spring Training complex.

I asked Kuo how he felt and he said, "Fine." Then I asked why he thought he was struggling on the mound.

"I expect perfection all the time and when I'm not perfect I don't cope very well," he said.

"Baseball's not geared to perfection," I told him, then recounted what has been said a million times about the sport. "Baseball's a game of failure."

Kuo smiled. He knew.

"So what else is bothering you?" I asked.

"Nothing."

"Do you feel okay physically?"

"Yes."

"Can I do anything for you?" I asked

"No."

"You have any feel for when you may start pitching again?"

All I got was a shrug of the shoulders.

I told him how much I appreciated everything he had gone through, how proud he should be of what he had accomplished, and how he could do it again.

All he did was smile.

"Well, anything else?" I asked.

"Thank you for coming here to talk to me."

As he left the office, I thought: Not much left for this guy. And my instincts were proven correct. Kuo came back to the club on June 21 and worked twenty-two innings the rest of the season, allowing twenty-two runs. He never pitched in the major leagues again.

A HALF HOUR EARLIER, I had met with another talented, and at that point frustrating, reliever.

Kenley Jansen was an amazing story that began in 2010 as he transitioned from being a nonroster catcher and potential Rule 5 draft or release candidate to a major-league relief pitcher and then later to one of the best closers in baseball.

A native of Curacao, Kenley was a promising defensive catcher who started for the Netherlands in the 2009 World Baseball Classic and was selected for the Futures Game, which features baseball's top prospects at the annual All-Star break. Kenley struggled offensively.

We were at a critical point with Jansen in 2010. We either had to put him on our major-league roster or risk losing him to the Rule 5 draft, which is designed to stop minor-league players from being stashed too long in any one organization. A player who is signed at age eighteen or younger can be drafted by another team if the team that signed him hasn't promoted him to the forty-man roster after five minor-league seasons. Players who are nineteen or older when they sign can be selected after four years, if not protected.

Every spring I encouraged the player development staff to think about players who perhaps had one or two exceptional tools but weren't going to be good enough to play in the big leagues at the position they were presently playing.

Midway through the 2009 season, our director of player development, De Jon Watson, and his staff decided to see if they could salvage Jansen's career by making him a pitcher. He had a great arm but had never been on the mound professionally.

Jansen appeared in eleven games late in the 2009 season for our

High-A club at Inland Empire and had uninspiring numbers but showed that power arm, and the player development staff thought they may have discovered something. He gave up fourteen hits, eleven walks, and six earned runs in 11⅔ innings. But he struck out nineteen. So we decided to see what he could do in 2010. All he did was tear through the California League with a 1.50 ERA and twenty-eight strikeouts in eighteen innings, then looked even better at Double-A Chattanooga, where he went 4-0 with eight saves and fifty strikeouts in twenty-seven innings.

We brought him to the majors on July 24, 2010, and he struck out two in a perfect inning of work in a 3–2 win over the Mets at Dodger Stadium. His statistics the rest of the year were impressive. He worked twenty-seven innings in twenty-five games, had four saves, an ERA of 0.67, allowed just twelve hits, and struck out forty-one of the 109 batters he faced.

As impressive as his numbers were, Jansen still needed a lot of work. He was easy to run on. His secondary pitches were virtually nonexistent.

Kenley made the Opening Day roster in 2011 but clearly hadn't worked on his game enough during the off-season or spring. He gave up four runs on four hits and a pair of walks in one inning against the San Francisco Giants in the second game of the season. Seventeen days later, he gave up five earned runs in a third of an inning in a 10–1 loss to the Braves.

But before and after those disasters, Jansen had some respectable outings. And all the while, we were being rocked with injuries in the bullpen. Jonathan Broxton, who was supposed to be our closer, was down. Kuo was dealing with his anxieties in Arizona. Vicente Padilla, who had stepped into the closer's role briefly, was recovering from forearm surgery. Blake Hawksworth, whom we had acquired in a trade with St. Louis during the winter, went on the disabled list with a groin strain.

By mid-May, we had eleven players on the disabled list and Jansen, despite his erratic performance, was being used deeper and deeper in games. Then, on May 23, we went into the bottom of the ninth inning against Houston with 3–1 lead and Mattingly called on Jansen to close. Kenley started out okay, striking out Chris Johnson, giving up a single to Billy Hall, and striking out Matt Downs. Then the game began to unravel. Hall took second base on what was scored as catcher's indifference but is described more accurately as just another example of Jansen's inability to freeze runners. Angel Sanchez walked. Then Hall, who at that point in his career had the speed of a sundial, took off on the front end of a double steal. No throw. Runners on second and third, two outs. Michael Bourn ran the count full, then laced a double to right to drive in Hall and Sanchez and tie the score at three. Jansen followed by getting two quick strikes on Clint Barmes, only to hit him with a pitch. Finally, Hunter Pence put an end to the nightmare with a single to left that scored Bourn and sent the Astros home with a 4–3 win.

In two-thirds of an inning, Jansen threw thirty-eight pitches—thirty-six of them fastballs—and let runners steal and take bases on him at will.

A few days later, Kenley asked manager Don Mattingly when Padilla was coming off the disabled list, knowing that would mean someone would be sent back to the minor leagues. Jansen already had been sent back to the minors, briefly, earlier in the month to work on his secondary pitches and holding runners on base. He wasn't happy about the demotion but was called back quickly when Broxton went on the DL. Now he was worried—rightly so—that he might be bound for Chattanooga again.

Mattingly told Jansen he expected Padilla back "soon," and almost immediately Kenley said his shoulder was hurting.

At that point, we couldn't afford to waste time and a roster space on relievers who weren't going to pitch, whether they were hurt or not. We put Jansen on the disabled list. Almost as soon as he was officially out for fifteen days—and drawing major-league pay instead of a minor-league salary—Jansen said his shoulder felt fine.

So now he is in Arizona and I am going to meet with him just before my session with Kuo. This happens to be "weigh-in" day for the players and Jansen has come in seven pounds heavier than his last weigh-in, a week before. Here's a young pitcher who has enjoyed some success in the major leagues, but hasn't yet shown the discipline to work on improving the holes in his game.

"Kenley, let me ask you something," I said as the two of us sat in the trainer's room on the minor-league side of Camelback Ranch. "If you and I were just friends who loved and understood baseball, and if I told you I had a pitcher who gained seven pounds in a week, who had just one pitch he trusted in a big-league game, who couldn't stop any runner from stealing a base, and who lacked confidence, what should I do with that pitcher?"

"He shouldn't be in the big leagues," he said.

"Well, that's you right now," I said.

"Me?"

"Yes, you."

We talked for another fifteen minutes. Actually, to be more accurate, I spoke for another fourteen and a half minutes.

Kenley nodded and said nothing.

Finally, at the end, Kenley said he appreciated hearing the truth from me. He said he didn't want to be ordinary. He wanted to be great for a great team . . . All the right things.

Time will tell, I thought.

And time did tell.

Just fifteen days later, Kenley returned to the majors on June 18, 2011, with a scoreless inning of work against the Astros. Including that outing, he appeared in thirty games the rest of the season. He allowed just two earned runs, struck out sixty-one, had seven holds, and four saves.

From the beginning of the 2012 season through 2016, Kenley appeared in 333 games and pitched 328 innings, allowing only 204 hits and 78 walks while striking out 495 hitters and setting the Dodgers' all-time saves record.

He was anything but ordinary.

On the contrary, his last five seasons with the Dodgers were Hall of Fame worthy. Not bad for a converted catcher.

MOST DAYS, I'm so busy I simply forget to eat. This isn't one of them. I'm hungry. Just as I'm walking into a place near Camelback Ranch, my cellphone rings. It's Josh Rawitch, our then vice president for communications, and he's got news that quickly takes my appetite away. A newly hired intern has posted on the Internet a confidential report I've prepared for our amateur scouts in advance of the amateur draft, which starts in seventy-four hours. The report is an organizational recap in which I discuss the major-league club and our top prospects, including what I consider to be our strengths and weaknesses and timelines when I expect key players to be ready for the big leagues.

Confidential?

Not anymore.

A college student is given a golden opportunity to see how a major-league draft room works. He is allowed to listen to scouts discuss high school and college players with the general manager. And, with this dream access, he decides it's so cool that he needs to tell the world about it, including revealing confidential details that affect scores of lives and careers. Who does that?

Needless to say, this is the intern's last day with the Dodgers' organization. He didn't last one week.

. . .

TWO HOURS after the amateur scouting debacle, I am preparing to go to Phoenix Sky Harbor Airport to fly back to Los Angeles and I get another call. This one is from trainer Stan Conte, who has juggled sixteen moves to the disabled list in the first eight weeks of the season. Stan tells me Padilla won't be activated as planned today. His neck hurts and he says he can't go. We had planned on him taking Jon Garland's spot in the rotation. Garland, who has never been on the disabled list in eleven seasons as a major leaguer until this spring, is having severe shoulder problems that will eventually require surgery. He isn't even with the team in Cincy. So, now with Padilla scrapped, we are short a pitcher. I call De Jon Watson and ask him to send John Ely from our Triple-A club and get him to Cincinnati as soon as possible.

Padilla, an interesting sort, is a tough read. Gifted with a power arm and above-average pitching intellect, he was released by the Texas Rangers with two months to go in the 2009 season. It didn't matter that the Rangers were in contention or that Padilla still had millions left on a contract. He had worn out his welcome in Texas.

YEARS EARLIER, while I was in San Francisco, the Giants needed starting pitching. Philadelphia called and offered Padilla for Kirk Rueter, who was in the final weeks of a stellar career and wasn't pitching at all. I went to Felipe Alou, the manager and a truly good soul, and asked about Padilla.

Felipe said, "I like the pitcher. I do not like the man."

In 2009, the Dodgers were in dire need of pitching late in the year so we had to take a flyer on Padilla when he was released by Texas. We signed him for $85,000 to cover the last six weeks of the season. We needed a starter, even one that Texas, a contender, had just released and was paying millions to not be on the team.

"I need a starting pitcher, Vicente, and you need a job," I told Padilla. "If you get released by two contending teams within weeks of one another, your free agent value will be zero. I will give you a chance, but one slipup and you will be gone before the sun rises on another day.

"Are we clear?" I added.

"You will see the real Vicente Padilla, I promise," he vowed.

I wasn't sure what he meant, but I was gambling it was going to be good for all of us.

It was, and the Dodgers wound up keeping him for two more seasons, where he was more good than bad.

Adam Katz happened to be the agent for Padilla and Kenley, so I called him to fill him in on both players. He appreciated the conversation I had with Jansen and was stunned to hear Padilla couldn't pitch. Adam had begged me to sign Padilla and vowed to do everything within his power to keep Vicente on the straight and narrow. I like Adam. I have known him since he represented Sammy Sosa when Sosa and I were in Chicago together. Adam is the kind of agent you can have an open dialogue with as long as you never forget that he works for the player. After years of hard-line negotiating, Adam and I decided we would work in a "cooperative effort" on any player issues.

"Thanks for letting me know about the conversation with Jansen," Katz says. "I'll call you back in a couple minutes and get to the bottom of the Padilla situation. Promise. I can't believe he isn't pitching."

I look at my watch. It's 3:17 p.m. Pacific.

Our game in Cincinnati is starting in less than an hour. This is a big trip for us.

We've struggled offensively and wasted some good starting pitching. Three-fourths of our infield and five of our top relievers are all injured at the same time. The Reds are the defending National League Central champs. We have three games with them, three in Philadelphia against the defending National League East champions, and four against our division rivals, the Colorado Rockies. When this year's schedule came out last August, I knew this trip was going to be a test. I couldn't have guessed we would start it with eight players on the disabled list—and about to make it ten.

We are fifteen minutes into the first game of this pivotal trip when Rafael Furcal comes in to make a terrific play on a grounder hit by Drew Stubbs, Cincinnati's leadoff man. Two innings later, Furcal is out of the lineup with an oblique strain he suffered on the throw. We've just gotten Raffy back. He broke a thumb sliding head-first into third base in a 6–1 win over the Giants on April 11 and didn't return until May 22, just twelve days ago. Now we are scrambling again.

I get a text message from Lovelace: "Let's think about Gordon for Furcal."

Gordon is Dee Gordon, son of former major-league pitcher Tom "Flash" Gordon, and our top infield prospect.

Before my flight takes off, I send a text to former major-league infielder Jose Vizcaino, who, along with our minor-league roving infield instructor, Matt Martin, has been working with Gordon at shortstop and has a great relationship with the kid. Jose was primarily a shortstop, but played all four infield positions in an eighteen-year career that started with the Dodgers and included stints with the Cubs, Mets, Indians, Giants, Yankees, Astros, and Cardinals. He was the first player I traded for when I was with the Cubs. We got him from the Dodgers. Years later, we acquired him when I was with the Giants. He is a good man, one who made the most of his talents and has the championship rings to prove it.

At this point in his development, Gordon is a very good prospect, but shortstop is a difficult position to play at the major-league level and Dee has played fewer than fifty games at Triple-A. If I am going to bring him to the big leagues slightly before I feel he's ready, I want him to have as much support as possible.

As my plane pushes back from the gate at Sky Harbor Airport, I text Jose to be ready to fly to Cincinnati first thing in the morning.

When I land in Los Angeles, the game in Cincinnati is over. We lost 2–1. We've scored one run in two games after what had looked like a breakout stretch when we scored twenty-three in three games. It's frustrating.

Around 9 p.m. Pacific time, I'm back in Los Angeles. I call our Triple-A manager, Lo Bundy, and leave a message to call back about Gordon. Bundy and the Albuquerque Isotopes are in Memphis, so it's 11 p.m. there. They've already finished tonight's game and have a bus to catch at 4:45 a.m. to go to the airport for a flight to Austin and another bus ride to Round Rock, Texas, where they will be playing the next night.

While I am waiting to hear back from Lo, I get Mattingly and Lovelace on the phone. It's midnight in Cincinnati. We are a few minutes into discussing our options when Bundy calls and gives me his personal briefing on Gordon. I relay his thoughts to Don and Vance, then hang up and call Conte to get an update on Furcal. Stan doesn't answer. I'm worried he's on the top stanchion of the Roebling Suspension Bridge in Cincinnati about to become the seventeenth member of the team to go on the DL himself.

I call Todd Tomczak, our assistant trainer. I tell him I really need Stan. If Furcal is going on the disabled list, I have to get a player to Cincinnati in the morning.

My next call is to Scott Akasaki. I ask him to look into flights from Memphis to Cincinnati that will allow us to get a player in town before tomorrow's game at 4 p.m. Eastern time. Scott knows there is an 8:25 a.m. flight because he's already booked a seat for John Ely, the pitcher we called up a few hours ago when Padilla declared he couldn't go.

Speaking of Padilla, I realize I haven't heard back from Adam Katz. He was supposed to call me "in a couple minutes" to give me a fill on Padilla. That was six hours ago.

At 9:15, I am back on the phone with Mattingly and Lovelace when Conte calls. He tells me he's 90 percent sure Furcal is headed to the DL, but he wants to do one more check in the morning before making a final decision. I tell him fine, but do it before 7:30 a.m. Cincinnati time because I need to make a call to the boys in Memphis.

While all this is going on, I have another ball in the air. Juan Uribe, whom we signed to a three-year, $21 million contract in the winter to serve as protection at second, third, and short, is ready to come off the disabled list. He is rehabbing at Class-A Rancho Cucamonga, in California. I have Vance call Manny Mota, who is with Uribe in Rancho, and ask if Juan can get to Cincinnati in time for Sunday's game.

The answer comes back: No. He wants to play one more rehab game before being activated. Besides, his family is coming to town and he wants to visit with them.

Oh really, I think. Nice move. Take another day. We're only paying you $27,000 a day to visit with your family.

WITH THE URIBE OPTION OUT, I call Scott and tell him Conte will examine Furcal at 7:30 a.m. Cincinnati time. I've decided I'm not going to call up Gordon. Instead, I'll bring up Ivan DeJesus Jr., a former second-round draft pick, who made the big-league club out of Spring Training but struggled and had just been sent back to

Triple-A on May 13. I tell Scott that as soon as Conte makes a final decision on Furcal, he will have to make sure DeJesus gets on the right plane—either one headed to Texas or the one with Ely bound for Cincinnati.

About 11:30 p.m. Memphis time, I call Lo Bundy and tell him I'm putting Gordon on hold and tell him about the DeJesus travel options.

Lo goes quiet for a second. "We have to be able to get DeJesus's gear sorted out before we take the four forty-five bus to the airport. Don't worry. We'll get it done."

"Don't take any Ambien," I jokingly tell Bundy. "You'll miss the bus in five hours."

"Naw, Ned," Lo says. "This is one of those nights where you watch TV till three or so, then get a shower and head to the lobby."

As soon as I get off the phone with Bundy, I text Vizcaino and let him know we are going to wait on Gordon. He doesn't have to fly to Cincinnati in the morning. It's 9:45 p.m. his time.

I call De Jon and bring him up to speed on everything. He's involved in all these moves, but since I personally called Bundy for a review of Gordon, I wanted to get back to De Jon and make sure he knows everything that went into the decision to call up DeJesus. We end our call with a recap of the intern's blog publishing our confidential draft information.

"I still can't believe it," De Jon says.

JUST BEFORE 1 A.M. CINCINNATI TIME, I call Lovelace and Mattingly one more time to tie up the loose ends and discuss our next move. Marcus Thames is supposed to be coming off the DL in a few days and we need to decide how we make room on the roster. Vance and Don are sitting in Don's hotel room. I ask Vance if he saw the blog.

"Brother, I was furious," he says. "Where do we find people with so little common sense and integrity? My blood was boiling. I can only imagine what you were feeling."

Numb. That's what I was feeling.

I CHECK WITH AKASAKI one more time. He tells me the travel arrangements are all set. DeJesus will be at the Memphis airport heading to Cincy and the big leagues or following his Triple-A teammates to Round Rock on a later flight.

Finally, time to wind down a little. I watch some television—baseball highlights, hockey highlights. Game 2 of the NHL Stanley Cup finals will be tomorrow in Vancouver. The email messages and calls are quiet. It's 3 a.m. in Cincinnati, midnight in L.A. I'm thinking perhaps we bring Gordon to Philly in a few days. Better alert Vizcaino again.

I fall asleep.

The demands of the job made it difficult to shut my mind off most nights. From early February through late October I'd get a few days off, but even those were filled with tough decisions, emotional phone calls, and worries about everything from a pitcher's elbow to a minor-league prospect's work ethic. There is a constant internal monologue. It's just how it is. Most of the time, I ate when I could and shifted my thoughts from one topic to another as quickly as possible. I missed family outings and time with friends and loved ones. Even when I carved out a little personal time, I was still tethered to my cellphone and inbox. I prepared every day for the unexpected not knowing what I'd be called on to fix, but knowing I'd be called on to fix something. I'm not complaining, just explaining.

A major-league general manager multitasks and juggles all day, every day. I'd lay my head on the pillow at the end of a typical eighteen-hour day knowing I had a half a dozen major decisions looming in the morning. Then there'd be another eighteen-hour day and maybe a twenty-two-hour one after that. As exhausting as it all was, trying to fall asleep was a nightly challenge.

I'm awake at 5 a.m. the day after, with two hours of sleep, to find an email from Conte. Furcal is headed to the DL. Another email from Scott confirms DeJesus and Ely are on their way to Cincinnati. I send a text to Adam Katz about Padilla.

"Anything?"

Crickets.

ONE FINAL NOTE ON PADILLA: After pitching the final two months of the season with the Dodgers, we have an interest in signing him as a free agent. It is November and I am driving south on 110 past the University of Southern California campus and Los Angeles Coliseum when my phone rings. It's Adam.

"What's up?" I ask.

"Padilla has been involved in a shooting accident in Nicaragua. I think he will be okay," Katz offers.

"What happened?"

"Apparently, he was at a shooting range with a buddy and his gun went off and the bullet went into his leg."

"Oh, that's all?" I reply, shaking my head.

"He still wants to pitch for you, so I hope this doesn't stop you from signing him," Adam says.

"We'll see, Adam. Call me after hunting season ends down there. If it ever does end."

We signed Vicente a few months later.

I DIDN'T KNOW IT at the time, of course, but that one "Day in the Life" came almost exactly midway through my nine years as general manager of the Los Angeles Dodgers. I had crazier days. Lots crazier. But rarely did I have one much less crazy. This day shows the many decisions and people depended upon to help a team be successful.

The Big Chair isn't a recliner. It's a hot seat that never relents. You're strapped in 24/7 waiting for the next jolt of electricity—not knowing when it will come or where it will come from.

Chaos and crisis management. Pick a day. Any day. That was a day in my life.

Eighteen
TICKET TO THE STARS

. . . .

I have been blessed to meet some amazing people in my career; the names and numbers in my cellphone stagger me. The list of baseball greats I've had dinner or drinks with would fill a wing of the Hall of Fame: Mickey Mantle, Roger Maris, Billy Martin, Willie Mays, Ron Santo, Ernie Banks, Billy Williams, Fergie Jenkins, Barry Bonds, Clayton Kershaw, Mike Piazza, Sandy Koufax. There are dozens more great people as well as a long list of National Hockey League executives and players I have befriended.

So you'd think, then, the general manager of the Los Angeles Dodgers would be right at home with big-time celebrities, but that's not the case. I can be sometimes flaky when it comes to dealing with the pop culture world. When it comes to baseball and hockey, I'm there; however, when it comes to movie stars and television personalities, not so much.

I met Ray Liotta and didn't know who he was even though he had been a Hollywood star for years and had been in movies about the Italian mafia and baseball. I had similar incidents with TV personality Katie Couric and another star who is a great baseball fan, Will Ferrell. It was never out of disrespect. I would have had a much better chance of identifying them if they had numbers on their backs.

IT WAS SOMEWHAT IRONIC that in 2012 I prodded my dear friend Tom Sherak, president of the Academy of Motion Picture Arts and Sciences, to take me to the Academy Awards show. We sat in the fourth row, center section. Seated around me were Brad Pitt, George Clooney, Meryl Streep, Michelle Williams, Tom Cruise, Martin Scorsese, and Steven Spielberg, to name a few. I needed a scorecard to tell who was who.

The show came as the McCourt ownership era was winding down and new owners were on the way. Hardly the time to take it easy, but I also figured it was a once-in-a-lifetime opportunity and I had missed enough of life. I would miss nothing the next day in Spring Training. On Saturday, the day before the show, I called Frank to tell him I planned to leave Sunday morning's workout at Camelback Ranch a little early to fly back to L.A. It was more courtesy than anything else, since I wasn't exactly covering first base on pickoffs or shagging fly balls. I told him I had a chance to go to the Oscars. Frank was surprised, but didn't make a big deal of it. He actually encouraged me not to worry about the Dodgers for a day— or at least for a few hours.

BASEBALL WAS MY FRONT-ROW TICKET to the stars. The game allowed me to go to the Academy Awards, to meet A-list Hollywood and TV stars—some of whom I forgot I met. But maybe the greatest starstruck blessing my career gave me was one magical evening with Frank Sinatra.

Tom Dreesen made it happen. Dreesen is from the south suburbs of Chicago. He is a gifted comedian and a true Cubs fan, two passions that, for most of his life, went hand in hand. We became friends soon after I joined the Cubs.

Tom appeared on *The Tonight Show* many times and opened for Sinatra for more than a decade. From time to time, Tom would ring me up for Cubs tickets, and I once even arranged for him, forty-eight at the time, to serve as bat boy for the Cubs.

On Thursday, May 14, 1992, the Cubs were in San Francisco on an off day. When Tom called, my first thought was he was calling for tickets, which would be fine since we were playing in cold and blustery Candlestick Park the next three nights and that meant there'd be plenty of empty seats. But Tom didn't need tickets, he had tickets to give.

"Hey, my friend, I have two tickets for our show tonight," Dreesen said, referring to a Sinatra concert where he'd be the opening act. "We are playing in Redwood City and I wanted to know if you would like to come down for the show."

Billy Connors, the Cubs pitching coach, and I met Tom at the Fairmont hotel and rode in his limousine to Redwood City. Frank was about an hour behind us getting to the arena. I heard him in the dressing room next door and told Tom I was going to say hello.

"Ned, he's not the kind of guy who is going to want someone just stopping in to say hello. I can't let you do it."

I was disappointed, but grudgingly agreed and hoped there might be another opportunity.

The performances were great.

We all left together for the ride back to the city and our limos were parked next to each other. Sure enough, there was Frank, separated only by a car door. I got up to say hello.

"You can't do that," Tom warned. "We need to get out of here and beat the traffic."

"Tom," I said, "when am I ever going to have a better chance to meet Frank Sinatra?"

Tom was silent.

"How long have you known Frank?"

"I've known Frank a very long time and we have been friends for a long time," he said.

"And where do you spend Christmas, New Year's, and other holidays?"

"At Frank's house."

"So, you consider him a good friend?"

"Absolutely. A great friend."

"But not a good enough friend to introduce Billy and me to him?"

Silence.

"I tell you what," Tom said. "We are going to dinner at Tommy Toy's restaurant. They are shutting it down for Frank. If he is in a good mood when he meets the owner, the maître d', the chef, I will bring you back. You say hello and then you two have got to go."

It sounded great. We had a chance.

Sure enough, that's what happened.

We stood in a short receiving line and met the great Sinatra. I thanked him for his music and for his time. Billy and I began to work our way out of the private room and were just about to the door when I heard this voice—*The* Voice.

"Where are you guys going? You're not going to stay for dinner?"

"We just wanted to say hello and say thank you," I said.

"I'm asking you to stay for dinner. Are you going to insult me and say no?"

First, you didn't say no to Frank. Second, this would be one of the most historically cool evenings of my life.

We sat at a round table for eight with Frank, Tom, and some of their close friends. The dinner lasted a couple of hours. The conversation varied from movies, entertainers, baseball, to childhood memories. Frank was beyond gracious—and funny.

About an hour in, Frank looked at Tom and said, "Who the fuck are these two guys?"

Billy, taking a sip of water at the time, choked for a second.

Tom chuckled, reintroduced us, and settled the room a little.

THANKS TO MY CAREER in baseball, I later met a man who had an incredible influence on Sinatra's career—Mo Ostin. Born in 1927, Mo moved from Brooklyn to Los Angeles when he was fourteen. He earned a degree from UCLA in 1951, and took a low-level position at a record company name Clef, a jazz label that became Verve Records.

One day at Verve, Mo was told to find an attorney to help the company. He wound up hiring Milton "Mickey" Rudin, whose clients included none other than Frank Sinatra. Rudin and Frank, who would work together from 1955 until 1987, both took an immediate liking to Mo and later hired him as president when they started their own label, Reprise Records.

Under Mo, Reprise had a lineup that included Sinatra, Ella Fitzgerald, Sammy Davis Jr., and the Kinks. Mo went to the Monterey Pop Festival in 1967 and signed a left-handed guitarist and vocalist by the name of Jimi Hendrix.

Ostin eventually became president of Reprise's parent company, Warner Bros., where he put together a lineup that was music's equivalent of the 1927 Yankees' Murderer's Row. He signed or worked with Dean Martin, Louie Armstrong, Miles Davis, Quincy Jones, George Harrison, John Lennon, the Beach Boys, Neil Young, Paul Simon, James Taylor, Eric Clapton, the Who, U2, the Grateful Dead, the Eagles, Madonna, Rod Stewart, George Benson, ZZ Top, Steely Dan, Prince, Frank Zappa, Van Halen, Joni Mitchell, Red Hot Chili Peppers—and comedians Steve Martin, Richard Pryor, and Bill Cosby.

I met Mo through Bob Daly, former chairman of the Dodgers,

who also had a tremendous career at CBS and, with Mo, at Warner Bros. A few weeks after Opening Day 2015, Bob brought Mo to lunch, and after a half hour or so of banter about the coming season, I turned the conversation from baseball to entertainment.

"Mo, you knew Sinatra as well as just about anybody," I said. "What was he really like?"

"There was no one like Frank," Mo said, smiling at the memories. "I was with him for years, from 1960 until he died. Every room he walked in, he brought electricity. You knew you were in the company of someone gifted and special. He had a charisma like no one else I ever met."

Mo told me he became friends with all the guys from the Rat Pack, and reminisced about sitting at the front table with his wife one opening night at the Sands Hotel in Las Vegas. Joining the Ostins at the VIP table were Marilyn Monroe, Ava Gardner, Peter Lawford, and Peter's wife, Patricia Kennedy Lawford.

"Marilyn would come to Frank's recording sessions," Mo said. "She would sit as close to me as you are. She loved Frank."

"Was she as striking as everyone says?" I asked.

"Without a doubt, very much so," he said. "But Ava Gardner. Wow! She was the most beautiful woman I ever met in Hollywood. Not only was she beautiful, she was sexy. She was the one girl who had control over Frank. He never was as vulnerable as when he was with Ava—or trying to be with Ava."

Hearing firsthand accounts of the life and loves of Frank Sinatra was spellbinding. I remember wishing my dad, my uncles, and my childhood buddies from Franklin Park could be with me when suddenly I realized, with goose-bump chills, that this was the thirty-third anniversary of my dad's death—April 27, 2015.

Do coincidences like this really just happen? I wondered to myself. I don't think so. This was a spiritual moment for me.

"Had you been in L.A. when Frank was alive, you two would have become good friends," Mo offered. "He loved sports, and he always liked being around good people. "Plus you being a *paisan*—it would have been a natural."

I'D LIKE TO THINK Mo was right. Frank and I could have been friends. And I got a hint of the possibility during that 1992 dinner I had with Sinatra in San Francisco when he offered up a little secret.

"You know I grew up in Hoboken, New Jersey," Frank said. "It was right across the Hudson River from the Polo Grounds. Although I am a great friend of Tommy Lasorda—I love Tommy—and while I've lived in L.A. a very long time, I really grew up a Giants fan."

Oh my, I thought. *If Lasorda only knew.*

Well, years later, I made sure he did.

The Giants were in Los Angeles for a nationally televised game Saturday, September 5, 1998. Orel Hershiser was pitching for the Giants against Tommy's Dodgers. If Hershiser in black and orange wasn't already enough of a backdrop for a tough day for Tommy, there was more.

Sabean and I had no place to sit due to the overflow press contingent. We were invited to sit with Tommy in his booth.

Sabean wanted no part of it.

I told him we didn't have much choice except to disrespect Lasorda and have no place to sit.

Sabean relented.

We sat with Tommy and three innings in, I began to tell Tommy the story. "Tommy, did you know Frank Sinatra was a Giants fan?"

You would have thought I said, No more free food. Telling

Tommy that his pal Ol' Blue Eyes was a closet Giants fan was far worse than telling him he had to pick up a check—which he was famous for not doing. "Who told you that?" he yelled.

I didn't know what to say. While I had laid the bad news out there, I couldn't bring myself to reveal my source was Frank himself. Tommy kept hammering away. After another inning of back-and-forth, Tommy couldn't take it anymore and demanded one last time that I tell him who told me this blasphemy.

"I really don't want to tell you, Tommy," I said. "This isn't going to be good."

"Fuckin' tell me."

"I can't," I said.

"You'd better fuckin' tell me," he said as he began to get out of his chair.

"Well," I began, "when I was with the Cubs, I had a chance to have dinner with Frank, and he told me."

Tommy wasn't amused. On the contrary, he was crushed and furious. He got up and stood over me cursing and questioning the validity of it all.

I was praying the national broadcast cameras wouldn't pan to the booth at that moment.

Can you just hear it?

"There's Giants assistant GM Ned Colletti telling Tommy Lasorda that Frank Sinatra was really a Giants fan."

I told Tommy I had no reason to make up the story. The dinner with Frank, and his confession, came long before I ever had any allegiance to the Giants.

Tommy wasn't in any mood to hear another word. "You guys," he fumed. "You can't sit here with me anymore. You need to leave right fuckin' now. Get the fuck out of here."

As we walked down the concourse, Sabean looked at me and said, "You couldn't have told that story a few innings earlier?"

Nineteen

A NEW BEGINNING . . .
GET THE HARDWARE

. . . .

I had walked that concourse as a visiting executive for decades and then walked it as the general manager of the Dodgers. Some days that concourse wasn't long enough and many days it was filled with far too many people who had too many questions. Suddenly, literally overnight, one set of questions disappeared.

ON MAY 1, 2012, exactly five months after Frank McCourt shocked everyone by agreeing to sell the Dodgers, he officially turned the organization over to Guggenheim Baseball Management. It was important for Frank to find owners he believed would be great owners for the franchise. He fought hard, certainly, to obtain the best financial deal, but also the best people as well, starting with Mark Walter, Earvin "Magic" Johnson, and Stan Kasten.

Two days before, on Sunday, April 29, the new owners addressed the team for the first time. We were wrapping up a 4-2 home stand that included a three-game sweep of the Washington Nationals and newly promoted rookie sensation Bryce Harper. One month into a new season, a new beginning, our record was 16-6, tied with the Texas Rangers for best in the majors.

As incredibly successful as they had been their entire professional lives, the new owners were very excited as they entered the clubhouse as a group to meet the team.

Stan did most of the talking, an early glimpse into his take-charge personality. The players couldn't have been happier.

"It's cool to put names to the faces," pitcher Clayton Kershaw told the *Los Angeles Times* after the meeting. "It sounds like they're very committed, which is always awesome to hear from your ownership. He [Kasten] kept talking about winning, so that was another common goal of ours. It's always good to get familiar with your bosses. It's definitely good to see they have the right intentions."

The intentions were right, but the fates weren't with us.

Exactly two weeks after the new owners introduced themselves to the team, a dream season started to slowly unravel.

On Mother's Day, Sunday, May 13, 2012, Matt Kemp injured an already sore hamstring and was forced to go on the disabled list. He would miss fifty-eight of the next fifty-nine games.

Five days after Kemp went down, second baseman Mark Ellis had his legs cut out from under him on a hard slide by St. Louis infielder Tyler Greene in the seventh inning of a tie game against the Cardinals at Dodger Stadium. Ellis stayed in the game and lined out in the bottom of the seventh inning, but was removed before the start of the eighth. Ellis, never one to exaggerate, told trainer Sue Falsone his leg was really hurting. Falsone, in her first season as the first female head trainer of any of the four U.S. major professional leagues, examined Ellis and immediately ordered her staff to take him to the hospital, where Ellis underwent emergency surgery. The blood flow to Ellis's lower leg had been cut off by the blunt trauma—a freak injury that sometimes is seen in car crash victims, but rarely among athletes. Dr. Neal ElAttrache said that without surgery, Ellis was just hours from losing his leg.

Even with Kemp and Ellis—two key starters—out of the lineup, we managed to hold our own for a few weeks. As late as June 19, we still had the best record in all of baseball. As late as June 25, we had the best record in the National League.

Then, on June 27, we lost a third valuable starter. Andre Ethier suffered a strained left oblique when he tried to check his swing on a pitch from Giants starter Tim Lincecum in San Francisco. The next day, we fell out of first place for the first time all season.

Obviously, with three of our eight regulars on the disabled list, we needed to figure out how to shore things up. Guggenheim sure made that financially easier.

Shortly after new ownership took over, Stan Kasten had come to me and urged us to "think bold." He said we shouldn't be afraid to go back and look at players we had an interest in in the past, but weren't able to afford either because our farm system wasn't in great shape or because of financial limitations.

The first player who came to mind—a guy we really wanted, but never could have afforded on Frank's watch—was Adrian Gonzalez.

In early May, just after Kasten basically gave us free rein, I called Boston GM Ben Cherington.

General managers exchange calls all year long. There are hot times of the season—trading deadlines, just before the GM meetings, and at the Winter Meetings—and there are moderate periods. Typically, it takes until May for a team to settle in and for the GM and staff to begin thinking about deals. But you lay groundwork all year long. Most deals take months to consummate and nearly all begin with a small seed that gets planted with little chance of growing immediately. As time goes on, and as standings change and injuries begin to shift a team's future, a soft idea in April may turn into a blockbuster in August.

I was doing little more than a "checking in" when I called Cherington in early May. But I did bring up Adrian's name. The Red Sox had gotten off to a bad start in what was destined to be a terrible year. They had been in last place in the American League East since the second week of the season and would finish in last place, twenty-six games behind the Yankees.

"I really can't do that," Cherington said when I brought up Gonzalez four weeks into the season. "You know, it would be a white flag. It would be really giving up on this team and this season. I just can't do that."

I said, "Well, file it and maybe down the road, if you change your mind, you know you can make a call to us and we'll see where it goes."

AS THE SEASON MOVED ON, and our injuries piled up, I encouraged my staff to stay in touch with every team, reminding them of Kasten's edict to "think bold."

Ragazzo focused on the Marlins. Rags had a good relationship with Orrin Freeman, who played college baseball at USC and went to work for the Marlins in 1991, the year the franchise began. He was the Marlins' director of scouting from 1995 to 1998 before being named special assistant to the general manager.

Just after the All-Star break, and just before the 2012 nonwaiver trade deadline, Rags came to me and said, "I think there may be a chance the Marlins will talk about Hanley Ramirez."

Ramirez, a three-time All-Star, the 2006 National League Rookie of the Year, and the 2009 NL MVP, was making $15 million with the Marlins. A stiff price, but we were in dire need of help at shortstop. Dee Gordon had joined the parade of injured players earlier in the month when he tore a ligament in his thumb sliding into third base. He would be out six weeks. But even before his injury, we knew we needed help at short. Given a chance to be a major-league regular for the first time in his career, Gordon was hitting just .229 with a dismal .280 on-base percentage when he went down. He also was leading the league with seventeen errors. He should have been playing second base, not short, and he and I had a number of conversations about the move. Dee resisted, firmly but respectfully, before finally agreeing to switch for the 2014 season. The move changed his life.

During the 2014–15 off-season, my successor, Andrew Friedman, traded Gordon to Miami and agreed to pay all of Dee's $2.5 million salary. All Gordon did was lead the National League in hitting (.333), hits (205), and stolen bases (58) and win a Gold Glove at second base. He cashed it all in by signing a five-year, $50 million contract with the Marlins in January 2016.

The morning after Dee signed his new contract he texted me: "Thank you, sir . . . I truly appreciate the tough love you gave me and for giving me an opportunity in 2015 . . . my family and I owe you Mr. Colletti."

That was a class move—one I never could have expected in 2012, when I was trying to trade for Hanley Ramirez to replace an injured Dee Gordon.

(Dee tested positive for a PED a month into the 2016 season, weeks after signing the life-changing contract.)

"Keep me in the loop and keep the conversations going," I told Ragazzo two weeks before the 2012 trade deadline.

A few days later, on Sunday, July 22, I was in Albuquerque with Stan Kasten and De Jon Watson, our head of player development, to watch our Triple-A team. Albuquerque has a beautiful ballpark, but the booth the team set aside for visiting Dodgers personnel is tiny—maybe six feet wide. The three of us—Kasten, Watson, and

I—were jammed in the booth when Ragazzo called with an update on Ramirez. I put Rags on speaker and couldn't help but chuckle at the comical site of three grown men squeezed together in a closet-sized room hunched over a tiny cellphone trying to hear the latest on a possible blockbuster trade.

"They're going to need Nate Eovaldi in the deal and they're not inclined to take any money back," Ragazzo said. "They've got offers with better prospects coming where people want them to eat some of Hanley's money. The money is a key component to them."

Eovaldi was one of our better pitching prospects. He made his major-league debut in August 2011 at age twenty-one with a win over the Arizona Diamondbacks. He didn't make the roster out of Spring Training in 2012 but was called up in late May after a solid two months at Double-A Chattanooga. He was struggling with the big club, going winless in his first seven starts before beating the Diamondbacks on July 16. The day the Marlins told Ragazzo they needed Eovaldi, he started against the New York Mets, going 4⅓ innings, striking out seven, walking one, and allowing just one run.

"Okay," I told Ragazzo after he finished filling us in. "Keep it moving and let's find out where it's going."

The next day, Monday, July 23, 2012, I flew to Phoenix to watch our Rookie League team play. I'm on the phone a lot with Ragazzo when, suddenly, things begin to really heat up. So now, instead of Rags and Orrin Freeman talking, it's me and Marlins' GM Mike Hill. We are getting closer and closer, but I know there is another team involved.

USA Today writer Bob Nightengale reported the other team was Oakland, which to almost everyone's surprise was making a run for the playoffs. So it made sense they might be in on a big trade. The A's had better prospects, but they weren't in a position to swallow

Hanley's salary. If we were going get him, money was going to be the key, just as Rags had said, and I let Stan know it.

"You can't let money be an issue when you can pick up somebody like Hanley Ramirez," Kasten said.

Whew. What a crazy turnaround from the days when Frank turned down a chance to get Cy Young winner CC Sabathia because of taking on added payroll.

That night, on my way to a Rookie League game across town, I decided to stop in at my favorite restaurant in Arizona, Don & Charlie's in Scottsdale. Before I went in, I called Mike Hill one more time from the parking lot. We discussed adding lefty reliever Randy Choate and us sending him minor leaguer Scott McGough. I called De Jon to get his read on McGough. We were on the verge of a deal pending a conversation with Hanley and medical approvals for all four players.

I ended the call and went into the restaurant, which has enough sports memorabilia to rival just about any place but Cooperstown. Meanwhile, my cell battery was showing red. It had less than five percent of its charge left. So I asked Don Carson, one of the owners, and a longtime friend, if he happened to know anyone who had a charger.

"I'll ask around," Don said.

Carson went from table to table asking his customers if anyone had a charger for my phone model. Sure enough, one kind soul had a charger in his car and left his dinner to go get it for me—not knowing he was playing a key role in a big major-league trade that was about to go down.

From Don's restaurant, I drove to beautiful Salt River Fields at Talking Stick to watch our Arizona League rookie team play the D-backs' rookies. The deal for Hanley finally came within a couple of phone calls of being completed. We started exchanging medical information. We were picking up the remainder of Hanley's con-tract, but I told Mike that Mattingly and I needed to talk to Ramirez personally before we closed the deal.

Miami had forced Ramirez to move from his normal position, at shortstop, to third base earlier in the season after signing free agent shortstop Jose Reyes. Ramirez wasn't happy about the move but swallowed his pride and was playing third. We knew we needed him at short, but thought we might use him at third, too, if Juan Uribe, our regular third baseman, continued a frustrating season-and-a-half-long hitting slump.

"Before I can do this, I've got to talk to Hanley and I've got to have Donnie on the phone," I told Hill. "We have to be assured he's going to do whatever we need him to do—play short, play third. We're not going to acquire him and then not have him play where we need him or give Donnie a difficult time, because we still have a lot of things in flux."

Late that night, a little after 11 p.m. West Coast time, 2 a.m. Miami time, Mattingly and I got Ramirez on the phone. Donnie asked Hanley what his thoughts were on playing wherever we asked him to play.

"Look, I'll do whatever you want me to do," he said. "I really don't want to move back and forth, game by game, between two positions. But whatever you need me to do, I'll do."

That was what we needed to hear from Hanley. So we were good there.

The four-player trade was complete, a trade the *Los Angeles Times* hailed as a "Stunning Deal."

We planned to announce the trade Wednesday morning, July 25, but within five or ten minutes of hanging up with Mike Hill, the news exploded all over Twitter. Someone had leaked it and now I had to get hold of Eovaldi. I like Nate and how he approaches the game. I really liked having him with the Dodgers, so I didn't want him finding out about the trade from somebody else—or worse, from Twitter. He was with the team in St. Louis and I called his room about one thirty in the morning, Central time, to give him the news. I woke him up. It was a tough call.

I asked Lovelace, pitching coach Rick Honeycutt, and Mattingly to go to Eovaldi's room and follow up my phone call. I knew he'd be in shock and I wanted them to be there to answer any questions he might have. Nate's a great kid and he's got a chance to have a great career, but we had to give him up to get better. And we still had a ways to go.

HANLEY PLAYED HIS FIRST GAME for the Dodgers—starting at third base—on Thursday, July 26, 2012, in St. Louis, and the team traveled to San Francisco for a three-game series the next day. I went up to San Francisco but stayed busy working the phones. We still needed relief help. On Sunday, Lovelace and I skipped the last game of the Giants series and flew back to Los Angeles to settle into the final forty-eight-hour stretch before Tuesday's trade deadline. When we hit the ground in L.A., we walked into a media storm of rumors that the Seattle Mariners were about to trade their ex-closer Brandon League.

It was getting to that time of the year when I'd need more than one phone. In the days leading up to and through the July 31 deadline, I'd be juggling three phone lines—the cell I carried all year long, a second mobile I'd add for special calls, and the office landline. Then, in the final hours before the deadline, I would have Lovelace and Ragazzo in my office with their phones as well.

I had talked to Seattle GM Jack Zduriencik a few times about League, but the conversations never went very deep. It was not uncommon for deals that had been lightly discussed and dismissed earlier to come to life in the last hours before a deadline, and I was hoping that would be the case in my talks with Zduriencik about Brandon.

Before I made any decision, I needed all the scouts on standby and available. Rick and Vance not only helped fine-tune my thinking, but also reached out to the scouts and had them on the line so I could talk to them in an instant. I read all their reports, and I would have heard them discuss the player perhaps a week earlier, but I wanted to hear it again. I wanted to hear the inflection in their voices. I wanted conviction one way or another. I needed to get to the core of their belief and evaluation process. Information was king and the clocks were ticking.

Along with Rick and Vance and the scouts, I would bring in Billy Mueller, Jose Vizcaino, Aaron Sele, Juan Castro, Mark Sweeney, and Josh Bard at the trade deadline. They knew the players—who in the Dodgers' farm system would be a major-league player and who wouldn't; who would make it in a smaller market but never be a player under the spotlight of a major market like L.A. Their opinions were important.

I thought League was somebody who could help our club and at the same time allow us to go get Shane Victorino from Philadelphia. I knew from a number of conversations with Phillies GM Ruben Amaro that he really wanted Josh Lindblom, a former second-round draft pick of ours who was evolving into a solid middle reliever at age twenty-five. I was willing to give up Lindblom to get Victorino, but I really couldn't trade Josh until I had another arm that could pitch the late innings of games. So when I heard the rumors about League, I immediately sent a text to Zduriencik. We wouldn't have been able to deal for Victorino if we hadn't added League because we were going to have to trade Lindblom. In the small world of baseball, all three players—Josh, Vic, and League—were represented by the same agency group from Brooklyn, Sam and Seth, the Levinson brothers. Three players from three cities and teams located on two coasts playing in two leagues, and all are involved in two trades that are coupled together.

"Hey, if you have any interest in moving League, we have an interest in doing a deal."

"Well, I'm about to do a deal, but what do you have in mind?" he sent back.

"Tell me what you need. I've got sincere interest and we're willing to work out a deal."

Within hours, we had it done. We sent the Mariners two prospects: Logan Bawcom, a twenty-three-year-old right-handed reliever who was 3-3 with a 2.60 ERA at Double-A Chattanooga, and Leon Landry, a star outfielder on the 2009 Louisiana State University national championship baseball team who was leading the Class-A California League in hitting at the time of the trade.

Neither did much after we traded them. Bawcom was 7-8 with a 4.21 ERA from the time we dealt him through the 2014 season. Landry, who showed such promise at High-A, struggled at the next level. He moved up to Double-A Jackson in 2013 and stayed there in 2014, batting just .248 with a .288 on-base percentage and a dismal .347 slugging percentage.

League had five losses and six blown saves for Seattle before losing his closer's job on July 1, but we thought he could help us. And we were right. He saved six games and won two others for us in September. But when he came to us, he was making $5 million—more than fifty times what we were paying the two minor leaguers we gave up for him. So I remember telling Stan Kasten just before we closed the deal that I was going to ask Zduriencik to help out with League's salary. I was going to ask him to pick up a half-million dollars. After all, it was how we had done business for a long time.

I honestly believe if I had told Kasten I was going to make myself the closer, he couldn't have looked more puzzled.

"With all the deals we're making, and going to make, and all the [advertising and sponsor] signage we're adding here in the next year, you're going to ask Jack for half a million dollars?" Kasten said, his voice rising. "He'll never speak to you again. Forget about the money."

THE NEXT MORNING, with little more than thirty hours to go until the nonwaiver trade deadline, we went to work hard on Victorino. Now that we had extra relief help, I could afford to offer Lindblom. Ruben Amaro and I were on the phone most of the day Monday and into the night. The Phillies weren't happy about the medical records on one of the pitchers we were going to add to the deal with Lindblom, so we were going back and forth on other prospects.

Stan Kasten was there the whole time. He was deeply involved in the internal discussions. But about eleven thirty that night, he said he was going to go back to his apartment and get some sleep. "Give me a call," he said. "You've got my cell number. Gimme a call and keep me up to date."

Shortly after that, about midnight, we think we have a deal that might work. So I try to call Stan. No answer. The call goes to his voicemail. I'm trying him every fifteen minutes. Midnight. Twelve fifteen. Twelve thirty. And so on. Now it's two o'clock and still I'm getting no answer. I'm hoping he made it back to the apartment, but there's no way to know.

Finally, at about four o'clock L.A. time, with the sun coming up in Philadelphia, Ruben and I decide to take a recess. We're real close to a deal, but we're not really there yet. And I still can't reach Stan. So I head home for a quick nap. As I pull into my garage, I take a quarter of an Ambien to get me started. I take a little more of the pill when I get inside and set the alarm for six thirty. Next thing I know, the alarm is screaming and I'm lying on my bed with my clothes on. I'm still wearing my suit coat, shirt, pants. No cowboy boots, though. At least I got those off.

I shower, change, and get back to Dodger Stadium five hours before the 1 p.m. West Coast deadline. We finally agree to send Lindblom and right-handed starter Ethan Martin, a former first-round pick, and a player to be named later to Philadelphia for Victorino.

We are elated. In one week, we've brought in an All-Star middle-of-the-order bat who can shore up our infield at short and third. We've added a proven left-handed relief specialist and a veteran closer who can pitch the back end of games for us. In Victorino, we have a leadoff man with a gung-ho attitude who can play center until Kemp comes back and then easily slide over to left or right as needed.

That would have been a productive off-season's worth of work. It was a phenomenal one week. And we still weren't done.

OUR ROTATION WAS a little wobbly with the loss of Eovaldi. We could use another starter and I knew a few would be coming up on the waiver wire. The Phillies led the way, putting Cliff Lee and Joe Blanton on the wire. We claimed them both. Lee was going to cost about $90 million if we got him, but Kasten was there thought by thought and was comfortable with the numbers.

Players on the waiver wire can be pulled back by their team if they are claimed by another team. But there is a deadline, and about five minutes before the deadline, Ruben Amaro called. "You're not going to get Cliff Lee, but if you want, you can get Joe Blanton," he said matter-of-factly.

So Ruben had pulled Cliff Lee back and we started talking about Blanton. I was having lunch at Il Pastaio, my favorite restaurant in

Beverly Hills, when we finally made a deal. Il Pastaio is run by a good group of guys from Sicily, where my relatives are from, and serves some of the best pasta I've ever had. I stepped away from the table and agreed to send the Phillies the proverbial player to be named later, in return for Blanton. That player turned out to be minor-league pitcher Ryan O'Sullivan, a starter turned reliever, who went over to Philadelphia's High-A team in Clearwater, Florida, on August 16, 2012, a little less than two weeks after we made the deal.

BEFORE THE TRADE DEADLINE PASSED, I had been talking to Cherington in Boston about some kind of package. We really wanted Adrian Gonzalez and Carl Crawford. Cherington wanted desperately to unload Josh Beckett. I didn't want Beckett unless I had to take him to get Gonzalez and I didn't feel a lot of pressure to do a deal before the deadline. I knew the Red Sox would put Gonzalez and Crawford on waivers and I knew they would clear because of their salaries. Gonzalez was making $21 million. Crawford was making $19.5 million and was hurting. He had a sore elbow that kept him out of all but thirty-one games of the 2012 season and eventually required Tommy John surgery.

So I let the nonwaiver trade deadline pass, but I kept the lines open with Cherington. He kept pushing Beckett, but Beckett had left his start the night of the nonwaiver deadline, July 31, after just 2⅔ innings. He had back spasms that forced him to miss his next start and stalled any possible trade talks.

In the meantime, Jerry Hairston, our super utility player, finally realized he couldn't go anymore after fighting a sore hip for three months. He was mired in a 3-for-27 slump on August 13 when he agreed to go on the disabled list and he later underwent season-ending surgery. So now I was looking for someone who could play several positions—someone like Boston's Nick Punto.

While I was talking to Cherington, Stan and Mark Walter had their own communications going with the Boston ownership group—John Henry and Larry Lucchino. Mark and Stan were as candid as they could be with their Boston counterparts. "Look, we're not afraid of the money. You give us who you need. We're not afraid of the money."

After one of those conversations, Stan came to me and said, "You know what? I think you're going to hear from Ben in the next coupla days."

And I did.

Aside from the fact that Adrian Gonzalez averaged .297 with 31 homers and 103 RBI during the previous six seasons, we had two other major reasons for wanting him.

First was the dearth of quality first basemen available in the free agent market after the season. We clearly were done with James Loney. Besides his crazy and still-unexplained freeway episode in January, he stopped producing on the field. He was batting just .248 with a grand total of two home runs as of August 13, the day Hairston went on the DL. We knew James wasn't part of our future and there didn't seem to be any great options on the horizon. The most promising free agent first baseman available during the 2012–13 off-season probably was going to be Adam LaRoche, who was on his way to hitting 35 home runs and driving in 100 for the Washington Nationals. We weren't certain he was going to be available and, candidly, we didn't have any real interest in the rest of the first basemen who were coming out.

The other big reason was Adrian's obvious marketing appeal. A native of San Diego whose father played on the Mexican national team, Gonzalez, bilingual and handsome, was the perfect hero for L.A.'s huge Latino community. And tied to that was a new television deal ownership was about to negotiate. Adding someone like Gonzalez, with the allure he would have in our market, would transform the television negotiations from a position of hope and limited credibility to one of strength and unquestioned credibility.

On Thursday, August 23, 2012, Ben Cherington and I finally were close on a deal to bring Gonzalez, Crawford, Beckett, and Punto to the Dodgers when Stan and Mark came into the GM booth during the fifth inning.

"How we doing?" Kasten asked.

"Well, you know, we're walking toward it," I said, and told Stan and Mark that I thought we could get some financial relief back because we were about to take on all $262 million worth of salary from the four players.

"We really don't want to lose this deal," Kasten said. "We need Adrian. We need Carl, even though we know he's not going to be with us the rest of this season [after his Tommy John surgery]. We need these players because we don't have these kinds of guys in our system. We're short. We know we're short. We need to shore it up and I think that this would be a sign to our fan base—with this deal and the Hanley acquisition—that we mean business."

I got it. Stan and Mark were right. We needed this deal. But $262 million is a crazy amount to have to take on. The three of us left the GM booth and walked toward my office.

"I'm going to try and get some more financial relief," I told them.

"No! Just make the deal," Walter told me.

"Look," I said, "I really believe we're going to be able to make this deal and I can get some, you know, some—what's the word here?—sizable, or considerable, financial relief back."

They weren't happy and they were sitting across from my desk when I got Cherington on the phone. "Ben, I'm willing to do this, but we need to get this down closer to two hundred million," I said.

Cherington balked, and when Mark and Stan heard the silence they looked as if they were going to grab the phone out of my hand.

Finally, Ben said, "I don't think we're going to be able to do that. This deal's gonna go away. We can't be paying sixty-two million and give up these players. We're telling our fan base we're out of it, we're done."

The conversation wound down quickly and I hung up.

Walter and Kasten were looking at me with daggers. "You better not have lost this deal," Kasten said.

"I didn't lose the deal," I said. "We still have a deal to be made here. Give me some time, I'll call him back."

Forty-five tense minutes later, I called Cherington back. "Where are you at?" I asked.

"We're not giving you sixty-two million and the players," he said flat out.

"Well, you can't expect us to take on Carl Crawford when he just had Tommy John surgery and he has no chance of playing the last five weeks of this season. He ain't gonna play till, maybe, May next year. We need twelve million dollars of relief."

It turned out Crawford was in the Opening Day lineup in 2013 thanks to a lot of hard work by Carl and our training staff. But we didn't know that would be the case at the time.

"You know what?" I asked Cherington. "We'll go down to two-fifty, but that's all we're going to do. We'll pay it down because of Carl's injury and not knowing what Carl's going to be able to do early in the season next year. I'll give you a little while to think about it, but we need to know tonight."

The two guys on the other side of my desk were glaring. "You better not have lost this deal over twelve million dollars," Kasten said.

"Twelve million dollars is a lot of money," I said.

Mark Walter looked at me and said, "Ned, it *is* a lot of money. But, you know what? I know I can make money. I know we can make money. So I'm not going to let a deal like this go by the wayside for twelve million dollars even though you're right. It is a lot of money. And I know where you're from, how hard your life was when you were young. I know what you've been through here before we arrived. I respect all of that. But we can't let this go. We are going to turn these millions into billions."

Fifteen minutes later, I called Cherington back.

He agreed to the $250 million.

I couldn't help but break into a colossal smile. "There, I just saved us twelve million dollars," I said, and with a theatrical aside, added, "Even though it's really not that much money."

We were all smiling in Los Angeles and I'm sure there were smiles all around in Boston, too.

WE STILL HAD THE PHYSICALS to go through and that took all day Friday, August 24. Meanwhile, word about the deal started to leak and I got a phone call from Dan Halem, senior vice president and general counsel for Major League Baseball. "Ned, I need to ask you something," Halem said after a few minutes of polite chatter. "The commissioner's asked me to call you."

"What's that, Dan?"

"I'm only asking this because you have a penchant for getting everybody to pay everybody's contract," Halem said. "Please don't tell me the Red Sox are paying a substantial amount of these contracts because I don't know if that's gonna fly or not."

I told him the Red Sox were paying $12 million of the $262 million.

"Thank goodness," Halem said. "That, I think, we can handle."

I said, "Good, but we're not there yet. We still have a lot of physicals to complete."

Boy, did we have a bunch of physicals to run through. Nine of them: Gonzalez, Crawford, Beckett, and Punto from the Sox; James Loney and four prospects from the Dodgers—pitchers Allen Webster and Rubby De La Rosa, infielder Ivan DeJesus Jr., and outfielder–first baseman Jerry Sands.

Physicals are always important, but sometimes time prohibits a thorough look. Many trades are completed with one trainer speaking to another after reviewing medical information—without ever laying eyes on a player or doing an X-ray or MRI. One trainer needs to trust and know the other trainer—know who has no problem lying and who is thorough and honorable.

Baseball may be the national pastime, may be a family game, and may be as American as apple pie. But baseball is also a billion-dollar business of ruthless individuals. You need to learn who you can trust and who you can't. By the time we even came close to wrapping up the physicals, it was too late to make any formal announcement even though the news was all over the media. The Red Sox players cleared waivers. But on our end, Sands and De La Rosa hadn't, so they would need to be players to be named later. And we still had one potential speed bump ahead: As a player with ten years' major-league experience, five with the Sox, Beckett had a built-in no-trade clause. And while Crawford didn't have the same five/ten protection, he did have a limited no-trade clause in his contract and the Dodgers were on the list of teams he could reject. Adrian had a limited no-trade clause in his contract as well, but the Dodgers weren't one of the teams on his list.

First thing Saturday morning, Boston time, Ben Cherington called Beckett and Crawford to get them to agree to the trade. He needed their approval in writing. And he was getting it. Finally, we were ready to announce the deal.

Needless to say, we were incredibly excited. The Guggenheim guys were so fired up, they ordered "the Hardware" to Boston right away. "The Hardware" was what they called the private corporate jet. They sent it to Logan International Airport—the airport the McCourt family helped build—to pick up Adrian, Nick, and Josh.

We still were waiting to make a formal announcement when I jumped the gun. I gave the go-ahead for the plane to take off for Los Angeles. We had a home game at six o'clock that night, Pacific time, and I wanted the new guys in the lineup if at all possible.

The Hardware had barely cleared Logan's airspace when my cellphone rang. It was Joe Torre, newly named executive vice president of operations for Major League Baseball. "Are you flying these guys to L.A.?"

I said we were.

"Do you know Commissioner Selig is still debating whether or not to approve the deal and the cash?" Torre asked.

"Well, obviously, I didn't know that, Joe." I knew it wasn't official, but I must have felt the commissioner's office was good with the deal after my conversation with Halem. "I admit, I made a mistake, Joe."

"All right," Torre said. "Let me talk to the commissioner and I hope that, you know, nothing comes out of this fine-wise or a rejection."

I offered to turn the plane around if the commissioner wanted.

"Gimme a little while," Torre said.

A few minutes later he called back. "Okay, the commissioner's approved it, but I gotta tell ya, he's not too happy with you guys jumping the gun on getting the players there."

A few hours later, Dodger Stadium was electric. Clayton Kershaw was on the mound. He gave up three hits and struck out eight in eight innings. But the real magic came in the bottom of the first inning when Adrian Gonzalez, in his first at-bat as a Dodger, hit a three-run homer off Josh Johnson. Pandemonium! Welcome to Hollywood, A-Gone!

. . .

ONE INTERESTING SIDELIGHT OF THE trade was how the media reported it. Every reference I ever saw said the Dodgers acquired
Adrian Gonzalez, Josh Beckett, Carl Crawford, *and* Nick Punto. It
was understandable given the All-Star caliber of the other three
players, but I felt bad for Nick Punto. It was always . . . *and* Nick
Punto. When we met, I told him I thought Nick was his middle
name. I figured his first name was "And."

Twenty

WILD HORSE

• • • • • • • • • • • • • •

Baseball America called it a "puzzling deal." A front-office executive called it "crazy."

"I don't know what's going on in Dodger land," he was quoted as saying. "They must have seen something."

We had, indeed, seen something. We had seen Yasiel Puig—the Wild Horse, as the great Vin Scully would nickname him.

Well, I hadn't seen him yet, but three very good evaluators had laid eyes on him—Logan White, Paul Fryer, and Mike Brito had seen Puig in Mexico and were convinced he was worth the $42 million his handlers wanted even though Puig hadn't played organized baseball in more than a year.

"What are the Dodgers thinking?" Baseball America reporter Ben Badler wrote. "Those who have seen Puig seem lukewarm on his talent. He has good bat speed and generates plus raw power, but scouts have expressed concerns about his hitting approach."

That worrisome hitting approach did surface, when he didn't adjust to great pitching after a couple of seasons. But the opening act was stellar. Puig produced a .305 batting average, a .502 slugging percentage, and an .888 OPS (on-base plus slugging) during his first two seasons in the majors, before injuries derailed him in

2015. Among National League players who appeared in at least 250 games during the 2013 and 2014 seasons, only Andrew McCutchen had a higher batting average and slugging percentage. And Mc-Cutchen won the NL MVP in 2013 and finished third in 2014.

Getting the Dodgers deeply involved once again in the international talent market had been a priority of mine for years. The Dodgers were forerunners, along with Toronto, in scouting and signing players from Latin America. L.A. greats Pedro and Ramon Martinez, Adrian Beltre, Raul Mondesi, Jose Vizcaino, and Pedro Astacio were just a very few who came from the Dominican Republic.

In 1982, my first year in baseball, the percentage of Latin American players in the minor leagues was approximately 7 percent; in 2015, the percentage was close to 40 percent.

By the time I was named GM of the Dodgers, a prominent key to organizational success lay in the international market, especially if teams drafted late in the first round. But for most of the McCourt years, the priority was helping the big-league club with a trade to buy for today at a cost in the future. The July 2 signing date for international players was just in front of the trading deadline and that worked to our disadvantage. Many of my conversations with ownership put me in an either/or position—either spend money to help the big club and make us better now, or invest in the international market and risk losing at the big-league level. There wasn't enough money to win now and build for the future.

On the international market, specifically in the Dominican Republic, the process went something like this: A *buscón* (agent) would bring a stable of soon-to-be sixteen-year-old players to several teams' complexes, work them out, then sign them with the highest bidder. The *buscónes* knew which teams had the money to spend and which didn't. The Boston Red Sox, for example, might have $500,000 to spend on a single player, while the Dodgers didn't have that in their international budget for the year. So what happened? The *buscónes* simply stayed away from the Dodgers. They didn't even bother to bring their best players to Campo Las Palmas, the Dodgers' academy in Guerra, northeast of the capital, Santo Domingo. The Dodgers once had been the trailblazers for baseball in the Dominican. And now we found ourselves shut out in one of the most talent-rich areas in the world.

In a twenty-year period split between San Francisco and Los Angeles, I was part of a midseason sell-off just once—in 2011, the final year of the McCourt era. Instead of scouring other teams for prominent big leaguers who might help our major-league club, I was sifting through organizations trying to find prospects for the player or two we were willing to move. What struck me that year was how many of the contending teams' best prospects were from Latin America.

We had fallen way behind even though we did sign pitchers Rubby De La Rosa, Pedro Baez, and Yimi Garcia. But were weren't signing true difference makers. We needed to be more aggressive in the international market.

So when the new owners came on board May 1, 2012, my first conversation—and nearly every one soon after that—focused on the need to tap the international markets, specifically Latin America.

With the new owners' approval, we decided to go after Jorge Soler, a five-tool prospect who had defected from Cuba in 2011. We were late in the game. The Cubs had been pursuing Soler hard and word started leaking they had a deal in place before we could make our strongest pitch. I was in Seattle with our club for an interleague weekend series, having breakfast at a coffee shop on Sunday, June 10, 2012, when I stepped outside around 10 a.m. and called Barry Praver, Soler's agent.

"He's going to sign somewhere else," Praver confided, then confirmed what I'd been hearing. "He is going to go to the Cubs."

I was disappointed, but I knew we'd turned a corner. We hadn't had a chance to make our best offer, but we'd made it clear the Dodgers were back in the game—willing, again, to make a strong financial bid for serious international talent. Word was out and within ten days it paid dividends.

I got a call from one of Yasiel Puig's agents. "I hear you liked Soler? We think we've got someone better."

I thanked the agent and told him I'd think about it and get back to him, but I knew the time had come to make a stand. Logan White called me and told me he had gotten a call from another agent, Gus Dominguez, about Puig.

It was like the Boston and Florida trades, when we added Adrian Gonzalez and Hanley Ramirez a month apart and began to restart the organization. We needed to regain the confidence of the fan base and reestablish the brand. Now we needed to get back into Latin America and reestablish our standing in that market.

For years, we couldn't even get players to come to our academy in the Dominican because we didn't have the money. Just look at 2011 for proof. That year, Texas Rangers spent $12.83 million on international signings. The Dodgers spent less than $200,000.

We needed a fireworks display to show we were back in business. And Yasiel Puig was a powder keg waiting to explode.

I sent White, Fryer, and Brito, who signed legendary Dodgers pitcher Fernando Valenzuela out of Mexico in 1979, to Mexico City to watch Puig work out. How Puig got to Mexico from Cuba is a story worthy of a book or two. Much has been written about it. The best I've seen was an article by Scott Eden in *ESPN the Magazine* in April 2014. Titled "No One Walks Off the Island," the lengthy, seven-chapter saga captured in fascinating detail how Puig failed numerous times to defect only to finally be spirited away in harrowing style by a group of armed men with ties to organized crime.

According to news reports, in March 2015, a forty-one-year-old

Miami businessman, Gilberto Suarez, was sentenced to one month in prison and five months' house arrest for his involvement in part of Puig's journey. Suarez had been paid $2.5 million to drive Puig from Mexico City to the U.S. border after Puig worked out in Mexico. I knew nothing about how Puig got from Cuba to Mexico or how he eventually got from Mexico City to the States. All I knew was his handlers said he was as good as Soler or better and they were willing to showcase him for us, and I knew, most important, that Major League Baseball had pronounced him eligible to be signed.

Several other teams also sent scouts to Mexico City to see Puig, and things quickly became unwieldy. At first, we couldn't figure out which of several agents was really Puig's representative. Puig was traveling from one city to another. Logan was trying to keep tabs on the moving pieces and also evaluate Puig in a very limited workout.

We didn't know who we should be dealing with. Then, when we started talking numbers, his price kept escalating by the hour. It was crazy. And we were under a lot of pressure to get a deal done since the rules for international signings were also changing in the days ahead.

With White as the point man on the ground, it came together with an added bonus. Before leaving Mexico, our scouts also laid eyes on then fifteen-year-old Julio Urias, who signed with the Dodgers after turning sixteen, in August 2012. During this same period, Corey Seager, whom we had drafted with our first pick in June, came to terms. Within a very short period of time, the Dodgers had new ownership and had added Seager, Urias, and Puig to the organization.

Major League Baseball was changing its international signing rules on July 2, 2012. And the changes were seismic. Beginning that day, spending on international signings was capped at $2.9 million a year; organizations exceeding that would be subjected to a penalty. That was going to put a serious crimp in the international market. Now, when we finally had the financial might to compete, we were being capped by a new system.

The Cubs beat the deadline by three weeks, signing Soler to a nine-year, $30 million deal. We signed Puig on June 28, 2012—four days before the deadline—for seven years at $42 million.

The day the signing was announced, everything changed for the Dodgers in Latin America, as I had hoped. *Buscónes* and players were waiting outside the gates of the complex, wanting to get a try-out. Puig would eventually have an impact on the field, but I don't know if any player we signed had a more profound impact on the way we were viewed by the *buscónes*, the players, and the competition. We were back in business in a major way thanks to that $42 million deal.

THE FIRST TIME I laid eyes on Puig was August 9, 2012, in Arizona. The Arizona Rookie League Dodgers were playing their counterparts from the Angels in Tempe. Puig went 1-for-3 with a triple, two runs scored, two runs batted in, a walk, and a strikeout—all in 110-degree heat. You could tell the tools were off the chart. The mannerisms were different. The excitement was different. Even his attitude was different. It was almost like you could hear him thinking: What am I doing here? I'm the best player on the field.

And he was better than everyone around him that day. But he still had to play. He still had to get in baseball shape, because he hadn't played in an organized game in more than fourteen months.

Baseball is a tough game. It's not like hockey or football or a contact sport of that nature, but there are still a lot of different things your body needs to be prepared to do. So we knew we had to bring Puig along physically. At the same time, we had people who were helping him transition to this country. We tried to teach him about customs, language, eating properly, and many other real-life concerns that most people take for granted. We knew he was proud and had a carefree personality at that point in time—and he would confirm that more than a few times in the coming years.

Puig batted .400, with four home runs, three triples, and eleven RBI, in nine games at the Arizona League level before moving on to our High-A club in Rancho Cucamonga, California, where he hit .327 in fourteen games.

We were focused on three things: (1) getting him physically in condition to play every day, which is difficult at that point in the season, (2) getting him as much game exposure as possible, trying to round off some of the rough edges offensively, defensively, and on the bases, while at the same time, (3) trying to get him acclimated to American culture as quickly as possible. That was a lot to try to accomplish simultaneously. It was quite an immersion—for Puig and for us.

When the minor-league season ended, we decided to send Puig to Winter Ball in Puerto Rico to get him more playing time. That turned out to be a great experience for Puig. He didn't tear up the league stats-wise, batting just .232 with nineteen strikeouts in twenty games. But I think he learned a lot in Puerto Rico. Raffy Chavez, then our minor-league pitching coordinator, was the pitching coach for Mayaguez, the team Puig played for that winter. Raffy kept an eye on Yasiel and taught him a lot about competing against veteran players. When you are playing in the Arizona Rookie League or the California League, everybody is basically the same age. But you go to Winter Ball when you're twenty-one years old, and suddenly you're competing with players who are thirty-seven, thirty-two, twenty-seven, twenty-five—players who have won awards in the big leagues, who have titles in the big leagues. That's a different ball game. I think it was a good experience for Puig because he came in to Spring Training a few months later and lit up the place.

What he did was amazing. Think about it. Somebody who lived where he lived, under the rule of Fidel Castro, making twenty dollars a month or something like that; someone who tried to escape time and again, and finally makes it in a crazy, terrifying way—now suddenly he is free and he has a lot of coin in his pocket. That's pretty dramatic. It would be mind-boggling for just about anybody. Then, on top of all that, he comes to Spring Training with the pressure to perform in front of his peers—or those he wants to be his peers. And what does he do? He tears it up.

One of the Dodger bloggers proclaimed Puig had the "best spring training ever." That was a bit breathless, but it was indeed a tremendous spring. Puig batted .517 with an .828 slugging percentage in 58 at-bats.

In spite of that dazzling performance, we decided to send Puig down to the minors to start the 2013 season. Nobody welcomed the move more than Mattingly, Puig's future manager, who was going to have a lot of roster juggling to do if Puig was on the major-league one.

It was almost as if Donnie wasn't comfortable with adding Puig to an already crowded outfield mix. Especially if Puig was a flash and needed to be sent back down—the thinking being you've banished a veteran to the bench and given a rookie the veteran's job—and now you want the veteran to come back and play. Besides talent and contracts and health, which went into making out lineups and rosters, egos were also a prominent trait, to be dealt with always.

I think Mattingly wasn't sure he wanted the pressure of deciding whether to play a high-performing rookie over proven veterans like Matt Kemp, Carl Crawford, and Andre Ethier. He seemed relieved when we agreed to send Puig to Double-A Chattanooga. There never was a player added to the roster that I didn't have Donnie approve first.

Puig's time in Chattanooga was short but eventful. On April 28, three and a half weeks into the season, Chattanooga police arrested Puig at one o'clock in the morning driving 97 miles an hour in a 50 mph zone. He told police the BMW SUV he was driving belonged to a friend and passenger who had been drinking. Puig was charged with speeding and reckless driving. The charges, which were ultimately dropped, were pending when we called him up to the big leagues.

We were in Colorado the first weekend in June and we were struggling. We lost four of five games, to fall nine games under .500, and both Kemp and Crawford were out with injuries. I was a little worried about calling Puig up, but we needed an outfielder and I didn't have much choice. I'd known sooner or later this day would come and we tried to prepare Puig as best we could.

I'd had a couple conversations with him on the phone and relayed some of my thoughts to him through his manager, Jody Reed. I'd told Puig he needed to play hard every day because he had a tendency to take it easy some days. He already had a reputation of being a complainer—telling his manager how he didn't feel right, how he wanted the day off. He was just difficult sometimes. I'd heard less than complimentary opinions about his relationship with his teammates, who thought he was big-leaguing them before he even got to the big leagues. We'd tried to fast-forward him as much as possible—support him on and off the field—but there was only so much we could do. And now, circumstances forced me to bring him up.

That first game, June 3, 2013, was amazing. Puig batted leadoff against the San Diego Padres and went 2-for-4 with a pair of singles off former Dodgers lefty Eric Stults. But the exclamation point to the beginning of a major-league career came in the top of the ninth inning with one out and Chris Denorfia on first base as the potential tying run in a 2–1 game. Brandon League was on the mound for us, having just walked Denorfia on five pitches, and followed that with two balls to San Diego's giant first baseman, Kyle Blanks. The next pitch, Blanks lofted a fly ball to deep right field that looked like trouble. Puig backpedaled to make a one-handed catch on the warning track, then unleashed a laser throw—one writer rightly described it as a "ridiculous throw"—to double up a dumbfounded Denorfia off first base and end the game. I still have a vivid memory of seeing the look on Andre Ethier's face after the throw. Ethier was playing center field and the only way I can describe the way he looked was like a kid who gets the gift of a lifetime on Christmas morning. Pure wide-eyed joy and wonder.

In a way, that day was like Christmas for all of us. Puig went on to bat .319, hit 19 home runs in 104 games, finish second in the Rookie of the Year voting, and help turn a team that was nine games under .500 into one that finished 92-70 and won the National League West.

THE RECKLESS-DRIVING CHARGES filed against Puig for his Chattanooga speeding arrest in April were dismissed on November 6, 2013, after he performed twelve hours of community service in Los Angeles. But seven weeks later he was arrested again, this time in Florida, driving 110 miles an hour in a Mercedes with his mother in the backseat. The reckless driving charges in that case also were dropped when prosecutors said they were unable to prove Puig put any other drivers in harm's way. The speeding charges remained, however, and he was forced to pay a fine.

I had a talk with Puig after his rookie season, before the Chattanooga charges were dropped and the Florida charges were filed. I told him he'd had a tremendous year and I was staggered by all he had gone through in the past year and a half. But I told him he needed to make good choices. Be careful with what you decide to do, I told him.

"You know, where I'm from we don't worry about tomorrow," Puig said with a shrug and a chuckle.

I smiled and said, "Yeah, I understand, but we can't just burn it all down every single day. And you don't live there anymore."

A few weeks after that conversation and before Puig's December arrest, I was in my office at Dodger Stadium one night and realized the field was lit up. I looked through the shades to see all kinds of kids out there playing baseball on a big-league field. Puig had arranged it. This time I was the one who shrugged and chuckled. How cool is that, I thought.

Then came the December arrest in Florida and I called Puig.

"Yasiel, what are you doing?" I said. "You know, I just watched you weeks ago have all these kids out to Dodger Stadium. I've heard where you stop on the side of the road in Los Angeles when you see kids playing and you talk to them and throw BP to them. You're becoming a hero to these kids. What happens if you end up in a bad accident because of your speeding? What are you gonna tell the kids? How are you gonna do this?"

Yasiel was genuinely contrite. He was broken up about it. And he began to settle down some after that talk—although there was still a lot of fine-tuning to do.

WHILE HIS OFF-THE-FIELD ANTICS QUIETED, Yasiel still had serious issues—especially with his manager. Puig and Mattingly never meshed and twice in a span of two months during the 2014 season nearly came to blows.

The first was on June 3, 2014—a year to the day after Puig's incredible Dodgers debut. The team was seven games back of the

San Francisco Giants and scuffling with a 13-17 home record. Before a night game at Dodger Stadium against the Chicago White Sox, closer Kenley Jansen was working on his pickoff moves—which, frankly, needed some serious work—when he and Hanley Ramirez got into a shouting match. Hanley, who was covering second base on the pickoff moves, said something and the two started to square off. Mattingly, clearly frustrated with his fractured and underperforming team, saw the looming confrontation and snapped.

The fists never flew, but Mattingly was in a fiery mood and Yasiel Puig picked a bad time to provoke him.

I witnessed the Jansen-Ramirez blowup from the GM booth and went to Mattingly's office after batting practice to talk to him about it. Donnie was fit to be tied.

"Hey, what's going on?" I asked.

"This fucking guy!" he yells, his face red with anger.

"Which fucking guy?" I asked. "Hanley or Kenley?"

"Hanley? Kenley? That's nothing. Fucking Puig, that's who. Fucking guy!"

Puig, who had a track record of showing up late, had done it again. The team was already in uniform stretching before batting practice when Puig came out of the clubhouse in shorts, his sliding pants, and shower shoes, and did a TV interview. His teammates, to a man, looked at him with an expression that could only be translated to "Who the hell do you think you are?"

"I've got him coming in here in a minute to get this on the table," Mattingly said. "We can't have this. This has been going on too long." Just as Donnie finished those words, third base coach Lo Bundy peeked through the doorway and said, "He's not coming."

"Tell him he better get in here," Mattingly told Bundy. "Ned's in here now. Ned needs to see him, too."

Two minutes later, Dodger legend Manny Mota comes in with Puig and closes the door. I'm in a little chair adjacent to Don's desk and next to me are four Dodger Stadium seats, into which Manny and Yasiel sit.

Puig started the conversation, looking at me and saying, "I'm glad you're here because I want you to hear what I need to say."

Then he turned and pointed at Mattingly. "Why do you pick on me all the time? Why is it always me? You got eight other guys. They ain't listening to you. They're not doing what you're asking. They come when they want, do what they want. But you pick on me every day. You always pick on me."

Donnie stood up behind his desk, and his face even more flushed. "You don't know if I have other people in this office," he says. "You don't know. You can't say I don't discipline these other guys. Like they don't know you're in here right now. You don't know when they're in here. That's a lot of bullshit. I don't treat anybody any differently."

Puig interrupted and fired back, "Bullshit. It's always me. It's always me. You pick on me because I'm the easy one—because those other guys, you don't wanna have to mess with."

Then, it was my turn. "Enough! E-fucking-nuff!" I yelled, looking Puig in the eye. "You're out of fucking line. You're out of line."

Donnie didn't say a word. He just watched me.

"You're out of line to make those accusations about the manager," I continued to yell at Puig. "It's disrespectful. When did you get here?"

Puig glumly acknowledged he'd been late.

"You're wrong," I tell him. "Did you come out in uniform ready to stretch?"

"No, I didn't."

"So you're wrong. It doesn't matter about anybody else. You are wrong. This is about you and what you did—not what happens with other people or doesn't happen with other people. It's you. I've supported you. I've looked out for you. I've backed you every chance I get with a lot of potentially damaging situations. But I won't go for this. You get here on time. You need to make this a priority. This is what you are going to need to do starting now. You're going to be here on time and be a good example for everybody else. I don't want to hear you've got any issues with other people. Other than that, I have nothing for you. If you can't do that, then the next move is mine and you won't like it."

That was the end of that meeting.

Puig left Donnie's office and went 2-for-4 with a double and a walk to raise his batting average to .343 with an OPS of 1.042—more than two hundred points higher than anyone else on the team. But we lost to the White Sox 4–1 and our home record slumped to 13-18.

JUST FORTY-SIX DAYS LATER, we had turned things around as a team. We were in a virtual tie for first place with the Giants (.006 percentage points back) and were in St. Louis to play the rivals who knocked us out of the playoffs the year before—and would do it again in a few months.

The Saturday afternoon game was on national television and starting for the Cardinals was Joe Kelly—the same Joe Kelly who turned the 2013 National League Championship Series around with a 95-mph fastball into the ribs of hot-hitting Hanley Ramirez.

Kelly was at it again. With two outs in the top of the third and the Cardinals leading 4–0, Kelly plunked Puig with a pitch that nearly broke his left hand. Puig stayed in the game but the hand started swelling. In the top of the sixth inning, he led off against Kelly, hitting a weak pop foul to first base on the first pitch. Stan Conte, our vice president of medical services, went up to

Puig, looked at the hand, and asked Puig if he thought he could still play.

"Yeah, I can play defense, but I can't really hit," Puig told Conte, who relayed the information to Mattingly.

Going into the bottom of the seventh, Mattingly asked Puig if he could play defense for one more inning.

The next inning came around and word was that Puig wanted to hit. Don needed him to play defense only and wasn't going to have him hit with the hand hurting.

So Puig played right field in the bottom of the seventh inning. Nothing was hit his way and he came in the dugout, where Mattingly told him Kemp was going to pinch-hit when Puig was due up third in the top of the eighth.

Puig fought the change but the change was going to happen.

He grabbed a helmet and a bat and started walking up the dugout steps to go in the on-deck circle.

Mattingly looked around and said to Hanley Ramirez, "Hanley, help me here."

Hanley blocked the steps so Puig couldn't get past him.

Kemp said to Mattingly, "Am I hitting? What do you want me to do?"

"I want you to hit," Mattingly said.

"Well, if he walks out there, I'm not going out there, too," Kemp said. "What am I supposed to do? I'm not going to go out and wrestle this guy in the batter's box."

Fortunately, that never happened, because Mattingly and Puig started screaming at each other and disappeared down the tunnel leading to the clubhouse. Some of the people who witnessed the confrontation—people who had been involved in the game for more than twenty-five years—told me later they'd never seen anything like it.

You've got to measure that with a grain of salt because people always are saying they've never seen anything like this or that. But more than one witness told me that standoff was the worst thing they'd ever seen between a manager and a player.

I was sitting behind home plate with Ragazzo and Pat Corrales when I got a text from John Pratt, our major-league video coordinator. Pratt let me know Mattingly needed to see me in the clubhouse as soon as possible. From our seats, we couldn't see into the visitors' dugout, so we didn't have a clue what was happening.

Trevor Rosenthal was on the mound to close out a 4–2 Cardinals win when Rags, Pat, and I headed to the clubhouse. I wanted both of them with me. Corrales is fluent in Spanish and I knew I'd need him. And Rags is indispensable in a crisis. I knew Kemp pinch-hit for Puig. And I'd gotten a text from Conte telling me Puig's hand was hurt. Other than that, I was in the dark.

The three of us were in Donnie's office less than three minutes when Puig walked in with bench coach Tim Wallach. I could see Puig was somewhere between sad and furious. He sat down in Donnie's chair—not for any malicious or disrespectful reason. There just weren't any other seats available. Corrales was in the lone chair and Rags and I were on the only couch—a couch that, to this day, holds nothing but bad memories for me. And little did I know, weeks later, I'd be here again, at one of the lowest points in my career.

As soon as he sat down, Puig started in. "I was disrespected by the manager. I'm always disrespected by the manager. He wants me to go out there and play defense, but he won't let me hit."

Without any background, this wasn't making any sense to me. It was a rant that really didn't add up and I was about to ask Puig what he was talking about when Mattingly walked in. The game had just ended. I don't think I've ever seen a person as furious as Donnie was at the moment.

Donnie saw Puig sitting in his chair and almost ripped off his own jersey in rage. He pointed a jagged finger at Puig. "You motherfucker. I'm so tired of your shit!" he screamed. "You think you run this fucking team. You're a motherfucker!"

Those aren't words you should use with anyone, but they were particularly cutting to someone like Puig, who came from a different culture where the f-word and your mother are never to be used together. The vulgarity is a real flash point.

I remember thinking that these two giant men were going to go after each other right there on top of me. They were really gonna go. I had Pat Corrales to my right. Pat was a tough man who was in his early seventies. On the other side of me was Ragazzo, who was tough as nails but was clearly out of his weight class in this fight. And there's me, all five feet, eight inches of me, stuck helplessly between two professional athletes who were foaming at the mouth to get after each other. Not a good moment.

To Yasiel's credit, he calmed down. He actually teared up, quieted the storm, got out of the manager's chair, and left the room, tears flowing.

As soon as he left, Donnie went off on him. How selfish he is. How he doesn't pay attention. How he messes up in the outfield. A litany of sins and perceived slights.

As long as I have known Donnie, he has been one of the most dignified, thoughtful people I know in baseball. It was painful to see him go through this confrontation. I don't know anyone in the game who doesn't think of Donnie and think of the quality of respect when they hear his name.

But instances like this show the passion and the conflicts that develop between competitive adults earning a living at the highest level, with the brightest spotlight on them every day. It is part of the road that needs to be traversed during a baseball season that puts grown men—regarded as the best in the world at what they do—in the same room from Valentine's Day to October 1 or later.

The rest of that night, after another loss to the Cardinals—and Joe Kelly, to boot—melted into a medley of damage control phone calls. I called Stan Kasten and let him know what happened. Then I needed to reach Puig's agents, Adam Katz and Andy Mota, and hear their different versions of what went down and why. What had begun as a quiet dinner with Ragazzo and Corrales at the iconic Charley Gitto's in St. Louis turned into mayhem.

Adam and Andy were trying to calm down Puig, whom they had just begun representing. They felt compelled to defend their new client for a lot of reasons, including fear of losing him to another agent because they hadn't handled yet another problem that Puig didn't want to deal with.

I was in a crossroads position but one that is more commonplace than an outsider would imagine. I had a team of players who needed to be shown that respect is part of the program—that you can't pop off against a manager. I had a manager who was fed up—madder than I have ever seen him, and for good reason. And I had a young, talented player whom we were trying to groom to become a star, in a still relatively new environment—a star that people could one day look up to, rather than roll their eyes at. I understood Puig needed guidance, nurturing, and some patience. I also fully supported the manager, Mattingly.

Oh, and we were in the pennant race, too.

IT WILL BE INTERESTING to see how Puig's career turns out. He goes all-out about eighteen hours a day—on the field and off. We'll see if it takes its toll. I've drawn the analogy many times: If a young person grew up in Los Angeles as a Dodgers fan and was a good high school player—good enough to go to UCLA or Cal State–Fullerton or Loyola Marymount or USC—and that player was drafted in the first round and signed at twenty-one and within a year was in the big leagues, like Puig, and like Puig took the city by storm, took the league by storm, and was in the spotlight every day, that person would very likely have a challenging time adjusting as well. In this situation, add the fact that Puig came from a totally different environment, a vastly different world, and in some ways it's amazing he handled it as well as he did, even with the slipups.

People were puzzled when we signed him. They called us crazy; wanted to know what we could possibly be thinking.

We were thinking we just might have found a wild horse who could carry us back into the international game. And we were right. Not only did Yasiel make an impact on a major-league field, but his signing and the signal it sent to the Latin American market dramatically changed the view of the Dodgers in a matter of months.

Within a year, the Dodgers were the biggest player in Latin America. The front office and ownership signed more than forty international players, including Cuban right-hander Yadier Alvarez, whose $16 million bonus was the second largest ever given an international amateur behind the $31.5 million the Red Sox gave Cuban second baseman Yoan Moncada in 2014. An increased scouting presence, more attention to detail, and financial power allowed the doors that were once closed to open wide.

"What are the Dodgers thinking?" Ben Badler wrote when the Dodgers signed Puig. Obviously, Ben hadn't spent much time on the inside of the thought process and didn't know all the details.

Twenty-one
PRESENTATION

. . . .

F rom time to time during my tenure, which included Yasiel, there were days that brought to mind one of my key evaluation tools—presentation. Is the performance crisp, clean, full-on? There was never a doubt about the hustle of Yasiel. Few have ever played the game harder. Focus and sometimes presentation were a little tougher to always chronicle.

Yasiel signed in June 2012. That year turned out to be one of the most poignant in not only my Dodgers career, but also in the history of the franchise. New ownership came in; amateur scouting discovered Corey Seager in North Carolina and Puig and Julio Urias in Mexico.

In a span of five weeks in July and August, the Dodgers made five big trades, acquiring nine players. Ownership was all in. Of all the deals, none exhibited that more than the late August deal with the Boston Red Sox that netted four players and included ownership taking on $250 million in contract obligations.

Presentation had always been a staple of my evaluation process, especially ownership's historic commitment. And that screams for accountability from everyone. The pursuit of players was seemingly endless, and with each decision to add more veteran players and payroll, the measure of accountability and presentation became higher. I felt it was all of our duty to equal ownership's commitment with one that was at least its equal.

The Boston deal was the exclamation point to the five-month flurry in the attempt to rebuild on the fly. So we will start there in explaining what all the moves and uniform changes brought to bear.

Boston has a passionate fan base, which makes it a tough place to play—unless you win. It's a great sports town, but if you play for the Red Sox, you're under a microscope all the time. If you play for the Red Sox, eighty-one home games are like eighty-one Super Bowls. And it takes a toll.

By the time we made the big trade with the Red Sox in August 2012, Josh Beckett was done with Boston—and Boston was done with Josh Beckett.

The previous October, Beckett was at the heart of one of the ugliest periods in Red Sox history. Boston had been on pace to win one hundred games and contend for its third World Series in seven years when, suddenly, the team slithered into an epic collapse. The Red Sox went 7-20 in September, blew a nine-game lead, and failed to make the playoffs.

Beckett was 1-3 with a 5.48 ERA during that stretch. Worse, a scathing postseason article in *The Boston Globe* singled out Beckett and fellow starters John Lackey and Jon Lester for the bulk of the blame in what the newspaper dubbed a "lost September." *Globe* writer Bob Hohler, an investigative reporter who wrote a book on the life and death of Christa McAuliffe, the New Hampshire teacher who died in the space shuttle Challenger explosion in 1986, broke the news that Beckett, Lackey, and Lester abandoned their teammates during the ugly slide. He said that on nights they weren't starting, the three pitchers left the dugout to drink beer, order in fast-food fried chicken, and play video games on a big screen in the clubhouse.

Interestingly, the Cubs, in the process of assembling a World Series champion in 2016, signed both Lester and Lackey to multi-year contracts. And the person in charge of that decision was former Red Sox GM Theo Epstein. To me, this was a perfect illustration of how what happens behind closed doors is often perceived differently on the outside. It also underscores how the combination of personalities can be affected, negatively or positively, by the combination of the people in the room and where they are in their own careers and lives. The architects of teams always take that into consideration—but whether they can pull it off is another issue.

Hohler's story created an uproar, not only in Boston, but nationwide. Beckett did his best to lie low and let the storm pass, then early in the 2012 season was back at the center of another miserable controversy. He skipped his first start in May with a sore elbow, but was spotted playing golf on an off day. When Beckett did pitch again, on May 10, he gave up seven earned runs in 2⅓ innings against the Cleveland Indians and was booed lustily at Fenway Park. The Red Sox fell to 12-19, seven and a half games out of first place, and Beckett was Beantown's favorite goat.

After the game, Beckett admitted he was terrible, but defended his decision to play golf. "I spend my off days the way I want to spend them," Beckett told reporters.

Gordon Edes, a longtime baseball writer for the *Globe* who moved over to the Red Sox beat for ESPNBoston.com in 2009, followed up with a pointed question. "Given that you skipped a start with what was described as a tight lat muscle, do people have the right to question why you were golfing?"

Beckett's reply: "Not on my off day."

Edes persisted: "Do you understand the perception that leaves when the team is playing as poorly as it is?"

"We get eighteen off days a year," Beckett said. "I think we deserve a little time to ourselves."

Bad move.

If Beckett thought the Indians hit him hard, all he had to do was wait for the media to pounce.

"After spending two days in the center of the maelstrom over his decision to hit the links last week when he was ostensibly injured, Beckett had nothing when it mattered, getting shelled . . . in an 8–3 loss to the Indians that redefined ugly," wrote John Tomase of the *Boston Herald*. "Afterward, Beckett redefined stubborn in his refusal to even acknowledge a perception problem."

Nick Cafardo of the *Globe* was even more direct, writing as if he were having a one-on-one sit-down with Beckett.

"Shouldn't you exercise a little discretion? I mean, you already have the beer and fried chicken stigma. You didn't tell your manager about the lat discomfort before he left you in for 126 pitches. Then you have to skip a start. And then you play golf?"

Things never got better for Beckett after that. He was 3-7 from May 15 to August 19 and was forced to skip another start just before we acquired him on August 25, 2012.

Given his public controversies, his ineffectual pitching of late, and his $15.75 million salary, I wasn't crazy about having to take Beckett to get the two guys I really wanted: Gonzalez "and" Punto. But the first night he was with us, Beckett started winning me over.

We have a team rule that players must wear a sport coat or suit when we travel. It's part of the presentation—an important symbol of professionalism and pride. After Josh agreed to waive his no-trade clause to come to Los Angeles, he, Gonzalez, and Punto had packed hurriedly and jumped on the Guggenheim corporate jet to get to Dodger Stadium for a Saturday night game. The following day would be an afternoon pre-getaway game, followed by a charter flight to Denver for a series against the Rockies. Beckett and the rest of the team got out of Dodger Stadium just before midnight Saturday and needed to be back about 9 a.m. Sunday with bags packed.

I left the stadium just before midnight and decided to stop for a quick cocktail after an incredibly exciting and emotionally draining day. I had just sat down when my cellphone rang.

It's Josh Beckett and I am thinking . . . I don't know what I was thinking, but this is his first day and here comes a midnight call. I stand up, walk outside to answer the phone, and hear Josh.

"Yeah, what's up?" I say.

"Hey, I don't want you to think I'm a troublemaker. I don't want you to think I'm disrespectful. But I've got a problem," he says, sounding genuinely concerned. "We raced out of Fenway so quick today. I packed a bag, but I neglected to bring a sport coat with me.

"I need to be at the ballpark at nine o'clock tomorrow. I don't want to break any rules. I don't want to be late because I'm off getting a sport coat on a Sunday morning. But I don't want to be there without a sport coat. So, tell me if you want me to find a sport coat and be late, if you want me to send the clubhouse kid out to get a sport coat for me, or if you'll give me a pass without the sport coat?"

"I'm inclined to give you a pass," I offered. "Let me talk to Donnie."

I told Mattingly about the call and said Beckett clearly was nervous about the first impression he was presenting. We talked it over and decided to make a one-time exemption.

On the flight the next day, Beckett took a bit of a tough time from the rest of the team, but everybody got a good laugh out of it all. Little did we know laughs were going to be hard to come by the rest of the season.

WE WON THE FIRST GAME with the new guys from Boston, but lost on Sunday, August 26. Still, we were just two games back of the San Francisco Giants heading to Colorado and Beckett's first start in a Dodger uniform. He pitched well enough, going 5⅔ innings, striking out six, and only allowing three earned runs. But Jeff Francis set the tone for the final month of the season by shutting down our offense. He allowed just three hits en route to a 10–0 win and I had a bad feeling about where we were headed.

I had an even worse feeling less than twenty-four hours later when Kemp went down, again, for the third time in the season. In the bottom of the first inning, he crashed full-speed into a partially padded wall in center field, rolled onto his back on the warning track, and needed nearly ten minutes to recover. He stayed in the game, and as circumstance would have it, the very next batter blooped one into center field. Matt had to make a hard head-first dive on a looping single. He stayed around for one more hitter, then left with what was originally diagnosed as a bruised knee and a jaw that needed to be X-rayed. In fact, Kemp had badly hurt his shoulder and would require surgery in October.

After missing fifty-one games earlier in the season, and not yet aware he would need surgery, Kemp insisted on staying in the lineup the rest of the way. He missed only three more games but struggled at the plate. When he hit the wall, he was batting .337. After the crash, he hit .214 with 33 strikeouts in 112 at-bats.

But Matt wasn't alone. The revamped offense with Hanley Ramirez, Adrian Gonzalez, and Shane Victorino was equally punchless. On August 25, the day of the Boston trade, we were two games out of first place. In the next month, the team won only ten of twenty-six games, was shut out five times, and fell a distant eleven games behind the Giants.

More than a few writers, sports talking heads, and fans speculated that we destroyed the chemistry of a winning clubhouse by bringing in too many new players. Not counting Crawford, who wouldn't be available until 2013, we added eight players: Hanley, Adrian, Beckett, Victorino, Choate, League, Blanton, and Punto.

I kept hearing: "You added too many players. They can't play together. It's not a team."

Some of that may be true, but the number of players who were hurt or playing hurt put the Dodgers on the clock. The season was going to be too long not to make the deals we made and in most cases the players added were going to be with us in the coming years.

Camaraderie is important, but we didn't bring in any bad apples—and that includes Beckett. He was a good addition to the clubhouse and was still good enough on the mound to throw the twenty-fourth no-hitter in Dodgers' history in 2014. I just think the folks who were harping about us bringing in too many new players were searching for an excuse—looking for a way to explain why we didn't produce offensively.

I always tried to assemble a team of players who worked hard, played hard, and exhibited grit—players who would sacrifice for the good of the group. It wasn't always possible to have twenty-five players with that DNA—especially given the dynamics of how deals are done in Major League Baseball. But that was the goal.

Chemistry is always important, but no one really knows if winning creates chemistry or chemistry creates winning. In my view winning creates chemistry.

THERE WAS MORE TO IT than met the eye. Remember, we also were trying to rebuild credibility in Los Angeles after the previous ownership had diluted the brand and revenues. The 2012 Dodgers began the season with a midlevel player payroll of approximately $90 million. After fifteen consecutive years of exceeding three million fans at Dodger Stadium, our attendance had dropped by 800,000 from 2009 to 2011, when the club drew 2,935,139. The people had spoken. We paid a price and part of the rebuild required making some unconventional moves—like changing a third of the roster in a month and taking on historic amounts of contractual obligations. I knew we were dealing with dynamics that were going to be unprecedented and challenging. I said exactly that to Mark and Stan moments before we made the Boston deal. We were coming out of an historically bad situation and ownership had a franchise-changing television deal to negotiate in the months ahead. There was a lot at stake.

To negotiate the record $8.35 billion Time Warner Cable television deal later that off-season, the team needed a drastic makeover and we needed to grab the attention of the fan base and business community. The people who made up the organization helped make it happen.

"To see what we were faced with last year at this time and to see where we started the season, it's kind of funny," Andre Ethier told ESPNLosAngeles.com. "They said they'd do whatever it takes to win and they're definitely proving that now."

On Sunday, September 16, three weeks after the Boston trade, we lost to St. Louis in twelve innings in the final game of the home stand at Dodger Stadium before a three-city road trip. Cardinal rookie Shelby Miller, who would become a nemesis for us in 2013, pitched a scoreless inning to get his first major-league win.

The loss just reinforced a feeling I'd had for the previous week or so. I was getting more and more aggravated with our presentation—how we play the game, how we go about it. I have many faults. I'm far from perfect. And one of my faults, sometimes, is having too much patience. Sometimes it's a blessing. Sometimes it's a curse. But watching this time, I knew I was beginning to run out of patience.

We had fifteen games to play when we flew to Washington,

D.C., for three against the Nationals. The first game was rained out, so we had a doubleheader on Wednesday, September 19.

In the first game, Jordan Zimmerman held us to one run through six innings and rookie Bryce Harper tripled and scored a run to beat us 3–1.

Beckett started the nightcap and he was cruising. He had allowed just two hits through seven innings and had a 6–0 lead. He'd thrown only sixty-eight pitches, but he had only pitched into the eighth inning three times all season.

Early in his career, Beckett was one of the best pitchers in baseball. A lot of innings later, a lot of hard work later, he was not the same guy. And I thought we had gotten enough out of Josh getting seven strong innings out of him, but he came out for the eighth and ten minutes later the score was tied.

On the second pitch of the inning, Michael Morse homered to right. Ian Desmond followed with a single to left. On the fifth pitch of the inning, Steve Lombardozzi hit a two-run homer to right— just the third home run of his career—to make it 6–3.

Beckett got catcher Jose Flores on a weak ground ball to third and would have had backup outfielder Corey Brown on a grounder to first, but Gonzalez muffed the ball.

At long last, Mattingly came and got Beckett, but Randy Choate gave up singles to the only two batters he faced and Ronald Belisario surrendered two more singles and hit a batter before finally getting out of the inning. We had just blown a six-run lead.

With the score tied at six, Kemp led off the ninth inning with a tiebreaking home run to deep center off Nationals closer Tyler Clippard, who had earned his thirty-second save in the first game of the doubleheader. We had a win and narrowly avoided a doubleheader sweep, but it was ugly and I needed to have a heart-to-heart with Donnie.

I hadn't had a lot of talks like this with Mattingly. But when I did, I tried to lead him to a thought and not mandate anything—just as Frank did with me for years. I didn't like to mandate because I wasn't managing the team, Donnie was. But it was my job to suggest. It was my job to look from thirty thousand feet. It was my job to see the game and the team, in a different way from the manager.

The manager's view is rarely longer than day-to-day. The GM needs to look at today, tomorrow, next week, next month, next season, three and five seasons down the road. And the GM can sometimes see what the manager can't—and vice versa.

Many times a manager and coaching staff will like a player because he is easy to get along with and is compliant. Players who have an edge against leadership or who aren't the brightest will at some point typically run afoul of the manager and/or a coach or two. Therefore, personality enters into some decision making, which is just human nature. But the job every day is to figure out how to win a game even if a manager doesn't get along with a certain player.

When it came to playing time and lineup choices, I always deferred to the manager. Many times I would suggest an idea I wanted him to consider, but I never put a lineup on his desk. If I needed to tell him whom to play and where to hit them in the order, I had the wrong manager. I have a lot of information before a game, but once the game begins, different factors come into play and I'm not privy to them all. But I could see the way our players were going about their work those final weeks of 2012 and I needed to talk to Donnie about it.

I WENT DOWN to the visitors' clubhouse at Nationals Park and walked into the manager's office. Stan Kasten was there. I didn't want to have this type of conversation in front of Stan because I didn't want to cast any doubt on Don in Stan's eyes. So I held off, figuring I'd take up the strategy part later. But I did tell Mattingly, "You know what? The presentation right now . . . It's not how you played or what you stand for. And I know it's not what I stand for. But right now, it's a reflection of both of us and the coaching staff—how we play. And I'm telling you, we need to adjust it and, please, hold these guys accountable."

The next game, the offense took another day off and we lost 4–1. The Nationals clinched a playoff spot with the victory and I was not happy.

Our flight from Washington, D.C., to Cincinnati, where we were headed for a weekend series, was delayed by weather. We were on the tarmac a long time and we didn't get to the Westin in Cincinnati until about four in the morning. Most of the team was in the lobby waiting for elevators when two men outside the Dodgers' traveling party started pushing their way through to get to the front. Turns out they were with Guns N' Roses, who played a concert that night. At that point in the season and that time of the morning, it didn't matter who the men were or why they were pushing their way into the elevator. Our players were tired and frustrated and in no mood to take anything from anyone. The next thing I knew, we almost had a lobby brawl, but there were about forty Dodgers personnel and only two members of the band's traveling party. So it calmed down quickly and everyone headed to their rooms.

Friday night, we beat the Reds 3–1. Kemp went 3-for-5 with a pair of RBI. Ronald Belisario got the win and League picked up his fourth save. We did okay, but, again, the presentation was spotty.

I had to get back to Los Angeles on Saturday, so I took a morning flight. But I asked our traveling secretary, Scott Akasaki, to have Kershaw call me. Kershaw had been battling a sore hip and we'd preferred to shut him down, but he wanted to pitch the Sunday night ESPN game.

Clayton reached me at home in Manhattan Beach and I started trying to talk him out of pitching.

"Look," I said. "You don't have anything to prove to me. You're the kind of guy who would get carried out on a shield. But you can't do this. You can't risk anything. You've got a long career ahead of you. I want to win as badly as anybody. But I can't risk putting you out there if you're not feeling right."

Kershaw convinced me that he was fine and he could make the start.

I knew I wasn't going to convince him. "Clayton," I said, "if you feel one thing, if you feel a twinge, if you feel anything in that hip or in your arm because of trying to make up or compensate for that hip, Honeycutt, Mattingly, and Conte have to know. You can't throw one pitch, feel something, and say, 'Well, let me see if I really feel it, and throw another one.' You need to promise me if you feel one thing, you're done."

"You have my word," he said.

So, Sunday night, I was watching the game and the camera showed our dugout just before first pitch and our coaches were all there, but only two or three players.

I made a call to Lovelace. I knew he was sitting in the booth we always used in Cincinnati. The booth had a straight line of sight into the third-base dugout, the visitors' dugout.

"Vance, how many guys in our dugout?" I asked Lovelace.

"Boss, there's hardly anybody in the dugout."

"All right," I said, "let me know when they get there."

On another television channel the Houston Texans–Denver Broncos NFL game was on.

About two minutes after I hung up with Lovelace, he called back. "The dugout just filled up," he said.

"Interesting," I said. "You know what happened?"

"What?"

"The football game just ended."

The majority of the players were in the clubhouse watching a football game while Clayton Kershaw was getting ready to take the mound and possibly risk his career—including the financial where-withal of his future—to help our team win a game. And where were his teammates? In the clubhouse watching football.

I was disappointed and furious.

Clayton lasted five innings. He threw ninety-two pitches, struck out five, and, uncharacteristically, walked five, but we won 5–3. And now the team was headed to San Diego for our final three road games before wrapping up the season with a six-game home stand.

I drove down from L.A. for the first game of the Padres series. A lack of attention to detail was catching up to us. We lost 2–1 to a bad San Diego team. In the top of the sixth inning, down 2–0, Matt Kemp got hit by a pitch with one out. He went to second on a single by Adrian Gonzalez, then made a base-running mistake without thinking it through. Hanley Ramirez tapped a weak ground ball to third. Kemp raced to third and rounded the bag, thinking the throw was going to first. Instead, San Diego third baseman Chase Headley wheeled and fired a bullet to shortstop Everth Cabrera, who had slipped in behind Kemp. Instead of bases loaded with one out, the Dodgers now had runners on first and second with two outs. Shane Victorino walked, but Luis Cruz grounded out to end the inning.

I was watching our presentation—our body language, our approach to the game. Players were walking to their positions. The team was lifeless. We weren't making the plays winning teams make and I was thinking the new ownership group, which just gave us the blessing to acquire many new players and their contracts, was watching this.

I couldn't wait any longer to address what I was watching. I'd already waited too long. I knew it. And it only made me more frustrated. I'd dropped hints. I'd expressed myself in very diplomatic ways. Now I was going to need to change approaches.

At San Diego's Petco Park, inside the visitors' clubhouse is a long hallway. At the end of the hallway is the manager's office and about twenty feet farther to the left and around the corner is the visiting coaches' room. I let the media go into Mattingly's office and I walked past to the coaches' room. I waited for all the coaches to get into the coaches' room. All but Honeycutt were in the room. Rick was talking with a pitcher. I closed the door. Trey Hillman, our bench coach, was in the room. So were Davey Lopes, Kenny Howell, Dave Hansen, and Tim Wallach.

One of my weaknesses is believing people will do what they are supposed to do, and so I wait sometimes until issues fester. I try to stay away from moments like this because I know once I reach a point, I will be ultrapassionate. I would rather have conversations to lead someone to take action before I get to this point. But now it was too late.

"I cannot watch this anymore," I began. "Our presentation. Our lack of effort. Our lack of thought process at the plate. Our refusal to execute and hustle is something losing teams do.

"You guys have all asked me for [contract] extensions. I love you all. Donnie and I hired you all. You're not his guys. You're not my guys. We're all in this together. We all have great respect for each other and the game. But I can tell you now: The only thing I can guarantee you right now is I'm not watching it anymore without telling you how disappointed the presentation makes me."

I paused a moment to catch my breath, then reiterated my words.

"You know what? Except for you, Trey, I've watched all you guys play," I said. "Davey, I've watched you play. I've known you since 1984, when the Cubs acquired you. Timmy, I watched you play all those years with the Expos and another few with the Dodgers. National League baseball. Kenny, I watched you pitch. Dave Hansen, I watched you learn one of the toughest jobs in baseball, which is to pinch-hit—to stay sharp and stay focused. I've watched all you guys and none of you played like this. None of you. None of you ever played with a lack of passion and a lack of focus. Not in front of me, you didn't. Right now, the guys you coach are playing with a lack of focus, a lack of energy, and a lack of passion. And it's a poor reflection on all of us.

"I'm hoping that one of you tells me I'm full of shit. That I'm fucked up. That I never played this game at this level. And so I don't know what I'm talking about. I'm begging you. Somebody tell me I'm wrong. Somebody, please, tell me I see it wrong. Tell me I don't see it the way you see it."

Silence.

More silence.

Finally, Tim Wallach said, "We were told not to, not to, uh, not be heavy-handed with them like previous coaches had been."

"Did I tell you that?" I asked Wallach.

"No," he said.

"I'm telling you how I need it to be done, right here, right now. You guys want to talk to me, you can talk to me now. You want to talk to me after I get out of here, you can call me anytime. After this one, I'll be awake all night. I can't stand watching us anymore. We've got eight games to go and we are not playing well enough. And it's really how we play more than anything. This new ownership group has given us a chance. We've acquired very good players. This cannot be ownership's payback.

"I tell you guys all the time. You can't control an umpire. You can't control a bad hop. You can't control what another player is going to do. You can't control what each other does. But you can control what you do. Our own effort is the only thing any of us have that is solely within our control. And that's what you guys need to do. Got it?"

When I finished, and the media was gone from the manager's office, I stopped in and told Donnie what I did. He looked upset but didn't say anything. The writers told me a few days later they could hear someone raising their voice through the venting system but couldn't put a name to the voice.

An hour later, I was in the lobby of the Omni hotel and Mattingly came in and walked over to me. "You know what? I wish you hadn't done that with the coaches. I guess you felt you needed to, but I wish you hadn't done that."

"I had no doubt I needed to," I told Donnie. "You're a tremendous person. You were a great player. You were drafted late. You fought your way through the minor leagues quickly. You won a batting title. You won an MVP. Your uniform number is retired in Yankee Stadium. That stuff doesn't come without you working as hard as you worked. And I have nothing but respect for that. But these guys you're managing, they are taking advantage of you. They've taken advantage of you, your good nature, your heart, your willingness to let them be men. And you can't let it continue. Just my opinion."

Between my lobby conversation with Mattingly and four in the morning, I talked to every coach, either face-to-face or on the telephone. They all checked in. They all called. They all gave me their opinion.

The next day, Donnie addressed the team without me instructing him to. And after he did, three players came up to me on the field during batting practice.

"I don't know what you did. But whatever you did, it was long overdue and we needed to hear it," was the message from all of them.

We won that night 8–2. We won seven of our last eight games

and the day after the season ended I met with Mattingly, Hansen, Wallach, Lopes, and Hillman. I outlined what I thought we needed to do. Voices were raised. Emotions flared, fueled in no small part by my top lieutenants, Lovelace and Ragazzo.

Three hours later, the meeting ended and we all felt we were in agreement. Everybody shook hands. We hugged one another and wished one another well for the winter.

Later that day, we met with the pitching coaches, Honeycutt and Howell. The meeting wasn't nearly as confrontational. But it was definitive. And we all left on the same page.

Finally, I met one-on-one with Donnie. I wanted to clear the air—to explain that my comments had only been intended to make everybody as good as possible. I told Mattingly that if I didn't believe in him, I wouldn't have hired him, and I was the person who made the decision to promote him to the position without any previous managerial experience. I said I thought he had a chance to be a great manager and we were going to continue to work to that end.

Donnie asked me point-blank if I would pick up his option for 2014, so he wouldn't be working on the final year of his contract during the 2013 season.

I told him that we would consider it, but a decision would have to wait. I added that ownership was relatively new and everyone was under scrutiny. For now we would have to leave the contract where it was—one year and a club option.

He said he understood. That part of the conversation lasted less than a minute and we shook hands and went our separate ways.

The 2012 season had begun nine months earlier in Glendale, Arizona, amid a cloud of uncertainty about the ownership change. Within a couple of weeks the team was sold. Frank McCourt held his final executive staff meeting on April 30. The new owners, led by Mark and Stan, came in officially on May 1. They inherited a team with a payroll about half of what large-market clubs spent and less than half of what the New York Yankees had been spending for years.

While the new owners were coming in with a clean slate, the core of the organization had been through a lot. At one point during the McCourt era, a top executive kept a copy of the 2004 Dodger yearbook and crossed out pictures of employees who either had been fired or quit because of the chaos. There were more crossed-out pictures than not. The fan base basically went into seclusion. Players like Kemp, Ethier, Billingsley, and, to a lesser extent, Kershaw, who were around for it all, needed to perform at peak levels despite endless distractions. I was proud of how we had come through, but I know baseball is a results-driven business. And at the end of the 2012 season, the Dodgers were missing from the playoffs for a third straight year. That hadn't happened to a team I worked with since my Cubs days, and those were long in the rearview mirror. I was determined to give the fans and new ownership the one thing they all deserved: a team that played hard and with determination.

Twenty-two

A LITTLE LUCK . . .
A LOT OF DOUGH
(AND KOREAN WON)

. . . .

As disappointing as our offense had been down the stretch in 2012, we were confident Ramirez and Gonzalez were the productive middle-of-the-order bats they'd always been and would have a big impact over a full season in 2013. We knew we'd be getting a proven leadoff hitter in Crawford, as soon as he was recovered from Tommy John surgery. We were counting on Kemp being healthy again and Ethier anchoring a solid lineup.

Pitching—specifically starting pitching—was our focus during the 2012–13 off-season.

While the games end in early fall, the GM's responsibilities continue on, day to day, week to week, month to month. The process of team building never ends. Ironically, the winter months, when the games are practically equidistant from the last one to the next one, are some of the busiest for the baseball operations' front office.

Besides evaluating the organization's players from the lowest level in the minor leagues to the big leagues, the off-season is a time for reshuffling and restocking, mainly through free agency. At the outset of the free agent market, prices are at a high. They slowly creep down after New Year's Day. If you know who is playing in the Super Bowl and a player hasn't signed yet, chances are he will be signing for far less than he expected. He may even be forced to accept a minor-league deal with an invitation to camp. There is some good bargain hunting at that point. And that bargain hunting can linger into the first couple of weeks of Spring Training.

After that, teams had better be well stocked and prepared for what lies ahead. We don't always know what is coming next, but we do know *something* is coming next and typically it is going to challenge a team's depth. And if the depth is thin, or not major-league caliber, it will be exposed within games.

A minor-league player is a minor-league player. The odds of finding a diamond in the rough who contributes to a big-league team for an extended period are slim. It rarely happens.

So if the GM and the front office haven't used their money well and haven't built an organization that can withstand an onslaught of injuries or individual declines in production, the price of adding depth becomes enormous once Spring Training is halfway through. Teams with a surplus of depth will be looking for $1.50 on the dollar in any deals.

We were looking for pitching depth early in the 2012–13 off-season.

Chad Billingsley had been our most effective pitcher from the All-Star break to mid-August 2012. He won six consecutive starts, with a 1.29 ERA from July 23 to August 19. But on August 24, 2012, Billingsley lasted just 3⅓ innings, gave up three runs on five hits and three walks, and left the game with a sore elbow. His season was done. He went on the disabled list the same day we made the big trade with the Red Sox.

Our doctors warned that Billingsley probably needed Tommy

John surgery, but Bills didn't want to be cut. He wanted to try to rehab the elbow and go with platelet-rich plasma (PRP) treatment injections, which had proven successful in cases where the ulnar collateral ligament of the elbow wasn't severely torn. But in many cases—and in Billingsley's case—the PRP treatments are merely a stopgap.

By early November, Billingsley left his rehab at Camelback Ranch in Arizona looking pretty good. But we still were leery. And, it turns out, with good reason. Billingsley pitched through Spring Training, but made just two starts in the 2013 regular season before finally undergoing Tommy John surgery on April 25.

Even if we were sure Bills would be back, we needed to add to our rotation.

Among the free agent starters we targeted was Anibal Sanchez, who had started 2012 with the Marlins and moved to the Detroit Tigers at the trade deadline. He was making $8 million and his numbers weren't impressive. On the year, he was 9-13, but his ERA was a respectable 3.86 and he had pitched well down the stretch and into the playoffs and World Series with the Tigers. He'd thrown seven shutout innings, striking out seven, to beat former Dodger and now Yankee starter Hiroki Kuroda in Game 2 of the American League Championship Series, and had given up just two earned runs in seven innings in a tough loss to the San Francisco Giants in Game 3 of the World Series.

Sanchez was represented by Gene Mato, an agent I'd never dealt with before and one who was working on his first big free agent contract. I found him really tough to deal with. He seemed to be trying to wait as long as possible to see if Sanchez could be the last free agent starter standing. He'd have meetings with us to see how far he could raise the bar, knowing he wasn't ready to take anything yet. To me, he seemed to want to just sit on the fringe and not make a mistake. So he waited, he waited, and he waited some more.

In the end, Sanchez ended up going back to Detroit, which I thought was unfortunate for him, because I thought he had better options—at least at the outset of talks.

MEANWHILE, WE PURSUED HYUN-JIN RYU, the top pitcher in the Korea Baseball Organization. A former Rookie of the Year and MVP in Korea, Ryu dominated the KBO, pitching for the Hanwha Eagles from 2006 to 2012, with appearances in the 2008 Beijing Olympics and the 2009 World Baseball Classic.

The Eagles agreed to "post" Ryu after the 2012 season, meaning U.S. teams would be allowed to bid for the right to negotiate with him. The team that offered the highest bid—officially known as the "posting fee"—would pay that amount to Hanwha in return for a thirty-day window in which to negotiate a separate contract with Ryu.

Our posting fee was $25,737,737.33—four cents below our bid.

As with most East Asian and Southeast Asian cultures, numbers often have special meanings.

In Korea, for example, the number four is an unlucky number. Four is *sa*, which is almost identical to the Korean word for death. In many ways, it's similar to the superstitions about thirteen in our culture. Major public buildings in Korea will skip the fourth floor, or, if there is a fourth floor, elevator buttons will simply use "F" instead of "4."

On the other hand, some numbers are considered especially lucky in Korea. Three (*sam*) and seven (*chil*) are two of the luckiest, invoking sentiments of success and good fortune. Our carefully crafted bid of $25,737,737.37 made a huge, happy impression on the folks at Hanwha and on November 9, 2012, we were given our thirty-day window to negotiate with Ryu. Of course, realistically, while the symbolism was catchy and important, the dollar amount also was the highest, which didn't hurt our chances, either.

. . .

RYU WAS REPRESENTED BY BORAS, which meant the negotiations were going to last all thirty days. When you deal with Scott on a thirty-day window, you may be negotiating the first twenty-nine days and twenty-three hours, but Scott's not negotiating until the final sixty minutes.

Sure enough, that's how it transpired. On the final Sunday afternoon, I was sitting in an office with a baseball operations staffer and our top Korean staffer, Martin Kim. On the phone in Korea was our longtime scout Byung-Hwan An, who had chosen a most unfortunate weekend to get married and was fielding calls hour after hour on his honeymoon night. Timing, Byung-Hwan, timing.

The deadline was 2 p.m. Los Angeles time, which was 7 a.m. in Korea.

Typical of negotiations with Boras, he started asking somewhere in the $90 million range and finished in the $30s. Also typical of Scott, we had a snafu at the end. We had settled on a six-year deal and Boras wanted Ryu to be able to get out after five years. And, of course, we were trying to lay as much money in year six as possible to entice him to stay the full term.

All the documentation had to be in the hands of MLB at the precise deadline. In the final minutes, I was on my cell with Scott, and the staffer was on the landline with MLB. We thought we had all the terms finalized and with fifteen, then ten seconds to go, Scott was arguing with me to move money around so if Ryu left a season early he would have earned more. We were looking for a balance, so if he did leave after five years, he would be leaving a lot on the table.

Finally, I said, "I have presented the deal we're going to do. I'm not necessarily hanging up on you, but this phone call is over."

All parties wanted the deal. The clock called an end to discussions. Scott and I had agreed on the value—the payment schedule was still up for debate when the call ended.

With that, the staffer told Major League Baseball's group we were done at the number we'd sent them. We were elated. We called Stan Kasten and he was happy about it. We called Mark Walter and the ownership group. They were happy about it. Martin Kim was happy and he was hearing from Korea that Ryu was ecstatic. He was screaming at the top of his lungs, just over the moon at the opportunity not only to pitch for the Dodgers in the United States, but also to become a millionaire overnight. He was making about $400,000 a year being the best pitcher in Korea. Now he was going to get $36 million over five or six years to be a starting pitcher for the Los Angeles Dodgers. And Byung-Hwa An's phone finally stopped ringing on his honeymoon.

About a half hour into the celebration, MLB called and said the players' union had turned in a different term sheet. While term sheets submitted by the clubs and players' agents sometimes contain small discrepancies, this one didn't seem small to me. But we had no time to hammer out the differences. We were not going to forfeit the deal.

It was that or lose the player, and we didn't want to do that. The commissioner's office and the MLBPA are not going to accept two different term sheets and the difference was not going to alter the deal enough to call it off.

Perhaps it was a strategic move by Scott to increase the contract value to his client—or, at least try to get as much as he could. He had not increased the monetary value of the deal, just the way it would be paid out. Scott's job is to get the most money and the most convenient, most powerful deal for his client no matter what he does to get it—within reason (or within some reason).

. . .

THE DAY BEFORE WE WRAPPED UP RYU, we also finished—pending a physical—a six-year, $147 million deal with 2009 American League Cy Young winner Zack Greinke.

Zack had been on our wish list for quite a while. We thought he was the best pitcher on the market that off-season and we wanted him badly. We were tired of going after the sixth- or seventh-best pitcher on the market every year, as we'd been forced to do during our financial down-holds. We needed to try and get somebody who could at least stand next to Clayton Kershaw, if not a step behind—an upper-echelon pitcher. Zack, in our mind, was the only one in the market.

I met with Zack's agent, Casey Close, at the General Managers' Meetings in Palm Springs in November. We went off campus to a nearby country club and sat in the lobby. We wanted to just express our interest and get some idea of what it would take and how long a deal Zack might want.

"It's going to be six years, at least, maybe seven years," Close said.

Casey is one of the sharpest and best agents I have dealt with. He also was representing Kershaw, the best Dodger pitcher since Sandy Koufax. And, while Kershaw's contract was still a year off, I had to be very selective in my words in dealing with Casey on Greinke.

This type of dynamic happens once in a while—especially with agencies that represent many players. It adds another component to the already complex negotiation process. Does the agent have other offers? Is he coming to you because your club is the only one offering the kind of deal he wants? How did previous negotiations go with the other clients of his that you signed? If there's been bad blood between an agent and a GM, both sides *have to make sure* the past doesn't carry over to the next round of negotiations with a different player.

Both the agent and the club representative have to be careful. If one of the players feels his value is higher than the previously signed player, the agent is in a tough position, and unless he has discussed the process and conversations at length—and early in the process—he may lose the player with the lower-valued deal. It's one scenario to have a different agent negotiate a higher-valued deal—it's quite a more difficult scenario when the same agent did both deals.

In the case of Clayton and Zack, we did want them both and knew we were markedly better with them both than with just Clayton. Had that not been the case, the club did increase its leverage some by at least having one of the two. Think of the leverage an agent would have if the first player eligible to leave did—the remaining player would have a tremendous amount of leverage if the team could lose them both. Fortunately, we had Zack signed before Clayton's negotiations began.

We told Casey we wouldn't be deterred by a long-term contract for Greinke. We knew other starting pitchers were getting deals in that range. We let Casey know we were prepared to move when he wanted to move. He said it was a big decision and Zack was going to have to meet personally with the finalists. We said we understood and we'd wait to hear from them.

We waited. And we waited.

I would call Casey about once a week to check in. He would say Zack's not ready yet.

Just before Thanksgiving, I called again and Casey said, "Maybe after the holiday, one of us can visit the other; let everybody get to know each other. You can ask Zack questions you have about him and he can ask questions he has about you and the organization."

Remember, Zack was once diagnosed with social anxiety disorder, a condition, he said, that plagued him from high school through his early major-league career. He missed all but three games of the 2006 season with the Kansas City Royals while he sought professional help. So I assumed when he came to meet with us he might want to bring along a support team in addition to his agent.

I was surprised, and impressed, when Close called. "Zack and his wife, Emily, will be out Tuesday," he said.

"Well, when are you coming out?" I asked.

"I'm not coming out," Close said. "Zack's going to come over by himself and meet you at the ballpark."

Impressive and interesting.

Of all the free agents I've dealt with, few—very few—would ever meet alone. Usually they had an entourage. Usually they had people to answer the tough questions for them—not let them get themselves in a box.

These meetings are meant to give both sides perspective on what they can expect. Few players are accustomed to these types of conversations and their comfort level is low. They are making a first impression on the personal side and neither player nor agent wants the team hearing or seeing something that would make them wary about the player's goals, priorities, competitiveness, stability, or lifestyle.

Many times in these meetings, the agent answers a majority of the questions. To me that's not a good sign. Even though the player has been somewhat "protected," the team isn't learning that much. I was always more comfortable with a player who asked questions and spoke out, whether I agreed with the answers or not. After all, these are job interviews. You don't come in to a job interview and say nothing except hello and goodbye.

I've walked away from players who didn't seem confident enough to hold a conversation. And on the flip side, I pursued players because their conversations sometimes broke a tie with other candidates who didn't offer much and left too much to chance; I was already taking enough of a chance.

In Greinke's case, he and his agent were confident enough for Zack to come out solo to meet with Don, Stan, and myself.

The four of us sat in Stan's office for about three hours and went through a variety of topics. Zack thought differently from most people I'd dealt with in the past. His memory was so sharp, his recall was astounding, and his filter nonexistent.

We went through our free agent amateur draft. We went through our lineup. He explained how he pitched to each one of our hitters. He explained how he thought some of the hitters we picked in the draft were good and some were bad. He liked Corey Seager, our first-round selection. He said he thought Milwaukee, where he had been pitching the day of the draft, should have taken Seager.

It was a different dialogue from anything I'd experienced with a free agent. We talked some basketball. He's a huge basketball fan.

About three hours in, we called a halt to the meeting and everybody left thinking it was going to be a pretty interesting fit. He wanted to know about our mind-set on the team, how we put it together, what we thought about the Boston trade, whether those guys all meshed.

We also talked about commitment. He was considering a long-term commitment and he wanted to make sure the new ownership was in it for the long haul—not just here to make a splash for a year or so and then bail out. I guess promises had been made when he was in Kansas City that he thought had fallen short. Stan assured him that wouldn't be the case in Los Angeles.

After that session, Casey Close and I continued to talk as the Winter Meetings approached.

AT THE 2012 WINTER MEETINGS in Nashville, Casey Close and I met every day except one. Our session on Wednesday night, the night before the meetings ended, turned very acrimonious. That happens.

Casey was in the $160 million range for seven years and we weren't going seven. We would go six. The meeting was so tense that I honestly didn't know if we would ever speak again about Zack. Casey stood up from the table, walked out of the suite, and slammed the door behind him.

Stan wasn't in on the session but came by just a couple of minutes later to get briefed. When I told him, he was angry. He was yelling. He wasn't as upset with me as he was with the whole process. While other executives who had worked with Stan warned me he was prone to explode, this was the first time he'd been loud and animated around me. The outburst lasted five minutes. He finished and walked out of the suite, slamming the door behind him. The door had been through a tough few minutes.

On Thursday, as I was leaving Nashville, I sent Casey a text: "Look, we haven't spoken for a day. You still have interest in continuing the negotiation? We're hoping. Let me know on Friday what you want to do."

On Friday, Casey replied saying he was still interested, but we would have to move off our number. I texted him back and said he would have to do the same. He sent back that he had some room to move so we should continue to talk.

The Ryu negotiations were coming to a head Sunday, so all day Saturday, December 8, 2012, I juggled the two deals. Luckily, though, I still had twenty-four hours for Ryu. I offered Zack a six-year deal, with the option to walk after three years if he wanted. In my mind, that was a powerful offer for the player. If his performance dipped, for whatever reason—injury, slump, whatever—he could refuse the option and keep the team on the hook for the full value and term of the contract. But it's also giving the player the best of both worlds, because if he continues to pitch great and salaries continue to rise, he can opt out and demand more money from us or go someplace else.

In the end, I think that's what won the day for us. The Texas Rangers made a hard run at Greinke and the money they offered was reportedly basically the same, but they wouldn't go for the opt-out clause. We needed something to separate us from the competition because we were battling a few issues, including an additional 10 percent state income tax charge in California compared to Texas.

Obviously, Greinke and Close wanted as much money in the first three years as they could get. We battled with that for a while, but finally struck a deal a little after five thirty Saturday night— pending a physical on Monday. I called Stan. He was happy. I informed Vance, Ragazzo, and Donnie.

By the time I finished the last of those calls, somebody in the Dallas area already had broken the story that the Dodgers had signed Zack Greinke. Whew. What a crazy world. Instant communication. And to think, when I first fell in love with baseball, I was always a day behind—and sometimes a game behind—on getting a Cubs score.

Zack's time in Los Angeles worked out. He exceeded all expectations, posting a 51-15 record during his three seasons, with three Top 10 Cy Young Award finishes, including a second-place finish in 2015. That season, Zack's last with the Dodgers, he was 19-3 with a 1.66 ERA in 222⅔ innings of work—one of the best seasons any pitcher had in decades. He then opted out and signed with Arizona for $206.5 million. The deal we signed in 2012 worked out for us and for the Greinkes. We wish every deal could be so wildly productive.

Even now, I would do the deal the same way. Nearly every pitcher has a shelf life. The key is to get the most productivity before injury or a decline in performance enters the equation.

ON MONDAY, DECEMBER 9, we announced Ryu. On Tuesday, we announced Zack. At both news conferences, Earvin Johnson introduced me, which was pretty cool. At the Greinke conference, Charlie Steiner introduced Earvin, who was going to introduce me. While Charlie was talking, Earvin was leaning over, asking me about Greinke. So I gave him my thoughts—four or five different points. But when Earvin got up to speak he used all my material. I was out of things to say and I was up next.

Earvin's a lot bigger than I am, and he's the boss. So I just thanked him for the great introduction and asked anybody if they had any questions—now that they knew how Earvin and I both felt about Zack.

Earvin was a very positive influence on the organization and the players. He told me early on that the clubhouse was for the players and the manager and staff. If I ever needed him to talk to a player, recruit a free agent, or just wanted advice on anything, he would always be there. He said he didn't want to be in the way and that he knew his place.

Earvin usually spoke to the club at Spring Training and his message was always one of the most insightful and powerful I'd heard. He knows how to be successful in life and in business. As a player he knew how to win in all environments—especially the most hostile ones, like the Garden in Boston or the Spectrum in Philly. He had made winning a life's work.

I was happy Earvin used all my material introducing Greinke at that first news conference. I really didn't have to say how I felt about Zack. It was obvious. At least I hoped it was. He is an exceptional pitcher and person. A class act. And we were lucky to have him.

Twenty-three
TOO GOOD TO BE TRUE

· · · · · · · · · · · · ·

A few hours before he planned to take five of his kids trick-or-treating on Halloween night 2012, onetime home run record holder Mark McGwire sat squirming in a chair at the posh Pelican Hill Resort in Newport Coast, California.

"Ned, I need to tell you something."

"What's that, Mark?"

"I'm really nervous."

We had asked permission from the St. Louis Cardinals two days earlier to talk to McGwire about a position as the hitting coach. Cardinals GM John Mozeliak already had offered Big Mac a contract for 2013, but agreed to let us talk. Like us, Mo had heard McGwire was beginning to tire of leaving his family home in Southern California while he spent a baseball spring and summer in Florida and St. Louis.

McGwire is a native of Southern California, played his college ball at USC, and was living in Irvine, fifty miles down the coast from Dodger Stadium. He had just turned forty-nine on October 1, and he and his wife, Stephanie, had five kids at home—Max, eleven; Mason, nine; and three-year-old triplets: Monet, Marlo, and Monroe.

We were looking for a hitting coach to replace Dave Hansen after our disappointing offensive performance in the second half of 2012. I started the search by asking our pitchers which teams' hitters regularly stymied our scouting reports. Which teams' hitters seemed to make the best adjustments?

"St. Louis," was the answer I got most often.

So Ragazzo and I drove down to Pelican Hill Resort to have a face-to-face with McGwire, who coached those relentless hitters.

The first fifteen minutes of our conversation were, frankly, awkward. I'd never met Mark before and he seemed to be all over the place as we tried to make small talk. Finally, he took a deep breath and confessed how nervous he was.

"I've never had a job interview before," he said. "I was a baseball player for a couple of decades—a collegiate player, minor-league player, major-league player. I got out of the game and Tony La Russa hired me as his hitting coach. I've known Tony for years, so it's not like we had an interview process to go through."

I looked at Mark and told him to relax. "We're looking to hire you, not to not hire you," I said. "Let's just have a conversation, free and easy. Don't worry about saying things in the right order or being too particular choosing your words. Just tell us what you think. I need to know your thought process and how you teach. You know, what you expect out of the hitters you are in charge of every day. That's what's vital to me."

From then on, we had a great meeting. We talked about Mark's maturation as a hitter—how injuries early in his career helped him become better. During his rehab, he had to learn a lot more about hitting. He had a great rookie year, fell off his sophomore year, got hurt, and really had to change his thought process and approach, which, in the end, turned him into one of the great sluggers of our time, albeit one who carries an asterisk.

We hired him the next day and he did a great job for us. He was a strong influence on Yasiel Puig when the Cuban defector made his sensational debut in 2013. Kemp loved working with him. We went from tenth in the National League in on-base percentage (OBP) and eighth in the league in batting average in 2012 to third in both categories in 2013 with McGwire as our hitting coach. In 2014, Big Mac's second year, we were even better—leading the league in OBP and finishing second in batting average.

OBVIOUSLY, WE COULDN'T INTERVIEW MARK without addressing the issue of steroids. On January 11, 2010, less than three months after he was hired as hitting coach in St. Louis, McGwire admitted publicly for the first time that he used performance-enhancing drugs for more than a decade during his playing career, including 1998, when he hit what was then a record seventy home runs in one season. McGwire apologized to the fans and to Commissioner Selig. He also telephoned a half-dozen former teammates as well as Pat Maris, widow of onetime home run king Roger Maris, to say how sorry he was. He'd made mistakes, but he owned up to them, publicly and privately, with class.

I didn't want to rehash the steroid issue with Mark, but I did ask him, given what he had confessed, if he thought he should be in the Hall of Fame. His answer reinforced to me that he is a humble man, who realizes he made a mistake—the same mistake that many of his peers made. But, unlike many of his peers, he is a man who can admit his mistake and recognize its consequences.

He said he felt by the criteria that was established, he should not be part of the Hall of Fame.

I thought that was one of the best answers I ever heard any athlete give when asked if he should be in the Hall. I thought it spoke volumes about the man. And based on his success with the Cardinals, we were excited to bring him to the Dodgers.

THE INTRODUCTION OF STEROIDS into professional sports changed everything. From a decision maker's perspective it made player acquisitions and signings very precarious. In some ways, it was fraudulent.

There was no way to know if a player was on steroids. You could watch body size change over time and you could see performance trends rise to new heights, but did you really know? As I studied trends, I found there were players I had signed off of their good years who suddenly stopped performing at those levels—when the contract they signed was based upon what they had recently accomplished, accompanied by the expectation that it would continue.

When players were about to enter their "walk year," which is what the final year of a contract is called when a player becomes a free agent the next season, some performances spiked remarkably. But you couldn't ask, you couldn't test, you didn't know. It was all left to guesswork and trying to figure out if performance would continue at the level you paid for. My tenure in the game began before the PED era and continued through testing and suspensions and the supposed cleanup. Through it all, I never saw any player do anything.

But did it alter decision making? Without a doubt. It is hard enough to predict future performance when large sums of money can easily change someone's perspective. It is impossible to predict decline through an injury that hasn't happened yet. When you add PEDs to the equation, it means a player you are signing who is using PEDs may not be the player who will be performing for you— that *is* akin to fraud.

It wasn't just the home run hitters or the hard-throwing pitchers. In my assumption it was also the twenty-sixth man trying to be the twenty-fifth man and make the major-league roster; the thirteenth pitcher on a twelve-pitcher staff; the career minor leaguer trying for that one shot at the big leagues. Check out the Mitchell Report names; not all were potential Hall of Fame candidates. Players looked around and saw other players doing it and not being stopped and probably figured it was worth it to follow along. And as salaries continue to escalate, the reward takes a measurably higher standing than the risk.

Like just about every executive in Major League Baseball, I've been asked about steroids time and again. When did players start using them? Did we turn a blind eye? Should we throw out all the records from the steroid era? Should any of the players who juiced ever be allowed into the Hall of Fame?

I don't know if anyone knows the day steroids came into the game. The consensus seems to be the mid to late 1990s—maybe after the strike of 1994–95. Only the pioneering players would know for sure.

Obviously, we can all read about players who either turned up in the Mitchell Report or tested positive or are on lists of people who bought illegal drugs. So I know it happened. And I know it happened with players who played for the Giants and the Dodgers. While I saw bodies change, I never saw anybody do anything illegal. I never saw a needle. I never saw a gel or a cream. I never saw a patch.

That said, I did work inside baseball when hitters put up sixty-six home runs, seventy home runs, seventy-three home runs; where failed starting pitchers turned into dominant closers and strung together accomplishments that had never occurred before— accomplishments that never happened before in the history of the game, in more than a hundred years of baseball. I saw accomplishments that made me say to myself, This guy is too good to be true. I said it in all innocence, but in too many cases it turned out he *was* too good to be true.

I said it too many times about too many players. How many? I can't tell you. I think it would be interesting to know—if everybody came clean and admitted whether they did or they didn't; whether they did it once or whether they did it every day. I think it would be very interesting. I think it would also be heartbreaking to a lot of fans to see the volume of players who used PEDs. But do I know for sure? I don't.

A lot of times the difference between Triple-A and the big leagues is really the consistency of performance. More than a few minor-league players come up, have a great week, and then, when the ink gets around, when the scouting reports get around, everything changes. Well, there were times when the ink was getting around and it wasn't changing anything. PEDs probably had a lot to do with that. Do I know that for sure? Just an educated guess.

What I do know—and this is not to mitigate the sins or damage in any way—is that it wasn't just the Mark McGwires and others who were putting up Hall of Fame–type numbers. It was players trying to keep their careers alive, trying to make it to the big leagues, trying to get enough time in the big leagues for a better pension, trying to get a contract that would get them to the arbitration stage, where they could start making millions of dollars, not just hundreds of thousands. It was players who needed a boost to get to free agency and sign the five-, six-, seven-year deal for $20 million or $25 million a year and then, when they got there, backed off to save their bodies from whatever long-term effects those drugs had.

All of that created a false reality where teams signed players based on performance established during a short period of time—usually coinciding with the player's drive to become a free agent or arbitration eligible—and then wound up with a different player and performance.

Sometimes, as an evaluator, you wondered about the physical and statistical changes and passed on a player because of them.

Other times, you wondered, talked yourself into it, and took a chance. Winning is at such a premium and talent is always such a rare commodity that I found myself signing players who I didn't know for certain were clean. But if I didn't sign them some other GM would and if it turned out that the player was clean, or didn't get caught, my team would be at a disadvantage. The police work wasn't my job.

As April 2016 came to a close, Major League Baseball announced Dee Gordon had tested positive for PEDs and suspended him for eighty games. I was stunned.

Drafted by the Dodgers, Dee was gifted with speed, quickness, and an ebullient personality. He also was slightly built, which the grind of a baseball season challenged.

Dee was at Dodger Stadium when his suspension was announced. He was traded to Miami in 2014—one of the first deals made by my successor, Andrew Friedman.

As a Dodger, Dee struggled to play every day at a consistent level and to keep the needed strength and weight to sustain a strong performance throughout a major-league season.

Until 2015, his career had gone backward—from being the leadoff hitter and shortstop for the Dodgers in 2011 to a part-time player in 2012 and 2013. On the morning after the Cardinals eliminated us from the 2013 NLCS, I met with Dee in the lobby of the St. Louis Westin hotel.

I told him I believed he needed to learn to play second base. I told him that I believed changing positions would be his best opportunity to play in the big leagues—shorter throws, more time to make plays, less grind on the body. To his credit, he went to Winter Ball twice that off-season and learned the position. He had a decent first year at second base for the Dodgers in 2014, but again, his performance tailed off during the second half. His on-base percentage went from .344 before the All-Star break to .300 after the break. His batting average dropped from .292 to .284.

After he was traded to the less pressurized environment of South Florida, Dee won the National League Batting Championship, won a Gold Glove for his defense at second base, and led the league in stolen bases in 2015. An impressive trifecta. For the first time in his career, his performance was steady all year, with a .338 batting average before the break and .327 after, and an OBP of .359 and .358.

The Marlins rewarded him with a five-year, $50 million contract.

Just four days before Dee was suspended, I met up with him when the Marlins came in to play a series at Dodger Stadium. He looked the same—perhaps a little stronger, a little more mature. But the locker room pregame music was blaring and he was smiling and laughing as always. He was the same Dee Gordon I'd known since he was a young prospect trying to make an impact and leave a positive impression.

I congratulated Dee on the upturn in his career and the new contract. He thanked me for my help and instructive conversations. We wished each other well.

Little did I know as I walked away that Dee Gordon 2.0 was too good to be true.

THE QUEST FOR STARDOM, a big-league career, and financial riches are at the heart of PED usage.

When I first started in 1982, Billy Buckner was the highest-paid Cub. He was making $400,000. That year, Dallas Green traded for Larry Bowa, who was making $500,000. I believe we signed Fergie Jenkins to his last contract, trying to get him to three hundred wins. He was making less than $200,000. Fast-forward. The minimum salary in 2017 was $535,000—more than Bowa, the highest-paid Cubs player, made thirty-five years earlier. Bowa wasn't a Hall of Famer and the value of the dollar thirty-five years earlier was a lot different. But think of it: a kid comes up from the minors in 2017 and makes more than a player who, just a generation earlier, was a five-time All-Star, earned two Gold Gloves, won a World Series championship, and finished his career with 2,191 hits.

In 1982, Philadelphia's third baseman Mike Schmidt, on a Hall of Fame path, was believed to be the highest-paid player, making $1.5 million. In 2015–16, players who were good players, not great players, started signing contracts in the $150–175 million range with average annual values in the mid $20 millions. On the high side today, $30-plus million annual salaries dot the landscape.

Signings of that value continue to raise the floor for the average player, the free agent player, the specialty player, the salary arbitration eligible player.

In my opinion, Major League Baseball needs to further tighten the noose on players who continue to try to sneak through the testing program. Clubs should have the right to void a multiyear contract of players who test positive.

Gordon lost $1.65 million of his salary in 2016, but he still will make $48.35 million of the $50 million contract he signed with Miami. Wouldn't it be fairer if the Marlins had the right to reconsider the signing decision once Dee served his suspension? Will Dee win another batting title and not test positive months later? Was the player who signed that $50 million contract a clean player? What about the effect his absence from the lineup has on the team results? Is that fair to the Marlins?

No team ever paid a player in counterfeit money. But more than a few teams were forced to pay counterfeit players.

Personally, I favor a lifetime ban without pay for players who cheat. Allow them to appeal, but if the facts prove they cheated, they are gone from the game.

If baseball won't impose a lifetime ban without pay, then clubs, at the very least, should be allowed to renegotiate or void those long-term contracts that set up players like Gordon for life.

MONEY MAY HAVE LED PLAYERS to PEDs, but the big money is responsible for some other prominent, challenging changes in the game, as well. In my mind, the explosion of salaries has helped skyrocket the number of players who go on the DL. The money's simply too good. The money's too big to make a player want to pitch through pain, to play through an injury. They don't want to risk it. If a starting pitcher can make a great living and limit his starts to five or six innings, instead of seven or eight or nine innings—and, really, those last couple of innings of every start are going to be the more stressful innings of an appearance—he might save himself a year or two during the course of his career. You may have a year or two or three left in your arm when, normally, you would be done. What's that worth? Thirty million? Ten million a year? We're talking life-changing money. In many cases, you're talking about a lot of people who grew up in homes where, maybe, the mom and dad both worked and, maybe, earned $100,000 gross between them. Now you've got their son making $100,000 a day for 187 days a season. That can't help but lead to profound changes.

The power of the players' union, guaranteed contracts, the size of the paychecks—they've all changed the hunger of today's athletes. Too often, managers, coaches, general managers, player development people will tell a player, "Hey, we need you to do this, we need you to do that," only to be met with a shrug or a roll of the eyes. "Really? I really have to do that?"

And what can we do? A player has to do something so staggeringly belligerent, so far over the line, to be suspended. Players these days operate with such wide latitude, it allows them to do sometimes as little as possible to stay on a team. Many times a player's effort will be in the lower half of a percentile. But however little he puts out, his paycheck comes in at 100 percent. Only the bad hops bounce in Major League Baseball; the paychecks don't.

I believe a lot of players today feel it would be nice to win a championship, but, if not, well, so what? What's the worst that could happen? A team has a bad season and a player goes home with maybe $15 million. That's not exactly the end of the world. And what's the worst that can happen to him next year? He'll probably get a couple million dollars' raise.

A hundred years ago, ownership ruled the game. Players had very few rights, and players did not have a choice to move from team to team for more money or a better opportunity. Superstars of the game were not treated fairly, were not paid commensurate with their abilities, let alone in line with what the owners were making. Some people feel that disparity led to the Black Sox Scandal of 1919. It led to different leagues. It led to holdouts. And it led to yet another attempt at a players' union, which became one of the most powerful unions in the land.

From about the mid-1960s, things started to slowly change. By the time the late 1980s had arrived, things were really changing. And by the time you got to the 1990s and beyond, we were well on the other side of the pendulum.

In 2005, three teams had payrolls exceeding $100 million. In 2015, twenty-two of the thirty teams had payrolls more than $100 million. And only six teams entered the 2014 season with payrolls under $90 million.

And spending big doesn't always equate to winning big. Four of the six teams with payrolls under $90 million in 2015 made the postseason at least once since 2013. Of the nine teams with the highest payrolls, five missed the playoffs and three finished in last place.

While payrolls have exploded, so, too, have revenues and franchise values. In 1981, the Tribune Company purchased the Cubs and Wrigley Field for $20.5 million. In 2009, the Cubs sold for a reported $845 million. In 2004, the Dodgers sold for $431 million, and in 2012, the team sold for $2.15 billion. *Forbes* reported that the industry would most likely surpass the $10 billion annual revenue mark in 2016.

How do we get back to somewhere in the middle? The game would have to shut down for that to happen. Do we need to get to the middle? Probably not if revenues, particularly the national television revenues and team cable television contracts, continue to soar. Does that mean this is the best balance the game will have? Considering the revenues, maybe this is the middle.

I FEEL SORRY for the fans who lived through the steroid era. So many numbers the players put up from the 1990s through early 2000s were synthetic as well. So much of the history everyone watched was fabricated. I can't help but think of all the computer-generated special effects on TV, the movies, and electronic games. The special effects are amazing, but you know they're fake. That's what baseball was like. It takes away so much from the game. And, no question, it takes away from the Hall of Fame.

I was a sportswriter early in my career, but I focused on hockey, not baseball. I never came close to serving the ten consecutive seasons as an accredited baseball writer that would have qualified me to vote for the Hall of Fame. In some cases, the voters are casting votes on assumptions and sheer speculation about players who may or may not have used steroids. They don't have all the facts and they probably never will.

I find it a very interesting debate—who should be in the Hall and who shouldn't. But I believe it has also become a witch hunt. You've got players who never tested positive, never were part of the Mitchell Report, never showed up on any lists at any drug factory, and now the sportswriters are making themselves judge and jury. I think that's totally unfair. I think the era was so saturated with players who used PEDs that it's difficult for me to come up with a right answer. Do you punish somebody—even if his name is in the Mitchell Report—who was putting up preposterous numbers at the plate against pitchers who were just as juiced? In a lot of ways, there was a level playing field among the best players in the game during the steroid era.

Was it wrong? Yes. Was it breaking the law? Yes. But that's a different arena. That's for the grand juries, the courts, and the prosecutors to handle. Induction into the Hall of Fame or not? That's a difficult question.

And what about amphetamines? Amphetamines are banned, too, but Hall of Fame voters tend to gloss over the issue. There is no way to know how long amphetamines have been around the game. There is a good chance that players took amphetamines for decades. When you look at the schedule, with 162 games in 187 days, or 154 games back before 1961 in probably 160-some days, how do players do that? How do they play a game that starts at 8:05 p.m. in New York on a Sunday night, play till 11:30 p.m., take off from Kennedy Airport at 2 a.m., fly six hours to the West Coast, get to bed at 8 or 9 in the morning, and play that night? How do they do that day after day *without* taking something that's going to help them physically regroup? But that's illegal, too. What do you do about all those records when "greenies" were readily available in every clubhouse? We all know the stories about clubhouses with two coffeepots—one "leaded" with amphetamines, and one "unleaded" with just regular coffee. Did any of the writers let that sway their Hall of Fame votes?

I spent eleven seasons with the Giants and Barry Bonds. My relationship with Barry was pretty much the same as many others in the first year or so. I said hello to him my first Spring Training in Scottsdale in 1995. I said hello about five more times that season. Not once did he acknowledge me.

During Spring Training 1996, I was walking through the clubhouse when Barry called out to me.

I was surprised.

"Hey, Ned. How come you never say hello?"

"Barry, I said hello to you a half-dozen times last year and you never once acknowledged me. That's okay. I don't need you to talk to me. All I want is for you to play as hard as you can—to give the team your best—and you've always done that."

That was the beginning of a very decent friendship. From time to time, my charitable endeavors included Barry, and he never disappointed. He didn't want anyone to know what he did for charity. He wasn't doing it for attention. But as long as he knew it was legit and as long as he trusted you, he was cordial and kind.

Barry never tested positive for steroids. He tested positive for being nonresponsive to the media. He tested positive for not being a teammate who would lead the group hug. He tested positive for being unapproachable. He appeared arrogant, aloof, nasty, difficult. But if you earned his trust, and never violated it, he was loyal and kind. If you violated that trust, you would never be allowed anywhere near him.

The relationship between top front office executives and a star player is always interesting. A star tends to take on a role. Sometimes he will engage a GM or assistant GM regularly, offering suggestions on how to make the team better or any number of topics.

Sometimes the star player says hello to the GM in mid-February and goodbye after the final out of the season with little more than a nod or a glance in between.

After our first season together, Barry and I developed an interesting relationship. We talked often and the conversations were sometimes compelling. Not all the conversations were baseball related, either. It got to the point where if I was walking by his locker—or the four locker spaces he used—before a home game, I had better have time because there was a fifty-fifty chance a conversation was going to start in which I would find myself needing to sit down at some point.

I think Barry was conflicted. He was burned early in his career when he was told time and again he was signing an autograph for a "sick kid" or something similar and then found the item for sale at a memorabilia shop. He helped friends, including longtime friends, who betrayed him. All of it, in my opinion, led Barry to wonder whether kindness was a sign of weakness. Being unapproachable was easier than being taken advantage of.

Still, I saw Barry do numerous kind and charitable acts that he didn't want anyone to know about. I saw him work with young hitters and leave a batting coach in awe because of his intelligence and teaching style. But, again, Barry didn't want the outside world to know about it.

Shortly after Barry hit his 660th home run, the Giants invited Hank Aaron and Willie Mays to the park celebrating three of the four players to reach that home run total (with the deceased Babe Ruth being the fourth). The Giants had Mays and Aaron autographing baseballs. Barry declined, not knowing who was going to be the recipients of the baseballs. Two days later, Mike Murphy, the Giants' longtime clubhouse manager, came into an office where Brian Sabean and I were sitting. He gave us each two baseballs signed by the trio and said, "These are the only ones Barry is signing now. He says you two have always treated him well and with respect." It was quite the honor, though one we hadn't asked for or expected. But that was Barry.

Two months after I left the Giants for the Dodgers in November 2005, Barry was given an award at an annual dinner for scouts in Beverly Hills. "Before I thank everyone," Barry said when he accepted the award, "I want to tell the people of L.A. how fortunate they are to have their new general manager. Ned Colletti is one of the best I know and much of our success in San Francisco was due to him. So although I'm a Giant and I don't like the Dodgers, I do like Ned and wish him the best here."

I was honored. I still am.

I don't know that Barry ever will be enshrined in Cooperstown. I do know that I saw him as a rookie and I saw him twenty-two years later as his career ended. He was the best hitter I ever saw and one of the best outfielders—especially in an underrated position like left field.

In 1998, while McGwire and Sammy Sosa were taking most of the applause for their home runs, Barry sat back and watched. I saw him nearly every day. And while body sizes were changing around the game, his looked similar to how he looked in Pittsburgh. He was a little bigger, but he was also thirty years old, not twenty-two. Still, he was smaller at the time compared to some, including those who were suddenly breaking records that had stood for generations. I didn't believe it was my place to discuss whether anyone was doing anything suspicious or illegal.

Did Barry decide to start using steroids when he saw McGwire and Sosa break records and gain increased adulation and notoriety? Did he start earlier, later, or not at all? I don't know for sure. I do know that in the first fourteen years he played in the majors, from 1986 to 1999, most of which was well before the so-called steroid era, this is what he accomplished:

Ninety-nine or more runs scored nine times; thirty or more doubles eight times; twenty or more home runs twelve times; thirty or more home runs nine times; forty or more home runs three times; one hundred or more RBI eight times (plus eighty-one RBI in the 112-game strike-shortened season of 1994); a .400+ on-base percentage nine consecutive seasons; a .500+ slugging percentage ten consecutive seasons, six of them with .600+; 250 or more total bases eleven times, including four with more than 310; more walks than strikeouts in eleven consecutive seasons; twenty-five or more stolen bases twelve times; thirty-five or more stolen bases five times; a .900+ OPS ten consecutive seasons, including eight in a row over 1.000; eight All-Star selections; three MVPs; eight Gold Gloves; seven Silver Slugger awards. Again, that was before the 2000 season.

And from 1990–99, he finished first or second in WAR (Wins Above Replacement) seven times.

During Barry's first fourteen years in the majors, he played 2,000 games, had 2,010 base hits, hit 445 home runs, drove in 1,299 runs, amassed 423 doubles, stole 460 bases, had slash lines of .288/.409/.559 with an OPS of .968. He accomplished all of that before anyone even thought of pointing a finger at him regarding steroid use.

Those staggering numbers don't even count his last eight seasons, when many fans and media believed that Barry was juiced. In those eight years, Barry won four more MVP awards and finished second to teammate Jeff Kent in 2000. He set the single-season home run record (73) and the career home run mark (762), despite being walked and pitched around at a record pace.

Barry was a very smart hitter—borderline genius with his ability to recall and ability to transform practice and preparation and put it to use when the game began. He understood the mechanics of a swing and how the body worked better than anyone else I encountered. Once or twice in Spring Training, he would spend a day in minor-league camp with hitters and watch and teach. Players and staff alike marveled at what he could see and convey. Yet, today, the voters speak loudly every January when the Hall of Fame votes are counted.

The media reveled when Barry was going through the BALCO investigations and the Mitchell Report innuendo. He was a fallen hero who ignored them, didn't spend time with them, and didn't care about their daily needs and professional responsibilities. That's still the way many feel.

I once asked Barry why he made it so tough for those around him, the media, some of his teammates—himself as well.

"Ned, all I want to do is play baseball," he said. "People can judge me by how I play baseball. Without baseball, they wouldn't know me or care about what I was doing. I'd just rather keep it all about me playing."

Of course, that wasn't possible. And players with lesser numbers who tested positive for performance-enhancing drugs but apologized publicly get far more Hall of Fame votes.

I think the Hall of Fame vote is such a complex topic that either clear, transparent, and precise rules need to be established or the voters should give up their subjective stranglehold on the selection process. Chances are pretty good that someone already elected is as guilty of using illegal drugs as those who have been locked out.

I hope one day Barry is forgiven and is enshrined. In my opinion, he was Hall of Fame–worthy long before the steroid era began. Bonds gained 53.8 percent of the 2017 vote, a fairly sizable jump from the year before, when he had 44.3 percent and 36.8 percent in 2015, but still 21.2 percent and ninety-four voters shy of induction after five years on the ballot.

IF BARRY WAS one of the greatest left-handed hitters of all time, Manny Ramirez had to be considered one of the greatest right-handed hitters—at least of his era—until that fateful May 7 in 2009. It was that day when it was announced that Manny had tested positive for a PED. *The New York Times* reported that he tested positive for using human chorionic gonadotropin (HCG), a fertility drug for women that has been known to be used by athletes to generate the body's production of testosterone after steroid use.

Manny hadn't agreed to terms with the Dodgers until early March, missing the first couple of weeks of Spring Training. I thought nothing of it until the positive test came back and it was revealed that he had tested positive during Spring Training, according to the *Los Angeles Times*.

Could it be that he was waiting as long as he could to sign, so when he did report and was tested, traces of the HCG would not be evident? It is one of the many questions that will likely remain unanswered.

In his first three months as a Dodger—the last two of the 2008 season and the first month of 2009—he had combined to hit twenty-three homers and drive in seventy-three runs, while batting more than .350, in approximately half a season. Those numbers are staggering. Too good to be true?

I bet the Hall of Fame voters will certainly think so. In 2017, Manny's first year on the ballot, he received 23.8 percent of the vote.

ONE MORE OBSERVATION about the Hall of Fame. Ron Santo, one of my heroes, finally was inducted into the Hall of Fame in 2012—more than a year after he died. What did Ronnie accomplish on a baseball field during the last year of his life that suddenly made him Hall-worthy? What an injustice that he never got to experience his dream coming true. I think it was other men's egos, other men's reluctance to add to the group that they were a part of, that kept Ron out of the Hall of Fame for so long.

Look at his numbers. He hit at least 25 home runs seven straight years and 342 in his career, drove in more than 100 runs four times, led the league in walks four times, won five consecutive Gold Gloves at third base, was named to the All-Star team nine times, and played in 2,243 big-league games. How many players do that today? It's rare, incredibly rare. And Ron did it while battling diabetes throughout his career. A routine physical exam at the start of his minor-league career revealed Santo had type 1 juvenile diabetes. At the time, in 1959, the life expectancy of someone with juvenile diabetes was twenty-five years. Ronnie was eighteen.

Santo's teammates knew about his diabetes, but not right away. He first revealed it to them in 1963, the first year he made the National League All-Star team, but asked them to respect his privacy. They did. The first time he acknowledged his diabetes publicly was on Ron Santo Day at Wrigley Field—August 28, 1971, near the end of his career. He said then that the disease never affected his play, but privately he told me a different story. He said many times he would have a diabetic reaction in the midst of a game. Sometimes his vision would blur to the point that when he focused he would see three pitchers on the mound. "I learned to concentrate on the middle one," he told me.

What Santo accomplished was remarkable, especially considering he was diabetic. He was a great leader on a run of very good Cubs teams. I think it was preposterous he didn't make it years earlier and even more so that they decided to induct him posthumously—when he wasn't around to enjoy it, to know about it, and partake in it. Tell me the logic behind that. It is one of the most profound injustices.

Ron Santo was a man who was too good to be true—for all the right reasons.

Twenty-four
SEPTEMBER OF MY YEARS

• • • • • • • • • • • • •

One day you turn around and it's summer . . .
Next day you turn around and it's fall . . .
FRANK SINATRA, *"THE SEPTEMBER OF MY YEARS"*

I never had the opportunity to meet Tim Russert, the gregarious longtime host of NBC's *Meet the Press*, who died of a heart attack in 2008 at the age of fifty-eight. But his death helped put my life in perspective. That and a million other occurrences along the wandering road of life.

Days after Russert's death, my children, Lou and Jenna, gave me a Father's Day gift: Russert's bestselling memoir, *Big Russ and Me: Father & Son Lessons of Life.* The book was a beautiful tribute to his father, a sanitation worker from Buffalo, New York.

Three months after I received the book, I began reading it. I was sitting in a Pittsburgh hotel room after a game. The season had been tough, but within a span of two weeks from late August to mid-September, we had gone from four and a half games back of the first-place Arizona Diamondbacks to four and a half in front. I was exhausted. I had watched every baseball highlight I could watch. I'd played our game back and forth in my mind so many times. I couldn't do it again. It was getting late, probably after 1 a.m., when I finally cracked open the book and immediately started missing my kids.

Early in the book, Tim Russert writes about his son, Luke, and his deep, soulful love for him. Tim tells the story about Luke going away to Boston College and how much he missed him. They were best friends, talking on the phone two or three times a day, every day.

The story goes that Luke comes home at Christmas and is trying on a shirt he received as a gift. His undershirt rides up and his parents see something on his side—a tattoo. Russert and his wife are less than happy about Luke defacing his body and let him know it, until their son shows them the tattoo. Inked to his side are the initials of his father and grandfather. Luke tells his dad that he always wanted him by his side.

That's as far as I got that night. It's tough to read through tears.

A couple of months later, I called my son, Lou, and said I had a question to ask him. I told him he could answer right away or he could think about the answer since the question was going to be one he would never expect.

Lou said simply, "Go for it."

"Lou, if I went and got a tattoo of my dad's initials on my side, would you do the same thing?"

"You're right," Lou chuckled. "Never in a thousand years would I have expected you to ask me to get a tattoo. But I'm good with it, so, yeah, I'll do it with you."

I'D MET A LOCAL TATTOO ARTIST, Landon Heying, who was a big Dodger fan. His shop was even called True Blue Tattoo. Landon once tried to convince me to get a tattoo of a World Series trophy to cover my entire back. I gave the suggestion serious consideration and said no, one second later.

Lou was flying in from Chicago for our tattoo session and as the day approached I started thinking about doing something a little more personal. I began looking for old letters from my dad so Heying could copy his handwriting. I asked my mother if she had any old letters. By this time, she was suffering from moderate dementia and would forget from day to day what I'd asked her. My dad had been dead twenty-five years by this time so my mother was my best shot at finding something, but after a dozen tries, I gave up and tried to re-create from memory the way dad wrote "N" and the "L," which stands for Louis, and his "C". I thought my attempts were close, but I knew they weren't the real thing. I wanted so badly to have the initials in his handwriting. I thought it made it at least twice as special.

The night before the 10 a.m. Monday tattoo appointment, I was cleaning out a closet at my place in Manhattan Beach when I came across a gift from heaven. Inside were a couple dozen packets of old home movies of my birthday and Christmas celebrations from fifty years earlier. Each of the packets had been hand-labeled by my dad.

The next day Lou and I got our tattoos. On my left side are my dad's initials in his handwriting. Lou did the same thing and also got his mom's initials on his side.

During my next trip to Chicago, I visited my mom and showed her the art on my side. Her reaction was no different from Tim and Maureen Russert's at Christmas when Luke showed them the markings on his side. She was upset—even though I was fifty-four years old. But she quickly softened and said it was a nice, classy display of respect and affection, albeit one she never expected. I asked her to write her name and initials on the back of one of my business cards and told her I'd be getting her initials on my other side. Begrudgingly, she did.

On the Dodgers' last trip into San Francisco in 2014—fifteen months after my mom died—I had Dolores Jeanne Colletti's initials tattooed on my right side in her handwriting. So, for the rest of my days, I have my parents by my side. That is something that is comforting and special as the September of my years begins to nuzzle me.

LIKE THE SONG SAYS, I've been a man of *wand'ring* ways. And now I find myself reaching back for yesterdays. It's amazing how many of them came on the road. I've always had a love of travel. Being able to couple that with my love for baseball was a blessing that brought unimagined and unbeatable life experiences and education. I was privileged to have held conversations with the best strategists and players in Major League Baseball for decades.

The road is a lonely place. I typically spent six weeks in a hotel during Spring Training and another 120 nights in rented rooms across the country. The number of nights a year I spent in hotels was about 165—then multiply that number by 35 years.

Along with the lonely nights in hotel rooms, the strolls around town in the morning, the dinners and late-night conversations, come the friendships and kinships.

One of the great blessings of a baseball life, especially with time on the road, was the privilege to hold conversations with the best strategists and players in the game.

People who love sports and baseball would pay to sit, listen, and talk about pitching with Sandy Koufax—hear how he challenged the great Mays and how Mays approached him one day and Don Drysdale the next. Conversations with Koufax and Kershaw, Maddux and Bonds, Omar Vizquel and Manny Ramirez, were amazing gifts. They were as magnificent to me as Michelangelo or Monet would be to an art lover, in the flesh.

And the conversations with managers—Lasorda, Torre, Zimmer, Frey, Baker, and Felipe Alou. For me, they were as intriguing as discussions with Generals Douglas MacArthur and Colin Powell might be for students of the military academies.

Or how about sitting in a New York City saloon like the old Runyon's or the Lodge on Chicago's Division Street with Harry Caray drinking until people were waking to begin their workdays? Harry's stories of Stan Musial, Dizzy Dean, and owners Bill Veeck and Charlie Finley made those crazy characters come to life. Harry had more than fifty years of baseball lore fermented in saloons and distilled through long, long nights.

"Once in a while," the legendary Caray said to me, "you owe it to yourself."

I had those opportunities hundreds of times with all those men and many others.

Maddux had a photographic memory. He remembered what he did pretty much each time he faced a certain hitter and knew if he could exploit the same weakness or needed to find a new approach to correct a mistake. He talked about throwing from the stretch in his pregame warm-ups because "the most important pitches I will make in the game will be out of the stretch."

Vizquel was the first shortstop who I recall removing his hat when he was running with his back to the infield for a short fly ball anywhere from the left field line to short center field. Why? I asked.

"Because when you are running with your back to the hitter, waiting for the ball to appear over your head, I believe I can pick the ball up thirty feet sooner if the bill of the cap isn't blocking my view."

Bonds, like Maddux, had a photographic memory. He may not have known a pitcher's name, but he knew a pitcher's release point, how his ball moved, and what he liked to throw in any particular count. I saw Barry look foolish on pitches early in a game or early in a season and learn from his mistakes better than any player I was ever around. A pitcher would remember he got Bonds out a certain way and try to go back to the well. More times than not, the ball ended up in McCovey Cove, the inlet of San Francisco Bay just over the right field wall.

I would see Barry after games when he did that and he would look at me and give me that great smile of his and just wink.

Manny would come to the ballpark at noon and hit for an hour before going back home for lunch and a pregame nap. When you talked to Manny, he seemed simple and unassuming. In reality, he was sly as a fox. He was a student of the game. He scrutinized pitchers and dissected hitting. In my mind, he was just behind Bonds in the mental aspect of the game.

Take a baseball, hold it straight out, and drop it. In the time it takes for the ball to hit the ground, that's how long a hitter has to decide what is coming his way—a 96-mph fastball, an 88-mph slider, a 76-mph curveball; whether it's in the strike zone or not, whether to swing or not. Manny and Barry were geniuses at putting that Rubik's Cube of physics and ability together every day of their amazing careers.

MANAGERS LASORDA AND TORRE are both in the National Baseball Hall of Fame in Cooperstown. Tommy paid his dues as a minor-league manager and then as a coach on Walter Alston's staff in Los Angeles. He was a master motivator.

In September 1981, Tommy's Dodgers went on a five-game losing streak to fall out from a game in front of the second-place Cincinnati Reds to two and a half back. Lasorda called a team meeting and railed to his players with a story about one of the great teams in baseball history—the 1927 New York Yankees. Tommy talked about how even that great team had weathered an eight-game losing streak on their way to winning the World Series. A five-game streak was nothing, Tommy screamed. Let's get going!

When the meeting was over, a coach told Tommy he didn't know the 1927 Yankees lost eight straight.

"I don't know that they did," Lasorda said. "But those players don't know either and now they think they're capable of great things."

The 1981 Dodgers won the World Series.

Oh, and by the way, the 1927 Yankees never lost eight in a row. Their longest losing streak was four games in August, when they were already fourteen games ahead of the Washington Senators. From 1923 to 1940, the Yankees lost eight in a row only once— early in the 1940 season, when they struggled to a third-place finish behind the Detroit Tigers and Cleveland Indians.

I SAW TOMMY from many different perspectives. First, for years, as the ebullient enemy manager of the Dodgers when I was with the Cubs and Giants. Later, I worked with him as a fellow Dodger executive whose office was no farther from mine than the distance from home plate to first base. Through it all, I made a point never to forgot what this man accomplished. He had an 0-4 record with a 6.48 ERA in 58⅓ big-league innings, yet he went on to become a legend in the game. That is impressive and worthy of great respect.

Tommy was sometimes a caricature, and always a character. He was never one to be shy about passing on a dinner check. He would bring fifteen to twenty coaches and staff members to a road city restaurant and act like he was sitting in his own kitchen, oblivious to the reality that somebody had to pick up the tab. I think it would be accurate to say that for forty years nobody paid less and ate more at some of the best high-end places across the country. One of Tommy's nicknames was "Crime" because crime doesn't pay.

As an opposing executive, I always felt his teams would be well prepared. He preached culture and staying together as a unit through whatever storms a season presented. I also had a closer look at Tommy when his teams would play in the postseason and I would assist the national TV broadcast. Many of my fondest memories involve Lasorda, who was always sharp, shrewd, and streetwise.

One was in 1988. I was completing my seventh year in baseball and was brought in during the postseason to help NBC with its national World Series telecast. The job entailed bringing players to the network's pregame show, keeping track of available players and changes during the game, then going to the dugout the final inning to bring the hero of the game to a spot near the camera for an on-field interview.

Many times it meant working in a booth with Vin Scully and Joe Garagiola Sr. during the game and helping Bob Costas or Marv Albert pre- and postgame. It couldn't get much better.

IN THE OPENING GAME of the 1988 World Series, I was in the Oakland dugout, ten feet from A's manager Tony La Russa, when Kirk Gibson hit the walk-off home run against a friend of mine, Dennis Eckersley.

Costas declared in the next day's pregame show that, despite Gibson's dramatic home run, the Dodgers, in his opinion, had the worst-hitting lineup in the history of the World Series. He granted they were riddled with injuries, but insisted the lineup the Dodgers were fielding was utterly unimpressive.

Word spread to Lasorda. And he addressed Costas's remarks in a team meeting before Game 2. Tommy was always looking for a motivational hook. The one Costas handed him was big enough to land Moby-Dick.

Hershiser pitched masterfully in the second game. He threw a three-hit shutout and had three hits and an RBI himself. I was in the L.A. dugout as the game was winding down, fully expecting to grab Hershiser as hero of the game.

Word came down from the NBC truck that they wanted Lasorda on with Costas postgame. The producers felt the one-on-one showdown was a made-for-television moment.

If Tommy won't do it, I asked, who was their second choice? Orel, they said.

As the Dodgers walked off the field up two games to none, I met Tommy at the third base coach's box and asked him if he would go on the air.

"Ned, what do you want me to do?" he asked as the crowd roared so loudly I had a better chance lip-reading than hearing.

"NBC would like you to go on now for a short postgame show."

"NBC?" he bellowed. "Are you fucking kidding me? They can kiss my ass. I ain't doing anything for those fuckers. Who wants me?"

"Well, they want Costas to interview you," I said, knowing what his reaction would be.

"Costas? Fuckin' Costas? You got to be fuckin' shitting me. I wouldn't piss on him if he were on fire."

"I get it," I said. "I just needed to know because I've got to get someone else."

I started walking toward Orel.

Tommy grabbed my arm. "Where are you going?"

"They said if you didn't want to do it I need to get Hershiser."

"Hershiser?" Tommy screamed. "Fuck Hershiser. I'll do it!"

I WAS LUCKY enough to spend scores of days sitting in the manager's office with Lasorda and Torre before games. The same with Don Zimmer and Jim Frey in my Cubs days.

Zim and Frey knew each other since they were teenagers in

Cincinnati. They dated Jean and Joan and later married them—high school sweethearts who stayed together through the travel, the minor leagues, the injuries, the sacrifices, and the celebrations. The Freys and the Zimmers combined for more than 120 years of marriage.

Zimmer signed with Brooklyn and played in the 1955 World Series, the only championship Brooklyn ever celebrated. He was a teammate of Jackie Robinson, Gil Hodges, Pee Wee Reese, and Duke Snider. He was part of the greatest era in Brooklyn Dodgers baseball. And he later played for the expansion New York Mets and iconic manager Casey Stengel.

Before he went to the Mets in 1962, Zimmer played for the Cubs. He was in the first game I ever attended at Wrigley Field, with my dad and 6,205 other fans on April 15, 1961. After Zim's playing career, he managed in every division in baseball and was at third base coaching when the Red Sox's Carlton Fisk hit the historic home run in Game 6 of the 1975 World Series.

In 1978, Zim was the Red Sox manager when Yankee shortstop Bucky Dent hit the home run that beat the Red Sox in an historic playoff game at Fenway Park. And years later, when Zim was coaching for Torre and the Yankees, he rented a house in North Jersey from guess who? Bucky Dent.

"Every room I went in there was a picture of Bucky hitting that fuckin' home run," Zim said. "I turned all those pictures around so I didn't have to relive that moment any more than I already had."

Frey was a minor-league player and manager, then joined Earl Weaver's coaching staff in Baltimore for an amazing run. In the 1970s, the Orioles won more than one hundred games three times and ninety or more five other times. Baltimore won five division championships and appeared in three World Series in a decade.

After making less than $10,000 a year and trying to support a family of five, Frey cashed in on his success in Baltimore and signed on to manage the Kansas City Royals. He took them to the 1980 World Series, where his opposing manager was Dallas Green of the Phillies—my first boss.

In 1984, Frey and Green and Zimmer combined to lead the Cubs to their first postseason appearance since the 1945 World Series.

I will forever cherish my times with Zimmer. He could be gruff. He could be surly. But once you got past gruff and surly, the man had a huge heart and was a classic character in a game filled with characters. He was in the game for sixty-five years, finishing as a coach/advisor on Joe Maddon's staff in Tampa.

I don't know where to start in describing him. He was Casey Stengel–ish in his use of the English language.

While managing the Cubs, he was on a diet and was a little late to the ballpark one day because he was, in his words, getting his pants "altercated."

I was his driver to horse racetracks all over the National League. He loved the ponies.

On June 12, 1986, Dallas Green called Frey and Zimmer to his office at ten in the morning. Jimmy was being fired as the manager of the Cubs. Frey went in and Zim sat in my office waiting for his meeting. When Jimmy came out, he said he'd been let go and that he would call me later that night.

Zim looked at me and said, "Well, pal, I'll either be the next manager of the Cubs or I'm getting fired, too."

No more than three minutes later, Zim popped his head into my office and said, "Well, kid, it was a quinella. I'll talk to you later."

They both had been let go and Zim, true to form, found the perfect horse-racing term to sum it up—quinella, where a bettor has to pick the first- and second-place finishers.

One morning, when Zim was still with the Cubs, we landed in Philadelphia about 4 a.m., after a night game in St. Louis. Zim had a car waiting at the airport to take him and coach Joe Altobelli to Atlantic City, New Jersey. I was the driver. We passed over the Walt Whitman Bridge into South Jersey, where wooded landscapes replaced the cityscapes. As the sun began to rise, deer came out of the woods and wandered close to the turnpike.

Zim looked at me from the passenger seat and said, "Would you look at the size of those dogs?"

My buddy was a classic.

THERE IS A BROTHERHOOD on the road. We are all away from someone we love and miss, while the allure of the game beckons to a nomadic life. There never was much time for sightseeing. Typically, we would leave for the ballpark early, sometimes shortly after lunch for a game that would not start for another five hours or so.

I always spent time in the manager's office, the clubhouses, and dugouts, where players, managers, and coaches discussed their craft. I did it because I wanted to learn and loved to listen. Once I had earned their respect, I would add a story or two. I learned a very long time ago that I gained more by listening than talking. One of my favorite lines came from Jose Martinez, who was a coach for the Cubs from 1988 to '94.

"*Compadre,*" Jose would say, "too many people like to talk too much. The mouth is the window to the mind and sometimes it's better to keep the window shut."

When the games ended, when a long night was turning into the next day, there were always late dinners and drinks in the restaurants and saloons that catered to the night shift of professional sports. I never lost sight of how special those times were or what amazing opportunities they presented. What a treasure it was to have dinner at any of the many restaurants in my hometown, neighborhood Italian spots like Tufano's or Mario's Table, or any of the cluster of spots on State and Rush streets, or in Il Vagabondo on Manhattan's East Side, or Sodini's in San Francisco's North Beach section, or Gitto's in St. Louis, both downtown and at the Hill— where Yogi Berra and Joe Garagiola Sr. grew up along with an aspiring announcer named Harry Christopher Carabina. Over the years, dozens of spots ended up being comfortable, where the owners and bartenders and servers knew your name even though you might be there once a year.

No one in baseball spends more solitary nights on the road than scouts. Scouting is not as sexy as *Moneyball* or sabermetrics. The best sabermetric people can tell a story with numbers. But only a few can watch a young person play baseball and project the future. I've always used both methods. Information is king, but qualitative information can be as telling and quantitative.

I've known hundreds of scouts, including my own son. They live on the road, driving thirty to forty thousand miles a year—and that's nowadays, when fewer kids are playing baseball and teams have more scouts. Go back sixty years ago when scouts drove upward of fifty-thousand-plus miles a year and slept on the side of the road, before the Interstate Highway System was even born.

There might not be a group I respect more than scouts. They are baseball's front line, doing some of the toughest work for some of the lowest pay, with few opportunities for real advancement.

Over the years, I have tried to stay in contact with my scouts as much as possible. One of the few upsides of Los Angeles traffic is the downtime it opens for communication. I lived twenty-two miles from Dodger Stadium. Eighteen of that was inner-city highway. Most days, my commute was forty-five minutes to an hour, for nearly all of which I would be on the phone with scouts—starting with the ones on the East Coast, then working my way to the Midwest, and finally the West.

I felt it was important to keep my scouts in the loop, make them part of the group. They were on the road alone nearly every day for eight months. That can get old. A friendly voice on the phone can mean a lot to them.

Like postal workers, scouts endure every type of weather. In the upper Midwest and Northeast, some travel with snowmobile suits in the trunks of their cars. In the Deep South, rain gear and insect repellent are essentials. In some of the tougher inner cities, the police will lock the players, umpires, family members, fans, and scouts inside the premises to keep everyone safe.

Wherever baseball is played, scouts are there. They travel internationally to the jungles of the Dominican Republic and politically unstable Venezuela. They are in the Netherlands, Australia, Japan, Korea, and everywhere in between.

Baseball's annual June draft is the focus of amateur scouts, who scour the United States, Canada, and Puerto Rico for talent and then face an uphill fight to have their work translate into something real. They have to convince their bosses, at the upper levels of the front office, to agree with them. Then the other twenty-nine major-league organizations need to pass on their pick. Then the amateur player has to sign. The whole process is the equivalent of successfully herding two dozen cats from home plate to first base. Plus, it's one tough way to raise a family and earn a living.

ONE OF MY FAVORITE SCOUTS was Joe DiCarlo, who spent forty years in the game, the last thirteen with the San Francisco Giants, before he died in 2008 at age seventy-three. DiCarlo was a classic. Once, when he was scouting in Puerto Rico, Joe left his dentures—both uppers and lowers—in his hotel room. I can't imagine how you could do that, but Joe did and then didn't want to spend the money on a new set. He went the last twelve years of his life without replacing his teeth.

Another time Joe was rushing to a game in a city he wasn't familiar with. He flew in and got on the bus to take him to a rental car location. After an hour on the bus, he asked the driver how much longer until they got there. The driver looked at him and gave him the bad news: "Sir, you are on the airport employee shuttle."

ALL SCOUTS ARE GOOD STORYTELLERS, but one of the best—both telling stories and scouting—was Hugh Alexander, a legend who worked for the Indians, White Sox, Dodgers, Phillies, and Cubs in a sixty-year career.

Hughie was eighteen years old in 1936 when he signed with the Cleveland Indians and batted .348 with 28 home runs in 122 games for the Fargo-Moorhead Twins in the Class D Northern League. The next year he was even better, earning a call-up to the big leagues in August after hitting 29 home runs and batting .344 in seventy-nine games with the Class C Springfield (Ohio) Indians. Alexander appeared in seven games with Cleveland and managed just one hit in eleven at-bats, but showed enough promise that he was expected to earn a starting job in the big leagues in 1938.

A native of Seminole, Oklahoma, Hugh went home for the off-season to work in the oil fields. At dusk one December evening, his flannel shirt got caught in an oil well rig gear, dragging his left hand and half his arm into the machinery.

"There was no one around," he told me several times at baseball's annual Winter Meetings, since the dates always coincided with the anniversary of his accident.

"I got to a house and banged on the door," Hughie said. "A woman answered. The women in town were afraid of the oil workers. Then she saw my arm and really didn't know what to do. She threw me the keys to a truck. I had no choice but to drive to the nearest town, about fourteen miles away. I was bleeding to death.

"I found a Native American doctor. He took one look and told me he couldn't save my arm, but would try to save my life. He gave me two shots of whiskey and a towel to bite down on. And then he took this saw and he cut my arm off right here," he said, pointing to the spot where his arm ended and his shirt continued. "And you know what? That son of a bitch hurt."

Right there a promising baseball career ended and a legendary scouting career began.

By Hughie's count, he figures he was the twentieth scout in baseball history. Today there are more than a thousand scouts.

I asked Hugh what territory Cleveland gave him to start his scouting career.

"I had Texas and New Mexico and Louisiana," he said.

Today most teams have four scouts in Texas, one in Louisiana, and New Mexico is part of another scout's territory. But there was more.

"And everything north to Canada."

The first player Alexander Hughie signed was Allie Reynolds, who won 182 games with Cleveland and the Yankees. He also signed Dale Mitchell, the last hitter in the 1956 World Series perfect game thrown by Don Larsen. And there were nearly sixty more he either scouted or had a part of signing, including three-fourths of the historic Dodgers infield: Steve Garvey, Davey Lopes, and Bill Russell; plus Hall of Fame pitcher Don Sutton and towering and powerful Frank Howard.

Alexander began scouting decades before the Rule 4 June Draft. In his first twenty-five years, scouts could sign age-eligible players on the spot. He told me he knew players' mothers typically had the most influence in the decision making, so he focused on easing their minds that the organization would look after their boys. Hughie had a persuasive, engaging personality and many times won the mom over when the dad had agreed in principle with another scout and team.

Hughie worked every angle and always competed to win, especially since he could no longer compete on the field. When he switched from amateur scouting to professional scouting, he was instrumental in helping the Philadelphia Phillies string together three division championships from 1976 to 1978, a World Series championship in 1980, and a National League pennant in 1983.

There was only one like him.

I knew of him when he worked for Philadelphia and got to become his friend and confidant when he came to the Cubs.

It's difficult to get a scout to admit a mistake, a player he missed who turned into a big leaguer. But Hughie had one of the classic misses. I heard him tell the story many times. He was in Oklahoma to see a young football star/athlete.

"I get a tip from a buddy of mine that there is this young player," Hugh said. "I drive over to his high school. As I'm getting out of the car, I notice this dark thunderstorm rolling across the plains to the west. I've also got another game to get to that's a full day's drive away. I walk in and visit the athletic director. He tells me the young man is seventeen and had a bad football injury and he already has arthritis in his legs. Plus his family had suffered many deaths among the young male members of the family. I go back outside. The storm is getting closer, the wind is changing direction, the breeze is cooling down, and tomorrow's game destination isn't getting any closer. I decide to drive on, reminding myself that it is tough enough to play baseball healthy, let alone with injuries and arthritis. I pull a piece of paper out of my shirt pocket. It has the name of the player I had come to see. I crumpled it up and let it fly out of my hand across the school parking lot. I can still see the wind taking it across the parking lot. It had one name on it: Mickey Mantle."

When Hugh Alexander died in 2000, at eighty-three, *The New York Times* published a seven-hundred-word obituary written by respected historian Richard Goldstein. Not bad for an old scout.

THE ROAD IS WHERE one of my most special baseball friendships developed and grew—my relationship with Brian Sabean.

When I was with the Giants, Sabean and I spent a lot of time on the road with the big-league club. Most days included a two-hour walk—sometimes in the afternoon, but more times than not we walked after games and a cocktail or two.

From August 30 to September 8, 1996, we were on a three-city trip to New York, Montreal, and Cincinnati. Sabes would become the general manager of the Giants at the end of the month and I would be named assistant GM. Both Montreal and New York are wonderful walking cities and have a late-night culture.

It was on one of those late-night walks along Rue Crescent in Montreal that we decided to make the tough choice of trading Matt Williams. Giants ownership was choking on the huge salaries they had given to Matt and Barry Bonds. Between the two of them, they accounted for nearly half the team payroll. We had to trade one or the other. And we needed to reload the big-league club after consecutive poor seasons. Matt was a fan favorite and a fixture in San Francisco and when we finally traded him that November, the backlash was vicious. But, in the end, just about everyone would agree we made the right call—mainly because we had acquired a player named Jeff Kent in the deal and used the money we saved on Matt's salary to sign other players.

Brian and I made those late-night walks for more than a decade. We talked into the wee hours of the morning and got up early to do it all over again. It was how we became better at what we were doing and built better teams along the way.

SABEAN WASN'T JUST GOOD as a general manager. He was great. So great, in fact, I think he deserves to be in the Hall of Fame.

Only five general managers, or presidents, of major-league clubs are in the Hall of Fame. The most recent two are Pat Gillick and John Schuerholz. Pat built the Toronto Blue Jays franchise from the ground up and won back-to-back World Series in 1992–93. He was also at the helm when the Phillies won the World Series in 2008. He was enshrined in 2011. John won two World Series titles—one in Kansas City in 1985 and one in Atlanta in 1995. He built sixteen division championship teams. The other four executives were inducted between 1920 and 1960—Branch Rickey, Larry MacPhail, Ed Barrow, and George Weiss. Sabean and Theo Epstein should be next.

Before Sabean came to the Giants in 1993, he was responsible for the draft and player development with the New York Yankees. From 1986 through 1992, his draft picks included Derek Jeter, Jorge Posada, Andy Pettitte, J. T. Snow, and Sterling Hitchcock, who was traded to acquire Tino Martinez. He played a role in the international signing of the great Mariano Rivera. Those players helped the Yankees reach the World Series six times—and win four times—in eight years from 1996 to 2003.

With the Giants, Sabean built four World Series teams beginning in 2002. Three of those teams—2010, 2012, and 2014—were world champions.

In other words, Brian played a major role with ten World Series teams in nineteen years, including seven that won it all.

Sabean did more than bring winning teams to San Francisco. His work and the accompanying success reenergized the franchise. In the forty years the Giants called blustery Candlestick Park home, attendance surpassed two million just three times. Two of those three seasons came while Sabean was in the upper echelon of the baseball operations department. Fan interest was so low the franchise was nearly relocated to Toronto and then Tampa.

Beginning in 2000, the Giants moved downtown to a magnificent, privately funded stadium. They have drawn 2.8 million fans twice since then, and more than three million fans every other year. Thanks to the champions Sabean built, the swell of fans who turned out to see them, and some brilliant marketing, the Giants expect to pay off the twenty-year mortgage on AT&T Park early.

Put it all together and I think my ol' late-night walking buddy deserves a plaque in Cooperstown.

THERE ARE LONG NINTH INNINGS. There are long at-bats. There are long flights. There are long days.

But somehow, the years flash by in an instant. We never really know when we are in the September of our years. For most of us, life suddenly begins changing. You look up and you are sixty. Where did it all go? Professional sports, Major League Baseball, is an intoxicating profession. But it takes its toll. You sacrifice most everything else in your life. The demands of the job compromise your family time, your leisure time, your health, and your life balance.

At the top of the profession, in the Big Chair as a major-league general manager, there is no down time. Every now and then you find time to put your duties off to the side for a few hours, but you can never put them away. So you go on and on and hope someday you can return home safely when the games are over.

One of the most poignant lines I ever read that captured my feelings on the push and pull of grinding professional demands was written by Jim Murray, the great *Los Angeles Times* columnist. Murray wrote for the *Times* from 1961 until his death in 1998. He was to journalism what Vin Scully was to broadcasting. How blessed the people of Los Angeles have been. For thirty-seven years, readers and viewers in the City of Angels had access to the best sports columnist and the best sports broadcaster. And they were and are simply the best. Humble, genuine, and immensely gifted.

Murray won enough awards during his career to fill a small locker room, but none more remarkable than the Pulitzer Prize he was awarded in 1990 for the collective work of his columns. Only two other sportswriters in history—Red Smith and David Anderson, both of *The New York Times*—were ever awarded Pulitzers for commentary.

I admired Murray's writing for decades, all the way back to my sportswriting days in Philadelphia. But of all the words he crafted, the most memorable to me came in a column he wrote reflecting on his long career. He wrote that while he had the chance to see the world and cover the greatest athletes and events of his time, the privilege came with a price. "Writing a column is like riding a tiger. You don't really want to stay on but you really don't want to get off."

That's how I felt. So many times, I told myself I needed to cut back. I needed more balance in my life. But the siren call of the job kept me climbing on airplanes and going to games. I told myself I'd catch up later. But I knew I was lying to myself. Time never comes back around.

And then you look up and your children are no longer little people. They are older than you were when they were born. Your hair, if you even have hair, is gray. And your friends are dying. I guess that's the September of your years.

FOR DECADES, I lived squarely in the hub. Phone calls, text messages, emails flowed continuously—an estimated 150 communications a day. Then one day, it changed. The communication went from drinking from a fire hose to an occasional drip from a leaky faucet. I went from being in the mainstream to being incommunicado down a quiet river.

More and more I've tried to take stock of where I am and where I'm headed, but never so vividly as during the days leading to my sixtieth birthday and thirty-third major-league season.

My friends, my buddies, my sports heroes were beginning to die. Between January 28, 2014, and Opening Day, April 4, 2015, I said goodbye to eight wonderful men.

There was somewhat of a respite before Dallas Green, the man who opened the first door to my baseball career, died, on March 22, 2017. Everyone needs a chance, and Dallas was the person who provided me with a life-changing one in 1982 and then another opportunity in 1984, when he moved me into the baseball operations side.

The somber stretch began on a Tuesday afternoon in late January 2014 when I drove to Calabasas, California, to hug and say goodbye to Tom Sherak, one of the best people I ever met. Tom led the league in titles and friends: husband, dad, grandfather, brother, actor, producer, film distributor, president of the Academy of Motion Pictures Arts and Sciences, networking master, fundraiser for the underserved or those in need. He was an advocate for humanity.

"Tom," I said one day on the phone, "do you realize this is the one hundredth straight phone call in which you have asked me for something?"

"It might be," he replied, "but let me know when I ask you for something for me."

He was right. He was a conduit for hundreds of people. He was dying of prostate cancer, despite a decade of desperate treatments, but he never thought of himself. If you had a common cold, he wanted to help you feel better.

More than a thousand people, many of them the power elite of

Hollywood, turned out for his funeral in Woodland Hills on January 30, 2014. His children eulogized him with amazing love. His wife, Madeleine, brought many to tears as she spoke of the life she and Tom built after meeting on a blind date in 1967. But, for me, some of the most touching words came from Sherak's longtime friend Rabbi Uri Herscher. His rabbi started by saying Tom probably had a few words of advice for God about how He could improve things in heaven. "And God should listen," Herscher said to loud laughter. Rabbi Herscher took in the crowd of mourners, which included people of many faiths and many industries, and paused from his written remarks and detoured right from his heart. "I look at all of you," he said. "I see people who I know don't like each other. I see people who have gone out of their way to not see each other for twenty years. I see you today sitting in the same pew. That is what Tom Sherak does."

He was right. That's what Tom Sherak did in a magnificent life. Part of me was buried that day. And I wasn't the only one who felt that way.

IN THE NEXT FIFTEEN MONTHS, I lost good friends Jimmy Fregosi, Jose Martinez, Don Zimmer, Ernie Banks, Gary Woods, Billy DeLury, and hockey legend Jean Beliveau, who reminded me of Vin Scully—talent, grace, and class. They were unique in their gifts of talent and in their treatment of people. I was privileged to have them in my life.

DeLury may be the one most fans know the least about. Billy never wore a Dodgers uniform, but he was as big a part of the franchise as anyone who ever did. The great Scully more than once described DeLury as "a Dodger from head to toe." Billy worked for the Dodgers from September 1, 1950, until the day he left this earth, April 5, 2015, the eve of Opening Day, just shy of sixty-five years. On his final day, he was hospitalized and early that evening took a walk to a veranda where he could see the distant lights of Dodger Stadium—for one last time, as it turned out.

Billy was the son of a vegetable truck driver and grew up in the tenements before coming to Ebbets Field looking for work as an office boy when he was seventeen.

When he died, you could see the sadness in the eyes of Sandy Koufax and Scully, his buddies for sixty-plus years. You could hear it in the voice of Joey Amalfitano, former player, coach, manager, scout, instructor. "Former" is a very common title in front of many baseball positions. But "former" never applied to Billy—not when it came to being a Dodger and not when it came to being a friend.

DeLury was a special man. He drove his wife's car during the time we worked together with the Dodgers. It reminded Billy of the love of his life, Ellie DeLury, who preceded him in death by many years. Billy also buried his son, William DeLury III.

I met Billy, who was slightly built, my first year in major-league baseball. He had many jobs with the Dodgers, but the one he was most remembered for was traveling secretary during Tommy Lasorda's managing tenure.

He was wise and sharp all the way to his final day. He could read people and he knew who was real and who was a phony. Often, an executive or a player would walk by and Billy's eyes would catch mine. He would ever so slowly shake his head from left to right, saying, without words, Be careful. Don't trust that guy.

When I became GM in November 2005, my first three calls were to Vin Scully, Sandy Koufax, and Billy DeLury.

DURING THE SUMMER OF 2012, Rick Ragazzo and I were going to meet at the elevator at the Ritz-Carlton hotel in Phoenix and go out to the ballpark early. On the concierge floor, having tea at two thirty in the afternoon, were Billy and Vin. Rags and I stopped by their table.

I'm not sure how the topic came up but the two men began telling their story of October 3, 1951, when Bobby Thomson homered off Ralph Branca and, in walk-off fashion, the New York Giants defeated the Brooklyn Dodgers in a three-game playoff to win the National League pennant at the Polo Grounds. It is one of the most famous moments in baseball history.

Billy was in his first full season and was helping in the ticket department. Vin was in his second year of broadcasting Dodgers baseball. When the Dodgers scored three times in the top of the eighth to go up 4–1, Billy left to return to the Dodgers offices at 215 Montague Street in Brooklyn to start working on World Series tickets.

The Polo Grounds, home field to the Giants, was located at the very northern tip of Harlem, 157th Street and Eighth Avenue. In order to get back to Brooklyn, Billy had to ride the subway south to the bottom of Manhattan and change trains to head east to the stop under Montague Street.

"So I leave and I get on the subway," Billy was saying. "We have a four-to-one lead and it's the top of the ninth. I get on a train and I'm heading south and there is no one on the train. It seemed like everyone in New York was watching or listening to the game. The winner was going to play the Yankees in the World Series, so you can imagine what a special time this was in New York.

"The train gets down to the bottom of Manhattan and I get off. I'm standing on the platform waiting for the train to take me to Brooklyn. There's one other person on the platform and he's had a lot to drink. He's stumbling around and saying 'How about them Giants. What a team.' I'm thinking he's loaded and he's just babbling, trying to make everyone think the Giants won.

"The train to Brooklyn shows up and I get on and head over to

Montague Street. I enter the building—it was an office building, not Ebbets Field—and I headed for the elevator. In those days, there were elevator operators. The elevators were like steel cages and someone would close the big door and push the button and take you to the floor you needed. So I get on the elevator and the operator pushes the black round button with the number three on it. He looks at me and says, 'Billy, what are you doing here?'

"I say, 'I came back to start to work on getting the World Series tickets ready.' He looks at me and says, 'Oh, Billy. You guys lost.' To this day, I still can't believe I heard those words. I didn't come back to work for a week. I was crushed."

Vin was part of the radio/television crew broadcasting the game. His partners were the legendary Red Barber and Connie Desmond, who were broadcasting the final innings.

"I was standing behind Red and Connie, watching the game unfold," Vin said. "We are broadcasting the game and I can't believe what I've just seen. Ann, Ralph's wife to be, was sitting downstairs. We had become very good friends. When the ball was hit, I immediately looked down at Ann. The ball left the ballpark, she opened her purse, and rather calmly took out a handkerchief, closed the purse, opened the handkerchief, and buried her face in the handkerchief. It was such a memorable and sad moment.

"But you know, baseball teaches us all that nothing is guaranteed. After doing the postgame wrap-up I walk down the stairs and begin working my way across the field to the clubhouse. At the Polo Grounds the clubhouses were next to each other in center field— more than five hundred feet from home plate. So the Giants fans are beside themselves. They are all over the field.

"I make my way from behind the plate, across the field to center field to the Dodgers' clubhouse and I am climbing the stairs to the entrance. On the stairs is Ralph Branca, my closest friend on the team. He is sprawled out on the stairs, facedown, and he is sobbing.

He had just given up the home run that, at least to that point, and maybe still, was the most famous home run in baseball history. I am at a loss to know what to say, so I don't say anything. But now I have to step over Ralph to get up the stairs to the clubhouse. I make my way inside and the room is so deathly quiet. But through the thin wall that separated the two clubhouses, you could hear the Giants celebrating as loud as loud can be.

"I needed to find a quiet place and let the players be. I went into the little training room and there on the training table sat Jackie Robinson and sitting on a chair was Pee Wee Reese, the captain. Pee Wee looked over at Jackie and said, 'You know, Jack, the one thing I don't understand?' And Jackie said, 'What's that, Pee Wee?' 'Why this game hasn't driven me crazy.'

"And that was it. We took a long ride back to Brooklyn."

I KNEW MY LIFE was changing when I started losing people whose careers, and knowledge, and personal kindness helped instill the burning love I have for the game of baseball. Education from books is wonderful, but I believe real wisdom comes with age and from those who take the time to share their life lessons and stories. Unfortunately, I don't think enough people appreciate that.

My first three stops in the big leagues were tremendous—my hometown Chicago Cubs, a world-class city of San Francisco and the Giants, and a marquee franchise—the Los Angeles Dodgers. My greatest personal failing was not enjoying it more and savoring the accomplishments for a minute instead of looking immediately for the next challenge.

Roland Hemond, a wonderful person and baseball general manager for nearly twenty-five years, told me to enjoy every celebration and win because there would be plenty of struggles. He was right.

From time to time, I heeded his advice. But I didn't do it nearly enough.

Earlier in my life, after I left Chicago for the West Coast, I had said goodbye to Jim Finks, Harry Caray, Jack Brickhouse, Vince Lloyd, Lou Boudreau, and Ronnie Santo. All these men were involved in sports, some on the executive level and some in the broadcasting world. When I was young, listening to or watching a baseball game was a big treat. I couldn't get enough of the storytelling—no matter how long the games went, or how good or bad the teams played. I was blessed that so many of the people who fueled my love for the game in my youth became friends in my adulthood. Like so many experiences of my life, I still find it truly unbelievable.

And then, they start to leave. You look around and you don't hear the familiar voices or see the familiar faces. You only see and hear your memories. And year by year, you find yourself telling stories about people your listener never knew, will never have a chance to know, and may not even know who they were.

If you are blessed with a relatively long life, I encourage you to not wait to do good. Don't wait to tell the people you respect what they mean to you. Don't wait to help others. Care about those around you. Nothing lasts forever and one day these days suddenly will become the good old days. Now is the time.

Live life to the fullest. Don't live it recklessly. Live it to the fullest, with passion, pure effort, and a heart that beats for others.

Twenty-five
YOU'RE IN TROUBLE

• • • • • • • • • • • • •

Matt Adams had just hit the first home run by a left-handed batter off Clayton Kershaw all season. A three-run home run that gave the St. Louis Cardinals a 3–2 win over the Los Angeles Dodgers in Game 4 of the 2014 National League Division Series. We'd just lost yet another flash point. Another one-on-one showdown. In this one defining baseball moment, their guy was better than our guy. And, this one time, our guy was as good as they get.

I was sick to my stomach. Fans, players, wives, coaches—a lot of people—were sick to their stomachs. But, with all due respect, no one can imagine how I felt. I went downstairs to the visiting manager's office—the same office I was in a year before after another gut-wrenching defeat to the same St. Louis Cardinals—the same office I was in just weeks earlier when Puig and Mattingly almost had a physical altercation in one of the most contentious confrontations I ever saw between a player and a manager in my three decades in baseball.

I don't have a lot of happy memories in that office.

Within minutes after Carl Crawford grounded out with the tying and go-ahead runs on base, I was sitting in that same tiny, antiseptic office, on that same miserable couch, feeling as disappointed and exhausted as I had ever felt in my career. Don and the rest of the staff went to the coaches' locker room and into the clubhouse, but Bill Plaschke, the veteran columnist of the *Los Angeles Times*, spotted me as he made his way to the clubhouse and took a quick detour.

"I think you're going to be in trouble here," Plaschke said without any foreplay.

"Really?" I said, my voice tired and somewhat surprised.

"Yeah, I'm hearing it from people who know—people in the upper ranks," Plaschke said.

"Really?" I repeated.

"Yep."

Five minutes—maybe ten—after a stunning, gut-wrenching loss, and before I could even commiserate with anyone in the Dodgers organization, an outsider was giving me inside information about my future. My loyalty to people, my value for process and for trying to handle everything and everyone with dignity and class, wasn't being matched if this verbal exchange was accurate.

It was disappointing that someone on the outside knew my fate before I did, but I didn't have the strength to battle what I had no chance to overcome. I was tired.

I immediately thought back to a conversation three weeks earlier at Dodger Stadium. I was walking back to the front offices with Stan Kasten after a game and Kasten said, "You've done a great job here. You've done tremendous stuff. We're going to get to the playoffs again and that's special and not easy to do." Then he said, "I understand a lot of your frustrations. You seem frustrated on a lot of ends. I'm going to help you with the frustrations and I'm going to take care of you when this is over."

I didn't really know what to take from the unexpected tone of the message. A bit uneasy about the comment, I said, "Thank you. I've got a contract. I don't need you to, quote, take care of me. I'm fine. But, thank you." I didn't really know what he was alluding to at the time. But I could at least offer myself an educated guess.

Then, two weeks later, just before the playoffs, he said almost the same thing. After we lost in unexpected fashion, and Plaschke drops his "you're in trouble" line, I knew my days with the Dodgers were numbered. But I've learned over the years to take things in stride. I've learned to try to spend my efforts on things I can control, to let go of the things I can't, unless I can find a way to wrestle back some control. So I lived with the Plaschke and Stan conversations for a couple of days.

We were eliminated on Tuesday night, October 7, 2014. We took the day off Wednesday.

The next day Stan and I came to the stadium to meet with Donnie and the coaching staff. By now, rumors were starting to bubble and Plaschke sent me a text saying he needed to talk to me. So I called a ten-minute recess in the meeting with Mattingly and the coaches and went into the hallway outside the clubhouse to call Bill.

"This is coming down," he says. "Andrew Friedman's their pick. This is gonna happen. The person I'm talking to is correct ninety-five percent of the time and he thinks there's at least a nine-in-ten chance this is happening."

I thanked Bill and went back to the meetings.

Stan, clearly aware of the rumors, seemed a little bit defensive when I passed him in a clubhouse hallway. "Don't worry about what you read," he told me. "Don't worry about all you are hearing."

The next day, I met with Stan at length in Magic Johnson's office at the stadium. We went over the entire baseball operations department. I gave him my candid feelings on where we were, who in the department had great upside, who I thought was pulling us down. When we finished going over everybody, Stan said we should get together for dinner during the weekend.

I agreed.

I guessed, correctly, that Stan was buying time to work out how to handle me, while at the same time talking to Andrew so he could announce everything at the same time.

By Sunday, I was ready to push the issue, so I sent Stan a text asking if he was up for dinner. I told him I'd arrange a place and get back to him.

For years, I've gone to Morton's on Figueroa in downtown L.A. for personal and professional dinners and meetings. The general manager, Jerry Bullock, is a longtime friend. I told him I needed a meeting space, a small private room.

When I arrived, Jerry had us in a banquet room that could have held sixty or seventy people. It was the same room I had used for the trading deadline in 2008 and 2009 when we had scouts in town and broke for dinner. This time it was Stan and me, alone, facing a giant television with the NLCS battle between San Francisco and St. Louis playing out on the screen. Stan ordered and I ordered. Stan seemed a bit uneasy. He was walking a lot in a room with just him and me. Then, without any small talk, he got down to business.

"I'm going to have to make personnel changes, including you," he said.

"Okay," I said.

"Don't say anything until I'm done talking," he said. "You've been very successful. I just think we need to redo things. We need a fresh start. We need a fresh look."

"I get it," I said.

"I'm going to extend your contract another year. I want you to stay. Hopefully, you'll stay. Mark Walter and I will extend you another year and give you a raise. As far as I'm concerned, you can go to the beach and never show up again or you can come back and I'll have different things for you."

He paused a second for the options to sink in.

"Andrew is a little bit uneasy with how you're going to feel. But you've told me before that it's more important for you to be part of a great organization and be part of a successful team than what's in it for you. Do you still feel that way?"

"Absolutely," I said.

"Well, then my hope is this will work out for all of us."

I said okay again and he said simply, "So, that's what I got." Then after another brief pause, he added one more thing. "If you get another opportunity—if that's what you really want—you should feel free to take it. I hope you don't. I hope that your opportunity here is strong enough for you. Know, though, that I will make it up to you in whatever you're paid at some other place if it's less than what you're getting paid now. We'll make up the difference."

I said, "Well, that's good. That's kind of you and Mark." And it truly was. I'm not sure how often that occurs, but it wasn't lost on me that Mark and Stan didn't need to extend my contract.

Business concluded and Stan and I finished eating. He left and I went to the restroom. The whole career-altering meeting took less than forty minutes and, just like that, my days as GM of the Dodgers were over.

Interesting how it goes. You sit down in a restaurant for half an hour, eat a quick meal, and have your professional life turned upside down. Even more interesting to me was the perception and transformation within baseball. Part of the reason a change occurred was the flourishing growth of analytics. And I was viewed as "old school" with my scouting philosophy.

Truth be told, it was simple analytics that separated me from others early in my career as then Cubs manager Frey asked me to keep track—by hand—of hitter and pitcher match-ups, clutch hitting, left/right matchups, and defensive positioning. We did it as computers were just coming into the game. Had I not embraced it and found use for numbers, my baseball career would have been short.

As analytics became more of a go-to requirement, I continued to embrace them. I just could never put sheer numbers ahead of the soul and personality of the human being inside the uniform. I used every piece of information I could in my decision making. I didn't brag about it or feel I needed to explain how the Giants, and then the Dodgers, came to their decisions. But I do understand the allure and the fascination with the numbers that the game produces. And it is not surprising, really, especially when you consider the fortunes earned by so many owners prior to their baseball experience. They live in worlds where analytics predict the futures of companies and products. Numbers are black and white. Those owners became millionaires and billionaires with formulas and calculations that crush the competition.

In my first years with the Cubs, the Tribune Company leadership didn't seem to appreciate the great scout Hugh Alexander—how someone with barely a high school education and a somewhat disheveled appearance could be brilliant at projecting baseball talent. The leadership of the Cubs' parent company was filled with MBAs from Northwestern and Michigan. Without question they knew how to grow the company and its stock. None of them looked like Hugh Alexander.

MONDAY MORNING, OCTOBER 13, 2014, news was starting to leak that I was going to be replaced. On Friday I had already told my two top aides, Ragazzo and Lovelace, that I was pretty sure we were done. When I arrived at the ballpark Monday, I told Ellen Harrigan, with whom I had worked closely all my Dodgers days. As astute and observant as Ellen had always been, she was stunned. Then I went to lunch with Rags and Lace and talked the whole thing over. I told them the Guggenheim people were great and they'd given us a good opportunity—that we shouldn't hold anything against them. Our moving on was just part of the natural order of the game. Disappointing, but destined. And we did so having won two straight divisions and leaving Andrew and company a farm system that was as good as any in baseball and that would help the Dodgers win two more NL West titles in 2015 and 2016.

The Dodgers called a news conference for 2 p.m. on Tuesday, October 14, almost one week to the minute after the first pitch of my final game as general manager. I planned to go to White Memorial Hospital in the morning to see DeLury, who at age eighty-one was doing his best to hold off the Grim Reaper. Before I could leave for the hospital, Stan called and said the news conference was being pushed up a few hours. I'd have to visit Billy later in the day.

So I went to the stadium, and when I got there Stan indicated he might not want me at the news conference. "We're a little bit cautious about having you talk to the media today."

"Why would that be?" I asked, genuinely puzzled.

"We don't want you to be upset. We don't want you to say anything you would regret saying."

I had been doing fine, all things considered. But now I was getting edgy. "You know, I've been in the job nine years," I said. "And, in that time, I've never run from anybody. And so now, on this particular day, with this particular topic, I'm not going to be available? I'm going to have people calling me for the next twenty-four hours trying to find out what happened. And if I don't return the call, then they're going to write whatever the person who leaked this to Bill Plaschke in the first place decides is the official version?" I told Stan I didn't want to be reading about other people's versions of the truth. I wanted to be available at the news conference. "I'd rather be the person who discusses what transpired here. With you there, too, of course, but me there, not running from the situation."

Kasten said he wanted to talk it over with the rest of the top brass and we went into his office. Inside were Tucker Kain, chief financial officer of the Dodgers and managing director of Guggenheim Baseball Management; Sam Fernandez, the longtime SVP and senior counsel; Lon Rosen, executive VP and chief marketing officer; Steve Brener, one of the top sports publicists in the country, who was a longtime Dodgers PR director before founding his own highly successful promotional agency; Joe Jareck, the sitting senior director of public relations; and Bob Wolfe, executive VP of the Dodgers and Kasten's longtime right-hand man. They were all sitting on a couch and chairs around a little coffee table and looking at me as if I were a dead man walking. They didn't know what to say, so I started the conversation rather cheerily: "Hey, guys, how we all doing today?" After a brief pause, I went on. "So, I understand there's a concern that I'm upset and I'm going to say something that might damage the organization and damage me. Why would that be?" I turned to Stan. "We had a conversation on Sunday about what's going to happen, including what's going to happen to me, right?" I turned to Sam Fernandez, whom I had known for decades.

I replayed the contractual discussion Stan and I had on Sunday evening. All concurred.

Yes, it was accurate.

"Then let's do this," I said. "Let's go have a press conference. Let's have some fun. I've got nothing to be ashamed of. We won five years out of nine. I navigated through one of the most cumbersome ownership situations in the history of sport. All different people, all different situations, all over the place. I've done that. I know we've fallen short of the World Series. I know where my shortcomings are. I know the free agent signings that have crushed us. I know what our drafts have been. I know it all. I lived it. I saturated my life with it. So let's talk about it. I have no problem talking about this. I'm not going to say anything bad about the Dodgers. I love the Dodgers."

The tense air in the room started to ease and I had one more thing to say.

"You guys and the group before you gave me this opportunity. I've come to love and respect what we've got. I want it to be great regardless of who is sitting in the general manager's chair. I have no problem saying it because it's what I feel. Let's be great. Let me help. Let me help Andrew be great."

We all left the room, with about an hour to kill before the news conference.

While we were waiting, Andrew called. As Stan had told me, Andrew clearly was uneasy that I would be upset at the change.

I assured him I was good. "I've got no hard feelings. No ill feelings toward anybody or anything. I'm here to help you if you want my help.

"When I got here, I didn't have somebody like me, willing to help. The seat had been open for weeks. The Dodgers didn't have a manager. We didn't have a coaching staff. We had four, maybe five, genuine big-league players. The team had lost ninety-one games the year before. You've got a good manager. You've got a coaching staff that knows how to win. You've got a team that won ninety-four games that should have won more. And you've got me if you want me. You have my word. All I want to do is help."

Andrew seemed somewhat relieved by the conversation.

The press conference took place in a small conference room. It was dignified and gracious.

Before I left Dodger Stadium, Lon Rosen called me into his office and offered a sincere thank-you for my efforts and also a potential opportunity. SportsNet LA—the Dodgers' television network—had expressed an interest in adding me to their studio analyst list. I was flattered. I told him I would have an interest, although everything was still very fresh in my mind. Thanks to Lon, and the decision makers at the network, it opened up another door for me, where I began a baseball television career that led to earning a local Emmy Award during my first year.

A few minutes later, the Tampa Bay Rays announced Friedman was leaving and we held our news conference at Dodger Stadium.

And shortly after that, I was in the car, driving to see DeLury in the hospital.

Twenty-six

BEAUTIFUL ENDINGS

• • • • • • • • • • • • •

*It's time for Dodgers baseball! Hi everybody, and a
very pleasant good [afternoon/evening] to you,
wherever you may be.*

VIN SCULLY'S SIGNATURE INTRODUCTION

O n September 24, 2016, the Dodgers—and a fan base that
reached beyond anyone's imagination—bid farewell to the
great Vin Scully.

Vin would be eighty-nine years old in sixty-six days. He was six
games away from finishing both his sixty-seventh year of broadcasting Dodgers baseball and his Hall of Fame career.

To say Vin Scully was a remarkable man would be the definition
of an understatement. Devotedly spiritual—the father of five, grandfather of sixteen, and great-grandfather of three—he was not only the
best baseball broadcaster in the history of the game, but also a symbol
of so much that was good and true, both today and in years gone by.

Vin began his career as a twenty-one-year-old in November
1949, broadcasting a college football game between Boston College
and Maryland from the roof of Fenway Park in freezing weather
without a hat or a coat. He has told the story hundreds of times.

"They didn't have a booth and I didn't want to disappoint anyone so I made do," he explained to me more than once. "The engineer set up a table on the roof and gave me fifty yards of cord and a microphone. I had left my jacket, sweater, and gloves back at the hotel, figuring I would be in a booth. It was one cold day, but I didn't complain. I was happy although I thought I did nothing more than an ordinary job. I didn't know if they would have me back."

He was wrong. His first employers wanted him back. So did every other employer for the next seven decades in a career that touched a mind-boggling span of baseball history.

Vin befriended Branch Rickey, who played in the major leagues in 1905 and went on to become one of the greatest baseball minds of all time. Rickey brought Jackie Robinson to the big leagues, breaking the color barrier and making history.

Scully knew the iconic Babe Ruth and Connie Mack, the legendary skipper of the Philadelphia Athletics. Mack was born in 1862, when Abraham Lincoln was president, and managed his last game in 1950, during Harry Truman's administration. So, in a way, Vin's connection to the game spanned more than a century and a half.

From 1950 through 2016, he met nearly every player and executive in baseball.

I once asked him how he managed to work for one team for sixty-seven years and be so content and peaceful. His answer was simple:

"I'm happy when I come to the ballpark," he said. "And I just like people."

Considering the length of his career and the almost unfathomable string of memorable moments he witnessed and broadcast, one might think it would be hard for Vin to pick his favorite. Not so. Ask him and he doesn't hesitate: October 4, 1955—the day the Dodgers shut out the Yankees 2–0 to win their first, and only, World Series in Brooklyn.

"To this day, that was the most special moment for me," he says. "There was a ground-out and the game was over and I said, 'The Brooklyn Dodgers are world champions.' That's all I said. And people came up to me the next winter and said, 'You were so brief and then didn't say anything else.'

"Well, I couldn't say anything else. I would have cried. I had come to know the players and had the utmost respect for what they had gone through year after year of getting beat and I knew what they had sacrificed. I couldn't utter another word."

Perhaps Vin's most historic call came on April 8, 1974, in Atlanta, Georgia, when he was behind the microphone for Hank Aaron's 715th career home run.

"What a marvelous moment for baseball," he said, the pride palpable in his words. "What a marvelous moment for Atlanta and the state of Georgia. What a marvelous moment for the country and for the world.

"A black man is getting a standing ovation in the Deep South for breaking the record of an all-time baseball idol, and it is a great moment for all of us."

There was so much beauty to Vin. He possessed so much passion and wisdom about the game and about life. He was kind and gentle to everyone I ever saw him meet, whether he knew them or not. He made strangers feel special. Had he chosen to become a writer, he would have won a Pulitzer Prize; had he chosen to be an actor, the Academy Award; had he chosen to be a humanitarian, the Nobel Peace Prize.

In the end, there was a veiled sadness in those last few weeks of his career. Vin was tired and it was time to draw the curtain, but that didn't make it any easier for the rest of us.

"People ask me what I'm going to do," he said during those final days behind the microphone. "Well, when you are retiring at eighty-nine, all you want to do is live. It's not like I'm sixty-five and have twenty more years or so to figure it out. Plus, with all the kids, grandkids, and great-grandkids, if I can't think of something to do, I am sure they will."

During the morning of his last game, on October 2, he sat in the visiting radio booth in AT&T Park in San Francisco, preparing for the broadcast. His wife, Sandi, was by his side, and fans were gathered just outside the window to the booth. Every five or ten minutes he would stand and wave and receive an ovation. Later that day, Willie Mays came to pay him a visit and the Giants presented him with a plaque that will hang permanently in the visiting radio booth commemorating the place he called his last game.

The tears that were shed, the honors bestowed, and the outpouring of love those final few weeks were more than a tribute to an historic broadcasting career. They marked the turning of a page in life's journey for millions—a heartfelt tribute from generations who grew up listening to Vin's beautiful stories; a reminder of simpler, seemingly purer times.

The world had changed so much since Vin broadcast his first game. One of the biggest changes—one today's generation probably can never appreciate—was the coming of the transistor radio in the 1960s. Suddenly, miraculously, Vin could be with you right there in the ballpark. What a beautiful gift.

IN VIN'S FINAL SEASON, the presidential race was between Hillary Clinton and Donald Trump. Race relations were roiling again. Police were being assassinated in the streets. The problems we deluded ourselves into believing were solved in the 1960s and '70s were front and center.

Vin was always there to get people through the tough times, no matter the decade: a war in Korea in the early 1950s, the Vietnam conflict in the 1960s, and Iran, Iraq, and Afghanistan during the last twenty years; through earthquakes in Northridge, riots in Watts, traffic on the 405.

Vin didn't just broadcast a baseball game: He would walk you through it—story by story, pitch by pitch. He brought the warmth of a mother's touch, the serenity of a father's protective hug. For some who listened—who didn't have a place to sleep, or food to eat, or had a loved one breathing for the last time—they always had Vin bringing them back with a secure feeling in his voice that told them somehow, everything was going to be all right.

On that beautiful September night in 2016 at Dodger Stadium, Vin was honored in a pregame ceremony that featured Sandy Koufax, Mark Walter, Kevin Costner, and Clayton Kershaw. At Vin's side, as always, was Sandi. The cameras caught Vin fighting back tears, then panned to the stands to show grown men and women sobbing.

The night the Dodgers organization honored Vin, festivities began at six thirty. I would say 90 percent of the fifty-five thousand seats were filled. If it had been the seventh game of the World Series, 90 percent of the fans wouldn't have made it yet due to heavy L.A. traffic.

For nearly an hour, the fanfare and well-wishes came at a breakneck pace. Vin was as classy and cordial as ever, but it was clear the ceremonies were taking a toll on him. He never sought the spotlight or the applause—just the opportunity to do what he loved doing.

As God would have it—as Vin would have it—the last play he called at Dodger Stadium was a walk-off homer by Charlie Culberson, a journeyman infielder, that clinched the National League Western Division Championship.

It was the fourth straight year the Dodgers had won the division and the focus was on the players. Much to his peace of mind, Vin faded from the center of attention. But not for long. As much as Vin probably would have liked to walk away and quietly drive home, the fans wouldn't let it happen. They showered the broadcast booth with yet another standing ovation and Vin returned the favor.

DURING THE SUMMER OF 2012, I asked Vin for a special favor. My daughter, Jenna, had interned with the Dodgers and knew Vin. Jenna was getting married on September 7. Vin would ask me about the wedding from time to time.

I never felt comfortable asking people I was around a lot to do me any special favors, but this one time I couldn't resist.

I asked Vin if he would introduce the wedding party on tape so we could play the recording at the wedding. He didn't hesitate. Within minutes, Jenna had a family heirloom.

When the wedding party was announced that night in a Chicago suburb two thousand miles east of Los Angeles, the guests couldn't believe it. Neither could my daughter or son-in-law, Chad Koskie. A special moment made more special by a special man.

DURING VIN'S LAST TWO SEASONS, I did pre- and postgame television for SportsNet LA. When I worked from Dodger Stadium, I had the great joy to sit down to dinner before games with Rick Monday, Charlie Steiner, and Vin Scully.

I had known Vin from my first days in baseball beginning in 1982, the year he was inducted into the broadcasters' wing of the National Baseball Hall of Fame. Beginning in 2006, I spent the next nine years with Vin, sometimes traveling together when he did road games as well as the home games. On nearly every flight, I would venture up to his seat, next to Billy DeLury, and we would discuss that day's game, or something one of us had seen years before, or perhaps literature, politics, movies, or restaurants.

I never took those moments for granted. Whether at thirty-five thousand feet, across a dinner table, or just simply through the airwaves, I knew at the time what a rare and great honor it was to share Vin's company.

ON NOVEMBER 29, 2016, Vin celebrated birthday number eighty-nine. Exactly one week earlier, he was in the East Room of the White House with Bruce Springsteen, Tom Hanks, Robert Redford, Robert De Niro, Michael Jordan, Kareem Abdul-Jabbar, Ellen DeGeneres, Cicely Tyson, Bill and Melinda Gates, Diana Ross, and nine other notable Americans to receive the Presidential Medal of Freedom from President Barack Obama. The Presidential Medal of Freedom is the nation's highest civilian honor—a tribute to the idea that all of us, no matter where we come from, have the opportunity to change this country for the better.

I called Vin on his birthday and congratulated him on the incredible honor.

"It was marvelous," he shared. "But let's not forget real life either. Last Tuesday at three p.m. Eastern time, President Obama is putting the Medal of Freedom around my neck—a tremendous honor. The next day I am back home at one p.m. Pacific and I'm at the grocery store looking for milk and bread. That's real life."

As the Dodgers were beating the Padres on Opening Day 2017, Vin was getting his car washed and running errands.

"I'm aware that I'm not where I've been for about 60,000 years," he told the *Los Angeles Times*. "But I'm just where I want to be."

ON MAY 4, 2017, the Dodgers added Vin to the Ring of Honor—the retired ten numbers of an iconic franchise.

Vin is the only non-player in the ring, still more than worthy.

"When I look at those numbers, I don't see numbers," he said. "I see faces. I hear voices. I see those numbers moving. There is a sense of looking back. That was my graduating class. Those are the ones who started me on my career."

For the first few years of my Dodgers' tenure, I spent many days, nights, and flights in his company—always knowing every opportunity was being spent with someone who was going to be a once-in-a-lifetime person.

Prior to the press conference, Vin and his wife, Sandi, and I had a few minutes to catch up. He was at peace, saying he was where he was supposed to be, spending time with the most precious part of life, his family, led by Sandi. Forever classy, forever caring.

"Well, how do you do, young man," he greeted me as he always did. "I hope you didn't come here today to see me because that wouldn't be necessary. But seriously, I hope you are doing great and that life is full of blessings for you."

There is a saying about a life well-lived. Vin's talent, character, integrity, and lasting impression on others exemplify, more than in anyone I know, a life well-lived.

That's Vin. Classy. Humble. A national treasure.

VIN SCULLY'S LIFE is a fairy tale come true. For generations, Cubs fans never knew fairy tales. There were no miracle comebacks. Most seasons of my life—most seasons of countless Cubs fans' lives—were a frustrating mix of Hall of Famers and nondescript players who always seemed doomed. Cursed. Lovable losers. Choke artists. Flops. Their Greek-like tragedies were haunted by goats, black cats, and one overly zealous fan. In reality, those hexes had less to do with decades of bad luck than a long line of poor starting pitchers, porous defenses, leaky bullpens, and clutch hitters who froze in the heat of the moment.

Every time the Cubs came close to contending, the national media flocked to Chicago to pen and air the same bad-luck dirge that had been written and talked about for decades. The Cubs were cursed. First the hex tavern owner William Sianis put on them in 1945, when ushers threw him and his billy goat out of Game 4 of the World Series. Then the black cat that sauntered past Ron Santo standing in the on-deck circle at Shea Stadium in 1969, heralding the start of an historic slide where the Cubs lost a five-game lead in six days and never recovered. Years later, it was first-row fan Steve Bartman, who reached for and deflected a foul ball that left fielder Moises Alou thought he could catch in Game 6 of the 2003 National League Championship Series. The Cubs were leading the best-of-seven series against the Florida Marlins three games to two and ahead 3–0 with one out in the eighth inning of the potential clincher when Bartman got a hand on the ball. Cursed. It was the same old story whenever the Cubs got close to the Promised Land.

Then came 2016.

A calculated, five-year plan that was put into place by Theo Epstein and owner Tom Ricketts changed everything.

Ricketts hired Epstein in October 2011, hoping Theo could do for the Cubs what he had done with the Red Sox—end a run of frustration and win the World Series. Remarkably, Theo did it in 2004, when his Red Sox won their first World Series in eighty-six years.

When he became president of the Cubs, Theo told Ricketts he was going to do a complete rebuild. He told the fan base they needed patience—something loyal Cubs fans had in plenty.

Theo started by trading away the few players he inherited who had value and accumulating prospects. He signed productive free agents to easily tradable contracts during the off-season, then waited for contending teams to get desperate and overpay at the trade deadline. With losing records its first few years under Theo, the Cubs had high draft picks and Theo used them to select some of the best players available.

How patient did Cubs fans need to be? From 2012 to 2014, Theo's Cubs lost 286 games. As brutal as the club had been through most of its history, no Cubs team had ever lost that many games in three consecutive seasons.

One of the top prospects Theo added was pitcher Kyle Hendricks, who came in a trade with Texas for Ryan Dempster, someone I had tried to acquire when I was running the Dodgers. Hendricks beat Clayton Kershaw and the Dodgers in Game 6 of the 2016 National League Championship to send the Cubs to the World Series for the first time in seventy-one years. He started Games 3 and 7 of the World Series, both wins for the Cubs, and allowed just one earned run in nine innings.

I caught up with Theo around the batting cage before Game 3 of the World Series and told him he ought to thank me for not giving him Allen Webster, the pitcher he wanted as part of the deal I tried to make for Dempster. He never would have had Dempster to send to Texas for Hendricks if we had made the deal.

"That's funny and true," he said. "And to think, the guy we were set on—the player you wouldn't trade—had an ERA of seven in Korea this past season. We 'settled' on Hendricks, who was throwing eighty-eight when we acquired him."

Webster, who actually had a 5.70 ERA—not a 7 ERA—for the Samsung Lions of the Korea Baseball Organization in 2016, would have changed Cubs history had I given Theo who he wanted. But he had a point. In any case, I was glad I held on to Webster. He was part of the package I put together three weeks later in the blockbuster trade that brought Adrian Gonzalez, Carl Crawford, Josh Beckett, and Nick Punto from Boston to Los Angeles.

Theo's patient and calculated approach to building his teams bore fruit and I was there to savor it.

On Friday night, October 28, 2016, the Cubs played a World Series game at Wrigley Field for the first time in seventy-one years.

The Series was tied at a game apiece when I flew to Chicago from Los Angeles the day before that historic game. My flight was filled and at least half the passengers were wearing Cubs swag. Every conversation I could hear centered on the Series, memories of Wrigley Field, or tales of long-suffering. Most people didn't have tickets. They were flying in just to be close to the fun. One couple had flown in from Asia, changed planes in L.A., and were on their way to the city I grew up in just to be within earshot of the ballpark. No doubt about it, this was no ordinary World Series. It was, without exaggerating, a once-in-a-lifetime experience. A once-in-three-lifetimes moment.

Between my sportswriting career and my Major League Baseball career, I had spent the previous forty years watching and dissecting sports, athletes, owners, fans, and games. I had spent the twenty years before my career watching and listening to as much sports as I could—day after day after day.

Nothing was as deeply moving as this.

I had been to fifteen World Series–clinching games, including games in Yankee Stadium when the Yankees won. I had been to Stanley Cup championship games in Minneapolis, Montreal, Boston, Los Angeles, San Jose, and in Chicago. I had been to NBA championship games and a couple of Super Bowls.

For me, that October weekend at Wrigley Field was a spiritual pilgrimage bathed in Indian summer warmth. I saw fans using chalk on the outfield walls facing Sheffield and Waveland avenues to scribble memorials to loved ones who never had a chance to see what the living were seeing. Tickets sold for thirty times their face value. A standing-room ticket was selling for $3,000—more than twice the $1,318 Cubs players took home in 1908 for their shares when they won the last World Series. People wept tears of joy because they were lucky enough to pay $30,000 for four tickets in the far reaches of the upper deck.

And to think, the first time I sat in the bleachers at Wrigley Field, it cost sixty cents.

A WEEK EARLIER, before the World Series, as the Dodgers-Cubs NLCS was playing out, the media jumped on the story about my uncle Frank not being able to attend the 1945 World Series because his older brothers, including my dad, thought he was too young at age eleven to spend the night sleeping against the Waveland Avenue wall awaiting a chance to buy tickets to the bleachers.

The story first appeared in the *Chicago Tribune*. Then Fox Television announcers Joe Buck and Ken Rosenthal mentioned it on air during Game 6 of the NLCS, turning the cameras on my uncle and me, who were watching my Dodgers get beat by his Cubs.

Chicago had a 5–0 lead going into the top of the ninth inning of that game. Even as hopeless as things looked for the Dodgers, Uncle Frank had seventy-one years of bad luck weighing on him.

"You better not mess this up for us," he said, grabbing my arm tight.

The irony of my presence in Wrigley Field with a Dodgers team that I helped construct being the final hurdle to a Cubs World Series appearance wasn't lost on me. Nor that it was my last game as an executive with the organization. Or, more important, who it was standing next to me when bedlam reigned and the Cubs became National League champions.

BEFORE THE THIRD GAME of the World Series, David Waldstein of *The New York Times* called and wanted to talk to my uncle. The story about my uncle's love for baseball and the Cubs was published the morning of Game 5. It detailed how seventy-one years earlier, my dad and two of his brothers had gone to Game 6 of the 1945 World Series this is contradicted on the previous page, where it says he was too young to stay out all night. Not only was my last surviving uncle about to fulfill his lifelong dream, but it was also recognized by *The New York Times*. It was a public acknowledgment of a close-knit family, the Collettis, whose members had suffered their share of loss but who cherished baseball and passed that passion from generation to generation.

THERE ARE FEW WORDS in professional sports that mean more than Game 7.

And that is where the Indians and the Cubs found themselves Wednesday night, November 2, 2016, after nine days and six-plus games of an excruciatingly tense World Series. With the Series tied at three games apiece, Chicago broke out to a 5–1 lead in the winner-take-all showdown—only to stumble over themselves yet again. There was a wild pitch that scored not one, but *two* runs for the Tribe in the bottom of the fifth inning.

With one out in the top of the sixth, thirty-nine-year-old Cubs catcher David Ross homered in his final major-league at-bat, allowing Chicago fans to breathe a little easier with a 6–3 lead. But they wouldn't breathe easily for long.

The Cubs were four outs from history when Cleveland rallied for three runs in the bottom of the eighth. A two-run homer by Rajai Davis tied the game at six. Those wearing Cubs blue sighed and swallowed hard, with that collective lump in their throats.

If you were old enough to remember, you had come to expect heroic misfortune. And here it was again.

All I could think of at that moment was 1969 when the Cubs began the season with a walk-off home run by Willie Smith on

Opening Day—a wild win that seemed a happy omen for a history-making run in the first year of divisional play.

Nineteen sixty-nine was a season for the ages—at least, until mid-August. As school beckoned Chicago's kids, the Cubs began a slow, painful, methodical collapse. On the morning of August 20, the day after Kenny Holtzman no-hit the Braves at Wrigley Field— and I found myself pictured on the sports page, having jumped the wall in celebration as a fifteen-year old—the Cubs led the St. Louis Cardinals by eight and a half games and the New York Mets by nine games.

Then everything fell apart. Cubs fans are comfortable with agony. It's part of their DNA. But what happened that September was almost too much to bear.

On September 7, a beautiful Sunday afternoon, I sat in the bleachers and watched as the Pirates' Willie Stargell homered onto Sheffield Avenue with the Cubs one strike from winning the game. The Cubs lost in eleven innings, 7–5. And I left Wrigley Field knowing that momentum was against my team and that the season was going to be too long for them to hold on. The Cubs headed out of town for a showdown series with the Mets that night and were leading now by just two and a half games. They lost both games in Shea Stadium and moved on to face Philadelphia.

That first night of the series, my buddies and I were hanging on the street corner of Panoramic Drive and Dora Street in Franklin Park, listening to the game from Philadelphia on a transistor radio. The day before, we had sent a telegram to Vince Lloyd and Lou Boudreau, the Cubs' radio broadcasting team, pulling for the Cubs to play better and win the pennant. Keep the faith. We sat on the street corner and listened in disbelief as Vince and Lou mentioned the telegram.

The Phillies were terrible that year. They lost ninety-nine games. But that Wednesday night, Philadelphia right-hander Rick Wise struck out six and allowed just three hits in a complete game 6–2 win—the eighth straight loss for the slumbering Cubs. For the first time in 156 days, the Cubs fell out of first place.

By the time the season ended, I was back in school, as a sophomore at East Leyden High. I remember sitting in the school basement—our study hall—reading the final standings in the sports section of the *Chicago Sun-Times*. I couldn't believe it. Second place, eight games behind the Mets, a mind-numbing seventeen-game turnaround—from nine up to eight back—in forty-three days.

Four players on that team—Billy Williams, Ron Santo, Ernie Banks, and Fergie Jenkins—were destined for Cooperstown, none of whom ever played in a World Series.

IN THE FALL OF 1984, I was a young executive with the Cubs when the team made history. In the days before Wild Card and Division Championship Series play, there was only a League Championship Series—a best-of-five showdown that determined which of two teams from the East and West divisions went to the World Series.

The Cubs went 96-66 that year to win the East and advance to the postseason for the first time since World War II. The San Diego Padres won the West with a 92-70 record and made the playoffs for the first time in franchise history.

Game 1 was played under a brilliant blue sky with the wind blowing out at a packed, raucous Wrigley Field. Cubs center fielder Bobby Dernier sent 36,282 fans into a frenzy by hitting the second pitch from Padres ace Eric Show into the bleachers. Nine pitches later, left fielder Gary Matthews homered and the rout was on. The Cubs would hit five home runs—including another by Matthews, one by Ron Cey, and, magically, one by starting pitcher Rick Sutcliffe, who had only four homers in his eighteen-year career.

The Cubs won 13–0, and followed up the win the next day with a strong pitching performance from left-hander Steve Trout.

After a travel day to the West Coast, the series resumed at Jack Murphy Stadium in San Diego on Thursday afternoon, October 4, 1984. The Cubs took a 1–0 lead in the second inning on a leadoff double by right fielder Keith Moreland and an RBI single by Cey.

Life was beautiful: The Cubs were up two games to none with a 1–0 lead in the potential pennant-clinching game. Dennis Eckersley, winner of six of his last eight regular season games, was on the mound. What could possibly go wrong?

Everything.

The Cubs were outscored 20–8 the final twenty-two innings of the series and lost all three games in San Diego. In the final game on Sunday, Chicago led 3–0 going into the bottom of the sixth when NL Cy Young winner Sutcliffe began to tire. He gave up back-to-back singles to Alan Wiggins and Tony Gwynn, then walked Steve Garvey to load the bases. A pair of sacrifice flies made it 3–2 and I could feel the air going out of the club. When a ground ball went under first baseman Leon Durham's glove in the seventh inning, the Cubs were dead. The Padres won the game 5–3 and went on to play in the World Series.

Agony. Part of my DNA. Part of every Cubs fan's DNA.

ANOTHER CUBS MELTDOWN I recalled as Game 7 of the 2016 World Series went to extra innings: In 2003, I was the assistant general manager with San Francisco and was interviewing for the GM position with the Cincinnati Reds. I arrived in Cincinnati the evening of Tuesday, October 7, as Game 1 of the NLCS between the Cubs and Florida Marlins was beginning. I sat in a hotel room at the Westin in downtown Cincinnati and couldn't believe what I was seeing: The television cameras panned Waveland and Sheffield avenues. The streets were full of people. Wrigley Field couldn't come close to holding the masses. I had been to Wrigley Field for nearly 1,500 games and had never seen the streets filled with people—*during* a game.

The Cubs lost 9–8 in eleven innings, but won the next three to close within a game of the World Series again. They lost Game 5 in Miami and headed back to Wrigley Field for Game 6 with two of the best starting pitchers in the National League—Mark Prior and Kerry Wood—ready to go. I brought my family and, of course, my uncle Frank.

As the Cubs led 3–0 heading into the eighth inning of Game 6, the crowd roared with anticipation. History, at last. Six outs to go.

Then, true to form, the Cubs gave up eight runs—partly because of Bartman's now-infamous lunge, but more from their own bumbling. Moments after the Bartman bobble, shortstop Alex Gonzalez muffed a potential double-play ball and right fielder Sammy Sosa overthrew a cutoff man. The Cubs lost 8–3.

My uncle cried.

The next evening the Cubs jumped to a 5–3 lead after four innings in Game 7—only to lose 9–6.

My uncle wept.

IN 2008, I FELT a little better when my Dodgers caused another round of misery for Cubs fans. Chicago won ninety-seven games that year, most in the National League. The Dodgers rallied to make the playoffs with a mere eighty-four wins after we brought in Manny Ramirez, Casey Blake, and Greg Maddux in a series of second-half trades.

The Cubs jumped out 2–0 in the second inning of Game 1 in Chicago on a home run by Mark DeRosa. The 42,099 fans inside Wrigley Field and another 30,000 or more outside were crazy happy. I sat there in a suite in the midst of all the delirium with my inner circle of Dodgers executives and my buddy Mike Murphy, the longtime Bleacher Bum turned Chicago sports radio personality.

Murph and I basically grew up in Wrigley Field during the late 1960s, but never knew each other until the day my Cubs career began in January 1982. Back when we were younger, fewer than a thousand fans came to the Cubs games. The television cameras of WGN would pan the stands and show someone down the right field line reading a book, with no one else in the picture. A foul ball would go into the upper deck and one of the two Andy Frain security ushers stationed up there would walk over, pick it up, and drop it in a bucket. The upper deck was closed most of those seasons except for Opening Day and the occasional big game.

An hour or so after DeRosa homered, James Loney hit a grand slam into the center field basket—the basket originally installed to protect Murph and the Bleacher Bums, who would walk the wall during the games. The Dodgers won that game 7–2, won 10–3 the next night, and went on to sweep.

More agony for Cubs fans.

BUT THEN CAME 2016. The Cubs had a magical playoff run through the Giants and the Dodgers to make the World Series. Standing in the way of their first world championship in 108 years were the Cleveland Indians—poster boys for futility itself. They hadn't won a World Series since 1948.

Neither the baseball gods nor Hollywood scriptwriters could have directed the Series any better. Game 7 was tied in Cleveland after nine innings. Extra innings were about to begin when rain fell and the umpires halted play. Tension. Excitement. Two teams with a combined 176 years of World Series frustration.

As my old friend Harry Caray would say: "Holy cow!"

The rain delay cooled the momentum Cleveland was building after Davis's emotional game-tying, two-run homer. And the Cubs used it to fire themselves up. As they headed back to their dugout to wait out the rain delay, right-fielder Jason Heyward, who had signed a $184 million free agent contract and then hit just .230 with seven home runs his first season in Chicago, pulled his teammates into the team's weight room. No coaches. No front office executives. Just teammates. Heyward quietly but passionately rallied the team around him. "I just wanted them to know how good they were, how good we are," he later told *USA Today*. "[I wanted them to] know how proud of them I was and that I loved them."

When the game resumed after a seventeen-minute delay, the Cubs scored twice, to take an 8–6 lead. But the Indians refused to go quietly. They scored once and had the tying run on third when light-hitting infielder Michael Martinez made the final out of a classic World Series.

As many as 15,000 Cubs fans had ventured 350 miles east to Cleveland—some leaving Chicago the morning of Game 7 in hopes of finding a ticket or just being in the neighborhood of potential history. They were delirious with joy.

When the Cubs won, the feeling was euphoric and blissful—nothing else seemed to matter. As I sat high atop the upper deck of Progressive Field with my son, Lou, and his friend Bill Dwoinen, I paused to reflect for a moment. I had grown up with the Cubs. I was part of the franchise, blessed to begin my baseball career with my hometown team—my favorite team. Now another baseball season was over. And it was the most remarkable season in a long, wonderful stretch—for me and for millions of others. The Cubs had won the World Series, 39,466 days since the last championship.

Most fans know a major-league baseball has 108 stitches. The Cubs went 108 years between titles. Games at Wrigley Field during the World Series started at 7:08 p.m., which in military time is

19:08—the last year the Cubs won a World Series. Numbers can be magical. One-oh-eight is a perfect stitch in time.

I WATCHED THE CLEVELAND FAITHFUL file out, agonized by falling short. The Cubs fans who stayed behind in Progressive Field were hugging and crying, generation with generation with generation, no doubt thinking of all those relatives and friends and former Cubs heroes who had died without having this moment in time.

When the game was over, the rain came down hard. No one cared. Lou, Bill, and I stayed in the park two hours. So did thousands of Cubs fans, all of whom were savoring what for many would be the most precious baseball memory of all time.

As I left Progressive Field, I checked my cellphone. There were a hundred text messages and emails from friends and baseball acquaintances congratulating me on seeing something that they all knew was special to me. Even though I had left Chicago twenty-two seasons earlier for the West Coast, those who knew my love and affinity for baseball also knew the Cubs winning a World Series set all other days apart.

I cried.

Those ten days from October 25 to November 3—the ten days it took to play the 2016 World Series—were the most wonderful days and nights of baseball of my life.

On November 4, 2016, an estimated five million people watched the World Series champion Chicago Cubs parade through the city. Various media reports hailed it as the seventh-largest peaceful gathering in world history—the largest ever in the United States.

For Cubs fans, it was worth the wait—especially for my uncle Frank, who whispered twelve glorious words to me on the phone after the Cubs win:

"Thank you for making the final years of my life so wonderful."

. . .

ON APRIL 10, 2017, the Cubs raised the World Series banner at Wrigley Field. The Dodgers were the visiting team and would be for the next three days. Two days later, the Cubs players, staff, and executives received the most exclusive and significant ring in World Series history—each containing 108 diamonds.

Twenty-seven

THE DODGER SWAY

. . . .

Many may feel that my greatest failing was not getting to, and winning, the World Series during my Dodgers tenure. It was a huge disappointment. As I reflect on my career, I see that my greatest failing was not being able to completely change a fractured culture—not being able to fully rekindle "the Dodger Way."

There are many variations and definitions of culture. To me, culture begins with leadership and encompasses everyone in one selfless mission, one united goal. It is about all the people. Commitment is a key fundamental. A litmus test for culture is whether people are all in, all the time, where they are more selfless than selfish and become comfortable with the uncomfortable.

When I came to L.A. from San Francisco in November 2005, Giants managing general partner Peter Magowan effectively blocked me from hiring any people I had worked with previously in San Francisco. Had my destination not been the hated rival Dodgers, there is a chance he would have let me take the customary couple of employees. But as I wrote earlier, Peter wasn't pleased he had to let me go four hundred miles to the south.

With a six-week void between the end of the season, and a near three-week void since Paul DePodesta had left and my hiring, Frank McCourt provided contracts to the staff who remained with the Dodgers.

While I did inherit a farm system that was about to produce a handful of major-league players, I also inherited a front office that worked with Paul, who had put together a team that sleepwalked through a 71-91 record (59-89 after a 12-2 start), the second-worst performance by a Dodgers club since World War II. Only 17 of the 132 teams in franchise history from 1884 through 2016 had lower winning percentages.

When I came in, the front office was a mishmash of regimes dating back decades. The baseball operations staff was comprised of people who had been with the club as far back as the Al Campanis days (1968–87). We had baseball operations staff hired by Fred Claire (1987–98), Kevin Malone (1998–2001), Danny Evans (2001–04), and, of course, Paul (2004–05). What I didn't have was anyone I hired.

There is a need by the GM to know and trust the staff implicitly. It takes time and sometimes there is a failure to determine who is who. When a GM joins a new organization they typically bring two or three people they know and trust completely to help provide the GM with insight. Familiarity offers the opportunity for people to speak the same language and understand immediately the expectations. Many words have different meanings and variations. But when people have worked side by side, there isn't a question about what the words mean and what vision looks like.

For forty-two seasons the Dodgers had but two managers. Walt Alston managed from 1954 to 1976; Lasorda managed from 1976 to 1996. Bill Russell, Glenn Hoffman, Davey Johnson, and Jim Tracy managed from 1996 to 2005. Only Tracy lasted as long as five seasons. My hires, Grady Little (two seasons), Joe Torre (three seasons), and Don Mattingly (four seasons while I was the GM and five seasons in total, in which his teams all finished over .500), added to the turnover in a key position.

One of the longest-running, most successful cultures in American professional sports had been fractured. For a franchise that had been the class of the National League for decades to win only one postseason game between the final game of the 1988 World Series and the first game of the 2008 Division Championship Series proved something was amiss. In the eighteen seasons preceding my arrival in L.A., the team qualified for the postseason just three times: 1995, 1996, and 2004.

In my first seven seasons as an assistant GM in San Francisco, the Giants made four postseason appearances, in 1997, 2000, 2002, and 2003, and were eliminated twice on the final day of the season—all with a payroll between 30 percent and 50 percent lower than the Dodgers. Just before that seven-year run, the 1996 Giants were 68-94. So it wasn't like the franchise was about to bloom before Sabean became GM and I became the assistant GM. The Giants needed to reboot. Sabean, Magowan, and Larry Baer made it happen. A winning culture took root.

Sabean has led the Giants baseball operation since 1997. Baer has been at the top level of management since 1992. Dusty Baker managed the franchise for ten seasons, Felipe Alou retired after four years, and Bruce Bochy has been in place since 2007. In the twenty-four seasons beginning in 1993, the Giants have had three managers; the Dodgers have had nine. Since 1997, the Giants have had one leader of the baseball department: Sabean. The Dodgers have had eight, including two interim GMs—Lasorda (1998) and Dave Wallace (2001).

The San Francisco Giants had a one-for-all, all-for-one culture. It didn't happen overnight and the people who worked within it were a variety of ages with different experiences. I didn't build that culture, but I helped bring it together and I know what it looks and acts like. The Giants had some down years, at least in terms of wins and losses, finishing under .500 from 2005 to 2008, my last year and the first three years after I left. But they turned it around and won three World Series in five years from 2010 to 2014. And a review from 1997 through 2016 shows that overall, they've been terrific—twenty good-to-great years. Through it all, the Giants organization built and maintained a culture of class, relentlessness, pursuit of unified excellence, and camaraderie.

The lack of a dynamic, all-for-one, one-for-all culture during the McCourt era didn't help. Too often we were limited in our options. When Joe was close to retiring from managing our best choice was Don. While I respected and admired Don and saw him work tirelessly as a coach, he also fell within the price range we could afford. In a market like L.A., it is very difficult to bring someone in who has never managed before, no matter who it is or how great their potential. And in a market like L.A., the stress, expectation, and strain on a manager should probably equate to the upper-third range in salary, like Joe, not the lower-third like Grady and Don.

Mattingly's outburst at a season-ending 2013 press conference (which in my opinion should have been handled behind closed doors) could have escalated into a YouTube classic had I responded with equal frustration and angst. I kept my cool. Donnie and I were simply where we were at that point in time. Ownership had changed since Don and I were both hired and they had every right to evaluate everyone. But if we had a strong culture, would a public showdown like that ever happen? Typically, there are challenges throughout an organization. Rarely are they discussed at a press conference that turns into one employee questioning and challenging his boss and ownership in front of the media.

When I came to Los Angeles, not only wasn't I allowed to bring anyone with me, but I found myself with people who thought they should have been hired to lead the Dodgers. Some people got past it; some never did and resented it. They weren't necessarily against me, personally, although I can't say that was a universal feeling. But a few, I felt—as did others—were focused primarily on their personal advancement. The position of general manager is difficult enough when everyone is pulling in the same direction. When that's not the case, it is nearly impossible to sustain any success.

For the most part, many of the people I inherited weren't happy with what had transpired through the years. That creates divisions and silos in an organization. I felt I had people whose first reaction when I discussed a project, a goal, a new idea was "How does this help me?" If it helped them and some of it happened to overflow and help the organization, fine. But if it doesn't help them first, their hearts weren't fully in it.

I believe leaders need to see not only today, but the midterm view and the long view, as well. You can never forget an organization is about the people. I always strove to remember that and to let the people know they were important. I admit I was far from perfect.

People are fed with communication, are nurtured by a chance to improve their own standing, and will be far more productive as a "we" environment versus an "I" environment. Patience and accountability are key for staff to encompass as they strive to advance. In an industry like baseball, jobs are in such great demand and opportunities for promotion are far fewer than in other professions.

I was always impressed by those who were dedicated to the good of the group, first and foremost. I never coveted Brian's GM position. I was drawn to the people who would take on more responsibility because they wanted to help the department become as great as it could be, while trying to impact people and the product alike in a positive way—no matter their level of experience or compensation. It took me a while to integrate that somewhat in L.A. I was never able to reconstruct what I had witnessed four hundred miles to the north. That was one of my shortcomings.

Without an infrastructure of people I knew and trusted completely, I was isolated during my first season with the Dodgers. I didn't have an inner circle to work with and was inheriting a ninety-one-loss team in my first opportunity to be a GM. Even my manager, Grady, who I hired, was new to me. The players rallied and many new personalities and talents were brought in and melded—winning eighty-eight games and tying San Diego for first place in the NL West.

The closest I had to a real confidant was Frank McCourt. While I'm grateful for the time I had with him and the opportunity he gave me, it is not ideal to have your inner circle be one person and that one person be your boss and the owner of the team. There's no substitute for putting together your own group of good people, for surrounding yourself with colleagues who hold themselves accountable, who embrace responsibility, and who genuinely put the good of the group ahead of themselves. It's rare, but it is key to long-term success.

I don't have all the answers. But I feel I helped a lot of people. I've worked in a lot of different positions—from low man in the media relations department to the general manager's chair and many positions in between. I was never the smartest intellectual person in any room, but I worked and watched and listened and learned. I learned long ago that that was the only way I could be successful. As in many businesses, there are always the naysayers, the doubters, who will try and erode someone else's self-confidence. I never believed I was always right, but I kept my effort and due diligence pure and after a while I needed to build a tough exterior and never doubt myself. I was going to make mistakes but I needed to hone and mature my own self-confidence. Believing in someone starts with them believing in themselves.

I didn't have as much amateur scouting experience as some, or as much time in player development, but I touched on those areas a lot before becoming a general manager. And I had also seen the final product at the big leagues for twenty-five seasons before becoming a GM, where the shortcomings of a player—be those shortcomings physical, intellectual, or emotional—come home to roost, usually at the most crucial times within a season.

Too often during my years with the Dodgers, we drafted talented players who, as it turned out, did not become World Series championship–caliber major leaguers. The big-league season is a very trying and challenging quest. Players have to be willing to fight through adversity, through physical injury, and through weariness. I'm not talking about physically fighting; rather, the ability to fight on a daily basis, to "grind," as the cliché goes, separates teams at the end. Talent and grit win.

There are flash points in a season—especially in September and October—where the difference between winning and losing comes down to one-on-one battles. The winner is usually the player who has the grit and fortitude to win the fight. We lost many of those battles.

A poignant example of this was the 2008 National League Championship Series against the Phillies. We lost in five games and never scored a run after the sixth inning of any game. In the first inning of Game 2 in raucous Citizens Bank Park, the Phillies' Brett Myers threw a pitch over the head of our best player, Manny Ramirez.

The Phillies were basically challenging the Dodgers: "It's on now, boys."

Word spread on the bench to settle things the next half inning. Pitcher Chad Billingsley could have done it. He didn't.

By the time the third inning of Game 2 was complete, the Phillies led 8–2 and were on the way to a two-games-to-none series lead.

It took until the third inning of the next game for Dodgers pitcher Hideki Kuroda to defend his teammates. That was the only game of the series the Dodgers won.

In the 2009 NLCS, a rematch also won by Philadelphia in five games, the Dodgers were outscored 20–10 from the seventh inning on. If it was a street fight, we would have been bloodied and lost that as well.

We had the same issues in the postseason in 2013 against St. Louis.

Just nine pitches into the 2013 NLCS, Cardinals starter Joe Kelly threw a 95-mph fastball inside to Hanley Ramirez, who was 8-for-16 with six extra-base hits and six RBI in the Division Championship Series against Atlanta.

Whether it was to move Hanley off the plate or out of the NLCS, I presume we will never know. The pitch broke Hanley's rib and changed both the complexion of our lineup and the series in an instant. There wasn't a return message until the eighth inning of Game 4, when Ronald Belisario hit pinch hitter Pete Kozma. No offense to Pete, but he hit .217 that season with one home run. He wasn't exactly Yadier Molina, Matt Holliday, or Carlos Beltran. St. Louis won the 2013 NLCS in six games and the 2014 National League Division Series in four. In those ten gut-wrenching games, we were outscored 19–7 after the sixth inning, including a 15–4 drubbing in the 2014 NLDS. There is no question we didn't win enough one-on-one battles, but part of the failure of 2014 falls to me for not assembling a better bullpen.

No individual could be blamed for our lingering failure in crucial situations, but I always valued players and scouts who put a premium on a player's psychological fortitude—a player's innate ability to bear down and win the one-on-one matchups. While players like that are hard to find, that's really where championship teams are defined. And while we were good enough to get into the postseason, we were lacking when it came to those final encounters late in the playoffs.

Early in the 2011 season, after six years of trying to make things work, I had the opportunity to begin making changes. As much as I knew it was the right call, I agonized over the decision on a personal level. I'll never forget how my life was shattered—how my family's lives were shattered—when Larry Himes fired me from the Cubs.

Far too often, people in positions of leadership fail to consider the personal side of professional decisions. When someone is fired, the trickle down is devastating. That's not to say no one should ever be fired. Sometimes changing personnel is best for everyone—for the person fired, for the person doing the firing, and, more important, for the organization.

The big shakeup never happened under my watch. I was the centerpiece of the next big shakeup in Dodgers history. In 2011, I spoke with some incredibly talented men and women who normally would have been eager to move to Los Angeles and work for the Dodgers. But not in 2011. The future of the franchise was as uncertain as it could possibly be: bankruptcy . . . the McCourt divorce . . . a pending sale . . . and new ownership with a different leadership group.

No one wanted to leave a stable job at another club for that much insecurity—not even if it meant climbing from a small-market club to the bright lights of Los Angeles. More than one of a handful of choices I wanted bowed out because of family concerns and the lack of organizational stability coupled with the cost of living in beautiful Southern California.

Instead of changing out personnel, we changed process. We regrouped and looked for another way to make the organization better. I decided to put different checks and balances into the system of player acquisition both on the professional and amateur sides.

I hired Dr. Dana Sinclair, a registered psychologist whose job it was to evaluate the mental strength and character of our players as well as potential draft picks. Dana did some impressive work.

Corey Seager comes to mind. Anyone who follows baseball knows Corey's talent. Logan White and the scouts did a very good job recognizing Corey. We also knew, thanks to Dana, when we drafted Seager that we had a player who wanted to go to battle one-on-one, whose willingness to sacrifice to be great was evident, and whose mind was able to slow the game and life down—traits of the greatest players in any sport. Those are the types of players championship teams have scattered throughout their clubhouses. Rookie All-Star Cody Bellinger, drafted in 2013, is another one.

As we reset our acquisition process and started to see the fruits of the change with Seager and other outstanding young people and players, the sand was running out of my Dodgers' GM hourglass. In my initial meetings with Andrew Friedman, who replaced me in October 2014, I told him I had failed to create the kind of culture that the Dodgers were known for from the 1950s through the 1980s. I told him, in my opinion, that that was my greatest failing, and his greatest challenge.

TWO YEARS LATER, IN 2016, the Dodgers hired first-time manager Dave Roberts. I thought he did a tremendous job in leading the team to its fourth straight NL West title and being named NL Manager of the Year. When a manager comes from within a coaching staff or from within the organization, his knowledge of the talent and personality of players and executives should be extensive. When a manager is hired from outside an organization and has not managed previously in the big leagues, the challenges are many—before the in-game situations can even be considered. The players in 2016 took on his personality, work ethic, and attention to detail. As evidenced by the 2016 and record-setting 2017 clubs, Roberts had installed a fresher, inspiring, championship culture.

ON THURSDAY, OCTOBER 16, 2014, as soon as the news conference announcing Andrew as my successor had been delivered, I drove to White Memorial Hospital and watched the NLCS game between the Cardinals and Giants on TV with Bill DeLury. We sat in the hospital room and I filled my longtime friend and confidant in on how everything had unfolded.

"Good," he said. "Good for you. Maybe you'll get some rest and some of your life back."

Then he said something very profound and poignant to me.

"You know they talk about the Dodger Way," said the man who lived it for sixty-six years. "Until people stop being selfish, it's never happening again. It hasn't been that way since the last couple years of the O'Malley era. I know eras change, but the foundation of success will always be the same.

"You gave it everything you had. You were successful. You brought a lot of pride back to a lot of people who had been here for a very long time. So, let it go. Make another chapter for yourself."

I'm on it, Billy. I'm on it.

Acknowledgments from Ned Colletti

When you have been blessed beyond measure, an acknowledgment of thanksgiving pours out of your soul.

My mom and dad, Dolores and Ned, were humble and simple, yet inspirational and wise. They had dreams for their children like every parent, but couldn't financially afford to pave the way. High school educated, they taught instead by their actions—their work ethic, and by being dependable, honorable, and genuine. Without them being who they are, I have nothing. And the same goes for my brother, Doug—dependable, honorable, genuine, and someone who epitomizes our parents better than I. Doug has been a member of the Chicago Bears radio broadcast crew for more than thirty years. To think that Ned and Dolores Colletti's sons and grandson have worked nearly eighty-five years in professional sports is something no one would have had the vision or the guts to predict.

I believe life's passion can be discovered early. Thankfully, I had my uncles Frank, Pasquale, and Joe. They loved baseball and passed it on to me in deep ways from the time I was five years old. As did the guys from the neighborhood: Robert Smith, Matt Heinzinger, Tom Kapusta. Mike Murphy, Roger Roeing, Bobby Ceddia, and those whose gift was street-earned wisdom, especially after my dad died: Ralph Parra, Art Artman, and Orv Wilkin. As well as those who added soul: Peter Schivarelli, Walt Parazaider, Lee Loughnane, Robert Lamm, and James Pankow.

In believing each person we encounter has a chance to change a life and a career, I begin with Gary Klasen, who hired me out of Northern Illinois University for Press Publications, a suburban Chicago newspaper chain. Gary also helped me with a position at the *Chicago Daily News*—a newspaper long gone now, but one in which great writers graced its pages. I worked for an advocate of prep sports, Taylor Bell, who gave me opportunity and confidence. And I sat at the feet of two esteemed sportswriters turned authors, John Schulian and Mike Downey, who, along with writer/author Ron Rapoport, became lifelong friends. My love for writing came from reading these gifted wordsmiths and was fostered by their crafting of thoughts and putting vision into words.

A gracious thank-you to the newspaper editors who taught me to write somewhat clearly and once in a while poignantly— Fowler Connell, "Commissioner" Fred Ortlip, Jim Gauger, Sebastian Saraceno, and Jim DeStefano, in particular. They taught me to make letters into words, words into sentences, sentences into paragraphs, paragraphs into stories, stories into books.

Thank you to Bob Ibach, who gave me the opportunity of a lifetime when he hired me to come home and work for the Chicago Cubs.

Ibach brought me to the Cubs' GM Dallas Green, who introduced me to Lee Elia, Billy Connors, John Vukovich, and the ultimate sports executive, Jim Finks. All of them took the time to mentor me, lead me, challenge me, and grow my baseball career, as did Dusty Baker, Felipe Alou, Grady Little, Joe Torre, and Don Mattingly. A couple of years into my career, Dallas hired Jimmy Frey to manage, who hired Don Zimmer to coach. Frey and Zimmer became two of my best friends. These baseball men define unselfish.

All of the years with the Cubs provided me with the experience to be hired in San Francisco, where Tony Seige was leaving and where his former boss Bob Quinn was hiring. Bob offered me a position on Tony's recommendation, and the man who made it all happen behind the scenes is the person to whom I owe as much professionally as anyone—Brian Sabean.

It is not exactly Tinker-to-Evers-to-Chance poetic. But it is Klasen-to-Bell-to-Ibach-to-Green-to-Sabean-to-McCourt when it comes to my career. All gave me something every person with a dream craves—opportunity.

I owe a debt of immense gratitude to Frank and Jamie McCourt, who provided me yet another opportunity that people who grow up where I grew up rarely, if ever, receive. Thank you as well to Mark Walter and Stan Kasten, who followed the McCourts and didn't have to keep me for a minute, but did. Gratitude and respect to my inner circle of Stan Conte, Vance Lovelace, and Rick Ragazzo, who stayed the course no matter how rocky or unpredictable the road became. And to Ellen Harrigan, the ballast of my Dodgers career, and Lon Rosen, who opened a door for me in television within minutes after the one closed on the Big Chair in the GM office.

To the Kadlecs, the Sodinis, the Pavinis, John Ortberg, the Seymours, Charisse Older, Peter Tilden, David Kipper, the late Tom Sherak and family, Bill Connor, and Gary Canter: a mere thank-you falls way short.

And to my cohorts in the Big Chairs all around North America— my hockey brethren—Brian Burke, Doug Wilson, Tony Granato, John McDonough, Dean Lombardi, Jay Blunk, Reid Mitchell, and Marshall Dickerson, who always had the time and the wisdom, and added the laughter, to open doors for me in a sport I've loved as much as baseball. Besides thanks, I offer this group a fitting toast, drunk from a Cup 35.25 inches tall.

I will be forever grateful to those who provided opportunity when my professional life reached the seventh inning: the best literary agent in the business, David Vigliano; and the team at Putnam: Kerri Kolen, my executive editor; and Sally Kim, Ivan Held, Christine Ball, Alexis Welby, Anabel Pasarow, Elena Hershey, and Ashley McClay. From the beginning David, Kerri, and Anabel all took a step with me that I didn't think possible, probable, or plausible. But here it is, impossible without the talented people of Putnam.

Coauthor and friend Joseph A. Reaves, who encouraged me to tell the stories that fill the pages, was invaluable. How he stayed the course with me, I will never fully understand. I am just very thankful that he did and that his wife, Lynne, let him.

I have saved the most poignant and loving thank-you for last. It would have been impossible to type everything you have already read through the tears: Gayle, Lou, and Jenna; and Chad, Becky, and Charlotte Grace. I married Gayle and we struggled, laughed, cried, and figured out how to do life together and apart. When you become a parent, you hope and pray both are capable—if there is a Cooperstown for mothers, Gayle is first ballot, a unanimous selection. While I went after a dream, she managed a home, children, family, and did far too much of it alone—impossible to think about that without tears. And Lou and Jenna, my greatest blessings, who fortunately took after their mother—I do not know any two people with more integrity and heart than my children. And with their spouses, Chad and Becky—everyone hit the jackpot. And then came Charlotte Grace, who became our first grandchild as the final touches were put on *The Big Chair*.

The lovers of baseball and sports also have earned a tip of the cap—a standing ovation. Without fans there are no games for pay, no sports careers to work toward, no fun and games in the toy department of life. The respect has been paid in huge dividends and I offer it back at least at one hundred cents on the dollar. It's been an amazing ride—one I haven't deserved nor ever taken for granted—but one I look back on in awe while I look forward to the chapters of life to come. None of it possible without the unfailing grace and majestic blessings from God.

With respect, immense gratitude, and deep love.

Acknowledgments from Joseph A. Reaves

First and foremost, I want to thank Ned Colletti for the opportunity to share his inspiring story. Ned and I have known each other since 1992, when I came home from a fourteen-year career as a foreign correspondent to become the *Chicago Tribune*'s Cubs beat writer. That bizarre transition puzzled most of my new colleagues, but Colletti was one of few—Harry Caray, future MLB.com columnist Barry Bloom, and Hall of Fame writer Jerome Holtzman were others—who immediately accepted me.

Years later, after I'd left baseball and returned from another stint overseas, Ned interviewed for the GM job in Los Angeles. He told me that Dodgers owner Frank McCourt caught him off guard during their interviews by asking what Colletti would do to perpetuate the Dodgers' history of innovation: signing Jackie Robinson, moving to the West Coast, introducing an academy in the Dominican Republic.

Ned said he paused and answered on impulse: "I'd be the first team to play a game in China and cultivate the Chinese market."

That answer probably had little to do with Colletti's hire, but not long after, Ned asked me to work with him. "You're the only guy I know who's worked inside the game and who's also worked and lived in China."

My years with the Dodgers were amazing. We played the first MLB game in China. We hosted the semifinals and finals of the 2009 World Baseball Classic to sellout crowds at Dodger Stadium. We went on a two-city tour of Taiwan. We sponsored tournaments in Brazil and Spain. We brought teams from Mexico, Korea, Italy, and Japan to our Arizona complex.

Frank McCourt made all those possible. For that, and more, he has my deep thanks. As does Frank's right-hand man, Jeff Ingram, who flew to Arizona to vet me when I was hired and supported me throughout my career.

McCourt did me another favor when he expanded my international duties to include developing strong relations between the Dodgers and their minor-league clubs. I visited each of those clubs three times a year, becoming friends with wonderful people who deepened my love of the game. My thanks to Ken Young, John Traub, and Nick LoBue in Albuquerque; Frank Burke, John Maedel, and Rich Mozingo in Chattanooga; Paul Barbeau, Scott Litle, and Emily Schafer in Midland, Michigan; Dale Hubbard, Jeff Hubbard, and Mike Melega in Tulsa; Bobby Brett, Brent Miles, and Grant Riddle in Rancho Cucamonga, California; and Dave Baggott, John E. Lindquist, and Ed Mattes in Ogden, Utah.

This book never would have been possible without the perspective of baseball's heart and soul—scouts, minor-league managers and coaches, unheralded front-office grinders. Among the best are: Bob Engle, Rick Ragazzo, Ellen Harrigan, Hide Sueyoshi, John Shoemaker, Bruce Hurst, Joe Walsh, Jose Vizcaino, Shawn Marette, Juan Bustabad, Rick Knapp, Vance Lovelace, Mitch Poole, Stan Conte, Ron Cey, Aaron Sele, and Billy Mueller.

Finally, my deepest thanks to my wife, Lynne, who has made it all possible and fun for four exciting decades.

INDEX